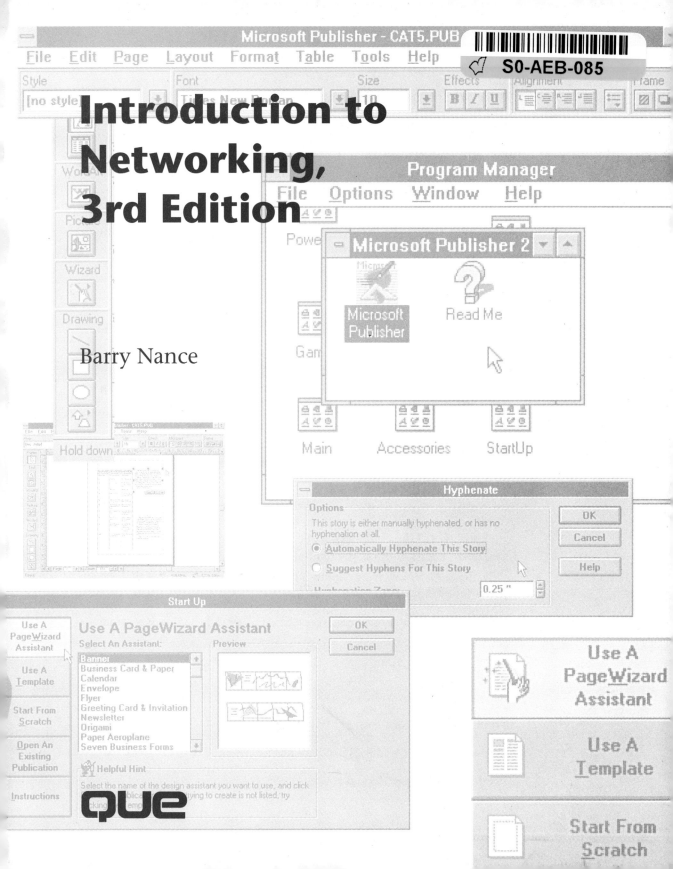

Introduction to Networking

Copyright © 1994 by Que® Corporation

Library of Congress Catalog No.: 94-66546

I5SBN: 1-56529-824-1

96 95 94   4 3 2

Interpretation of the printing code: the rightmost double-digit number is the year of the book's printing; the rightmost single-digit number is the number of the book's printing. For example, a printing code of 94-1 shows that the first printing of the book occurred in 1994.

Screens reproduced in this book were created using Collage Complete from Inner Media, Inc., Hollis, NH.

Publisher: David P. Ewing

Associate Publisher: Michael Miller

Publishing Director: Joseph B. Wikert

Managing Editor: Michael Cunningham

Product Marketing Manager: Greg Wiegand

Dedication

This book is for my wonderful family. They gave me both the motivation and the time to do this book.

Credits

Publishing Manager
Brad R. Koch

Acquisitions Editor
Angela J. Lee

Product Directors
C. Kazim Haidri
Robin Drake

Production Editor
Virginia Noble

Editors
Noelle Gasco
Susan Ross Moore
Andy Saff
Kathy Simpson

Technical Editor
Discovery Computing, Inc.

Book Designer
Amy Peppler-Adams

Cover Designer
Dan Armstrong

Production Team
Stephen Adams
Angela Bannan
Claudia Bell
Carol Bowers
Ayrika Bryant
Kim Cofer
Karen Dodson
Rich Evers
Brook Farling
Jenny Kucera
Bob LaRoche
Elizabeth Lewis
Stephanie Mineart
Nanci Sears Perry
Linda Quigley
Susan Shepard
Amy Steed
Rebecca Tapley
Michael Thomas

Indexer
Charlotte Clapp

Acquisitions Coordinator
Patricia J. Brooks

Editorial Assistant
Michelle Williams

Composed in *Stone Serif* and *MCPdigital* by Que Corporation

About the Author

Barry Nance, a columnist for *BYTE* magazine and a programmer for the past 20 years, is the author of *Network Programming in C* and *Using OS/2 2.1*, 3rd Edition, both published by Que Corporation. Barry is the Exchange Editor for the IBM Exchange on BIX, where you can reach him as "barryn."

Acknowledgments

I thank all the great people at Programming Resources Company for their help in writing this book.

Trademarks

Contents at a Glance

We'd Like to Hear from You!

As part of our continuing effort to produce books of the highest possible quality, Que would like to hear your comments. To stay competitive, we *really* want you, as a computer book reader and user, to let us know what you like or dislike most about this book or other Que products.

You can mail comments, ideas, or suggestions for improving future editions to the address below, or send us a fax at (317) 581-4663. For the on-line inclined, Macmillan Computer Publishing now has a forum on CompuServe (type **GO QUEBOOKS** at any prompt) through which our staff and authors are available for questions and comments. In addition to exploring our forum, please feel free to contact me personally on CompuServe at 74143,1574 to discuss your opinions of this book.

Thanks in advance—your comments will help us to continue publishing the best books available on computer topics in today's market.

Christopher Haidri
Product Development Specialist
Que Corporation
201 W. 103rd Street
Indianapolis, Indiana 46290
USA

Contents

3 Using Electronic Mail

63

II Building a Network   89

4 Using File Servers   91

8 Using LAN Manager, Windows NT, and LAN Server   223

IV Expanding a Network   299

11 Using Network Applications   301

12 **Managing Your Network**   **327**

Introduction

When computers are networked, they can do more work for people. People accomplish entire projects, consisting of many tasks, when they work in teams. You can think of a network as a team of computers, designed to support a team of people.

Setting up a team of people, coordinating tasks, managing problems, and monitoring progress are overhead jobs that must be done to help the team work together effectively. Networks similarly involve some overhead, but the result is worth the effort if—as with a team of people—the overhead tasks are done correctly and on time. This book helps you understand networks so that you can do your job better, as part of the team of people in your office.

Networking a group of computers is not as simple as mastering a single computer. Personal computers have become everyday commodities, to some extent. A personal computer is not quite as simple as a stereo component system or a television set, but a PC is a useful tool that you can master (and probably already have).

Networking computers, like managing a team of people, is a challenge. The vocabulary of local area networks is full of acronyms. The products that you can buy sometimes operate well together and sometimes do not. The prices you pay can range from less than a hundred dollars per computer to several thousand. The benefits you realize from networking computers may be nothing at all (or, in some instances, you may be even worse off with the network than without it), or the benefits may give you a tool whose usefulness transcends the functionality of the individual computers you have networked. Mindful of the potential rewards and benefits, and despite the risks, businesses are networking their computers at a rapid pace. With information like that found in this book, businesses are meeting the challenge of networking. Local area networks (LANs) are one of the fastest growing segments of the computer industry.

Perhaps you have been told that your computer at the office is becoming part of a local area network. Perhaps you run an office, small or large, and you have wondered whether a local area network would help people get their jobs done in your office. You may have been given the job of recommending a local area network or even installing one. Or perhaps you are just curious about how a network works or what a network can do for you. For these and similar situations, you will need an introduction to local area networks. This book is for you.

Personal computers (PCs) are replacing mainframes and minicomputers as the tool of choice for processing information. Over the past 10 years, the only serious obstacle to the personal computer revolution was finding a way to share information among several PCs. Mainframes and minicomputers had the overwhelming advantage of enabling people to share information because everyone accessed the single host computer where the information resided. LANs also enable personal computer users to share information—both the applications themselves and the data on which the application operates—and LANs are now an integral part of personal computing. What will become of the expensive mainframes and minicomputers? It may come as a shock to some people, but the inexorable trend toward local area networks is turning mainframes and minicomputers into mere file servers.

Why Network Computers?

The first use for networks, and the first use to which you probably will put a local area network, is the sharing of costly computer disk drives and printers. Early in the 1980s, Apple Computer's very popular Apple II computer was expensive. Large-capacity disk drives for the Apple II were likewise expensive. Local school systems wanted to purchase Apple II computers to help school-children learn, but the cost of the disk drives—even small ones—was prohibitive. And the computers were not nearly as useful without disk drives. A company named Corvus saw a need and began selling one of the first local area networks to local boards of education. The school system could purchase a single large-capacity disk drive; purchase Apple II computers without disk drives; connect the computers and the disk drive through a local area network; and give access to the single, shared disk drive to each Apple II user. The idea caught on rapidly. School systems found a way to afford computers for their students, and Corvus grew at a fantastic rate.

High-capacity, high-speed disk drives are not as expensive as they used to be. Today, of course, *high capacity* means hundreds of millions of bytes (*megabytes, or M*), or even billions of bytes (*gigabytes, or G*)—a far cry from the

5-million-byte and 10-million-byte Apple II disk drives purchased by the school systems. If you buy 10 computers at current prices, each with a 100-million-byte (100M) disk drive, the disk drive component of each computer will cost about $250—a total of $2,500 for all 10 computers. If you buy a single 1000M disk drive, you will pay about $1,000—a difference of $1,500. To network these 10 computers, you probably will spend more than $1,000 on network cards and software. The economics of local area networking have changed considerably since the days of Apple II computers and Corvus. So why would you network these 10 computers?

There are three answers to this question. The first says that 10 people probably do not need 1000M (1G) of disk space, because those people can share single copies of common files and applications rather than have individual copies on each computer. You can save money by buying a smaller single disk drive that all 10 people can share. You can save additional money by using the local area network to share a printer among the 10 people.

The second answer points to the people costs associated with personal computer use. If you use a local area network to share a single disk drive, you centralize the administration of the information on the disk. You can easily make backup copies of all the information on the shared disk—for example, for all 10 people. If each person were responsible for making his or her own backup copies, you would quickly find that some people would ignore the guidelines and not back up their disk drives. The department of 10 people (or perhaps an entire business) would run the risk of losing some of its valuable information. Along these same lines, the 10 people could use the local area network to share files and information. Without the network, a person would share files by copying those files to a floppy disk and walking the disk over to another person. (This is sometimes referred to as *sneakernet*.) With a LAN, people can give files of information to each other simply and easily.

The third answer contains the most sophisticated and complex reason for using a LAN. A growing number of personal computer software products recognize the presence of the local area network and are multiuser. These products are *LAN-aware:* the software coordinates the updates to a central file and enables many people to access the same information at the same time.

Local area networks can save a business money, but the savings in terms of computer hardware costs are a smaller part of the overall picture. The savings in people expense are the larger part.

Many times, using a local area network to run its business is a necessity for a company. The network enables the company to function because the enterprise absolutely needs to share information. Stores that rent videotapes are a prime example. The store needs to keep an accurate record of which video-tapes are rented and which ones are on the shelf. A minicomputer or main-frame computer, with a terminal for each sales clerk, would be an expensive solution. Instead, the store uses PCs, networked behind the counter, to keep track of the whereabouts of each videotape. Two or three clerks can keep each other informed by simply operating two or three personal computers and recording the rentals and returns. The network's file server holds the common database file of videotapes. Each time a clerk enters information, the clerk's PC updates the common database file on the file server.

Perhaps your company needs to share a CD-ROM disk drive, a plotter, a high-speed modem, or a fax machine. Many (but not all) configurations of local area networks support the sharing of these devices.

You can share disk drives and other devices on your local area network. You can share applications and information in a way that formerly was possible only with minicomputers and mainframes. And you can use a LAN for electronic mail, scheduling (of meetings, for example), and workgroup coordination.

This discussion of sharing files may have caused you some concern. You may very well have files that you consider private and that you do not want to share with other people. Fortunately, most networks provide several levels of security so that you can keep private files from prying eyes. The first level uses a password to verify the identity of the person who wants access to a file server. The next level of security enables you to "hide" files and entire direc-tories of files on a user-by-user basis. If your concern is that the file not be inadvertently modified or deleted, you can mark the file as *read-only* to ensure that the file remains intact.

What Is the Purpose of This Book?

By using illustrations, photographs, and clear, simple explanations, this book introduces you to local area networks. As you read further, you will learn what a LAN is, how to use a LAN, and how a LAN works. You will find considerations, suggestions, and recommendations for selecting LAN components. You will become well versed enough with LANs to avoid costly mistakes. You will get tips that help you use a LAN better and more produc-tively. And you will become acquainted with a number of popular network-ing products from companies like Novell, Microsoft, IBM, Artisoft (LANtastic), Performance Technology, Sun Microsystems, Thomas-Conrad, Apple Computer, Digital Equipment Corporation (DEC), Network General, and Xircom.

Who Should Read This Book?

You will find this book useful and informative if you are curious about networking computers. You do not have to have a network now. In fact, if you are in the process of selecting a local area network, you can use this book as a comprehensive guide during the selection process.

Perhaps you are getting a LAN in your office. You have some experience using a personal computer, and you want to know how the LAN will affect your work. If this is the case, you can use this book to prepare yourself for the new LAN. You will be ready to use the LAN productively when it arrives.

If your computer is already connected to others with a local area network, you can use this book to understand how the network operates. You can familiarize yourself with the different networking products so that you can get the most from your LAN.

What Is in This Book?

Part I of this book, "Understanding Networks," lays the foundation you will need in later chapters and tells you how you can benefit from a network. Chapter 1, "A Networking Overview," is an overview of local area networks. Chapter 2, "Sharing Computer Resources," discusses the sharing of disks, printers, CD-ROMs, modems, fax machines, applications, and data files. Chapter 3, "Using Electronic Mail," explains the use of the LAN as an officewide post office for interoffice mail.

Part II, "Building a Network," gives you nuts-and-bolts information about how networks function. Chapter 4, "Using File Servers," tells you what a file server is and how a server is different from other computers on the network. In Chapter 5, "Using Protocols, Cables, and Adapters," you see how the network connects all the computers into a cohesive unit. Chapter 6, "Using Workstations," discusses your personal computer's new role as a workstation on the network.

Part III, "Networking Software," comprehensively covers the products that bring the network to life—network operating systems. Each chapter discusses specific products and thoroughly acquaints you with the products' features. Chapter 7, "Using NetWare," leads off with a discussion of NetWare Version 2.2, Version 3.12, and the new Version 4.0. Chapter 8, "Using LAN Manager, Windows NT, and LAN Server," describes the major networking products from IBM and Microsoft. Chapter 9, "Using Peer LANs," brings you up-to-date on products that don't require you to have a separate file server, such as

Personal NetWare, NetWare Lite, Windows for Workgroups, and LANtastic. Chapter 10, "Using UNIX LANs," explores TCP/IP as well as some of the networking alternatives available in UNIX networking environments: Network File System (Sun Microsystems' NFS), PC Interface (Locus Computing), and POWERfusion and POWERserve (Performance Technology).

Part IV, "Expanding a Network," gives you a perspective on software and hardware products that help you get the most from your new LAN. Chapter 11, "Using Network Applications," explains how and why some software products are LAN-aware and some are not. Chapter 12, "Managing Your Network," is a thorough discussion of the tools you can use to manage, administer, and diagnose problems on the LAN. Chapter 13, "Analyzing Interoperability," provides an analytical look at why LAN products from different vendors do not always work well together. Finally, Chapter 14, "Building WANs from LANs," lets you explore the sharing of information across the city, across the nation, or even around the world through wide area networks (WANs).

The Appendix, "Understanding LAN Certification," describes the Novell and IBM programs in which you can enroll to achieve certification of your understanding of local area networking. Becoming a Certified NetWare Engineer (CNE) through Novell's program, for example, can open up job opportunities and may help increase your salary.

You'll find a Glossary near the end of this book.

What Should You Already Know?

This book is not a primer on personal computers. You should already have some familiarity with computers to get the most out of this book. In particular, you should know what a personal computer is, how to start and use an application on a personal computer, and what a disk file is. You do not need to know anything about networks themselves.

The first chapter, which is an overview of local area networks, will get you off the ground easily and simply. Turn the page and find out what a local area network can do for you!

Part I

Understanding Networks

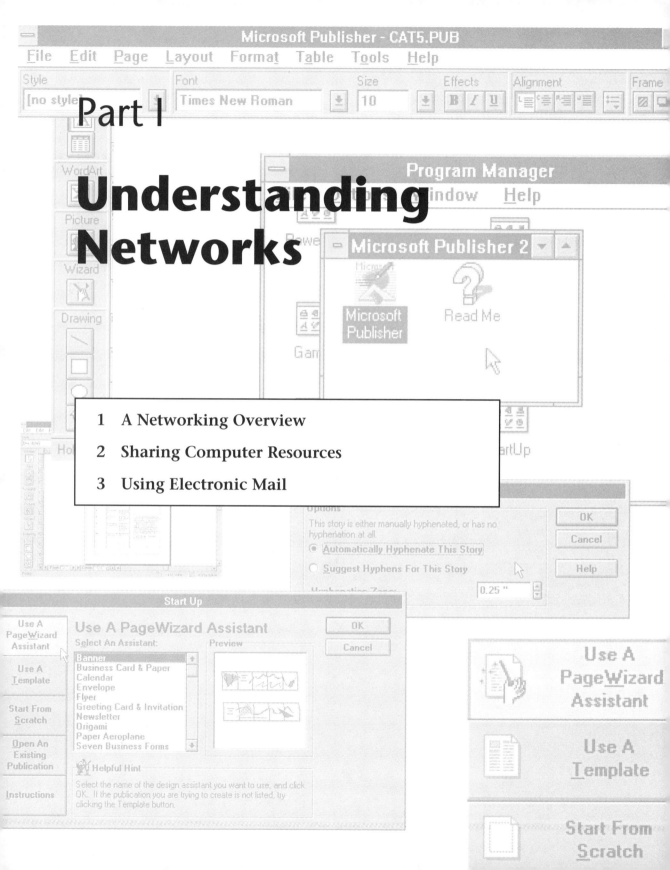

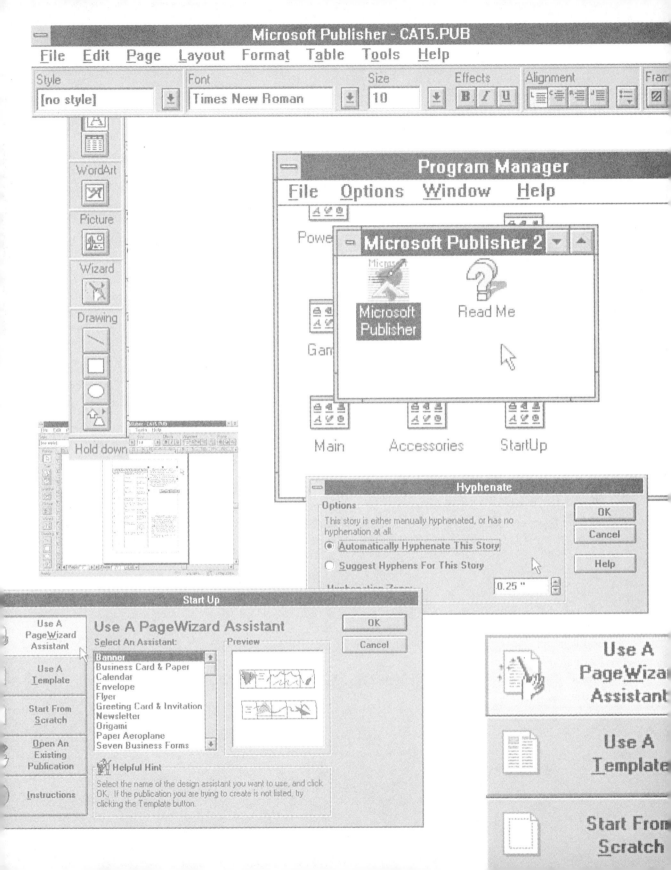

Chapter 1

A Networking Overview

A LAN is a local area network. Within a single building or similar geographical space, a LAN enables you to connect a group of personal computers together. People using the networked computers can share information. Without the LAN, you would have to copy files to a floppy disk and transport the disk to another person in order to share files (this is sometimes colorfully described as *sneakernet*—walking a floppy disk from your desk to someone else and delivering the disk by hand). The floppy disk method does not enable several people to access the same file at the same time. A LAN does give you this simultaneous-access capability, as long as you use application software designed for multiple users. Even without simultaneous access, however, a LAN is useful. In addition to easily sharing files, people on a LAN can share a printer, a CD-ROM disk drive, a modem, or even a fax machine.

In this chapter, you first find out what a LAN can do. Next, you explore the basics of what makes up a LAN. During your exploration, you become acquainted with workstations, file servers, LAN cables, and network adapters such as LANtastic, ARCnet, Ethernet, and Token Ring cards. After discovering what makes up the hardware side of LANs, you move on to LAN software components. You learn about network operating system software products such as NetWare, OS/2 LAN Server, LAN Manager, LANtastic, NetWare Lite, and Personal NetWare. After a brief discussion of application software, you learn about security, backing up files on a LAN, data redundancy, and power protection. The chapter concludes with some advice on when you should ask for help.

Understanding What a LAN Can Do

A LAN can do virtually everything a mainframe computer or minicomputer can do, but at a much lower cost. People can share computer resources and information, and they can work together on projects and tasks that require coordination and communication, even though those users may not be physically close. In addition, if the network crashes, a networked user may very well be able to continue working because that person's personal computer is still functioning. (A mainframe or minicomputer crash typically idles an entire department or company of people.) The next chapter, "Sharing Computer Resources," explains in more detail what LANs can do. The discussion in this chapter gives you basic concepts you should be familiar with before you encounter that detail.

You can do seven things with a LAN that you cannot easily do with non-networked, stand-alone personal computers:

1. *Share files.* A LAN enables many users to share a single copy of a file stored on a central file server computer or on one person's PC. An attorney's office, for example, may have a common pool of documents that various secretaries can access and update.

2. *Transfer files.* A LAN enables you to copy files quickly from machine to machine without having to exchange floppy disks.

3. *Access information and files.* A LAN enables anyone to run applications, such as the accounting software, from any of your office's workstations.

4. *Share applications.* A LAN enables two people to use the same copy of an application—for example, the Microsoft Word word processing program. Two people cannot edit the same document simultaneously, however.

5. *Simultaneously key data into an application.* A LAN-aware application program enables two people to key into it at once. Two people can key general ledger transactions at the same time, for example, with the program coordinating their work so that the two users do not interfere with each other. Note that only special LAN-aware versions of programs enable simultaneous keying. Ordinary computer programs enable only one person at a time to use the program on a given set of files.

6. *Share printers.* Using a LAN, you can share one or more expensive laser printers among several workstations.

> **Note**
>
> If printer sharing is your goal, an inexpensive printer switchbox may be all you need in order to connect multiple computers to a single printer.

7. *Use electronic mail.* You can use a LAN as a post office to send memos, reports, and typed messages to other people sitting at computers in other parts of the building. The telephone often is more convenient, but a LAN E-mail system takes messages when people are away from their phones, and it provides a paperless "interoffice memo" environment.

Understanding the Components of a LAN

A LAN is a combination of computers, LAN cables, network adapter cards, network operating system software, and LAN application software. (You sometimes will see *network operating system* abbreviated as *NOS*.) On a LAN, each personal computer is called a *workstation*, except for one or more computers designated as *file servers*. Each workstation and file server contains a network adapter card. LAN cables connect all the workstations and file servers. In addition to its local operating system (usually DOS), each workstation runs network software that enables the workstation to communicate with the file servers. In turn, the file servers run network software that communicates with the workstations and serves up files to those workstations. LAN-aware application software runs at each workstation, communicating with the file server when it needs to read and write files. Figure 1.1 illustrates the components that make up a LAN.

Workstations

A LAN is made up of computers. You will find two kinds of computers on a LAN: the workstations, usually manned by people; and the file servers, usually located in a separate room or closet. The workstation works only for the person sitting in front of it, whereas a file server enables many people to share its resources. Workstations usually are intermediate-speed AT-class machines with an 80286 or 80386 CPU. They may have 1M to 4M of RAM. Workstations often have good-quality color or gray-scale VGA monitors, as well as high-quality keyboards, but these are characteristics that make them easy to use and are not required to make the LAN work. A workstation usually has an inexpensive, slow, small hard disk.

Fig. 1.1
The components
of a LAN.

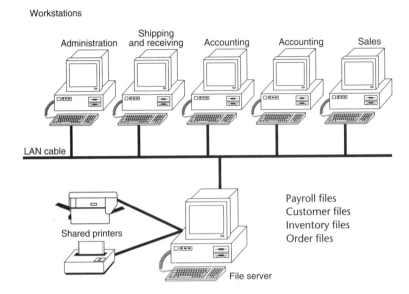

Some workstations, called *diskless workstations*, do not have a disk drive of their own. Such workstations rely completely on the LAN for their file access.

When you use a workstation, it appears and behaves in almost all respects like a stand-alone personal computer. If you inspect a workstation closely, you typically observe four characteristics that set it apart from a stand-alone computer:

- Extra messages appear on-screen while the computer starts up. These messages inform you that network software is loading at the workstation.

- You have to give the network software your user identification number (or account ID) and a password before you can use the LAN. This is the login procedure.

- After you log in to the LAN from a DOS-based workstation, you see additional drive letters that you can access. (On a Macintosh, you see additional folders; on a UNIX computer, you see additional file systems.)

- When you print memos or reports, a printer in a remote location on the LAN can produce your printouts.

Chapter 6, "Using Workstations," covers workstations in detail.

File Servers

In contrast to the workstations, a *file server* is a computer that serves all the workstations—primarily storing and retrieving data from files shared on its disks. File servers are usually fast 386-, 486-, or Pentium-based computers, running at 25 MHz or faster and with 8M or more of RAM. File servers usually have only monochrome monitors and inexpensive keyboards, because people do not interactively use file servers. The file server normally operates unattended. A file server almost always has one or more fast, expensive, large hard disks, however.

Servers must be high-quality, heavy-duty machines because, in serving the whole network, they do many times the work of an ordinary workstation computer. In particular, the file server's hard disk(s) need to be durable and reliable.

You most often will see a computer dedicated to the task of being a file server. Sometimes, on smaller LANs, the file server doubles as a workstation. Serving an entire network is a big job that does not leave much spare horsepower to handle workstation duties, however; and if an end user locks up the workstation that serves as the file server, your network also will lock up.

The file server may use a different operating system from that used by the workstations. NetWare is an example of a network operating system that runs only on file servers. (The portion of NetWare that does run on the workstation, which you'll hear people refer to variously as the requester, shell, NETX, or VLM, is there to help DOS, not to replace DOS.)

Under a heavy load, if there are 20 workstations and one server, each workstation can use only one twentieth of the server's resources. In practice, though, most workstations are idle most of the time, at least from a disk-file-access point of view. As long as no other workstation is using the server, your workstation can use 100 percent of the server's resources.

Chapter 4, "Using File Servers," explores file servers in more detail.

LAN Cables

LAN cable comes in different varieties. You may use thin coaxial wire (referred to as *Thinnet* or *CheaperNet*) or thick coaxial wire (*ThickNet*). You may use shielded twisted pair (*STP*), which looks like the wire that carries electricity inside the walls of your house, or unshielded twisted pair (*UTP*), which looks like telephone wire. You may even use fiber optic cable. Fiber optic cable works over longer distances than other types of cable, at faster speeds. But fiber optic cable installation and fiber-optic-based network adapters can be expensive. The kind of wire you use depends mostly on the kind of network adapter cards you choose. The next section discusses network adapter cards.

Each workstation is connected with cable to the other workstations and to the file server. Sometimes a single piece of cable wends from station to station, visiting all the servers and workstations along the way. This cabling arrangement is called a *bus* or *daisy-chain topology*, as shown in figure 1.2. (A *topology* is simply a description of the way the workstations and servers are physically connected.)

Sometimes a separate cable runs from a central place, such as a file server, to each workstation. Figure 1.3 shows this arrangement, called a *star*. Sometimes the cables branch out repeatedly from a root location, forming the *star-wired tree* shown in figure 1.4. Daisy-chained cabling schemes use the least cable but are the hardest to diagnose or bypass when problems occur.

If you have to run cables through walls or ceilings, installing the cable can be the most expensive part of setting up a LAN. At every branching point, special fittings connect the intersecting wires. Sometimes you also need various black boxes such as hubs, repeaters, or access units.

Fig. 1.2
The linear bus topology, attaching all network devices to a common cable.

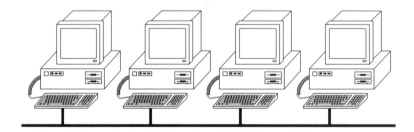

A few companies, such as Motorola, are pioneering a type of LAN that does not require cables at all. Such a *wireless LAN* uses infrared or radio waves to carry network signals from computer to computer.

Planning the cabling layout, cutting the cable, and installing the cables and fittings are jobs usually best left to experienced workers. If the fittings are not perfect, you may get electronic echoes on the network, which cause transmission errors. Coaxial cable will cost about 15 cents per foot, whereas shielded twisted pair will likely cost over a dollar per foot. This sounds like a big expense for a large LAN, but the cost of installing cable, at about $45 per hour, overshadows the cost of the cable itself. The only time you might consider installing LAN cable yourself is when you have a group of computers located on adjacent desks and you do not have to enter the walls or ceiling with the cable.

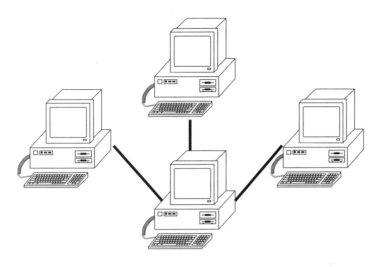

Fig. 1.3
The star topology, connecting the LAN's computers and devices with cables that radiate outward, usually from a file server.

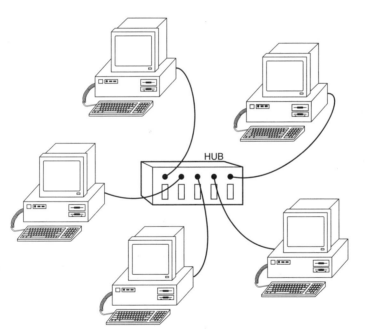

HUB

Fig. 1.4
The star-wired tree topology, linking the LAN's computers and devices to one or more central hubs, or access units.

Building codes almost always require you to use fireproof *plenum* cables. Chapter 5, "Using Protocols, Cables, and Adapters," explains LAN cables in detail. For now, you should know that plenum cables are more fire-resistant than some other cables. You would be very upset if you installed ordinary cable and were later told by the building inspector to rip out the cable and start over with the proper kind.

Network Adapters

A network adapter card, like a video display adapter card, fits in a slot in each workstation and file server. Your workstation sends requests through the network adapter to the file server. The workstation receives responses through the network adapter when the file server delivers all or a portion of a file to that workstation. The sending of these requests and responses is the LAN's equivalent of reading and writing files on your PC's local hard disk. If you're like most people, you probably think of reading and writing files in terms of loading or saving your work.

Only two network adapters may communicate with each other at the same time on a LAN. This means that other workstations have to wait their turn if one person's workstation is currently accessing the file server (processing the requests and responses that deliver a file to the workstation). Fortunately, such delays are usually not noticeable. The LAN gives the appearance of many workstations accessing the file server simultaneously.

LANtastic adapters have two connectors on the back to attach the incoming and outgoing cables. Ethernet connectors have a single T connector, a D-shaped 15-pin connector, a connector that looks like a telephone jack, or sometimes a combination of all three. Token Ring adapters have a 9-pin connector and sometimes a telephone jack outlet. Figure 1.5 shows a high-performance Token Ring adapter with both kinds of connectors.

Cards with two or more connectors enable you to choose from a wider variety of LAN cables. A Token Ring card with two connectors, for example, enables you to use shielded twisted pair (STP) or unshielded twisted pair (UTP, or telephone wire) cable.

The LAN adapter card listens to all the traffic going by on the cable, and fil-ters out just the messages destined for your workstation. The adapter hands them over to your workstation when the workstation is ready to attend to the messages. When the workstation wants to send a request to a server, the adapter card waits for a break in the cable traffic and inserts your message into the stream. The workstation also automatically verifies that the message arrived intact, and resends the message if it arrived garbled.

Adapters range in price from less than $100 to much more than $1,000. What do you get for your money? Primarily speed. The faster adapters can push data faster through the cable, which means that the file server will get a request more quickly and send back a response more quickly.

With a small LAN of four workstations and one server, blinding speed is not that important. However, if you have 100 workstations sharing one cable, speed can become a significant issue.

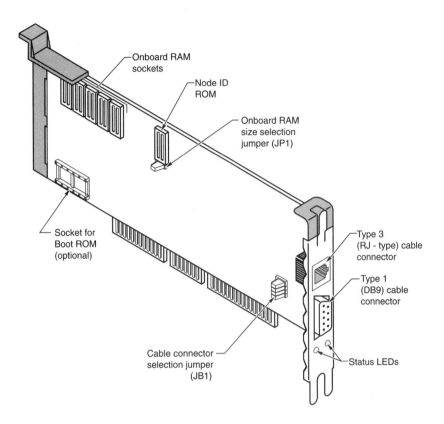

Fig. 1.5
The Thomas-Conrad 16/4 Token Ring adapter (with a 9-pin connector and a telephone wire connector).

Onboard RAM sockets

Node ID ROM

Onboard RAM size selection jumper (JP1)

Socket for Boot ROM (optional)

Type 3 (RJ - type) cable connector

Type 1 (DB9) cable connector

Cable connector selection jumper (JB1)

Status LEDs

Understanding Networks

Data Transfer Speeds on a LAN

Electrical engineers and technical people measure the speed of a network in *megabits per second* (mbps). Because a byte of information consists of 8 bits, you can divide the megabits per second rating by 8 to find out how many millions of characters (bytes) per second the network can theoretically handle. Suppose that you want to transfer an entire 3 1/2-inch 720K floppy disk's worth of information across a LAN. The rated speed of the LAN is 4 megabits per second. Dividing 4 mbps by 8 tells you that the LAN can theoretically transmit 500 kilobytes (500K) of data per second. This is equivalent to an average hard disk's transfer rate. The data from the 720K floppy disk will take at least a few seconds to transfer, as you can see from these rough calculations.

In practice, a LAN is slower than its rated speed. In fact, a LAN is no faster than its slowest component. If you were to transfer 720K of data from one workstation's hard disk to the file server, the elapsed time would include not only the transmission time but also the workstation hard disk retrieval time, the workstation processing time, and the file server's hard disk and server CPU processing times. The transfer rate of

(continues)

(continued)

your hard disk, which in this case is probably the slowest component involved in the copying of the data to the server, will govern the rate at which data flows to the file server. Other people's requests will interleave with your requests on the LAN, and the total transfer time may be longer because the other people are using the LAN at the same time you are.

If you transfer the data from a 720K floppy disk to the file server, you will see that it takes even longer. Floppy disk drives, as you know, are slower than hard disks. Your workstation will use the network in small bursts as it reads the data from the floppy disk. The workstation cannot send data across the LAN in this case any faster than it can read the data from the disk.

LANtastic Adapters

Artisoft makes both Ethernet and its own proprietary network adapter cards. Artisoft's proprietary model is called a LANtastic adapter, which is a little confusing because Artisoft also makes a network operating system called LANtastic. The LANtastic adapter operates at a rate of 2 megabits per second (2 mbps), and it uses four-conductor cable strung out in a snaking path that connects to all the workstations. Installation is easy if you do not have to put the cable inside walls or the ceiling.

Ethernet and Token Ring are industry standards, while the LANtastic adapter has a proprietary design. Most people choose Ethernet or Token Ring network adapters when building a new LAN.

ARCnet Adapters

ARCnet is one of the oldest types of LAN hardware. It was originally a proprietary scheme of the Datapoint Corporation, but today many companies make ARCnet-compatible cards. ARCnet is a little slow, but it is forgiving of minor errors in installation. ARCnet is known for solid reliability, and ARCnet cable and adapter problems are easy to diagnose. ARCnet costs less than Ethernet. ARCnet operates something like Token Ring, but at the slower rate of 2.5 megabits per second (2.5 mbps). The section "Token Ring Adapters" later in this chapter explains the basic principles on which ARCnet and Token Ring work.

Ethernet Adapters

Ethernet-based LANs enable you to interconnect a wide variety of equipment, including UNIX computers, Apple computers, IBM PCs, and IBM clones. You can buy Ethernet cards from dozens of competing manufacturers. Ethernet comes in three varieties (Thinnet, UTP, and ThickNet) depending on the thickness of the cabling you use. ThickNet cables can span a greater distance, but they are much more expensive. Ethernet operates at a rate of 10 megabits per second (10 mbps).

Between *data transfers* (requests and responses to and from the file server), Ethernet LANs remain quiet. After a workstation sends a request across the LAN cable, the cable falls silent again. What happens when two or more workstations (and/or file servers) attempt to use the LAN at the same time?

Suppose that one of the workstations wants to request something from the file server, just as the file server is sending a response to another workstation. A collision happens. (Remember that only two computers may communicate through the cable at a given moment.) Both computers—the file server and the workstation—back off and try again. Ethernet network adapters use something called *Carrier Sense, Multiple Access/Collision Detection* (CSMA/CD) to detect the collision, and they each back off a random amount of time. This method effectively enables one computer to go first. With higher amounts of traffic, the frequency of collisions rises higher and higher, and response times become worse and worse. An Ethernet network can actually spend more time recovering from collisions than sending data. IBM and Texas Instruments, recognizing Ethernet's traffic limitations, designed Token Ring to solve the problem.

Token Ring Adapters

Except for fiber optic cables/adapters, Token Ring is the most expensive type of LAN. Token Ring uses shielded or unshielded twisted pair cable. Token Ring's cost is justified when you have a great deal of traffic from many workstations. You will find Token Ring in large corporations with large LANs, especially if the LANs are attached to mainframe computers. Token Ring operates at a rate of 4 or 16 megabits per second (4 mbps or 16 mbps). As yet unannounced as this book goes to press, a 100 mbps version of Token Ring should become available soon.

On a Token Ring network, even when there is no traffic, all the workstations continuously play a game of "hot potato," passing an electronic token among themselves. The *token* is just a short message indicating that the network is idle.

If a workstation has nothing to send, as soon as it receives the token, it passes the token on to the next downstream workstation. Only when a workstation receives the token can it send a message on the LAN. If the LAN is busy, and you want your workstation to send a message to another workstation or server, you must wait patiently for the token to come around. Only then can your workstation send its message. The message circulates through the workstations and file servers on the LAN, all the way back to you, the sender. You then send a token to indicate that the network is idle again. During the circulation of the message, one of the workstations or file servers recognizes that the message is addressed to it and begins processing that message.

Token Ring is not as wasteful of LAN resources as this description makes it sound. The token takes almost no time at all to circulate through a LAN, even with 100 or 200 workstations. It is possible to assign priorities to certain workstations and file servers so that they get more frequent access to the LAN. And, of course, the token-passing scheme is much more tolerant of high traffic levels on the LAN than the collision-sensing Ethernet.

ARCnet and Token Ring are not compatible with one another, but ARCnet uses a similar token-passing scheme to control workstation and server access to the LAN.

Sometimes a station fumbles and "drops" the token. LAN stations watch each other and use a complex procedure to regenerate a lost token. Token Ring is quite a bit more complicated than Ethernet, and the LAN adapter cards are correspondingly more expensive.

Is Token Ring better than Ethernet? Should you use ARCnet? Or do you need high-speed, expensive fiber optic cables and equipment? The answer depends on the amount of your message traffic, which adapter cards are available for all the computers you have, and your budget. You'll find more detail on network adapters in Chapter 5, "Using Protocols, Cables, and Adapters."

LAN Software

In addition to LAN hardware, you must have a network operating system. PC DOS, Macintosh System 7, and UNIX cannot by themselves create a network. (Novell's DR DOS Version 7, however, does contain support for local area networks.) You use the network operating system's installation procedure to add network software to DOS or another operating system the workstation uses. On a server-based network, you install the network operating system on a separate, unattended PC. The unattended PC becomes the file server, and the network software you install on the workstation lets the workstation access the file server.

The most popular network operating system software is NetWare, from Novell. In addition to the network operating system, you'll probably want application software that takes advantage of your LAN and is LAN-aware. You won't have to upgrade all your software immediately, however. The network operating system can make the file server's hard disk and printer seem like a locally attached disk and printer.

Network Operating Systems

Just as you need DOS or some other operating system to manage applications in a stand-alone computer, you need a network operating system to control the flow of messages between workstations and servers. In the simplest case, this network software makes the disk drive on the server appear to be an extra drive (perhaps F) on each workstation. The network operating system also may make a LAN printer in another room appear to be locally attached to your workstation. Most ordinary computer programs are thus totally unaware of the LAN even though they use files on the remote drive F or print to the LAN printer through the LPT1 port.

On some networks, a separate, unattended computer acts as a file server. Such a network is a server-based LAN. On other smaller LANs, each workstation may be both a file server and a workstation at the same time. A network that has workstations which are also servers is a *peer-to-peer LAN* (sometimes called a *peer LAN*).

The network operating system (NOS) components on each workstation and on the file server communicate with each other through a computer language called a *protocol*. One common protocol is IBM's NetBIOS, short for *Network Basic Input Output System*. Several vendors besides IBM use NetBIOS. Another protocol is Novell's IPX, which stands for *Internetwork Packet Exchange*. You learn more about protocols in Chapter 5, "Using Protocols, Cables, and Adapters."

Here are of some network operating systems and their manufacturers:

Operating System	Manufacturer
AppleTalk	Apple
LANtastic	Artisoft
NetWare	Novell
NetWare Lite	Novell
Personal NetWare	Novell
Network File System (NFS)	Sun Microsystems
OS/2 LAN Manager	Microsoft
OS/2 LAN Server	IBM

(continues)

Operating System	Manufacturer
Windows NT Advanced Server	Microsoft
POWERFusion	Performance Technology
POWERLan	Performance Technology
Vines	Banyan
Windows for Workgroups	Microsoft

In the next few sections, you explore the highlights of some of these network operating systems: NetWare, the almost-twins LAN Server and LAN Manager, Windows NT Advanced Server, LANtastic, NetWare Lite and Personal NetWare, and Windows for Workgroups.

NetWare. Novell was one of the first companies to build LANs. The company used to offer both hardware and software, but in recent years Novell has concentrated on the software side of LANs. Novell's NetWare products are popular for several reasons:

- More applications will work on NetWare than on any other single brand of network.

- NetWare supports workstations using DOS, DOS and Windows, OS/2, UNIX, Windows NT, Macintosh System 7, and other operating systems.

- NetWare works with more types of network adapters than any other network operating system. You can select your hardware from dozens of vendors, picking the exact amount of power you need. You can use ARCnet, Ethernet, Token Ring, or almost any other type of network adapter with NetWare.

- NetWare LANs can grow to enormous size.

- NetWare LANs perform well.

- NetWare's security features are more than adequate for most LANs.

Chapter 7, "Using NetWare," discusses NetWare in more detail.

OS/2 LAN Server and LAN Manager. IBM and Microsoft developed OS/2 to be the successor to DOS. (In 1991, however, Microsoft stopped working on OS/2.) These companies wrote an operating system that can run multiple programs simultaneously, has more than 640K of RAM available to OS/2 applications, and performs well in difficult situations. These characteristics make OS/2 a powerful operating system for a file server environment.

While they developed OS/2, IBM and Microsoft also worked together to create file server software suitable for OS/2. IBM developed IBM LAN Server, and Microsoft developed LAN Manager, but you will find few differences in these products. The IBM programmers in Austin, Texas, and the Microsoft programmers in Redmond, Washington, shared their work constantly as they created their almost-twin network operating systems. Both companies want LAN Server and LAN Manager to outsell NetWare, but as yet, this has not happened.

Novell maintains a commanding lead in the LAN industry, but the IBM and Microsoft products do have an important attribute that makes the OS/2-based file server software attractive. An OS/2 file server is highly programmable when compared to a NetWare server and can do more than just manage files for workstations. An OS/2 computer, even while it acts as a file server, can run software that aids the workstations in special ways.

In a conventional workstation/server relationship, when a workstation needs to look through a large file for some data, all of the file—in message-sized pieces—must travel through the LAN cable to the workstation to be inspected. This process can cause quite a bit of LAN traffic and can slow down other workstations' access to the server. A better approach has the workstation tell the file server what it is looking for. The search for the data can occur directly in the server. When the server finds the data, it can return just that data to the workstation in only a few LAN messages. This software technology is called *client/server* architecture. Unfortunately, in most cases, the client/server approach requires the efforts of a programmer to implement the special processing that occurs inside the server.

Novell has something similar to OS/2 tasks, called VAPs (value added processes) for NetWare 2.2 and called NLMs (NetWare loadable modules) for NetWare Versions 3.12 and 4.0. But NetWare's file server environment is not as easily programmed as OS/2. OS/2 and the file server products LAN Server and LAN Manager are well suited to client/server applications.

Windows NT Advanced Server. Microsoft also sells another network operating system product, Windows NT Advanced Server (AS). Windows NT AS is a version of Microsoft's New Technology (NT) operating system. Like IBM's LAN Server, Advanced Server is a 32-bit network operating system. Unlike LAN Server, NT Advanced Server can be run on Intel, MIPS R4000, or DEC Alpha computers. Although CPU speed is rarely a bottleneck on file servers, you might choose to run Advanced Server on a symmetric multiprocessing (multiple CPU) computer. The extra CPU processing power might let you use the file server for additional client/server applications.

Advanced Server offers C2-level security, which means that the network operating system has a secure logon procedure, memory protection, auditing, and discretionary access control (the owner of a shared resource can monitor who is using the shared resource). Some corporate and military LANs require C-2 or higher security. In the area of reliability, Advanced Server uses a transaction-based file system that can back out of file updates if a series of related updates don't finish successfully. Advanced Server supports RAID (an acronym for *redundant array of inexpensive disks*) level 5, which helps provide greater data reliability by storing the same data on multiple disks. NT Advanced Server also recognizes signals from a UPS and comes with tape backup software.

Chapter 8, "Using LAN Manager, Windows NT, and LAN Server," describes these Microsoft and IBM networking products more fully.

LANtastic. The LANtastic network operating system from Artisoft is very popular because it is inexpensive, simple to install, and simple to operate. LANtastic supports many kinds of network adapters, including Ethernet, Token Ring, and Artisoft's own LANtastic adapters. LANtastic also uses only a small amount of the 640K of conventional memory to do its job. LANtastic's frugal use of RAM leaves room for you to run larger applications at your workstation than other network software does. LANtastic's network administration software offers both text mode and Windows interfaces through which you can configure and manage the LAN. LANtastic can work alongside NetWare on the same LAN, and LANtastic offers Apple Macintosh connectivity.

LANtastic runs on top of DOS; even the file server software is DOS-based. DOS is quite slow when it tries to manage large files, and LANtastic users suffer some penalty in performance as a result. For light duty (using word processing and spreadsheets and copying small files) on a network with only a few workstations, though, LANtastic can be a cost-effective alternative to more expensive network operating systems.

On very small LANs, you can even run applications on a LANtastic file server as if it were a workstation. For this reason, LANtastic is a peer LAN. If you are on a tight budget, you can save the cost of a separate file server computer by using LANtastic as a peer LAN. Be aware, though, that performance may not be entirely satisfactory because the file server is using DOS, and the server also is acting as a workstation. You also put your data somewhat at risk with a peer LAN. If someone is using an application at a workstation that is also a file server and that application crashes, your network will crash.

NetWare Lite and Personal NetWare. Not to be outdone in the small net-work market, Novell offers a peer LAN product called NetWare Lite. Like LANtastic, NetWare Lite can turn a server into a workstation. The risks and performance considerations are the same as with LANtastic. You can, of course, set aside a computer to act as just a file server and avoid some of the risks. NetWare Lite, however, is DOS-based, and a NetWare Lite server cannot share files with workstations as quickly as can regular NetWare.

NetWare Lite is inexpensive and easy to install, and it operates well within a larger NetWare LAN. In a department of 100 people who are on a NetWare LAN, you may use NetWare Lite to connect a small group of 5 or 10 of those people. These people could access the regular NetWare LAN, and at the same time, separately share information among their own computers with Lite.

In addition to offering NetWare Lite, Novell sells a peer LAN product called Personal NetWare. Personal NetWare offers many of the same basic features as NetWare Lite, including peer-to-peer sharing of files and printers. The more recent of the two products, Personal NetWare provides better integra-tion with both Microsoft Windows and Novell's own server-based NetWare products.

Windows for Workgroups. Microsoft noticed the success of two peer-to-peer network software products—Artisoft's LANtastic and Novell's NetWare Lite. Late in 1992, Microsoft released a version of Windows that incorporates built-in networking. Called Windows for Workgroups, the Windows-plus-network product enables you to share disk space, files, and printers through the point-and-click Windows interface.

Windows for Workgroups is a peer LAN; any PC that can run Windows in 386 Enhanced mode can share resources with other PCs. If a computer on the LAN can run Windows only in Standard mode, that computer can use shared resources but cannot share its own resources across the LAN. Similarly, DOS-only (non-Windows) workstations can use resources shared by Windows PCs running in 386 Enhanced mode. DOS-only workstations need to use the Windows for Workgroups' companion product, Workgroup Connection, to enable the use of the LAN's disk file and printer resources.

Not quite as quick and efficient as LANtastic or NetWare Lite, Windows for Workgroups is generally suitable for small LANs of 2 to 20 PCs. Nonetheless, you'll find that Windows for Workgroups is easy to install and use. The new menu items and toolbar icons in both File Manager and Print Manager make sharing and using resources with Windows for Workgroups almost painless. Windows for Workgroups includes an electronic mail application and a team-oriented scheduling application that can help your organization communicate better. If you already are accustomed to using Windows, have PCs that can run Windows in 386 Enhanced mode, and want to share files on a LAN, Windows for Workgroups can be an easy way to get started with networking.

Chapter 9, "Using Peer LANs," covers peer LAN networks in more detail.

Application Software

You need to buy new application software if you want to get the most benefit from your LAN. If your accounting package is not LAN-aware, for example, only one person at a time can use the software. You soon may find this too confining. You will want to think about upgrading to multiuser versions of some of the applications you use. Word processing software won't become multiuser until some time in the distant future, but developers of spreadsheet software are already designing their products for concurrent, multiuser access. Many database management software products allow multiple workstations to share a common database. And most vertical market software (computer programs written specifically for a particular business or industry) are inherently multiuser.

If you have a word processor, even if different people are not able to edit the same document from different workstations, you need to buy a license for each person who uses the software. The same goes for other kinds of single-user and multiuser applications, including DOS. Companies that have bought a single copy of a program and then used the copy on many machines may be in for a rude shock. A programmer can easily design an application to ask other workstations on the LAN if they are running the same copy of the software. This sort of copy protection is growing in use, while the kind that relies on encrypted floppy disks, deliberately damaged floppy disks, and parallel port devices is on the wane.

Ensuring LAN Security

When you have a LAN, you put everyone's files in one big container. Unless you make special provisions for security and privacy, anyone can look at—and modify—any file. Any user can easily rifle through the electronic desk and personal papers of any other user, including the president of the company. You may want to set up a security system on a LAN for four reasons:

- *Limiting damage.* Perhaps you know one of those butterfingered types who accidentally types *DEL *.** instead of *DIR *.** and then ends up destroying hundreds of files. If that person types the wrong thing on a LAN, he or she could wipe out all the other users' files in addition to his or her own files.

- *Protecting confidentiality.* If you know that anyone in the company, including the office gossip, can read any of your computer files at any time, you cannot store important files on the LAN. People who would never dream of rifling through the president's desk will nevertheless browse through others' LAN files.

- *Preventing fraud.* If all employees know they have access to the accounting system's accounts payable files, an unscrupulous person may be tempted to tell the computer to issue a check in his or her name.

- *Preventing malicious damage.* If a disgruntled employee has access to all the files on the LAN, he or she may corrupt or modify these files. By the time someone detects the damage, the company could find itself in dire financial straits. The capability to share files is a two-edged sword. It also implies the opportunity to corrupt or destroy files.

Using Passwords

The first key to security is the password. Each LAN user identifies himself or herself with a *password*—a secret word known only to that user. If properly used, passwords verify the identity of the person who logs on to the LAN. Proper password administration guidelines include encouraging people to use hard-to-guess passwords, asking people to change their passwords regularly, and asking people to keep their passwords secret.

Limiting Access

Another key to security is to limit access within the LAN on a directory-by-directory or server-by-server basis. With NetWare, for example, you can give a person the right to open and read files in a directory, but restrict him or her from modifying those files. Or you may make an entire directory off-limits. And if you want to protect important files even from your own typing errors, you can mark files as *read only* so that you cannot delete or modify the files.

Protecting Your Data

File servers, like other computers, sometimes fail. Whether the failure is the result of a loss of electrical power or of a hard disk crash, you will want to minimize the effect of a server failure. Your data is important to you, and it represents an investment of time and energy that you do not want to lose. This means that you need to get serious about file backup, data redundancy, and power protection.

File Backup

The method you use to make backup copies of your data will depend mostly on how much data you have. Floppy disks may do the job on a very small LAN, but in most cases, you will likely use a tape drive to copy files to a magnetic tape cartridge. If your data is critically important, you may forego the tape drive and use a *WORM* (write-once-read-many) drive. (A WORM drive has a laser that burns patterns of pits and holes into a glass or plastic disk; such recordings last a very long time.)

No matter what device you use to make backup copies, you should make frequent and regular copies of your data in case something happens to your computer or its data.

If you are the person in your office who makes backup copies, you can choose one of the following approaches, depending on how often your data changes, how important it is, and how much work you would have to do if you had to reenter it:

- *Occasional.* You may get by with occasionally copying individual files to one or more floppy disks. This approach is the least secure, but it is better than nothing. If you use this method, make sure that you label your disks. Disorganization is your enemy with this approach. And, if you have to restore a file, you may find that your backup copy is not as recent as you would like. If this happens, you will have to redo any work you have done since the backup copy was made. You may even find that the disk containing the backup copy is damaged, and you have to redo *all* the work of re-creating the data.

■ *Serious.* If you make backup copies regularly (perhaps more often than once a day), if you use a backup utility such as BACKUP.EXE, and if you use two sets of disks (or two tapes) to do your backups, you are in this category. You know exactly how much time has elapsed since your last backup copy was made. You know exactly which disks to use if you need to restore a file.

■ *Professional.* Data centers with multi-million-dollar mainframe computers use this method. You can, too. Essentially, you always have three copies of your data on three sets of disks (or magnetic tapes). To make your backup copies, you first identify each set of disks as A, B, or C. (For safety's sake, you should actually have two A sets, two B sets, and two C sets.) You rotate your use of the three sets of disks so that, if today's backup is labeled C, you have yesterday's backup copies on B and the previous day's on A. Then, tomorrow, you use the A set to make your backup copies. You may even extend this approach to a fourth set of disks and make sure that the oldest copy is taken *off-site* (to a different location) just in case something happens to the building in which your computer is located. (This backup method is sometimes known as the *grandfather/father/son scheme.*)

Data Redundancy

Backup also means redundancy. You are better off to have two medium-size file servers than one giant server. If a file server breaks down, you can get by temporarily with the other server. Of course, you should make the second server part of your backup procedure.

Manufacturers of file server computers recognize the need for data redundancy and offer models that contain *disk arrays*—multiple hard disks that mirror each other. If one hard disk dies, another carries on without a moment's hesitation. People refer to this multiple-disk duplication of data as *redundant array of inexpensive disks,* or RAID.

> **Caution**
>
> Multiple hard disks and multiple servers are not a substitute for a good file backup procedure.

Power Protection

Power failures happen unexpectedly. Sometimes they happen during a thunderstorm, but power failures happen at other times, too.

Nearly all software will, to some extent, corrupt the file it is working on at the time of a power failure. For a word processor, this means that you lose what you have keyed in since the last time you saved the file. For an accounting program, it may mean that you lose everything you keyed in since the last time you backed up the files to tape. To protect yourself, place your servers on an uninterruptible power system (UPS). You should not, however, place workstations and especially laser printers on a UPS along with the file server. The manufacturer rates a UPS according to the amount of electricity the UPS can supply to the devices you attach, and you shouldn't exceed that rating.

If the power fails, batteries will keep the server running for another 10 minutes—enough time to gracefully shut down the server without losing your files. In addition, a UPS isolates the server from spikes and sags in the supply of commercial electrical power. These spikes and sags may reboot a computer or cause the computer to malfunction temporarily. Such spikes or sags cause just as many problems as a full-fledged blackout. At times, very large spikes will permanently damage a computer. When commercial power fails, a UPS can tell the network operating system to close down the files, without human intervention.

You can use a lower-cost standby power system (SPS) to protect your equipment from blackouts, along with a power-line filter to help remove spikes and electrical noise from the supply of commercial power. By itself, an SPS does not protect you from spikes and sags, however.

Asking for Help

If you buy a lemon computer, you will be out, at most, a few thousand dollars. If you buy a lemon LAN, you may be out tens of thousands of dollars, or worse. Even if you buy a first-class LAN, you may buy one that is too complex or one that cannot grow with your organization. You may wind up throwing it out and starting over again. Even if you feel confident enough to choose a

LAN on your own, it may be wise to hire someone with experience for just a few hours of consultation to verify your plans. The expert also may be able to warn you of costs you forgot to budget.

Installing a LAN can be a humbling experience. You need to understand adapter card jumpers, I/O addresses, upper memory blocks (UMBs), IRQs, page frames, and other esoteric things. Most of the work of installing a LAN consists of resolving conflicts between the LAN hardware and the hardware you already have installed.

Summary

You now have a good understanding of local area networks. You know what a LAN can do, and you know the components of a LAN—workstations, file servers, cables, network adapter cards, and the all-important network operating system. You see security in a new light, and you realize the importance of making backup copies of the information on the LAN. You know why you need an uninterruptible power supply for the file server, and you have some guidelines for when you should ask for advice from an expert. You are well on your way to becoming a LAN expert yourself.

In the next chapter, you learn more about sharing disks, printers, CD-ROM drives, modems, fax machines, applications, and application data files on a LAN.

Chapter 2

Sharing Computer Resources

The sharing of computer resources—disks, printers, files, and devices—is the bread and butter of local area networks. Networks come in many sizes, and you can find a configuration to fit virtually every networking situation. You may have two computers that need to share only a single printer. You may have thousands of computers that need to share huge files at the same time they access a mainframe computer. Or, more likely, the combination of computers and devices you want to share is something between these two extremes. This chapter shows you how to find a network that fits your particular needs. You also learn how networks can be configured in a wide variety of ways to solve connectivity problems.

The most popular shared resource is a disk drive, and this chapter begins by explaining the different ways you can share a disk among several computers and people. After you explore the sharing of disks and disk space, you move on to printer sharing. From a simple printer switchbox to an array of print servers on a LAN, you learn how different printer sharing options enable you to send your printouts to a remote printer. You also discover why you need to be a good neighbor as you use the communal printer.

This chapter then tells how you can share a CD-ROM disk drive on a network. CD-ROMs are not ordinary disk drives and require special consideration to be shared successfully. And, speaking of special considerations, would you like to be able to share a fax machine on your LAN? You can, as you see in this chapter.

Connecting one or more modems to your LAN so that you can share access to other computers (a bulletin board system, a host computer, or an information system) is the area you explore next. For communications in the other direction, when remote users want to be able to use your LAN as if they were in your office, this chapter explains your options.

Sharing Disks and Files

Disk-sharing options range from simple PC-to-PC file-transfer utilities, such as LapLink or Brooklyn Bridge, to multiple-server configurations of NetWare and LAN Manager networks that include Apple Macintosh and UNIX computers, alongside the ubiquitous IBM PC and clones. In the next few sections of this book, you explore this wide range of options.

Sharing Files without a LAN

When you have two computers you want to connect temporarily so that you can copy a few files from one computer to the other, a simple serial link between the computers will do the job nicely. Figure 2.1 shows such a serial link between two PCs. Using the modem port (often labeled *RS-232*, *Serial*, or *COM1*) or perhaps the parallel (printer) port on each computer, you can use products like the following to copy those directories and files that you select from a menu:

> LapLink
> Traveling Software
> 18702 N. Creek Parkway
> Bothell, WA 98011
> (800) 662-2652
>
> Brooklyn Bridge
> Symantec Corp.
> 10201 Torre Avenue
> Cupertino, CA 95014
> (800) 441-7234
> (503) 345-3322
> Fax: (503) 334-7474

The software creates directories on the target computer as necessary. If you have several megabytes of files to transfer, plan on doing something else for a while after you start the transfer. This method of copying files is faster and more convenient than using floppy disks but much slower than accessing files through a local area network.

Peer-to-Peer Networks

To connect a small group of computers permanently, you will need more than a simple file-transfer utility. You step up to the first level of local area networks when you tie computers together on more than a temporary basis. At this first level, you do not need to set aside a personal computer to act as a file server. In fact, all the computers can be file servers and workstations at the same time; this environment is called *peer LAN*.

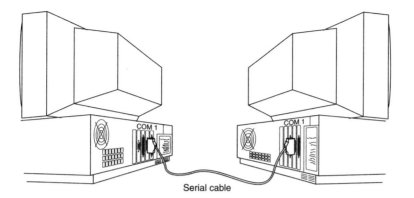

Fig. 2.1
Using a serial link
to transfer files.

Serial cable

Figure 2.2 depicts a peer LAN environment, in which three desktop computers each act as both a file server and a workstation. In a peer LAN, the disk
space and files on your computer become communal property. It can be un-
nerving at first to be sitting at your computer, working away, and see the
hard disk activity indicator light blinking as someone else accesses your disk
and its files. Or you may be annoyed to find that your computer is slower
than usual because you are sharing its resources. Peer LANs, however, are
cost-effective for small, lightly loaded networks. And peer LANs have an advantage over server-based LANs— you don't have to remember to copy a file
from your computer to a separate file server in order for other people to access that file. Depending on how you set up security, others may be able to
access files immediately after you create them.

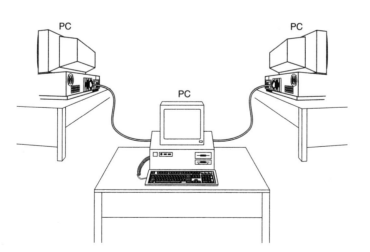

Fig. 2.2
Three peer LAN
computers, sharing
each other's hard
disks.

A list of peer LAN products, along with the companies that offer them, follows:

10NetPlus
Digital Communications Associates, Inc.
7887 Washington Village Drive
Dayton, OH 45459
(800) 358-1010

AppleTalk
Apple Computer
20525 Mariani Avenue
Cupertino, CA 95014
(408) 996-1010

EasyNet
LanMark
P.O. Box 246
Postal Station A
Mississauga, Ontario
Canada L5A 3G8
(416) 848-6865

GV LAN OS
Grapevine LAN Products
15323 Northeast 90th Street
Redmond, WA 98052
(206) 869-2707

LANsmart
D-Link Systems
5 Musick
Irvine, CA 92718
(714) 455-1688

LANsoft
ACCTON Technology
46750 Fremont Boulevard
Suite 104
Fremont, CA 94538
(415) 226-9800

LANStep
Hayes Microcomputer Products
P.O. Box 105203
Atlanta, GA 30348
(404) 441-1617

LANtastic
Artisoft
575 East River Road
Tucson, AZ 85704
(602) 293-6363

NET/30
Invisible Software
1165 Chess Drive
Suite D
Foster City, CA 94404
(415) 570-5967

NetWare Lite and Personal NetWare
Novell, Inc.
122 East 1700 South
Provo, UT 84606
(800) 453-1267

Network OS
CBIS
5875 Peachtree Industrial Boulevard
Building 100, Unit 170
Norcross, GA 30092
(404) 446-1332

POWERLan
Performance Technology
7800 IH 10, W.
800 Lincoln Center
San Antonio, TX 78230
(512) 524-0500
(512) 349-2000

ReadyLink
Compex
4055 East La Palma Avenue
Suite C
Anaheim, CA 92807
(714) 630-7302

WEB
WebCorp
3000 Bridgeway
Sausalito, CA 94965
(415) 331-1449

Windows for Workgroups
Microsoft Corporation
One Microsoft Way
Redmond, WA 98052
(800) 426-9400

Using Your PC as a Workstation and Server

A peer LAN makes your computer work much harder than it normally does.
Most peer LAN network operating systems are DOS-based, which means that
the network software has to use DOS to access the hard disk, just as your
applications do. When another user on the LAN runs an application that
reads or writes files located on your hard disk, the network operating system
steps in and takes momentary control of your computer. After satisfying the
other user's file request, the network operating system relinquishes control
back to the application you are running. For a small file, you may not even
notice that your hard disk has been accessed. If the file is large, however, it
may take several seconds or even minutes for DOS to locate all the portions
of the file. DOS can't handle large files quickly and efficiently.

When you start a computer that is both a workstation and a server, you see
DOS load, and then you see the network software load. Usually, the network
operating system loads as one or more TSRs (terminate-and-stay-resident
programs). Unless you have an 80386 computer and memory manager software, the network TSRs will take up part of the 640K of conventional
memory. You therefore will have somewhat less RAM in which to run your
applications. Memory usage can range from as little as 0K if you use a
memory manager to as much as 60K to 110K of RAM if the network software
must use a portion of the 640K.

On a network, you want to make sure that the SHARE.EXE program is loaded automatically at all computers. SHARE comes with DOS (not with the network operating system) and enables file sharing on your computer. If SHARE is not loaded, you may find that files become strangely corrupted.

Allowing Others to Access Your Computer

The network operating system enables you to assign names to your disk drives. You publish these names to the other users, who use networking commands such as NET USE to access the disks. You can automate this process by putting the networking commands in the AUTOEXEC.BAT files for the computers on the network. If you do this, the network will start up automatically when you power on all the computers.

What happens if you reboot your computer while another user is accessing it? Peer LAN network operating systems do the best they can in such a case. If you press Ctrl-Alt-Del, the network operating system asks whether you are sure you want to reboot. If you answer Yes, the NOS closes any files that other workstations have open, notifies the other workstations that the server which is your computer is no longer available, and enables the reboot to occur. If you use the power switch to reboot the computer, however, the network operating system has no warning. Another user on the network may at that moment be writing a file to your hard disk. The power interruption may very well cause that user's file to become corrupted, and you may have to run the DOS CHKDSK utility to repair the damage when you power back on. CHKDSK probably will not be able to salvage all of the file. The other user will have to redo some or all of his or her work.

Managing Disk Space

On a peer LAN, other people can use your hard disk as if it were their own. If you do not establish procedures and guidelines for disk space usage, these people can use up your disk space rapidly. You definitely will want to have procedures in your office for periodic housecleaning.

You can avoid the problem to some degree if you tell DOS to partition your hard disk into more than one logical drive. The extra partition will become a new DOS drive letter (D, for example). You can share the new drive letter on the LAN and let other people know the shared resource exists by publishing an alias for just that new drive letter. You then keep drive C for your own use. To do this, however, you should back up all the files on your computer before running the DOS FDISK and FORMAT commands.

Note that if you simply establish separate directories on the hard disk for public use, you cannot limit disk space usage. One directory can hold files that take up an entire disk.

Backing Up and Restoring Peer LAN Files

Even if people stick to using their own hard disks and use the peer LAN lightly or not at all to share files, the network can be the basis for a centralized backup procedure. From one workstation, you can make backup copies of the files on all the other workstations. Of course, you will want to implement the professional file backup scheme mentioned in Chapter 1, "A Networking Overview."

Note that you must share—and connect to—all the drives on all the computers in order to do a thorough backup. And note that the workstation performing the backup (to which the tape drive is attached) must have permission to access all the files in all the subdirectories you want backed up.

Handling Security and Administration on a Peer LAN

Most peer LANs implement security in two ways. First, a network administrator assigns account IDs (sometimes called user IDs) to the people who use the computers on the network. The administrator also sets up passwords for new accounts, but each person can later change his or her password to a secret combination of letters and numbers. To use the LAN, a person logs in by typing the account ID and password. As it is typed, the password does not appear on-screen. Account IDs and passwords ensure that only authorized people use the LAN, and they verify the identity of each person so that each person can be given different access rights or permissions on the network.

The second means of providing security is to assign permissions. Some peer LAN products use default permissions for new account IDs that enable a user to access everything on the network. The administrator then must name specifically each drive letter (alias) or directory that the new user should not access. Other peer LANs use default permissions that deny a new user any and all access to the LAN, and the administrator must, in this case, specifically name each drive letter or directory that the new user *can* access. Either way, network administrators are busy people in organizations that have a high employee turnover rate.

A special account ID exists to identify the network administrator. This special account ID sometimes is named *Supervisor* or *Manager.* Anyone who logs in with this account ID can delete not only files but also other account IDs. The password for this special account ID should be kept highly secret.

The network administrator has the responsibility of setting up new accounts, deleting old accounts, publishing new aliases for drive letters, and generally troubleshooting all the problems that happen on the network. The wise administrator sets up generalized BAT files that he or she can install on all the workstations to automate much of the access to the network. The administrator also keeps a special boot disk handy, with network software on it, in case a user accidentally renders a workstation unusable on the network.

Server-Based LANs

In contrast to peer LANs, server-based LANs offer better performance and increased reliability. Your first step up from a pure peer LAN environment is to dedicate one of the computers on the network as a file server and use the same peer LAN network operating system product to now have a server-based LAN.

> **Note**
>
> You will want to read your license agreement for the peer LAN network operating system to see whether you need to pay a different license fee for the software in this situation.

Naturally, using a peer LAN computer as a dedicated file server means that DOS is still in charge of the files on the server. If you want to go beyond DOS-based LANs, you need to take yet another step up. Network operating systems such as NetWare install themselves into the file server and replace DOS entirely. By managing the computer completely as a file server and by organizing the disk in a way that performs well for large files (which DOS cannot do), dedicated server-based network operating systems enable LANs to be larger and do more work. Figure 2.3 illustrates a server-based LAN. Notice in the figure that the file server is the central resource on the LAN that the other PCs (the workstations) access.

Fig. 2.3

A server-based
LAN.

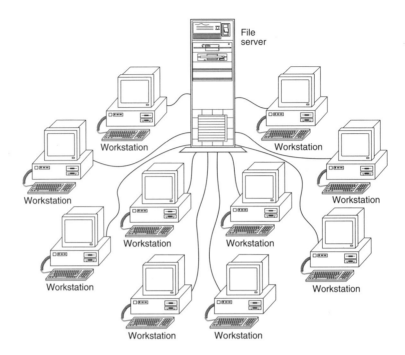

A list of dedicated-server LAN products, followed by the companies that offer them, follows:

AppleTalk
Apple Computer
20525 Mariani Avenue
Cupertino, CA 95014
(408) 996-1010

LAN Manager
Microsoft Corporation
One Microsoft Way
Redmond, WA 98052
(800) 426-9400

LAN Server
IBM Corporation
Old Orchard Road
Armonk, NY 10504
(800) 426-2468

NetWare
Novell, Inc.
122 East 1700 South
Provo, UT 84606
(800) 453-1267

VINES
Banyan Systems
120 Flanders Road
Westboro, MA 01581
(508) 898-1000

Using Your Workstation

As Chapter 1 explained, you see four major differences between a stand-alone computer and one that is a workstation on a LAN. You see extra messages at boot time, you have to use a login process to access the LAN, you have extra drive letters that represent the disk drive(s) on the file server(s), and you can send printouts to a remote printer. You see these differences whether you are on a peer LAN or a server-based LAN.

On a server-based LAN, however, you do not have to share your workstation's hard disk with other people. In fact, if you want to share a file with someone, you must copy the file to a file server (or create it on the server to begin with) before the other person can access the file. You can reboot your workstation without worrying about destroying someone's files. And the disk space on your local hard disk is yours to administer. Figure 2.4 shows a server-based LAN product, Banyan VINES.

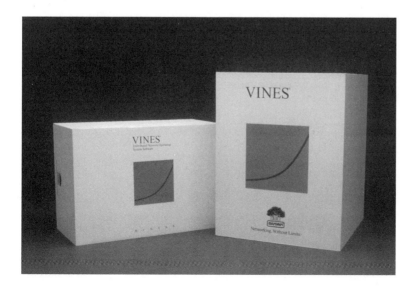

Fig. 2.4
The Banyan VINES network operating system is server-based.

Managing Disk Space

Managing the disk space on the file server is another matter. On most server-based networks, your network administrator has tools for controlling disk space usage. On a NetWare LAN, for example, the administrator (supervisor) can limit you to a certain number of megabytes of space. The administrator can easily get reports of disk space usage by account ID. If necessary, the administrator can even use NetWare's built-in accounting system to "charge" each department of people for the LAN disk space the group uses. (In practice, this is rarely done.)

Typically, you have a directory on the file server all to yourself, with your account ID as the name of the directory. You have all rights to this directory. You can share files with others by granting them the rights to see, open, and read files in your directory. These rights may even be the default rights set up by the network administrator as each new account ID is created.

Suppose that you are starting a special project at work and you will be working with a team of people on the project. The network administrator may create a special directory for you and give the entire team all rights to the directory—rights to see, create, read, write, and delete files, as well as to create directories within the project directory.

Backing Up and Restoring Files

The network administrator usually will take care of backing up and restoring files for the entire network. Because server-based networks can be quite large, both in terms of number of users and volume of files, the backup procedure almost certainly will fall into the professional category mentioned in Chapter 1. In fact, the LAN may have a computer with the sole purpose of making backup copies of file server files. Such a machine is a *backup server*.

A tape drive that uses 250M tapes may be out of its league on a large server-based network. You will find that gigabyte tape drives are more the norm on large networks. The following companies have products especially for large networks:

Emerald
12230 World Trade Drive
San Diego, CA 92128
(619) 673-2161

Mountain Network Solutions
240 East Hacienda Avenue
Campbell, CA 95008
(408) 379-4300

Palindrome
850 Diehl Road
Naperville, IL 60563
(708) 505-3300

Palindrome's The Network Archivist (TNA), for example, keeps track of the
last time a file was accessed. If disk space gets low, and if a file has not been
accessed in a long while, TNA will (at the network administrator's option)
delete the old file but leave a marker in its place. If a user accesses the file
marker, TNA alerts the network administrator to mount the tape containing
the file so that the file can be restored to the file server.

Many backup and restore products can even help the network administrator
manage hidden files containing account IDs, passwords, and other network-
specific data.

Using Faster, Larger Disks

Network disk drives and old closets have something in common. They tend
to fill up rapidly, and they never seem large enough. On a server-based network, large, heavy-duty disk drives are more the rule than the exception.
Many companies make disk drives, and almost all of them work fine on a
server-based network. Companies that specialize in larger, sturdier disk drives
include IBM, Seagate, Maxtor, Core, and Racet.

Handling Security and Administrative Issues

On a peer LAN, the network administrator position may be a part-time job
for someone (perhaps you). On a large server-based LAN, however, the network administrator position may be filled by one full-time employee, two
employees, or even more people. Almost every activity of such an administrator is related to seeing that the LAN's resources are shared fairly and productively among its users.

In addition to setting up new account IDs (and deleting old ones), an administrator uses his or her supervisory privileges to create new directories as
necessary, monitor disk space usage, make occasional LAN configuration
changes, and help people who are having trouble.

Server-based LANs use basically the same approach to security as peer LANs—
account IDs, passwords, and permissions—but in a more sophisticated way.
The administrator has more flexibility and options regarding how LAN resources are shared. On a NetWare LAN, for example, the administrator can
assign a greater variety of permissions (rights) among the LAN's users.

Disk space is only one of the resources a LAN can share, although clearly it is the most important. The next most popular LAN device that is shared is the printer.

Sharing Printers

In the simplest of cases, when you need to share a printer among a few computers but you do not want to share files, you do not need a LAN at all; a printer switchbox will suffice. At the opposite extreme, you may have multipart forms, address labels, word processing documents, and thousands of pages of reports to print—all produced by dozens of computer users. In the latter case, you definitely need a LAN. You may even dedicate one or more of the computers on the LAN to keeping the printers busy.

Using Printer Switchboxes

You can share a single printer among two or three computers quite easily, without setting up a LAN. As long as you do not need to share any other computer resource besides the printer, you can install a printer switchbox. The simplest switchbox is called an A/B box, because a computer user who needs to use the printer just reaches over to the box to flip a switch from the A position to the B position in order to gain access to the printer. The switchbox has two or more ports for incoming parallel or serial printer cables from the computers, and it has one outgoing port for the cable to the printer.

Figure 2.5 shows three PCs that print to a single printer through a printer switchbox. For a variation on this theme, you can purchase a switchbox that attempts to detect which computer wants to use the printer. As you may expect, such automatic devices do not always guess right about which characters go on which page when two computers try to print at the same time. Such devices can be handy, however, when you have people who find walking to a central switchbox from different rooms or offices unproductive and inconvenient. You should also be aware that some laser printer manufacturers recommend that you do not use their printers with printer switchboxes.

Pacific Data Products makes printer-sharing devices that work well and that fit right inside a Hewlett-Packard LaserJet printer. You can connect up to 10 computers to a single printer with the Pacific Connect Xi device. The company's DirectNet EX product connects up to three printers directly to a NetWare or TCP/IP-based network. For more information, contact the following:

Pacific Data Products
9125 Rehco Road
San Diego, CA 92121
(619) 552-0880

Using Print Servers

On a peer LAN, your computer can simultaneously be a workstation, a file server, and a print server. If you find yourself the keeper of the office's printer simply because it is attached to your peer LAN workstation/server, you will become a part-time printer attendant. You will clear paper jams, load a fresh supply of paper, change ribbons or toner cartridges, and stack the printed pages on a table for others to retrieve. Your workstation will perform more slowly because it is spending time printing for other people. If this happens to you and the printer is used a great deal, you may want to suggest that the office arrange a separate, dedicated computer—and an official part-time printer attendant—to take care of the printer.

The separate print server computer also can be a file server. Both peer LANs and server-based LANs can be set up this way. A file server can handle light to occasionally moderate printing chores without affecting its ability to serve files to the workstations on the LAN.

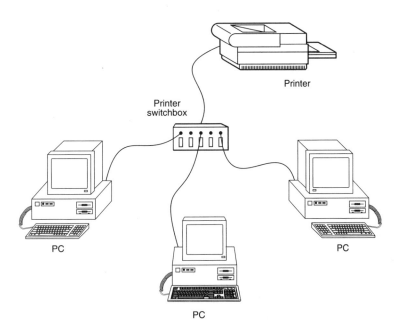

Fig. 2.5
Sharing a printer through a switchbox.

For moderate to heavy printer usage, your LAN will need a dedicated print server. This is especially true if you have more than one printer or if you have a high-speed laser printer (such as the Hewlett-Packard IVsi). Figure 2.6 illustrates a print server PC whose sole purpose is to drive a shared network printer.

Fig. 2.6
A dedicated print
server on the LAN.

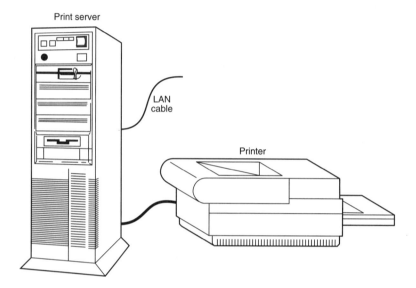

Redirecting Printouts

Whether or not your print server is dedicated, printing to the network printer is a matter of telling the network software that you want your printouts redirected across the network. With some networks, you issue a NET USE command to accomplish this. On a NetWare LAN, you issue the CAPTURE command.

A personal computer can have up to three printer ports, named LPT1, LPT2, and LPT3. If more than one network printer exists, the NET USE or CAPTURE command can associate these DOS printer port names with different network printers. The system administrator will publish a list of which printers are available and the printers' alias names. After you set up LPT1, LPT2, and LPT3 to redirect printouts to particular network printers, you simply tell your application software which printer port (and therefore which printer) to use.

Using Laser Printers

Laser printers are usually fast, heavy-duty, feature-laden devices. They lend themselves to LAN environments because of their speed and versatility. One person may print a memo on the network printer; the next person may print a wide, sideways-appearing (*landscape mode*) report or chart; and the third person's print job may consist of a *portrait mode* newsletter containing a great number of typefaces (*fonts*). The same printer produces all these printouts fairly quickly, without breaking stride.

Page-per-Minute Ratings

Printer manufacturers rate laser printer speed in terms of pages per minute. The rating is a best-case average; pages containing picture images or many fonts print more slowly. For instance, Hewlett-Packard rates its LaserJet IIP printer at 4 pages per minute and the IVsi at 17 pages per minute. Xerox rates its model 4045 printer at 6 pages per minute, the model 3700 at 24 pages per minute, and the model 4220 at 20 pages per minute. As you consider what sort of printer you want to share on your LAN, you will want to conservatively count on actually producing fewer pages per minute, depending on whether you print plain-paper reports (quick) or multiple-font-and-image newsletters (slow).

Duty Cycles

After a laser printer prints about 6,000 pages, you need to change the toner cartridge or refill the toner compartment. At 100,000 pages, depending on the printer, you may need to send the printer back to the factory to be overhauled (a service technician or repair depot may handle such matters for you, of course). In addition to these limitations, the laser printer needs to rest every so often. A laser printer cannot print continuously, 24 hours a day, without stopping. The period of time the printer can operate without stopping for a while is its *duty cycle*. This is usually expressed in terms of pages per month. The Hewlett-Packard IVsi, for example, has a duty cycle of 75,000 pages per month, whereas the H-P LaserJet IV should be used only to print fewer than 20,000 pages per month. If you have high-volume print requirements in your office, make sure that you investigate the duty cycle of a printer before you buy it. On a LAN, because many people share the printer, duty cycle and page-per-minute ratings become considerations you may not otherwise need to worry about. You wouldn't want, for example, to use the small H-P IIP as the shared printer in an office that prints large volumes of paper.

Font Cartridges and Downloadable Fonts

Fonts of different sizes and styles are popular add-ons for laser printers. People like to be able to choose just the right font to make their printouts look good. Fonts are available as files you download into the printer from a computer and as cartridges you insert in the printer.

On LANs with many users, the number of fonts everyone wants to use may exceed the number supported by the shared laser printer. You may be able to simply put more RAM into the laser printer, but at some point, you should count on establishing guidelines in your office for which fonts are available in the network printer. You also need to set up procedures for redownloading the fonts into the printer in case someone powers off the printer (to clear a paper jam, for example).

Using Dot-Matrix Printers

Dot-matrix printers are excellent for preprinted forms, multipart forms, and address labels. The process of aligning forms, which is not always done easily with a locally attached printer, becomes even more of a chore with a network printer. You may even find that you have to print a form, walk across the office to the printer to make adjustments, and then repeat the process if further alignment is called for. Dot-matrix printers also have rated speeds and duty cycles.

Practicing Printer-Sharing Etiquette

Unless your office is large enough to warrant hiring a printer attendant, sharing a network printer means that each person needs to be a good neighbor so that everyone gets fair use from the printer. When you walk over to the printer to retrieve your printout, you may discover that the printer is having trouble. The printer may only be out of paper, or the paper may have jammed inside the printer. The output tray may be full, or the printer may need a new toner cartridge (or a new ribbon). If you need to turn off the printer and then turn it back on again, you may need to download the printer's fonts again.

You can be a good neighbor in the way you print your output, too. The printer knows the last font it used and, unless told otherwise, continues to use that font for other print jobs. One person may walk away from the printer with a perfectly formatted, sideways-printed, small-font spreadsheet report. The next person, who simply wanted to print a plain-paper status report or memo, sighs in disgust to find that the report or memo resembles a spreadsheet. Even on a dot-matrix printer, the way you tear off the last form affects the next person. You should leave forms and labels in an aligned state.

Sharing CD-ROM Drives

CD-ROM disk drives are popular add-ons for stand-alone personal computers. Naturally, people also want to share these drives on a LAN. Your LAN may use CD-ROM disks that contain generally published material such as encyclopedia, dictionary, and almanac information. Or your LAN may use CD-ROM disks containing specialized data that is particular to your business. On many LANs, you can share such information and thus make it easier (and cheaper) for everyone to access the large volume of data on a single CD-ROM disk.

Several companies make CD-ROM drives, including Sony, Pioneer, NEC, Hitachi, Panasonic, Chinon, and Toshiba. In addition, companies including IBM, Storage Dimensions, Corel, and Racet offer *read/write optical drives.* A *write-once-read-many (WORM)* disk drive, such as the one made by Storage Dimensions, makes a good backup device on a LAN. Once you write data onto a WORM disk, you cannot erase the data—you've made a backup copy of your files that will last for a very long time. *Read/write magneto-optical* (MO) drives are also good devices for making backup copies of important files, but you have to be careful not to erase your backup copy of your files. All these disk drives use a laser, or a laser with magnetism, to record data.

Realizing That CD-ROMs Need Special Software

CD-ROMs and other optical drives use an internal data format that is unlike the format of DOS-based disks or even NetWare file server disks. You need special device drivers that understand this data format, which is sometimes called *High Sierra* but is more formally known as *ISO 9660.*

On stand-alone computers and most peer LANs, you can use the MSCDEX drivers written by Microsoft. These drivers come bundled with all CD-ROM drives. You can obtain an OS/2 CD-ROM driver from your CD-ROM manufacturer so that you can share a CD-ROM drive on an OS/2 LAN Server or LAN Manager network. On NetWare LANs, your options are more limited (it is difficult to make NetWare recognize ISO 9660 format disks). Corel, however, makes an optical drive that works with NetWare. Or you can use a product such as Map Assist to share the CD-ROM drive from another workstation rather than from the file server.

Using Optical Drives and Your LAN

CD-ROM disks and other read-only optical media hold hundreds of megabytes of data in permanent form (usually about 680M), prerecorded for your use. WORM disk cartridges are empty when you buy them, but once you store files on WORM disks, the recorded information is permanently etched on the disk. WORM disks usually are guaranteed for 10 years. (Both of these are good reasons to use a WORM drive as a LAN backup device.) A WORM cartridge typically holds 800M (400M on each side).

A read/write optical drive, however, behaves like an ordinary disk drive in an important way—you can read and write data on the disk. You can think of read/write optical drives, such as IBM's 3 1/2-inch 128M drive, as fast, very-high-capacity floppy disk drives. Like a floppy disk, the R/W optical disk cartridge is easily removed from the drive; you can implement an extra level of security by storing the disk in a safe place when the data is not in use.

CD-ROM, WORM, and read/write optical media are slower than a personal computer hard disk. You can use them to enhance your LAN, but you will not want to use them as your primary means of storing LAN data.

Using Modems and LAN Communications

On a LAN, communication is a two-way street. You can configure your LAN so that people can reach out to other computers from the LAN (bulletin board systems; an information service such as Prodigy, CompuServe, America Online, or Dow Jones News Retrieval; the Internet; or a host computer). And you can set things up so that people outside your office can access your LAN remotely through a communications link.

Occasionally Dialing Out

Perhaps your office just needs to share a modem for occasionally dialing into another computer system. If this is the case, a simple RS/232 switchbox may suffice. An RS/232 switchbox operates like the printer switchbox discussed earlier. Several serial cables lead from each of the personal computers (or workstations, as they may be part of a LAN) to the switchbox. A single serial cable connects the switchbox to the modem. When a person wants to use the modem, that person walks over to the switchbox, sets the switch to his or her computer, and proceeds to use the modem.

Frequently Dialing Out (Modem Pooling)

If people on your LAN need to access modems frequently, you can establish a pool of modems and use a communication server device from such companies as these:

> Cubix
> 2800 Lockheed Way
> Carson City, NV 89706
> (800) 829-0550

J&L Information Systems
9238 Deering Avenue
Chatsworth, CA 91311
(818) 709-1778

Network Products Corporation
1111 South Arroyo Parkway
Suite 450
Pasadena, CA 91105
(800) 638-7765

Or you can use a server device from another communications equipment vendor. Such a device connects to your LAN and enables several people to share modems or communications lines to a host computer.

Connecting through a Gateway Computer

Another option for handling outgoing communications from the LAN is the dedicated *gateway computer*. The gateway computer attaches to a host computer and handles multiple communications sessions at the same time. A person at a workstation runs software that uses one of those sessions. People at other workstations simultaneously use other sessions. Each workstation's software makes it look as if that computer is attached directly to the host, but the communications data actually is routed through one of the gateway computer's sessions. Figure 2.7 shows conceptually how each workstation on the LAN can have a host session through a gateway.

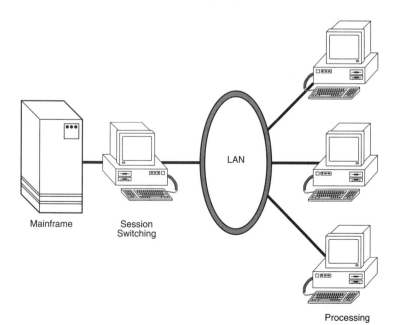

Fig. 2.7
Several LAN workstations can have host sessions through the gateway computer at the same time.

Mainframe   Session Switching   LAN   Processing

Several companies make gateway software and hardware products. Here are some of these companies:

Attachmate
13231 Southeast 36th Street
Bellevue, WA 98006
(800) 426-6283

Digital Communications Associates
1000 Alderman Drive
Alpharetta, GA 30201
(800) 241-4762

Eicon Technology
2196 32nd Avenue
Montreal, Canada H8T 3H7
(514) 631-2592

Gateway Communications
2941 Alton Avenue
Irvine, CA 92714
(800) 367-6555

Novell, Inc.
122 East 1700 South
Provo, UT 84606
(800) 453-1267

Wall Data
17769 Northeast 78th Place
Redmond WA 98052
(800) 433-3388

Dialing into the LAN

The simplest way to enable remote access to the LAN is to use remote control software. The remote user runs one copy of the software on his or her computer; a workstation on the LAN, with a modem attached, runs another copy. The remote user controls the workstation computer remotely, from his or her remote computer. The mirroring of screen and keyboard activity makes the remote user think that he or she is logged in to the LAN directly. In reality, the LAN workstation does all the work.

The remote control approach is simple, but it has drawbacks. While the remote user is communicating through the LAN workstation, that workstation cannot be used by anyone else. If you do not use fast modems, the remote user experiences slow response time. The remote PC becomes merely a terminal through which the screen and keyboard activity of the LAN-attached computer is mirrored. If an application changes the appearance of the screen frequently, or if the application uses graphics rather than text (as does Microsoft Windows), a remote control product is hard-pressed to keep up with the activity.

Here are the names of some of the software products that implement remote control, along with the names of the companies that offer them:

Carbon Copy
Microcom
500 River Ridge Drive
Norwood, MA 02062
(617) 551-1000

Close-Up
Norton-Lambert
P.O. Box 4085
Santa Barbara, CA 93140
(805) 964-6767

NETremote
Brightwork Development
766 Shrewsbury Avenue
Jerral Center West
Tinton Falls, NJ 07724
(800) 552-9876

pcANYWHERE
Symantec Corp.
10201 Torre Avenue
Cupertino, CA
95014
(408) 253-9600

Frequently Accessing Remote LANs

For anything beyond the most infrequent remote access to your LAN, remote control software is inadequate. When you're out of the office regularly, either traveling or working at a different location, you want to be able to access the LAN at the office quickly and reliably. Distance limitations won't let you string a LAN cable between your location and the main office; you will need to use a modem to connect with the LAN.

You have several alternatives when you want to log in to the LAN from a remote site. You can use a generalized remote control product, such as Microcom's Carbon Copy; you can use a special LAN remote control product, such as Novell's Access Server; you can buy a LAN-aware modem, such as the Shiva NetModem-E; or you can get Remote LAN Node, from Digital Communications Associates (DCA). CUBIX is another company that makes a product which implements remote access to the LAN and works well. Figure 2.8 shows a PC in a remote office connected through a telephone line to a LAN in the central office; the modems, modem server, and remote LAN software make the remote PC appear as just another workstation on the LAN. However, modems are slower than LANs, and the remote PC won't be able to access shared LAN files as quickly as a workstation that is directly attached to the LAN.

Fig. 2.8
Connecting to the LAN via modem from a remote site.

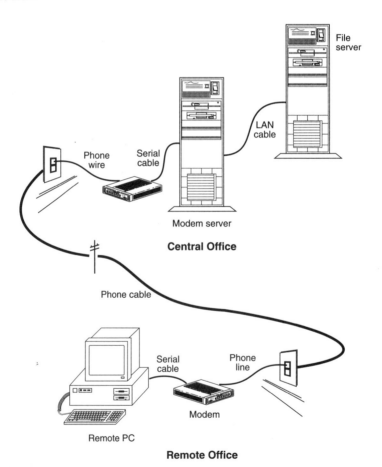

Generalized remote control software works by echoing the keypresses and screen images across the phone line. What you type gets played back by a computer in the office. The screen images appearing on that computer appear also on your remote PC. You need one PC in the office, each with its own modem, for each remote control session with a PC in a distant location. Performance can be sluggish as the remote control software shuttles screen image updates to you. Running Microsoft Windows through a remote control product can be painfully slow.

A *LAN-aware modem* eliminates the illusory "smoke and mirrors" of generalized remote control software and lets you actually become a node on the network from your remote site. The LAN-aware modem extends the LAN to you, despite the distance between you and the LAN. The two drawbacks to a LAN-aware modem are that you cannot use your existing modems and you are usually limited to the network operating systems the modem supports. The Shiva NetModem-E, for example, supports only NetWare and AppleTalk.

Looking at Access Server

Novell's Access Server is worth looking at. Access Server consists of software and special communications adapter boards. You supply a fast 80386 computer with 8M to 16M of RAM. Once installed, Access Server can manage several simultaneous communications sessions with remote users. Each user can use a small part of the Access Server computer. Unlike other workstations, the Access Server computer can perform multiple logins to the LAN, one for each remote user. The applications run by the remote user actually execute inside the Access Server computer.

Access Server takes the remote control design one step further by multi-tasking several mirrored sessions inside the central Access Server 386 or 486 PC. From your remote site, you control one of the sessions inside the Access Server computer. You can log in to an Access Server computer from a VT220 or other terminal, or with communications software such as Procomm Plus. With the remote control approach of Carbon Copy or Access Server, transferring files from your remote PC to the file server at the office can be problematic. Your remote PC is only a mirror of the processing that occurs in the PC at the office. You cannot run Microsoft Windows with Access Server, but you can use Access Server to dial into a NetWare LAN from even a dumb terminal. Access Server works only with NetWare LANs.

Considering Remote LAN Node

Like Access Server, Remote LAN Node (RLN) from DCA requires a dedicated PC on your network. RLN does not work through remote control, though;

RLN on the dedicated PC acts as a LAN bridge to give you the same kind of LAN connection as the other, locally attached nodes on the network. Your personal computer does the computational work. File service packets travel across the phone line to give you access to the remote file server. RLN is like a LAN-aware modem in this respect, but RLN doesn't require that you buy a unique kind of modem. The RLN server becomes a multiport LAN bridge that distributes file server data to remote clients.

The RLN server, itself a normal Ethernet node, forwards the requests for loading or saving files from your remote PC to the file server. Because the RLN server contains a single Ethernet card, RLN makes the file server believe that the requests come from the RLN server when, in fact, they originate in your remote PC. RLN supports a wide variety of network protocols and network operating systems, but only through Ethernet cards. You can use Network Driver Interface Specification (NDIS) or Open Datalink Interface (ODI) drivers supplied with RLN to connect to NetWare, UNIX, Banyan, LAN Server, or LAN Manager networks.

RLN's menu-driven installation and well-written documentation make quick work of getting RLN up and running. Configuration is a simple matter of specifying phone numbers, COM port usage, baud rate, and other communications parameters. On a client PC, the Remote LAN Node TSR takes up 55,872 bytes of RAM, and you can load RLN into high memory with a memory manager such as 386MAX, QEMM, or EMM386.

Performance depends primarily on the speed of the modems you use with RLN. Remote LAN Node works with Hayes-compatible modems, at speeds from 1200 baud to 38400 baud (if the remote workstation and RLN server PCs will handle the data rate, of course). At present, RLN does not work across X.25 links (Chapter 14, "Building WANs from LANs," explains X.25 in detail). MNP5 data-compressing modems help performance, and RLN itself implements compression at the packet level.

Because your RLN client workstation is essentially just another node on the LAN, you can copy files to and from the file server with the DOS COPY command. To do the same thing with remote control software such as Carbon Copy, pcANYWHERE, or Access Server, you have to invoke a special mode of the RC software and issue non-DOS commands.

After you are logged in to your LAN, your access to the file server and shared network printers becomes almost completely transparent. If you use Microsoft Windows, note that Remote LAN Node modifies your SYSTEM.INI and WIN.INI files to load Windows drivers that help the performance of the communications link while Windows is active. The Windows program files, data files, and most certainly the swap file should reside on your local hard disk. You wouldn't want to load these Windows files across a modem-based communications link.

Connecting LANs through Wide Area Networks

Even a multiple-user, dial-in facility like Access Server may not be enough in some cases. If you want a permanent connection between two geographically distant LANs, you need to create a wide area network (WAN) through a bridge or a router. Chapter 14, "Building WANs from LANs," discusses bridges, routers, and wide area networks in detail.

A *bridge* connects two LANs; each LAN may use a different protocol. You can install a bridge, for example, between an Ethernet LAN and a Token Ring LAN. The bridge transfers workstation and file server messages from one LAN to the next, as appropriate. The transfer may take place over phone lines, through modems. Naturally, the speed at which the modems operate governs the response times experienced by users on one LAN who access the other LAN. A *router*, in contrast to a bridge, shuttles workstation and file server LAN messages between LANs that use the same protocol (Ethernet to Ethernet, or Token Ring to Token Ring).

Companies that make LAN bridges and routers include Andrew Corporation, Microcom, Cisco, and Wellfleet.

Sharing Fax Machines

Fax machines are essential tools in offices today, just as are networks. The combination of the two is an interesting marriage of technologies.

If you do not have a LAN-based fax server, you typically take the following steps to send a document by fax:

1. You use a word processor or perhaps other application software to prepare the document you want to send by fax.

2. You print out the document pages and fill out a fax cover page.

3. You walk over to the fax machine, punch in the telephone number, and send the document.

When the fax machine prints an incoming document addressed to you, someone in the office may drop it off at your desk, or you may have to visit the fax machine periodically to retrieve your fax correspondence.

A LAN-based fax server saves both steps and paper. You can send fax documents directly from your workstation, without printing them first. The LAN-
based software prepares much of your cover page for you. The same word
processing software or other application software creates the document file,
but you send the printout to the LAN-based fax server rather than to a
printer. Under software control, the document goes into the fax queue to
wait its turn for transmission.

For incoming fax documents, the fax server device stores the image in a file
on a file server. You or an administrator can route the file to your workstation, where you view the image (the document) at your leisure. If you want
to print the fax, you can, but printing is optional.

On a small network, you may find that you don't need the sophistication or
power of a separate fax server. A simple fax/modem, connected to a workstation that's running LAN-aware fax software, might be sufficient.

If you think a LAN-based fax server would be a useful, timesaving, paper-
saving addition to your office, here are three products and their manufacturers that you will want to investigate:

> FAXPress
> Castelle
> 3255-3 Scott Boulevard
> Santa Clara, CA 95954
> (800) 359-7654

> FaxWorks LAN
> SofNet, Inc.
> 380 Interstate North Parkway
> Suite 150
> Atlanta, GA 30339
> (404) 984-8088

> NET Satisfaxion
> Intel
> PC Enhancements Division
> 5200 Northeast Elam Young Parkway
> Hillsboro, OR 97124
> (800) 538-3373

Castelle's FAXPress product, in addition to being a LAN-based fax server,
is a print server for networks that use NetWare. Figure 2.9 shows the FAXPress
product.

Fig. 2.9
Castelle's
FAXPress, which
can be both a fax
server and printer
server.

Summary

In this chapter, you covered the sharing of computer resources on a local area network. You learned various ways to share disk drives and disk space, from simple file-transfer utilities to peer LANs to server-based LANs. You now know why printing on a LAN can be different from printing on a stand-alone personal computer, and you are aware of the printer etiquette you should exercise to make the office run more smoothly.

You went beyond the sharing of hard disks and printers to explore turning a CD-ROM into an officewide source of information. You know ways to make fax documents easier to send and receive.

When people located in a different office need to access your LAN remotely, you understand the communications methods they can use. You also have a firm grasp of the considerations involved in setting up outgoing communications facilities to access other computers from your LAN.

In Chapter 3, you learn how electronic mail works, and you find out how you can use it to your best advantage.

Using Electronic Mail

Electronic mail is the most popular add-on feature for local area networks. You should have no trouble getting an E-mail product that is to your liking. Several commercial products exist. In some cases, the network operating system vendor bundles E-mail software with the network software. As you learn in this chapter, you can even find free E-mail applications to try out.

Electronic mail is a simple, yet potent, facility. When used office-wide, E-mail becomes more valuable and useful than the telephone for helping people communicate information. You can use E-mail to convey information that is difficult or impossible to read over the telephone, including reports, tables, statistics, charts, and images.

Electronic mail transcends the local area network; companies such as MCI Mail and CompuServe, as well as the Internet, offer dial-up E-mail services you can use nationwide or even worldwide. E-mail is not time-zone sensitive. You can carry on an E-mail conversation with someone halfway around the world, who may very well be sleeping as you reply to his or her mail.

In this chapter, you learn how electronic mail works, and you find out how you can use it to your best advantage. You explore two of the industry standards for E-mail: Action Technologies' Message Handling Service (MHS) and the CCITT X.400 specification. Next, you become acquainted with the electronic equivalent of address lists (so that you can send copies of a note to many people), and you discover the practical advantages of attaching files to your E-mail notes. You also learn about several of the popular E-mail products. The chapter closes with a look at *groupware*—the new class of software products designed to enhance the productivity of a team of people through E-mail and E-mail extensions.

An E-mail Overview

Electronic mail can replace both voice mail (answering machines) and inter-office memos. In its simplest form, E-mail consists of a mechanism for transferring a file of text from you to one or more people. On a LAN, this may take the form of merely copying a text file into a personal post office directory on the file server so that the recipient can open and read his or her mail. This simplest of approaches does nothing for privacy and security, however. Most products elaborate greatly on this approach, using file encryption or directory and file permissions to enforce security.

Electronic mail does not need to be LAN-based. You can subscribe to a number of commercial services that offer E-mail. To use one of these services, you simply dial a number with your modem, log on to the service, and begin using that service's E-mail commands. You can compose your messages on-line, but if the service charges on a connect-time basis, you may find it cheaper to compose your messages off-line and then quickly upload them to the service once you are on-line. These E-mail services include MCI Mail, CompuServe, BIX, Delphi, Prodigy, Western Union's EasyLink, AT&T Mail, the Internet, and others. Which service is best depends on your budget and, of course, on whether your correspondents are also on that same service.

Understanding E-mail Components

E-mail products show off the best features of a LAN-based computer. You can easily compose and route mail to all your correspondents, whether they're across the hall or across the country (through a modem). Under the hood, E-mail systems that use file servers are fairly straightforward. A central database contains the names and locations of all mail users. A second database holds individual mail messages and attached files. You will find that LANs are the most frequently used medium for routing E-mail from place to place. The more sophisticated packages also can send messages across longer distances—by way of a modem (over dial-up lines), through dedicated (leased) telephone lines, or through LAN bridges. Figure 3.1 illustrates one workstation sending an interoffice memo, electronically, to another workstation.

All E-mail software packages include a post office component and a user interface component. The software post office component, like the real U. S. Postal Service, takes a completed mail message, decodes the address, and sends the message to its destination. Depending on the address, your message may be routed across the office through the LAN, through other computer systems in your office to another LAN, or across the country through gateways and bridges. Software post offices should be invisible, reliable, and prompt. And, if you expect people in your office to use E-mail instead of interoffice paper memos (or instead of Federal Express), the product must have an intuitive interface.

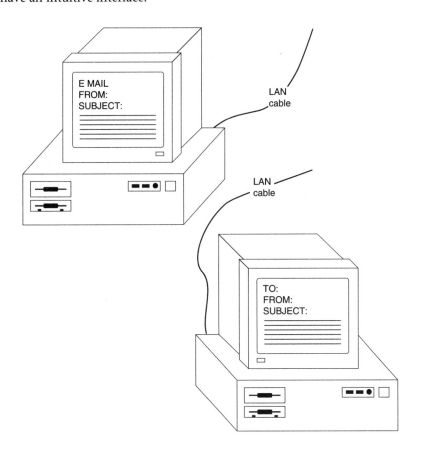

Fig. 3.1
Electronic mail can send interoffice memos from PC to PC.

The quality of the user interface is a primary factor in determining whether E-mail will fall into disuse or become an essential tool in the everyday operation of your office. If the software is overly obtuse or lacks the features people need to enable them to communicate information among themselves, the E-mail product will quickly begin gathering dust.

The text editor within the E-mail system must be friendly and easy enough to use for infrequent, novice E-mail users, and it must be fast and powerful for those who use the E-mail system many times each day. If the text editor imposes constraints on the size of a mail message you can type, the E-mail system must enable you to attach longer files that you have created with a word processor or other application. The text editor must enable you to quickly correct typing mistakes—even those in the mail header where the recipient's name and address show.

Looking at the Perfect E-mail Package

Everyone knows that effective communications contribute positively to the bottom line. If a business does not communicate well (with a remotely located sales staff, for example) the profit-and-loss picture may suffer accordingly. Companies that do well have learned the value of communications, including tools such as electronic mail products.

Phone tag is a frustrating game that no one likes to play. A good E-mail package helps you avoid the game by putting messages squarely on the desktop of the other person. With most E-mail packages, you can attach files that contain graphics images, a software update (executable file), or a lengthy report.

Most E-mail products are somewhat expensive (although you learn about two free ones later in this chapter). For a small LAN, price may be an overriding concern. In a large workgroup environment, however, where you are trying to establish electronic mail among many kinds of computers and networks, support and training will be your major expenses. If a vendor can offer a product that connects all your computers, along with support and training, you probably will find yourself doing business with that vendor.

Some E-mail products may provide security when accessed across the network from workstations, but may do nothing to prevent access from the server itself. You may need to lock your server in a secure place to prevent unauthorized tampering with the mail directories and files.

Generally speaking, electronic mail products are not particularly easy to install or maintain. You should consider E-mail software to be in the same class as file server software. Your network administrator should install the product, set up the user lists, and get the bridges connected (if appropriate). A system administrator should be able to manage an E-mail system easily, but for large installations that require bridges and gateways, help from an experienced installer is invaluable.

Another consideration is whether an E-mail system offers a mail front end for the different kinds of microcomputer systems and operating environments that everyone in your office is using. Some products offer front ends for

Macintosh, OS/2, Windows, and even NewWave users, in addition to the DOS version that virtually every system comes with. If you want to share mail with UNIX workstation users, you will want to be sure that the E-mail vendor offers a UUCP (UNIX-to-UNIX copy) or SMTP (Simple Mail Transfer Protocol) gateway. Through a UUCP or an SMTP gateway, UNIX users can send and receive E-mail to and from other computers.

Some E-mail products support a few specific types of network operating systems. Other products will work with any LAN that supports DOS file locking. All packages offer at least a rudimentary text editor, and some offer a graphics editor as well. Some products restrict the number and type of files you can attach. In addition, not all E-mail programs encrypt files—an important consideration if you don't want your mail read by others.

Some electronic mail products have add-ons you may want. These include a *voice mail* capability (annotating an E-mail message with a short sound recording), an *on-line conferencing* capability ("chatting" between workstations), and the capability to set up bulletin board areas where people can post public messages. Many products also enable you to call in and download your mail messages when you are out of the office.

Using Special Delivery

An *E-mail bridge* connects two similar E-mail systems. When your LAN post office software realizes it has to send a message to a separate post office, the originating post office must put the message into a special envelope and do some extra work to deliver the message to the other post office. To send the mail across town or across the country, the sending post office uses a company-wide address list to find the phone number of the other office. It then dials up the other post office and transfers the message through a modem. The receiving post office, after it has received the message and opened the special envelope, treats the resulting mail message like all the others it deals with locally. The receiving post office simply routes the incoming message to the addressee on the local LAN.

In contrast to an E-mail bridge, an *E-mail gateway* translates between different message formats when the two post offices use different mail systems. Sometimes this translation is simply the rearranging of address (and return address) information; however, the translation process may be much more involved. The translation almost always has to convert from one format of account identification to that of the other mail system.

You may need such a gateway if you do business through commercial E-mail services, such as Western Union's EasyLink or AT&T Mail. The gateway collects your outgoing messages, dials the E-mail provider on a periodic schedule, sends the outgoing messages, and picks up any incoming messages. Some services also provide their own gateway software that routes messages between LAN-based E-mail systems by way of the E-mail service.

Deciding Whether You Need E-mail

You may want to evaluate whether you actually need E-mail. Vendors of E-mail products will, of course, tell you that you need E-mail. E-mail can have a few drawbacks, however. For some products, for example, you need to be at your workstation to see the notification that you have something in your electronic in-basket. If you are away from your desk, you may miss the notification, and you will have to look in your in-basket to see what new mail you have. On a NetWare LAN, however, if the E-mail product uses the Send facility to notify you of incoming mail, the notification will sit at the bottom of your screen until you press Ctrl-Enter. On Macintosh-based E-mail systems, the Apple menu icons blink until you enter the E-mail system.

Another consideration is the size and organization of your office. If you have a fairly small office, with people who are located close to one another, E-mail may not be for you. Besides the cost of the E-mail product and the amount of file server disk space allocated to E-mail, you will incur administrative costs. For the small office, you may well find that a handwritten note or a tap on someone's shoulder is just as effective as E-mail. Technology for its own sake is sometimes not the answer.

If your company is geographically dispersed, if your office is large, if your workspace uses high partitions to separate people, or if you find it difficult to get the right people together to discuss your projects, E-mail may be the solution. In fact, if it sometimes takes more time to set up meetings in your office than the meetings themselves take, you will be interested not only in E-mail but in the workgroup scheduling software mentioned later in this chapter.

Using X.400, MHS, and Other Standards

E-mail systems do not adhere to a universal standard for addressing and sending messages. Such a standard exists, in the form of the CCITT (the international governing body on communications standards) X.400 specification, but X.400 is difficult and cumbersome to administer and use. Most E-mail products instead use a de facto standard created by Action Technologies, known as Message Handling Service (MHS).

X.400

The international E-mail interexchange standard, X.400, is so complex and costly to implement that currently only large enterprise-wide networks and commercial E-mail service providers use X.400 gateways.

X.400 is a CCITT standard; it defines how an intersystem mail message is addressed. When someone says "X.400," that person is usually referring not only to the addressing standard but also to a number of other CCITT E-mail standards. Among these are X.401, which describes the basic intersystem service elements, and X.411, which defines message-transfer protocols.

The most important member of the X.400 family of standards is X.410, which defines mail-handling protocols. X.410 deals with how Open Systems Interconnection (OSI) protocols work for E-mail applications. True E-mail interoperability is possible through these standards. Not all X.400 systems implement the standards properly, however. Some systems, for example, cannot reliably send binary files or Group 3 faxes (the most popular high-speed fax standard) from one network to another, even though such file transfer is part of the X.400 standard.

X.400 is becoming popular for international E-mail. U. S. Sprint, with its Telemail software, is a leader in providing overseas E-mail links. Administrators of Telemail networks, however, sometimes do not activate every connection with every possible E-mail domain, so you may not have access to overseas E-mail even if you use Telemail. However, some IBM proprietary E-mail systems do have X.400 gateways to Telemail.

Other obstacles to using X.400 exist. You must have a gateway from your LAN to an X.25 packet-switching network (like Telenet or Tymnet) in order to use X.400, and X.25 gateways are not common.

The X.400 Application Program Interface Association (APIA), founded in 1989, develops application programming interface standards between LAN E-mail systems, wide area network E-mail systems, gateways, and X.25 networks. Products using the X.400 API can connect your office's mail system to other mail systems. Such efforts are just beginning, and they will take years to bear fruit.

How do you address an X.400 E-mail message to someone? Basically, you format your text file with address elements defined in the standard. The E-mail system administrator assigns a unique originator/recipient name to every user. The format for an originator/recipient identifier follows:

keyword:value, keyword:value

Each keyword is an address element. Most E-mail systems use only a few address elements, but X.400 enables a system to use a dozen or more.

Every address contains certain common elements. For example, all X.400 addresses include an ADMD—Administrative Management Domain. An ADMD is a public-mail system (such as MCI Mail) that serves as a message-transfer system. A private mail domain (PRMD), such as a LAN E-mail system, can be attached to public networks like Telemail or MCI Mail.

A user name, user number, or a combination of first name and surname uniquely identifies an individual in his or her home mail system. A *WidgetMail* user, for example, who happens to work at the Widget Company, might be identified like this:

ADMD:MCIMail, PRMD:WidgetMail, FN:Barry, SN:Nance

The exact order in which the keywords and values appear does not matter.

As you can see from this scheme, keeping track of someone's E-mail address can require a sophisticated computer system and database. Knowing when you can use shortcut names and when you must use the elaborate form of the address is tricky. Fortunately, a new standard (labeled X.500 by the CCITT organization) addresses just this issue. A few years from now, X.500 will help you keep your mail messages from falling into a global dead-letter bin.

As defined by the CCITT, X.500 is a directory assistance system for computers. X.500 database systems will contain the E-mail addresses of all users with accounts in X.400-type systems around the world. Such a global directory will take a long time to appear, of course.

MHS

Before the Message Handling Service, each electronic mail product stored its messages in files formatted in such a way that other products could not use the files. The addressing schemes used to identify recipients were proprietary. Action Technologies published the MHS standard to overcome these limitations. Action Technologies also wrote software that implements MHS on NetWare LANs, and Novell bundles MHS with each copy of NetWare it sells.

An MHS gateway requires its own dedicated server, but MHS is a convenient way of moving information between E-mail systems. Because many vendors of E-mail products support MHS, MHS has become the least common denominator for interconnecting workgroup E-mail systems.

MHS provides a standard directory-and-file structure on the file server, into which any mail application can drop off messages. MHS puts the incoming messages in specific locations and manages the physical flow of messages between mail centers. When you install MHS, you create a publicly accessible server directory structure. Anyone on the network can create a message and give it to MHS for delivery. After you create the message, the MHS utility software sees the message and processes it.

A standard MHS packet is an ASCII text file containing several information items, each in a special format. A version number appears first and tells MHS that this is an MHS mail packet. The next line has the To field, and the following line has the From field. Your E-mail software has the responsibility of handling the addressing and providing complete MHS addresses.

If you address the message to a user on the same MHS server, the server simply copies the file to that user's MHS mailbox. This mailbox is different from the mailbox your E-mail software gives you. Periodically, an MHS E-mail software module polls the mailbox, looking for new messages. When the module finds a new message, the MHS module copies it from the MHS mailbox to the E-mail mailbox. If the address is for another mail center, MHS moves the message to an out-basket directory for further processing. At a time determined by the MHS scheduler, the MHS server picks up the out-basket mail and sorts it by destination. The server uses the modem to establish a connection to the other mail center and then transfers the mail to the remote MHS site.

In turn, the remote MHS server collects the messages and sorts them by address. After a mail message is sorted, it is handled like all other messages on that LAN. As far as a user at the remote site is concerned, the only difference is that delivery of mail is not instantaneous. The E-mail software does not have to know about gateways and bridges. It just puts an address (in an MHS-recognizable format) on the mail message and hands the message to MHS.

The MHS scheduler can execute programs as part of its periodic, scheduled processing. These programs are usually file converters or message formatters that help the messages appear in a format that another mail system can understand.

Action Technologies' Message Handling Service is less sophisticated than X.400, but MHS is more widely implemented in smaller workgroup environments that need to interconnect dissimilar E-mail systems. For more information on MHS, contact the following:

Action Technologies
2200 Powell Street
11th Floor
Emeryville, CA 94608
(800) 624-2162

Using Address Lists

You probably do not need an X.500 super-phone-book yet, but you do need a simple way to address a mail message to a given group of people. Most E-mail products enable you to establish address lists. You can use the name of the group (*Everyone*, *ProjectTeam*, or perhaps *Managers*) to refer to all the people in that group when you address your mail. Sometimes an E-mail product will use a network operating system's own groups. Pegasus Mail, a free electronic mail package from David Harris of Dunedin, New Zealand, is such a product (see the section "Pegasus Mail" later in this chapter).

Using a File Server as a Post Office

If the E-mail package your office selects becomes a frequently used, popular tool, you will find that the tons of interoffice paper mail used to circulate in your office now reside on the file server, in electronic form. Your office will save on paper costs, but at the expense of some disk space on the server.

The network administrator will keep an eye on disk space usage for the mail system. When it grows beyond a reasonable threshold, the administrator will circulate an E-mail message admonishing people to clean out their in-baskets and delete old mail.

Suppose that someone looks at his or her in-basket, sighs, and says, "I have too many old messages to delete one by one. I'll go into the mail directory and do a DELETE *.* DOS command to save myself time." This is the time your security system should take over. If a person can use a DELETE command in the mail directory, that person also may have file-read rights and be tempted to read other people's mail. Or, if the person does not realize that other people's mail messages exist in that directory, a DELETE *.* command could wipe out everyone's mailbox in the post office.

The mail directory on the file server is as important as any other directory. The interoffice memos in that directory are an important part of your business, and they deserve the same backup procedures you would implement for the other directories on the server.

Using E-mail Products

You have acquired a good understanding of E-mail concepts, standards, and practices. You are almost certainly curious to find out about specific E-mail products. The next few sections of this chapter will satisfy your curiosity. You learn about Pegasus Mail, cc:Mail, Microsoft Mail, Da Vinci eMAIL, and Higgins Mail.

Pegasus Mail

Pegasus Mail is free, works well, and is easy to install and use. It uses NetWare's own user identification and group names to send and receive mail. Unless you have a non-NetWare workgroup environment, and unless you need MHS or X.400, you owe it to yourself to try Pegasus Mail. Look for Pegasus on bulletin board systems in your area, on CompuServe, or on BIX (file name PMAIL21.EXE in LANs/Listings).

Pegasus works only on NetWare LANs. Using NetWare's own user identifications and groups, Pegasus needs no separate registration of mail users. You find out about incoming new mail in either of two ways. The NewMail program, which a system administrator usually puts in everyone's login script so that it executes whenever you log on, informs you of new mail. While logged on to the LAN, you receive notifications of new mail through NetWare's Send facility. Send puts a message at the bottom of your screen; you press Ctrl-Enter after you have read it. Figure 3.2 shows the main Pegasus Mail screen.

You can build personal address lists and distribution lists with Pegasus. Pegasus is highly configurable. Forwarding mail messages to other people is possible with Pegasus, as is archiving old mail. The text-mode version of Pegasus includes a capable text editor somewhat reminiscent of the WordStar word processor in both appearance and keystroke commands. There's also a Windows version of Pegasus.

Installation of Pegasus is merely a matter of copying a few selected files into a public directory from which everyone can find and execute the software. You can begin using Pegasus immediately.

Fig. 3.2
The main Pegasus
Mail screen.

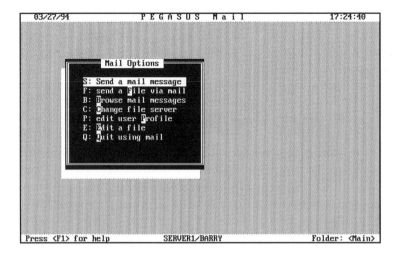

If you want to correspond with the author of Pegasus, David Harris, here is
his address:

David Harris
Pegasus Mail
P.O. Box 5451
Dunedin, New Zealand

cc:Mail

cc:Mail comes in DOS, Windows, OS/2, and Mac versions. cc:Mail offers optional gateways to many other types of E-mail systems, and the software uses
your network file server to provide mail services. It encrypts mail messages
and stores them as data files on the server hard disk. Installation and administration weren't easy with earlier versions of cc:Mail, but versions since 3.2
have added automatic installation and configuration features.

On a Macintosh, a desk accessory (DA) provides notification services, and a
separate application program manages your mailbox. When you first run
cc:Mail, the software gives you a Standard File dialog box that you use to
place the mail files on the server. cc:Mail then creates its Post_Office file.
Thereafter, you simply double-click this file to start cc:Mail. The software
stores information (the path to the server and your user name) in this file to
establish future connections. A set of icons gives you buttons that you click
to provide mail services such as reading, composing, and deleting messages.
Each button has an equivalent menu selection. You open highlighted mail
entries by clicking the mouse or pressing the Return key. Attached files are
document icons in a subwindow; double-clicking them tells cc:Mail to show

you the file's contents. You can view graphics files sent from the PC (cc:Mail saves them in PICT format). The Notify Desk Accessory polls the server at user-defined intervals for new messages. A small window or a chime tells you that you have new mail.

PC users run the Mail and Notify programs to manage their mailboxes. An optional TSR program alerts you to incoming messages. The Messenger module also can provide notification and sets up a hot key you can use to access mail services. Each time you run one of these cc:Mail modules, you supply the path to the mail directory, your mail name, and your password. Under Windows 3.0 and later, an icon of an addressed, stamped envelope represents the minimized Notify program. You use Notify to list the messages in your mailbox and to start cc:Mail.

The cc:Mail interface for the IBM PC and compatibles is different from the Mac interface, naturally. You navigate through a set of prompts and menu options to manage your mail. A built-in graphics editor enables you to draw images that you can attach to a message, and the Snapshot TSR enables you to capture and send screens from any application. Figure 3.3 shows the cc:Mail screen you use to send mail messages.

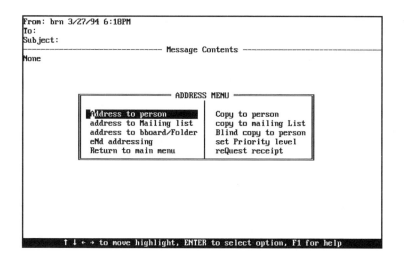

Fig. 3.3
The cc:Mail electronic mail product.

For more information on cc:Mail, contact the following:

Lotus Development Corporation
55 Cambridge Parkway
Cambridge, MA 02142
(617) 577-8500

Microsoft Mail

You can get Microsoft Mail in one of three editions to suit an organization of almost any size. For small LANs, the Mail application that is part of Windows for Workgroups lets you point and click to send your memos to others. Windows for Workgroups Mail is useful when you have from 3 to 25 people in an office who need to stay in touch with one another. For larger groups or for groups more geographically dispersed, you can get the Microsoft Mail and Schedule+ Extensions product. Or you may even find that you need the complete Microsoft Mail 3.1 product. Microsoft Mail 3.1 provides electronic mail within a LAN, between LANs connected by modems, or between LANs and outside mail services such as MCI Mail. Microsoft Mail 3.1 works with computers running the DOS, Windows, System 7 (Macintosh), and OS/2 operating systems.

To begin using Microsoft's electronic mail software products, you should first designate a member of your team as mail administrator. The administrator initializes the mail system by creating a post office on a file server computer and then adds the names of the team members to the address list for the post office. Thereafter, the administrator manages the disk space and the list of authorized mail system users.

The computer that you designate to hold the post office directory doesn't have to be the fastest machine in the office. You will, however, want to use a machine that stays powered on most of the time. If the post office computer isn't running when someone wants to send mail, the mail will be delayed.

Each person on the LAN manages his or her own disk space for saved mail messages; the mail administrator manages the disk space occupied by shared folders on the post office computer. A *shared folder* is a common, public access area that everyone in the workgroup can use. Each person on your team can open shared folders and view the mail messages in the shared folders, as well as create a new shared folder in the post office. The person gives other team members access to the new shared folder through access permissions (Read, Write, or Delete).

The mail administrator checks the status of shared folders to monitor the disk space those folders consume. When the mail administrator decides that the post office computer is low on available disk space, he or she can compress the disk space used by the folders. After compression, if the post office computer is still low on disk space, the administrator can encourage people to delete old mail messages or unused folders. The administrator can delete the entire post office, change the name of the post office, or move the post office directory to a new location.

Each workstation on the LAN has a private mail message file named MSMAIL.MMF. This message file is your private mailbox. When the Mail application software notices that you have incoming mail, Mail retrieves it from the team's post office directory and stores the message in your mail message file. If you find that you want to send mail but aren't connected to the LAN—perhaps you have a portable notebook computer and you're on a business trip—you can use Mail as you ordinarily would, even though you might be on an airplane or in a hotel room. Later, when you reconnect your notebook computer to the network, your Mail application can transmit your messages to the post office.

Windows for Workgroups electronic mail doesn't do a good job of allowing more than one person to access Mail from a single workstation. As noted, the MSMAIL.MMF file is a mailbox for all incoming mail on a workstation, rather than a file specific to each person who uses the workstation. You can set up a manual procedure for creating multiple instances of the MSMAIL.MMF file, but the procedure is somewhat tedious and error-prone. Microsoft recommends that two people who want to access Mail from the same workstation maintain their own MSMAIL files, using each person's initials as the file extension (MSMAIL.JJG and MSMAIL.RMY, for example). Microsoft recommends also that, before starting Mail, you copy the other person's MSMAIL file to MSMAIL.<initials> and then rename your copy of your personal MSMAIL file to MSMAIL.MMF. You must remember to do the copying and renaming operations before another person can access Mail.

You click the Compose icon or use the Compose Note menu item in the Mail menu to access the Send Note window. You use this window to address your message to one or more team members, indicate the subject of the memo, type the message, optionally specify how you want Mail to handle this particular message, and send the message to the recipient(s). When you send your note, the recipient's Mail application beeps, and the recipient sees a new message header appear in the inbox. The mail icon in the lower-right corner of the Mail window becomes a picture of an envelope in a mail slot, and the summary information on the bottom line of the Mail window changes to show that the recipient has a new, unread message. You can attach a file to your mail message, if you like. The file might be a spreadsheet, a chart, an image, or another DOS file that is related to your mail message. Figure 3.4 shows the initial Microsoft Mail screen.

Fig. 3.4
The initial
Microsoft Mail
screen.

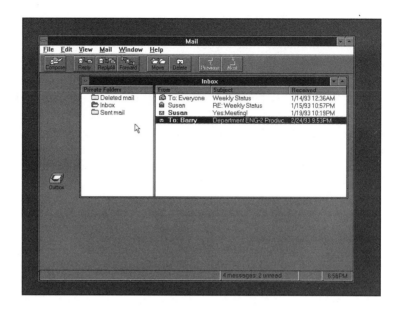

For more information about Microsoft Mail, contact the following:

Microsoft Corporation
One Microsoft Way
Redmond, WA 98052
(800) 426-9400

DaVinci eMAIL

DaVinci Systems has versions of eMail for DOS, Windows, OS/2, and NewWave environments. Under DOS, you can run eMail as a stand-alone application or, if you prefer, as a pop-up TSR program. The micro TSR mode that DaVinci Systems designed into eMail uses a hard disk swap file to store portions of the executable program. The result is that the eMail TSR takes up only 10K of RAM. You define a hot key sequence that swaps out your current application and loads eMail. When you exit eMail, the TSR restores the interrupted application where it left off. eMail can use the NetWare Send mechanism to notify you of incoming mail, or you can load a TSR that presents a one-line message at the bottom of the screen. Windows alerts appear for a definable amount of time (the default is 20 seconds) and then disappear.

The user interface of the DOS version is essentially a blank screen. You can press the F8 key to bring up option menus, but otherwise, eMail presents you with little information to go on. You will want to keep the manual at your side if you are an infrequent user of eMail. The Windows version, however, is easy to use; it puts the mail functions into drop-down menus just as you would expect in a Windows environment.

eMail enables you to attach files to messages. Under Windows, you can send the contents of the Windows Clipboard to other Windows users. You copy some information to the Clipboard, you attach the Clipboard data to your mail message, and the recipient simply pastes it into an application.

Security is not eMail's long suit, and you will want to take extra precautions for messages you send through eMail. The mail message files on the file server are easy for anyone to find. And messages are, by default, unencrypted. You must specifically request encryption when you send a mail message. Encrypted messages cannot be read by other people, and the recipient of such a message has to supply a password in order to read the message.

You can configure eMail on a user-by-user basis. eMail maintains personal information files that define how eMail operates on users' systems. A person can change the polling frequency for incoming messages and the alert procedure, and customize the frequency and duration of the message-alert sounds by changing the MAIL.INI file. You may want to use this feature in an office where computers are located close to one another, so that people can easily tell who has received mail.

For more information about eMail, contact the following:

DaVinci Systems
P.O. Box 17449
Raleigh, NC 27619
(800) 326-3556

Higgins Mail

Higgins Mail is a subset of Enable Software's workgroup scheduler software, and it runs on DOS and OS/2 computers. Higgins Mail uses an electronic slip of paper metaphor to help you manage your mail messages. The slips of paper that Higgins Mail displays on your computer screen correspond to your E-mail memos and notes.

If you have used Microsoft Word 5.0, with its Escape-for-menu, single-keypress-selects-option interface, you will be right at home with Higgins Mail. You press Esc to bring up the menu at the bottom of the screen, and then press the appropriate key to choose a menu option. When you select an edit function, the menu disappears. Pressing Esc switches you from the editing window back to the menu. Context-sensitive help messages constantly tell you where you are, what you are doing, and what you can do next.

The shared Higgins Mail database on the file server uses a proprietary storage format, and Higgins Mail encrypts the messages in the database. Higgins Mail is quite popular, and a number of gateways exist to transfer mail between Higgins Mail and other E-mail systems.

You establish nicknames (aliases) and full user names when you install Higgins Mail. The software maintains a list of registered mail users. When you send a mail message, Higgins Mail shows you a list of people in what it calls the default domain. A *domain* is a group of people and resources on the LAN. You choose recipients from the default list or select a different domain of names. Your mailing address on the LAN consists of three items in the following format:

Domain:Workgroup:UserID

The Higgins Mail software module that notifies you of incoming mail is called *Mailcall*. This is a small (3.5K) TSR that displays a message for 10 seconds or until you press a key. If the new mail remains unread by you, Mailcall periodically displays the same message to remind you that you have mail. If you are away from your desk when mail arrives, Higgins Mail ensures that you will find out about it when you return.

For more information about Higgins Mail, contact the following:

Enable Software
Northway Ten Executive Park
Ballston Lake, NY 12019
(800) 888-0684

Other E-mail Products

You may want to research other electronic mail products besides the ones mentioned in this chapter. If this is the case, you can use the following list of vendors as a starting point for your research:

Action Technologies
(The Coordinator)
1145 Atlantic Avenue
Suite 101
Alameda, CA 94501
(415) 521-6190
Fax: (415) 769-0596

Banyan Systems, Inc.
(Network Mail for VINES)
120 Flanders Road
Westborough, MA 01581
(508) 898-1000
Fax: (508) 898-1755

CE Software
(QuickMail)
P.O. Box 65580
West Des Moines, IA 50265
(800) 523-7638
(515) 224-1995
Fax: (515) 224-4534

Notework
(Notework)
72 Kent Street
Brookline, MA 02146
(617) 734-4317

Sitka Corporation
(InBox Plus)
950 Marina Village Parkway
Alameda, CA 94501
(800) 445-8677
(415) 769-9669
Fax: (415) 769-8771

SoftSwitch, Inc.
(Mailbridge and SoftSwitch Central E-mail gateways)
640 Lee Road
Wayne, PA 19087
(215) 640-9600
Fax: (215) 640-7550

VoxLink Corporation
(VoxVoice, VoxMail)
1516 Tyne Boulevard
Nashville, TN 37215
(615) 331-0275
Fax: (615) 331-2057

WordPerfect Corporation
(WordPerfect Office)
1555 N. Technology Way
Orem, UT 84057
(800) 321-4566

Understanding Networks

Going beyond Electronic Mail

You can use your LAN (and its gateways) to save paper by implementing interoffice electronic mail; once you have done that, you will want more. The next set of problems you can solve with your LAN deals with scheduling meetings and managing projects. You can maintain an officewide calendar of events on the LAN so that everyone knows when certain things will happen in the office (Mr. Haynes of the California sales office will be here on Tuesday, for example). You can extend the calendaring quite far; some applications enable you to coordinate people's schedules and set up meetings. This type of application is known as *groupware*, or workgroup software.

Scheduling Meetings

A group scheduler application acts as an electronic bulletin board. It provides a public place where you can post meeting announcements. If the software also knows each person's appointment calendar (the person keys it into the application and keeps it up to date), the software can resolve meeting and scheduling conflicts by looking at people's individual calendars. When you want to call a meeting, you enter an appointment in your calendar and give the names of the other people you need to talk to. Most group schedulers immediately notify the prospective attendees of the planned meeting. Each person can respond with "Fine, I'll be there" or "Sorry, I can't make it then." Electronic mail is an essential component of the process; it enables you to tell people why you feel the meeting is necessary.

Group schedulers have different ways of handling meeting conflicts. Some schedulers examine the other participants' calendars and show you conflicts before you set a meeting time. Others find open times on everyone's schedule and propose a meeting time.

Most group schedulers work by organizing participants into teams. When you schedule a meeting, you can enter the team's name as the attendee rather than list all the individuals. The scheduler then inspects each team member's appointment calendar to determine the best time for the meeting. Some group scheduler applications support rudimentary project-tracking as well. One popular group scheduler is Schedule+, from Microsoft; another popular scheduler is WP Office, from WordPerfect. Figure 3.5 shows the Microsoft Schedule+ product, and figure 3.6 shows WP Office.

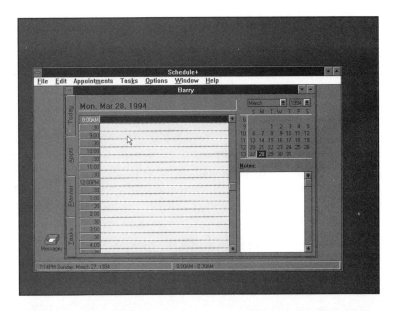

Fig. 3.5
Microsoft
Schedule+.

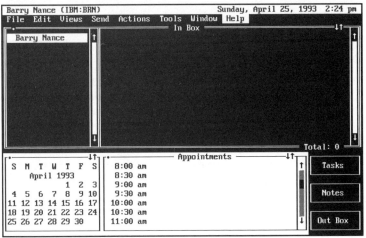

Fig. 3.6
WordPerfect's
WP Office.

Looking at WP Office

If you have only a few computers on a network and all of them are Intel-based PCs, you probably won't need the power and functionality of
WP Office. However, if your network environment includes DOS clients,
DOS-and-Windows clients, Macintosh clients, and perhaps a Data General,
UNIX, or VAX/VMS host computer, your LAN is a prime candidate for WP
Office. If you have more than 25 workstations, even if they all run the same
operating system, you should consider WP Office for your LAN.

WP Office works on several types of networks: NetWare, Banyan VINES, TOPS Network, IBM LAN Server, NOKIA PC-Net, 3Com 3+, 10Net, LANtastic, AT&T StarGROUP, DEC PCSA, and 3Com 3+ OPEN. A full installation of WP Office consumes about 7M of disk space for the central (post office) portion, about 5.5M for DOS files, and about 5.5M for Windows files.

WP Office 4.0 gives the members of your organization electronic mail, a calendar, a calculator, an appointment book, a task list, a team-oriented shared notes area, a shell menu, a clipboard, a notebook with auto-dial feature, a file manager, a macro editor, and a text editor. WP Office integrates these functions across the LAN in a way that lets you and your coworkers coordinate smoothly, despite the fact that you might be using different kinds of computers. The group scheduling software works across the LAN to help you make light work of setting up meetings and allocating resources such as audiovisual equipment. WP Office scans each person's (or resource's) appointment book to find acceptable meeting times. Invited attendees receive automatically generated E-mail requests to attend; each person can accept or decline with a click of the mouse.

You'll be right at home in WP Office if you are familiar with the usual WordPerfect function key layout (F3 for help, F5 to list, F7 to exit, and so on). If you don't use WordPerfect's word processor, you'll find the nearly-CUA-compliant menus (Alt-F for File, Alt-E for Edit, and so on) easy to use. New in Version 4.0 is mouse support for the DOS text-mode application modules. Of course, the Windows and Macintosh modules let you point and click when you want to send notes or update your task list. For the most part, entering personal appointments and arranging group meetings are simple fill-in-the-blanks processes. WP Office automates the job of searching for common free times when you want to hold a meeting. Personal appointments can be meetings, task list items you want to set aside time for, or other allocated blocks of time.

Even though using WP Office is a breeze, installing and configuring the software is not. Your network administrator will spend a significant amount of time getting WP Office ready for you to use. It may be time well spent, however; having the capability to share electronic mail and appointment books among different types of computers creates a level playing field out of what is usually a multiplatform mess.

The WP Office shell is a DOS menuing system that can be configured to manage all your applications, not just the suite of WP Office modules. If you find that you spend more time in one part of WP Office, you can select a different view in WP Office to give on-screen emphasis to that part—electronic mail, the calendar, or perhaps the task list.

The electronic mail gateway software that comes with WP Office supports wide area connections between WP Office LANs in addition to MHS, SMTP, and X.400; you also get remote modem-based access to WP Office when you are away from the office. If you write E-mail notes on a plane or in a hotel room without a modem, WP Office will send the notes automatically for you when you return to the office and connect to the LAN.

Identifying Groupware Vendors

If you want to explore the class of software known as groupware more closely, the following list of companies is a good place to start your research:

CaLANdar
Microsystems Software, Inc.
600 Worcester Road
Framingham, MA 01701
(508) 626-8511
Fax: (508) 626-8515

ClockWise
Phase II Software Corporation
444 Washington Street
Suite 407
Woburn, MA 01801
(800) 735-2557
(617) 937-0256
Fax: (617) 937-0098

The Coordinator II
Action Technologies, Inc.
1145 Atlantic Avenue
Alameda, CA 94501
(415) 521-6190
Fax: (415) 769-0596

Higgins Enable Software
Higgins Group
1150 Marina Village Parkway
Suite 101
Alameda, CA 94501
(800) 854-2807
(415) 865-9805
Fax: (415) 521-9779

Meeting Maker
On Technology, Inc.
155 Second Street
Cambridge, MA 02141
(617) 876-0900
Fax: (617) 876-0391

Network Scheduler II
PowerCore, Inc.
1 Diversatech Drive
Manteno, IL 60950
(800) 237-4754
(815) 468-3737
Fax: (815) 468-3867

OfficeWorks
Data Access Corporation
14000 Southwest 119 Avenue
Miami, FL 33186
(800) 451-3539
(305) 238-0012
Fax: (305) 238-0017

OnTime
Campbell Services, Inc.
21700 Northwestern Highway
Suite 1070
Southfield, MI 48075
(313) 559-5955
Fax: (313) 559-1034

Planisoft
ASD Software, Inc.
4650 Arrow Highway
Suite E-6
Montclair, CA 91763
(714) 624-2594
Fax: (714) 624-9574

Right Hand Man II
Futurus, Inc.
3131 North I-10 Service Road
Suite 401
Metairie, LA 70002
(800) 327-8296
(504) 837-1554
Fax: (504) 837-3429

Schedule+
Microsoft Corporation
1 Microsoft Way
Redmond, WA 98052
(800) 426-9400
(206) 882-8080
Fax: (206) 883-8101

Shoebox
R+R Associates, Inc.
39 Carwall Avenue
Mount Vernon, NY 10552
(914) 668-4057
Fax: (914) 668-9277

SuperTime
SuperTime, Inc.
2025 Sheppard Avenue E
Suite 2206
Willowdale
Toronto, Ontario
Canada M2J 1V7
(416) 499-3288
Fax: (416) 492-9192

Synchronize
CrossWind Technologies, Inc.
6630 Hwy. 9
Suite 201
Felton, CA 95018
(408) 335-4988
Fax: (408) 335-1086

Who-What-When Enterprise
Chronos Software
555 De Haro Street
Suite 240
San Francisco, CA 94107
(800) 999-1023
(415) 626-4244
Fax: (415) 626-5393

WordPerfect Office LAN
WordPerfect Corporation
1555 North Technology Way
Orem, UT 84057
(800) 451-5151
(801) 225-5000
Fax: (801) 222-5077

Summary

This chapter introduced you to electronic mail, one of the more significant uses to which you can put your LAN, after sharing files and printers. If you get the right E-mail product, you can dispense with the tons of interoffice mail that circulate the office in paper form. You can take a step toward the paperless office of the future through E-mail. You will find your electronic files and notes much easier to organize than their physical paper- and typewriter-oriented predecessors.

You have learned how electronic mail works, and you know how to use it to your best advantage. You now understand two of the industry standards for E-mail: MHS and the X.400 specification. You have familiarized yourself with several of the more popular electronic mail products. And you have looked over the horizon to discover the new class of LAN-aware application software, called groupware.

In the next chapter, you learn about file servers. You learn what a file server does, and you explore the components of a file server from both a hardware and a software point of view. You learn also about server-based and peer-to-peer network operating systems.

Part II

Building a Network

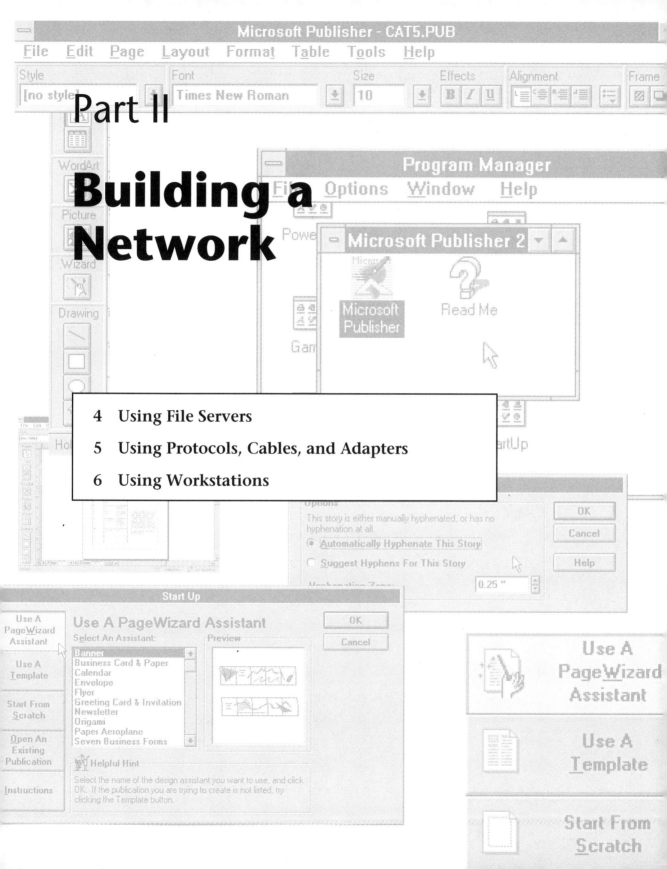

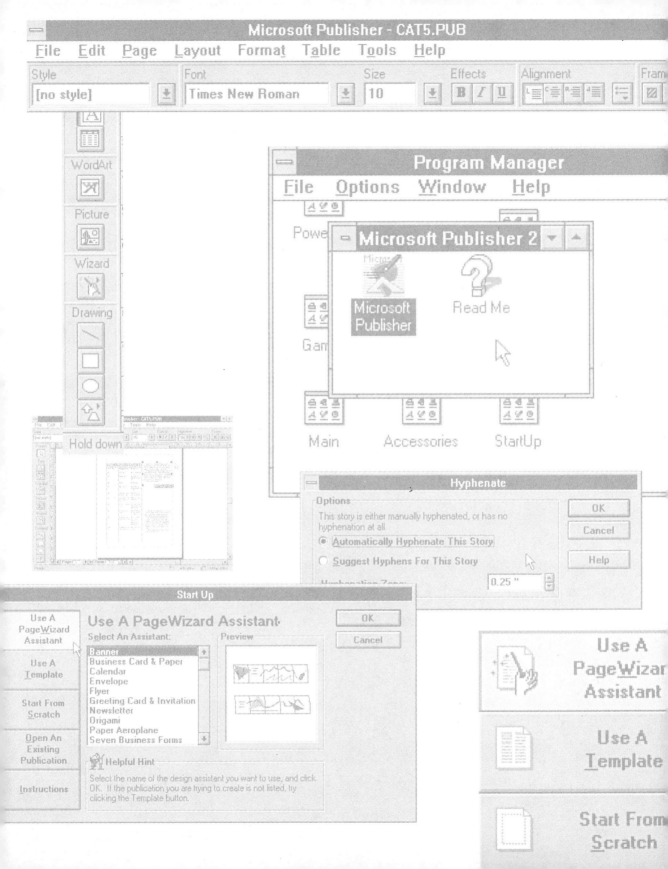

Chapter 4

Using File Servers

The file server is the Grand Central Station of your network. It is the only chef on duty in a busy restaurant. These metaphors only hint at how much work the file server has to do. The file server is a slave to its many masters, the workstations on the network.

In this chapter, you first get an overview of file servers. You find out what a file server actually does, and you discover the criteria for a good file server computer. Next, you explore the components of a file server, from both a hardware and a software point of view. After an introductory discussion of these components, you go over the individual parts in detail: hard disk, computer CPU chip, RAM (internal memory), network adapter card, power supply, keyboard, monitor, and mouse.

You then move on to examine the network operating system (NOS), which is the software that converts the personal computer into a file server. You first cover server-based network operating systems, and you then learn about peer-to-peer network operating systems. This chapter treats both kinds of LANs, server-based and peer-to-peer, in depth.

An uninterruptible power supply (UPS) is an important part of a LAN. In this chapter, you find out why.

Getting an Overview of File Servers

In Chapter 2, "Sharing Computer Resources," you looked at a LAN from the viewpoint of sharing disk space and printers. Now it is time to look at the LAN from the file server's point of view, to see how it shares these resources. First, you get a look at what a server does. Then you examine both the hardware and the software components of a file server.

Learning What a Server Does

The file server, whether or not it also acts as a workstation, doles out files to the other computers connected to it through the LAN. The server may also manage a printer to which everyone can send their printouts. The file server does this work only at the request of the workstations. The server does not behave arbitrarily. You can get unexpected results, however, if two people update the same file at the same time without using LAN-aware, multiuser applications.

Sharing Disk Space and Files

On a peer LAN, you know that your computer can be both a workstation and a file server to the other people on the network. On a server-based LAN, the file server is a separate, unattended computer that silently serves up disk space and files. Both types of servers perform the same basic functions. On a busy LAN, the following sample dialog of messages happens tens of times or hundreds of times each minute:

Workstation	File Server
Open file "SALES.WK1".	Okay; file is open.
Give me the contents of the file.	Okay; here is the data.
Close the file.	Okay; file is closed.

This dialog is typical of about 99 percent of the activity that occurs between workstations and a server on an average LAN. The LAN cable carries the dialog messages back and forth from the workstations and file server. The network operating system, with portions running in both the workstation and the file server, carries on the dialog. The network operating system gives the applications running at the workstation the illusion that the file server hard disk is just another drive letter. So that the workstation can treat the file server hard disk as just another drive letter, the network operating system does all the tasks DOS would do. These tasks occur over the LAN cable, rather than just locally inside the workstation.

File-Sharing Collisions

If two workstations both want SALES.WK1 at *approximately* the same time, and if the people at the two workstations both have rights to modify the file, trouble can erupt. Suppose that Joe loads the file into his spreadsheet program, types some new data in the worksheet, and saves the file. You do the same thing, but you type different data. You also type faster than Joe. You write your changes to the file quickly, but Joe—the slower typist—saves his changes a minute or two later. Clearly, Joe's changes take effect while yours are ignored. This is probably not what you intended to happen. You and Joe should coordinate the use of the file in order to avoid these problems.

If two workstations access SALES.WK1 at *exactly* the same time, the file server opens the file for one workstation but denies access to the other workstation. You may update the file without noticing a problem, but Joe may see this dreaded message:

```
Sharing Violation; Abort, Retry, or Ignore?
```

You can avoid file-sharing problems in a number of ways. The simplest method is to coordinate the update of the files (electronic mail can help you accomplish this). Another procedure involves giving people copies of files from one central source and having only one person responsible for updating the central file. Or you may have one person in charge of files in a manner similar to that of a public library. When the discussion turns to network operating systems later in this chapter, you will see how the NOS can help you enforce good file-sharing techniques.

II

Building a Network

Sharing a Printer

When you send your printouts to the LAN printer, the network operating system stores each one in a temporary *spool file* on the file server. Each spool file is a disk file whose contents correspond to the stream of data making up the printout, and the spool file can include downloadable fonts and graphics in addition to plain text. When the printer is finished printing someone's report or memo, the NOS sends the next spool file to the printer as a *print job* and deletes that temporary spool file. Typically, the network operating system prints a *banner page* or *job-separator page* between printouts to identify each one. The banner page shows the user ID of the person who wants to receive the printout, along with some other information about the print job.

In other words, the file server acts as a buffer for all the printouts. The server sends each printout to the printer, one by one. On a busy LAN, you may have to wait for other users' printouts to appear before the server prints yours. Unless you disable the banner page, your printout will be preceded by a page that identifies the printout as belonging to you.

Understanding the Components of a File Server

Before you delve into the finer details of file server operation, you will need a road map. In the next few sections, you get that road map in the form of brief descriptions of file server components. Subsequent sections deal with the parts of a file server in greater detail.

Surveying the Server Hardware

A typical file server consists of a personal computer that you dedicate to the task of sharing disk space, files, and a printer. On a larger network, you may instead use a personal computer especially built for file server work (a superserver), a minicomputer, or even a mainframe. No matter what sort of computer you choose to use as a server, the server and the workstations communicate with each other through network adapter cards and LAN cables.

Using PC-Based Servers. Personal computers come in all sizes, shapes, and speeds. You can choose exactly the amount of power you need in your file server. Not all network operating systems work with every configuration of personal computer, but the range is wide enough to give you a considerable set of choices. The speed of the computer and the size and speed of the hard disk are primary factors. The amount of RAM in the computer is a big factor, too. Other components—monitor, keyboard, and mouse—are less important, because most file servers operate as unattended machines.

When you set up an ordinary personal computer as a file server, you select a machine with a larger hard disk and more horsepower than other PCs in the office. You follow the directions that came with the network adapter card to install the adapter. You install the server portion of the network operating system on the PC, and you put the machine in a location where people are less likely to trip over its power cord or otherwise interfere with the server's operation. After attaching the LAN cable to the new server, you power up the PC in its new role as file server.

Using Superservers, Minicomputer Servers, and Mainframes. A *superserver* is a personal computer especially designed to be a file server. It looks and behaves much like a PC, but a superserver may have multiple hard disks that can act in tandem to provide a high degree of data redundancy. Files written to one disk are automatically *mirrored* on the other disk. If the first disk fails, the other disk takes over instantly. This gives the file server a certain level of fault tolerance. A superserver almost certainly has a fast CPU and a good deal of internal memory (32M, 64M, or more of RAM).

Your office may choose to use as the file server a minicomputer such as a Digital Equipment Corporation VAX computer or an IBM RS/6000 computer. In the case of a VAX, you may install the version of NetWare that Novell designed to run on VAX equipment. RS/6000 computers use AIX, IBM's brand of UNIX, as a base operating system. You may install Sun Microsystems' Network File System (NFS) or another UNIX-based network operating system on the RS/6000. No matter what type of minicomputer you use, you probably will be interested in having the minicomputer be a host computer as well as a file server. If the minicomputer's regular workload of application software interacts with the applications running on the workstations on the LAN, you have a client/server environment. In such an environment, some of the work gets done on the minicomputer, and some gets done on the LAN workstations.

You also can use a mainframe computer in a client/server role on a LAN, but of course, the programming and administrative costs are greater. At the present time, mainframe computers do not lend themselves very well to being used as file servers. This will change in the future (more than one NOS vendor is developing software to turn a mainframe into a file server), but in the meantime, mainframes require a substantial programming effort to play a role in a LAN.

Using Network Connections. Chapter 5, "Using Protocols, Cables, and Adapters," goes into detail about the network connections you establish to put the file server and all the workstations on the LAN. In brief, you put a network adapter card in the server and attach a LAN cable to the card. You will want to select a network adapter that uses the same protocols as the workstations' adapters, but you should consider using a more powerful adapter in the server. As the Grand Central Station of the LAN, the server gets more message traffic than the other computers. A network adapter for the file server may have more on-board memory and special controller chips that process messages faster. The adapter may require that you put it into a 16-bit or even a 32-bit slot in the computer.

Surveying the Server Software

After you set up a personal computer's hardware configuration to make it a server, you install the *network operating system (NOS)*. The NOS may enable the computer to continue to operate as a workstation in addition to being a server, or the NOS may "take over" the computer, turning the machine into only a file server.

II

Building a Network

Using Server-Based or Peer-to-Peer Systems. The network operating system you install on your server may be just one or a few TSR programs to enable the computer to share itself across the network. Such simple network software usually leaves the computer running DOS and able to act as a workstation at the same time it is a server. Such a system is called a *peer-to-peer* network operating system. However, the network operating system may not be DOS-based at all. The NOS may replace DOS completely once the system has been loaded into memory, or the NOS may use a high-power operating system such as OS/2 or UNIX in place of DOS. Such a network operating system is a *server-based* NOS.

Of course, you may install a peer-to-peer NOS but choose not to use the server computer as a workstation, enabling the computer to concentrate on its role as a file server. Configuring a PC in this way makes the computer a *dedicated server*. The file server still runs DOS, but you do not have to worry about the possibility that an application running on the server/workstation may crash and thus stop the entire network. A server-based NOS, by definition, is a dedicated server.

Deciding Which NOS Is Best for You. Server-based network operating systems are more expensive than their peer LAN counterparts, but such systems offer better performance, greater reliability, and higher levels of security. A server-based NOS also can enable you to connect more kinds of computers to the network. NetWare, for example, the most popular server-based NOS, supports Macintosh and UNIX computers at the same time that it supports DOS-based and OS/2-based computers.

If you are setting up a small LAN (with no more than perhaps 5 or 10 workstations), if that LAN will be used only for word processing chores and maybe some light record-keeping (database) work, and if you have only DOS-based computers to tie together, you may find that a peer LAN is your best choice. If you have more workstations, if the LAN will do more than share word processing document files, or if you have Mac or UNIX computers that you want to use on the network, you probably need a server-based NOS.

Looking at Criteria for a File Server

You need a place to store the files that you want to share among the workstations. You may turn one of the office's personal computers into a file server, or you may choose to use a different kind of computer—perhaps a minicomputer or a superserver—as the file server. Either way, you have four criteria to apply:

- You need fast access to the files on the server.

- You need the file server to have the capacity to hold files and records for many users.

- You need some measure of security for the files.

- You need the file server to be reliable.

If you choose something other than a PC to be a file server, you also need to verify that the computer is capable of being connected to the LAN and that it can behave as a file server. You will need to discuss LAN options with your minicomputer vendor, for example. However, if you use one of the PCs as a file server, you should choose a PC that is faster and has larger, faster disks than the other machines. Why do you need the file server to be a faster computer if the software applications run on each of the individual PCs on the LAN and not on some central machine? During busy periods, the server receives many requests for disk files and records; it takes a certain amount of CPU effort as well as disk rotation/access time to respond to each request. You want the requests to be serviced quickly so that each user gets the feeling that he or she is the only one using the file server at that moment.

You will not want to buy the fanciest color monitor, highest-quality keyboard, and most expensive mouse for a dedicated file server. A monochrome monitor will be adequate, because you will not interact with the server a great deal after you have installed the NOS and have the network up and running.

Understanding the Server Hardware

You now have a good, basic idea of the components of a file server. You know the general procedure you would use to turn a personal computer into a file server. You know the different types of network operating systems. You are familiar with the criteria for a good file server. Next, you look at each of these components in much greater detail. You begin by thinking about how the reliability of your file server will affect the work in your office.

Evaluating Hardware Reliability

As Chapter 1 mentioned, a file server does many times the work of an ordinary workstation. You may type on the server's keyboard only a couple of times a day, and you may glance at the server's monitor only a few times. The server CPU and hard disk, however, take the brunt of responding to the file service requests of all the workstations on the LAN.

If you consider your LAN an important investment in your office (it is hard to imagine otherwise), you will want to get the highest-quality computer you can afford for the file server. The CPU should be an 80486 or Pentium chip and should be one of the faster models. The hard disk should be large and fast. But the most important consideration is that the CPU, the motherboard on which the CPU is mounted, and the hard disk should be rugged and reliable. Do not skimp on these components. *Downtime* (when the network is not operating) can be expensive because people cannot access their shared files to get their work done. Higher-quality components will keep the LAN running without failure for longer periods of time.

In the same vein, you will want to set up a regular maintenance schedule for your file server. Over a few weeks, the fan at the back of the computer can move great volumes of air through the machine to keep it cool. The air may contain dust and dirt, which will accumulate inside the computer. You will want to clean the "dust bunnies" out of the server every month or two. You do not replace components in the server as part of your regular preventive maintenance, but you will want to know whether a part is beginning to fail. You may want to acquire diagnostic software or hardware to periodically check the health of your file server. (Chapter 12, "Managing Your Network," discusses the tools you can use to keep your file server fit and trim.)

The electricity the file server gets from the wall outlet may, from time to time, vary considerably in voltage (resulting in *sags* and *spikes*). In the interests of making your file server as reliable as possible, you will want to install an uninterruptible power supply (UPS) between the electric company and your server. The UPS will not only provide electricity in case of a power failure but also *condition the line* to protect the server from sags and spikes. You learn more about UPS equipment later in this chapter.

In general, you want to do whatever you can to make your network reliable, including placing the server away from public access areas.

Evaluating the File Server Hard Disk

The hard disk is the most important component of a file server. The hard disk stores the files of the people who use the LAN. Figure 4.1 illustrates a hard disk inside a file server. To a large extent, the reliability, access speed, and capacity of a server's hard disk determine whether people will be happy with the LAN and will use the LAN productively. The most common bottleneck in the average LAN is disk I/O time at the file server. And the most common complaint voiced by people on the average LAN is that the file server has run out of free disk space.

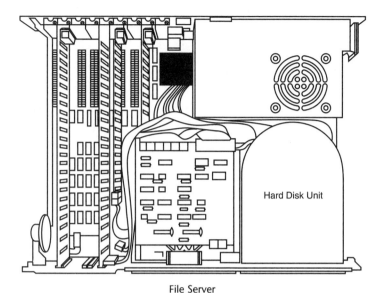

Fig. 4.1
Everyone on the LAN shares the file server's hard disk.

Hard Disk Unit

File Server

Evaluating Disk Speed

Disk access speed is determined by a number of factors, including the following:

- Recording method (MFM, RLL, ESDI, or SCSI)

- Type and on-board intelligence of the controller

- Type of hard disk (stepper band or voice coil)

- Interleave factor

- Location of the files on the disk (location affects how far the read/write head has to move in order to get to the file)

Generally, disk access speed is measured by two things: data transfer rate and average seek time. *Data transfer rate* expresses the number of bytes of data that the hard disk and its controller card can deliver to the computer. *Average seek time* represents the time taken by the disk to move the read/write head a small distance and then wait about a half revolution of the disk platter for a given sector to appear under the head. For comparative purposes, the type of disk that was installed as standard equipment by IBM in the IBM PC AT computer gives a data transfer rate of about 180K per second and an average seek time of 40 milliseconds. Third-party disks from companies like Connor Peripherals, Core, Maxtor (Storage Dimensions), Micropolis, Priam, Rodime,

II

Building a Network

and Racet are faster, operating in the 6- to 20-millisecond range for average seek time. And, of course, IBM offers speedy drives in the current crop of high-end PS/2 machines.

Evaluating Disk Capacity

Disk capacity tends to go hand in hand with speed; the larger drives are the faster drives. The designers of 500M to 1000M (and larger) drives are obviously thinking in terms of file servers as they engineer their latest, technologically advanced products. Some of these huge drives cost as much as the computer in which you put them, however. How much space do you need on your file server? How many drives should you buy, and how many file servers will you need?

A significant factor is that you are limited in the number of drives that can be installed in a given file server machine. Usually, you can install only two hard disks in a personal computer. (SCSI drives are less limiting in this respect.) A related consideration is that it is generally better to have several medium-sized disks in multiple servers than to have one huge disk in one server. You then have more read/write heads, more hard disk controllers, and more CPUs responding to user requests for files. You also can continue to use a second file server to keep the network going in case the other one fails.

A general rule of thumb is that you should allot 50M of disk storage space for each user on the LAN. This is only the roughest of guides, because you need to take a look at what you think the LAN will be used for and what types of applications the users will run. File server disks are quite a bit like closets and file cabinets—no matter how many you have, they tend to fill up fairly quickly. If you are the administrator of a LAN, you may want to keep the following tips in mind:

- Encourage people to use their local hard drives for executable files and for applications not shared on the LAN.

- Don't buy diskless workstations to try to save money.

- Don't let people store games on the file server.

- Set up a "retention period" scheme for different kinds of files on the network. Houseclean regularly; don't wait for the server to run out of space.

Evaluating Hard Disk Alternatives

Optical disks are another alternative for file servers. They use light to store data, or sometimes a combination of light and magnetism. With the proper software drivers, optical disks can be made to behave just like any other file server drive. Optical media are extremely durable and reliable. Until recently, optical disks had two major drawbacks that kept them from being more popular: they had a tendency to have slower access times than magnetic disks, and you could not erase files—the laser-burned holes were permanent. (These were called *write-once, read-many* drives, or *WORM* drives.) The situation is improving, however; companies such as Corel, Storage Dimensions, and Racet now offer rewritable optical disks that are network-compatible.

Evaluating the File Server CPU

The file server CPU tells the hard disk what to store and retrieve. The CPU is the next most important file server component after the hard disk. Unless your LAN will have only a few users and will never grow, a file server with a fast 80386 or 80486 CPU and plenty of RAM is a wise investment. The next section discusses server RAM.

The CPU chip in a computer executes the instructions given to it by the software you run. If you run an application, that application will run more quickly if the CPU is fast. Likewise, if you run a network operating system, that NOS will run more quickly if the CPU is fast. Figure 4.2 shows a server's CPU.

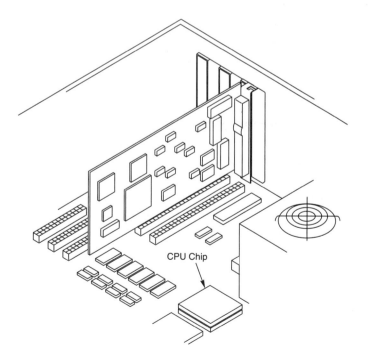

CPU Chip

Fig. 4.2
The file server's CPU processes file requests from all the workstations.

II

Building a Network

Some network operating systems absolutely require certain types of CPU chips. NetWare Version 2, for example, requires at least an 80286 CPU. NetWare Versions 3 and 4 require at least an 80386. IBM LAN Server Version 2 and Microsoft LAN Manager Version 2 require that OS/2 1.3 be running on the server computer; OS/2 1.3 requires an 80286 or later CPU. LAN Server 3.0 requires that the file server use OS/2 2.x, which runs only on 80386 or later CPUs.

Evaluating Server RAM

The network operating system loads into the computer's RAM, just as any other application does. You need to have enough RAM in the computer for the NOS to load and run. On a peer LAN, a few megabytes of RAM might be enough, whereas on a server-based LAN, you might install 32M, 64M, or more in your file server.

You can realize significant performance gains with a faster CPU and extra RAM because of something called *caching*. If the file server has sufficient memory installed, it can "remember" those portions of the hard disk that it has previously accessed. When the next user asks for the same file represented by those portions of the hard disk, the server can hand these to the next user without having to actually access the hard disk. Because the file server is able to avoid waiting for the hard disk to rotate into position, the server can do its job more quickly. The network operating system merely needs to look in the computer's RAM for the file data that a workstation has requested. Note that the network operating system's caching of file data is distinct from (and in addition to) any caching that might occur, because the hard disk or hard disk controller card has on-board memory.

Evaluating the Network Adapter Card

The server's network adapter card is the server's link to all the workstations on the LAN. All the requests for files enter the server through the network adapter, and all the response messages containing the requested files leave the server through the network adapter. Figure 4.3 shows a network adapter you might install in a file server. As you can imagine, the network adapter in the server is a busy component.

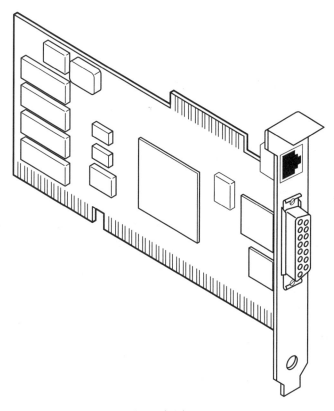

Network Adapter

All the network adapters on the LAN will use Ethernet, Token Ring, ARCnet, or some other protocol. Within one of these protocols, however, you can find network adapters that perform better than others. A network adapter may be faster at processing messages because it has a large amount of on-board memory (RAM), because it contains its own microprocessor, or perhaps because the adapter uses one of the larger (longer) computer slots and thus can transfer more data between itself and the CPU at one time. A faster, more capable network adapter is an ideal candidate for installation in the file server. Chapter 5, "Using Protocols, Cables, and Adapters," discusses network adapters in more detail.

Evaluating the Server's Power Supply

The innocuous power supply is usually a shiny box inside the computer. The power switch is part of the power supply. Electricity enters the computer through the power cord attached to the power supply. Inside the computer, small low-voltage wires carry current to the motherboard, floppy disk drives, and hard disks. The power supply has one or more fans that move air through the computer to cool the components.

In a file server, the power supply is an important but often overlooked item. Power supply failures and malfunctions cause problems elsewhere in the computer and are difficult to diagnose. Your file server may display a message indicating that a RAM chip has failed, and then stop; the cause of the problem may indeed be a failed RAM chip, or the problem may be in the power supply.

The fan(s) in the power supply sometimes stop working or become obstructed with dust and dirt. The computer overheats and either fails completely or acts strangely. Cleaning the fan(s)—after unplugging the computer from the wall outlet, of course—should be a part of the regular maintenance of your file server.

Power supplies vary considerably in quality. Some of the best ones are manufactured by the following company:

PC Power and Cooling
31510 Mountain Way
Bonsall, CA 92003
(800) 722-6555

Evaluating the Keyboard, Monitor, and Mouse

The keyboard, monitor, and mouse (if any) are not significant components on a file server computer. Often you can use lower-quality, less-expensive components for these parts. A typical file server runs unattended and may go for hours or days without interaction from you. You can power off the monitor for these long periods.

Note one caution about the keyboard, though; you ought to tuck the keyboard away so that falling objects (pencils or coffee mugs, for example) do not harm your network's file server.

Understanding the Server Software

Both server-based and peer LAN network operating systems can share disk space, disk files, and printers. In the next few sections, you discover how the network operating system enables you to share these resources.

Learning What the NOS Does

Conceptually, server-based and peer LAN network operating systems have three software components. The actual division of labor among the individual computer programs varies with the network operating system. Some simple products consist of a single computer program that embodies all three components. Other more complex NOS products divide the work among many computer programs and modules.

The first, lowest-level component provides connectivity and is always present. This network operating system module enables the workstation to communicate, through the network adapter cards and the LAN cable, across the LAN. This lowest level of software consists of network adapter driver computer programs.

Of the other two software elements, one is a workstation component, and the other resides in the file server. The workstation element creates request messages and sends them to a file server. Computers running the file server component can honor those requests.

Most of the requests from the workstation are file-oriented. Some are administrative in nature, having to do with logging in, logging out, and identifying who's who on the LAN.

Logging In to the Server

When you start up your computer, the network software loads into memory, but you cannot yet access the file server's hard disk. You need to log in by typing your user ID and password. On a NetWare LAN, for example, you can change to the file server drive letter (typically F) after loading the network software. You find yourself in the \LOGIN directory. You cannot access any other directory until you log in. One of the few files in the \LOGIN directory is LOGIN.EXE. When you run the LOGIN program, the software asks for your user ID and password. Figure 4.4 shows the login procedure on a NetWare LAN. The password does not appear on-screen as you type it. With IBM LAN Server and Microsoft LAN Manager, however, the LOGIN computer program resides on your workstation. The server is not even minimally available to you until you log in.

> **Note**
>
> As you learn in Chapter 7, "Using NetWare," and Chapter 8, "Using LAN Manager, Windows NT, and LAN Server," some network operating systems refer to the process of identifying yourself to the LAN as "logging in," and others refer to the process as "logging on."

Fig. 4.4

Logging in to a
NetWare LAN.

```
F:\LOGIN> login
Enter your login name: joel
Good evening, JOEL.

Drive  A:    maps to a local disk.
Drive  B:    maps to a local disk.
Drive  C:    maps to a local disk.
Drive  D:    maps to a local disk.
Drive  E:    maps to a local disk.
Drive  F: = SERVER1\SYS:  \JOEL

SEARCH1:   = C:\WINDOWS
SEARCH2:   = C:\DOS

F:\JOEL>
```

Even before you type your user ID and password, the workstation sends messages through the LAN cable. The very first of these messages is a *broadcast message*, directed to any and all computers on the LAN. This particular broadcast message asks file servers to identify themselves. When a file server responds, the workstation knows that it then can ask you for your user ID. If your workstation cannot find a file server, you see an error notification on your computer screen.

During the login process, the file server looks up the user ID in one of its internal tables. Your password, rights and permissions, workgroup ID (the name of the team you are on), default directory, disk space restrictions, and other network restrictions reside in these internal tables. Naturally, the password and other information exists in encrypted form to prevent tampering.

Other network-specific administrative tasks may take place during the login process. On a simple peer LAN, these tasks may be called out in the BAT file that turns the computer into a workstation. On a NetWare LAN, a *login script* tells the LOGIN.EXE program how to configure your workstation. NetWare LANs have system login scripts that apply to everyone, as well as individual login scripts that apply only to specific users.

Mapping Drives

Different personal computers contain different drive letter assignments, even before the network software loads. DOS assigns these initial drive letters based on the number of disk drives (both floppy and hard) in the computer and the number of partitions on the computer's hard disk(s). One computer may have a drive A (floppy) and a drive C (one hard disk partition). On another computer, DOS may assign drives A, B, C, and D, as well as other drive letters.

To complicate matters, the file server may contain multiple disk drives, and the network may have multiple file servers. How should the network software assign drive letters in such cases?

The process of assigning network drive letters is called *mapping drives*. On a NetWare LAN, you run the MAP.EXE utility program to assign drives. By default, NetWare begins assigning drive letters starting with F, or, if you already have several DOS-assigned drive letters on your computer, the next available drive letter. You can change the default assignment, as well as map additional nondefault network drives, by using MAP.EXE. Typically, a network administrator invokes MAP in the system login script so that everyone gets the same drive letter assignments when he or she logs in. Figure 4.5 shows the use of the MAP utility to map drive J to directory JOEL on volume SYS on the file server named SERVER1.

```
F:\JOEL> map

Drive  A:    maps to a local disk.
Drive  B:    maps to a local disk.
Drive  C:    maps to a local disk.
Drive  D:    maps to a local disk.
Drive  E:    maps to a local disk.

SEARCH1:  = C:\WINDOWS
SEARCH2:  = C:\DOS
SEARCH3:  = F:\PUBLIC [SERVER1\SYS:  \JOEL]

F:\JOEL> map root j:=server1\sys:joel

Drive  J: = SERVER1\SYS:JOEL  \

F:\JOEL>
```

Fig. 4.5
Mapping a drive letter to a file server directory.

On a LAN Server or LAN Manager network, you use the NET USE command to assign drives. Many peer LANs also use the NET USE command to assign drive letters. One peer LAN, WEB (from WebCorp), assigns a single drive W and then establishes each different server computer as a directory on this networked drive W. The name of a server's directory is based on the machine name you gave the server at installation time.

Macintosh computers do not map drive letters, of course. If you have a Mac, you will see additional folders you can access after you have logged in. The Chooser enables you to see these additional network resources. A UNIX-based computer, however, sees the network drive(s) as additional file systems. For example, with Network File System (NFS, developed by Sun Microsystems and offered by many makers of UNIX computers), the UNIX workstation mounts a network drive over an empty directory, thus making the UNIX mount command work almost the same for network drives as for local file systems.

Accessing and Sharing Files

After you have logged in and mapped the network drives as drive letters (or folders or file systems), you can access applications and data files on the network. You can also print to the shared LAN printer (as discussed later in this chapter). As you run applications to do your work, you should notice little or no difference between using your local hard disk and using the file server's hard disk(s).

Depending on how the network operating system implements its security features, however, you may observe that network files and directories behave differently from what you are accustomed to. On a NetWare LAN, for example, you may not have any rights at all in a particular directory. When you use the DOS DIR command, you see no files listed at all. Or, when you try to copy a file into that directory, you see an error message on your screen. You can run the NetWare utility RIGHTS.EXE to find out what rights, if any, you have in a directory.

Some DOS-based utilities and commands do not work on network drives. In particular, CHKDSK and disk diagnostic software such as Norton Utilities and PC Tools, when run at a workstation, cannot operate on network drives.

The file server itself can help you administer good file-sharing techniques. You can use the network operating system's rights and permissions capabilities to divide people into teams. Each team may be given its own public directory on the server. Coordination among the team members, perhaps in the form of a published procedure and personal assignments of responsibility for certain files, will go a long way toward preventing file-sharing problems.

A server-based network operating system typically uses something other than DOS to access the hard disk. The hard disk in a NetWare file server, for example, uses a method for storing and locating files that is fast and reliable. You cannot boot a NetWare file server with a DOS floppy disk and run the DOS CHKDSK utility on the hard disk. The hard disk does not use a formatting scheme that DOS recognizes. A DOS-based workstation, however, can use NetWare files as if they were DOS files, because the workstation and file server conspire to make the server's files look like DOS files. The workstation component transforms the responses from the server into DOS-like files. In contrast, a peer LAN typically does use DOS to access the hard disk.

Disk Sharing—A Technical Perspective

How does the network operating system make the file server's hard disk appear to be just another DOS-assigned drive letter? The answer is *redirection*.

Redirection of DOS function calls is the mechanism that makes file sharing possible. An application running on a workstation goes through the motions of asking DOS for some part of a disk file, but the network software intercepts the request and sends it to the file server. The file server does the actual disk I/O to obtain that part of the disk file and returns the result to the workstation. The network software on the workstation hands the disk file contents to the application, and in doing so, makes it look as though the workstation's copy of DOS had been the one to obtain the file contents. The application is unaware that the DOS function call it issued was handled by something other than DOS.

The network software performs several steps in order to send the request to the server and get back the response. The first step the workstation's network software does is to determine whether the network should handle a DOS file-read request or pass it along to DOS. The workstation network software does this by noting at file-open or file-creation time whether a network drive letter is in effect for the open or create call. Because the network software maintains an internal table of which drives are network devices, it is fairly easy for the workstation network operating system component to know whether a file-open or file-create call applies to a network drive. After the file is opened or created, the workstation's network software records the file's identity and knows to send any file-read or file-write requests to the file server. The local copy of DOS running at the workstation never knows about or accesses these files.

Suppose that the workstation's network software detects that a file-read request is for a file located on the file server. The network software turns the DOS function call into a network message. The format and size of this message vary with the different vendors' protocols, but its basic purpose—to request some file material from the file server—is the same for all network operating systems and protocols. The workstation network software then sends this message to the file server, through the network adapter card and LAN cable.

At the server, the receiving network adapter and adapter support software give the message to the file server portion of the network operating system. The NOS recognizes the message as a file-read request.

(continues)

II

Building a Network

(continued)

If another workstation's request is currently being processed by the server (a common occurrence on a busy LAN), the network operating system puts the file-read request in a queue for later handling. In its turn, the request is processed by the file-service portion of the network software running on the server. The desired sectors of the file are found in the server's cache memory or, if they are not in memory, are accessed directly from the server's hard disk.

When the file server does the I/O operation, it encounters one of three typical situations for a disk read: the requested bytes are read, end-of-file is detected, or only some of the requested bytes are read (this happens if more bytes were requested than actually exist). The file server creates a network message containing an indication of which of these three situations was encountered, appends the file data (if any) to the message, and then hands the result to the network support software for transmission back to the appropriate workstation.

When the workstation receives the response from the file server, its network software reverses the steps taken to send the file-read request. The network adapter processes the message containing the response by giving the message to the workstation's network software, and the network software emulates DOS by putting the file data into the application's buffer. The workstation's network software sets the CPU registers to indicate the number of bytes actually read, and returns control of the CPU to the application at the next instruction after the DOS function call.

Sharing a Printer

The network operating system redirects your printouts to the shared LAN printer in much the same way the NOS redirects your application's file I/O requests. The stream of print material becomes a series of LAN messages that flow from your workstation to the file server (or perhaps to a separate print server). The LAN messages containing the printout material become, in turn, a spool file on the server, which the network operating system queues for eventual printing.

Your workstation may have a locally attached printer (perhaps a dot-matrix model), and the LAN printer may be a high-speed laser printer. The network software enables you to print to either printer. In the next few sections, you explore how printer redirection works and what you need to know about using the LAN printer.

Accessing the LAN Printer. DOS-based computers support up to three printer ports, called LPT1, LPT2, and LPT3. If you have a locally attached workstation printer, it is connected to one of these printer ports (in some instances, your printer may connect to a serial port—COM1 or maybe COM2). You can print to your locally attached printer as soon as you start up your computer.

Before you print to the LAN printer, however, you must redirect one of your printer ports to the network. With LAN Server, LAN Manager, and many peer LAN products, you do this with the NET USE command. With NetWare, you use the CAPTURE command to redirect your printouts. Figure 4.6 shows the use of the CAPTURE command to create a connection between a PC's LPT1 port and the network printer named LASERJET. You may want to put the appropriate command into a BAT file, along with the other commands that turn your computer into a LAN workstation, so that you do not forget to issue them. If you send a printout to a printer port that has neither an attached local printer nor a redirected LAN printer, your computer may freeze. Even if it does not freeze, you will not get the printout you expected.

```
F:\JOEL> capture s=server1 q=laserjet nt nb noff
Device LPT1: re-routed to queue LASERJET on server SERVER1.

F:\JOEL> capture show

LPT1:  Capturing data to server SERVER1 queue LASERJET.
       User will not be notified after the files are printed.
       Capture Defaults:Enabled      Automatic Endcap:Enabled
       Banner :(None)                Form Feed       :No
       Copies :1                     Tabs            :No conversion
       Form   :0                     Timeout Count   :Disabled

LPT2:  Capturing Is Not Currently Active.

LPT3:  Capturing Is Not Currently Active.

F:\JOEL>
```

Fig. 4.6
Using the Net-Ware CAPTURE command.

If you have a locally attached printer, it probably uses LPT1. In this case, you may redirect LPT2 to the LAN printer. Or, if you have no local printer, you can redirect LPT1 to the LAN printer. You may even redirect all three printer ports to different LAN printers, if your LAN is large enough to have multiple shared printers.

When you send a printout to the LAN printer, the network software in your workstation considers the current printout to be a print job, separate from other print jobs you may have submitted. The network's spooling software processes each print job as each one reaches the top of the queue of pending print jobs.

II

Building a Network

Issuing Print Jobs. The network software at the file server or print server that manages the printer is called a *spooler*. The spooler receives your redirected printouts as streams of LAN messages and stores the printouts as temporary disk files. Each printout is a separate print job. Unless you specify otherwise, the network software prints a banner page, sometimes called a *job-separator page*, ahead of your printout to identify the printout as belonging to you.

If you print a memo or report from within a word processing application program and then print a subsequent report from a spreadsheet program, how does the LAN know that they are separate printouts? Typically, network operating systems use two methods to identify separate printouts. If the application uses DOS conventions to print, the network software sees the application open the DOS device named LPT1, write to that device, and then close the device. The close operation signals the end of the printout to the network software.

If, however, the application bypasses DOS to print, the network operating system does not detect the Open LPT1, Write to LPT1, Close LPT1 sequence. The NOS sees only a stream of print material go by, separated by long pauses between the times you tell your applications to print. Fortunately, the network operating system can time the pauses. If you tell the NOS to consider a pause of 10 seconds or longer as the end of a printout, the NOS dutifully waits those 10 seconds and then signals the end of that printout. If you do not specify a timeout period or if the timeout period is too short, the NOS will become confused about which printout is which. Keeping track of each printout is important to the spooler because the spooler does not want to mix pages of your printout with pages that other people have requested.

Using the Spooler. The print spooler module in the network operating system constantly switches its attention between two functions. One function consists of receiving print material in the form of LAN messages and storing that material as temporary disk files. The other function consists of knowing which disk file should be printed next and sending that next printout to the printer. After the spooler prints a file, it deletes that disk file. Each disk file is a separate print job. If both you and another person happen to print reports at the same time, the spooler accumulates each printout into a separate file. After detecting the end of each printout, the spooler prints first one report and then the other. Unless confused by timeout periods that are too short, the spooler will keep the pages of the printouts from getting mixed.

The spooler puts the most recently received printout at the end of a queue. Associated with each printout is information you have specified at the workstation, such as whether you want a banner page printed, whether you want the NOS to eject the last printed page (you may have already embedded a page-eject command at the end of your printout), and the type of paper the NOS should use to print your output. Each printout, as it is received from a workstation, goes to the end of the queue and waits for its turn to print. Most network operating systems provide utility commands you can issue to find out how far down in the queue your print job is. Many of these utilities also enable you to cancel a waiting print job or hold the job for later printing.

Using Different Fonts, Modes, and Printer Commands. People like to use different fonts (typefaces) in their memos and letters. Most laser printers and some dot-matrix printers support different fonts, of course. Most laser printers can even print reports "sideways"—in landscape mode—so that the long edge of the paper is the bottom rather than the side of the page.

Almost all printers stay in the most recently selected mode (portrait or landscape) and use the most recently selected font until told otherwise. On a shared LAN printer, if one person tells the printer to use a Letter Gothic font in landscape mode, the next person's printout may appear in that same mode and font, although this may not be what the next person intended.

All printers support commands that reset the printer to a default state. You should make a practice of sending such a reset command to the printer between printouts.

Ensuring Server Security

Chapter 1, "A Networking Overview," mentions the four reasons for implementing security on your LAN: limiting inadvertent damage, protecting confidentiality, preventing fraud, and reducing the chance of malicious damage by a disgruntled employee. The network operating system helps you protect the information stored on the LAN by requiring people to have user IDs and passwords and by allowing each person to have different access rights to different directories and files. One peer LAN product, POWERLan, from Performance Technology, even enables you to password-protect a shared LAN printer.

Establishing User IDs and Passwords

On the file server, the network operating system keeps track of each LAN user's login name (user ID), password (in encrypted form, of course), directory rights, and other attributes. The network operating system protects the files containing these attributes. You cannot edit these files with a text editor, for example.

II

Building a Network

On a NetWare LAN, these files collectively are called the *Bindery*. Other network operating systems simply refer to them as *system files*. To modify these files, you must use a utility program supplied with the network operating system.

When a network operating system's login process detects an invalid user ID and password, the NOS of course denies LAN access to the intruder. Some networks even enable the system administrator to specify that a given user ID can log in only once (rather than at several workstations concurrently), can log in only during certain hours of the day, or can log in only from certain workstations.

Granting Rights and Permissions

Even if every person on the LAN has the best of intentions as he or she gets work done, mistakes still happen. A DIR *.* command may turn into a DEL *.* command when typed. And sometimes a well-intended person will overzealously try to do LAN management tasks (such as copying a new application's executable files to a public area of the LAN) that can disrupt the day-to-day operation of the office. To prevent these and similar situations from happening, most network operating systems enable the system administrator to restrict the access rights of each user ID on a directory-by-directory basis.

NetWare, for example, implements the concept of *trustee rights*. The system administrator grants these rights to a person or group of persons to allow or disallow various levels of access to a directory and its subdirectories. Each directory has a *maximum rights mask* representing the highest level of privilege that any of the directory's trustees can be granted. Here are the eight rights expressed by the rights mask that each trustee may have:

- A user may read from open files.

- A user may write to open files.

- A user may open existing files.

- A user may create new files.

- A user may delete existing files.

- A user may act parentally—he or she may create, rename, and erase subdirectories, as well as set trustee rights and directory rights in the directory and its subdirectories.

- A user may search for files in the directory.

- A user may modify file attributes.

Assigning the Network Administrator

The utility program that the system administrator runs to add new user IDs to the LAN or to modify users' access rights requires, as you might expect, that the person running the program have special rights. Such rights by default exist for only a certain user ID. On NetWare LANs, this special User ID is *supervisor*. On LAN Server and LAN Manager networks, the special user ID is *admin*. The person in the office who knows the password for this special ID can perform network administration tasks on the LAN.

Creating New Users

One of the first tasks you perform on a new LAN, and one you perform each time your office hires new employees, is the adding of user IDs to the network. The utility program that the system administrator runs to create new user IDs is usually menu-driven and simple to use. Figure 4.7 illustrates the NetWare SYSCON utility for adding users and performing other administrative tasks on a NetWare LAN. Vendors of network operating systems know that system administrators are busy people who do not have time to look up complex commands and parameters.

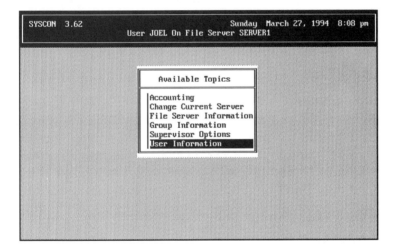

Fig. 4.7
NetWare administrators use SYSCON to manage many aspects of the LAN.

The basic process of adding a user ID, for all network operating systems, involves establishing the ID, its initial password, and its directory rights and other security attributes, and perhaps creating a *home directory* for the new user. The home directory usually has the same name as the user ID and is the default initial directory the user sees after logging in.

The process of removing a user from the LAN, when someone leaves the office, is simply the opposite of adding a new user. The system administrator removes the ID and deletes the user's home directory.

In addition, some network operating systems enable the system administrator to map the root directory for a new user (see the following section).

Mapping Drive Letters

The system administrator assigns the drive letters that everyone uses to access the file server. The administrator does this on a user-by-user basis for most peer LAN products. On a NetWare LAN, the administrator usually inserts entries in the networkwide system login script to establish the same drive letters for everyone.

On a large file server with a complex directory structure, the system administrator may find it convenient to map the drive letters differently for each user and provide each user with a different view of the server. By mapping a user's home directory as a root directory, for example, the system administrator can hide the rest of the file server from a user. The fully qualified name of the home directory might be F:\USERS\BARRY, but the administrator may map the root directory for user BARRY so that the user simply uses F:\ to refer to what is actually F:\USERS\BARRY. When one of BARRY's applications writes files to the root directory of drive F, that application is in reality writing to F:\USERS\BARRY.

Tracking Disk Space

The network administrator also must keep track of available disk space on the file server. With peer LAN products, because every workstation is potentially also a server, the administrator's job is multiplied by the number of workstations on the LAN. If a peer LAN has no administrator, each person needs to monitor his or her own available disk space. On a server-based LAN, the administrator can monitor disk space utilization on the single file server. Fortunately, a simple DOS DIR command is usually all it takes to reveal how much disk space remains on the server.

Most network operating systems do not enable you to limit the disk space that a person's files can occupy. NetWare is an exception; you can specify the maximum disk space that a particular user ID can use.

When available disk space becomes tight, it is usually the network administrator who (even after reminding people to delete obsolete files) has to houseclean the server's hard disk. It takes a surprising amount of time and effort to do this effectively.

Fixing a Failed Server

If the file server runs completely out of disk space, or if it fails as the result of a hardware malfunction, the network administrator has the unfortunate responsibility for putting the server back into service. The administrator may do some housecleaning, reboot the server, or troubleshoot a more difficult problem (which may affect only the file server or a segment of the entire LAN). In this last situation, the administrator probably will have to reconfigure the LAN so that a backup file server computer can be used until the primary server is repaired. Chapter 12, "Managing Your Network," discusses the tools and techniques an administrator can use to solve such problems.

Changing the Server Configuration

From time to time, the network administrator will need to change the file server configuration. The change may be as simple as adding memory (RAM) chips to the server, or as complex as adding a new hard disk or upgrading the network operating system. As you would expect, such tasks require planning and should be scheduled so that they cause the least disruption to the people in the office.

Comparing Server-Based LANs and Peer LANs

You now understand the differences between a server-based LAN and a peer LAN. Which one is best for your office? You know that a peer LAN is best suited for small, lightly loaded LANs. You should be aware of other considerations, however.

Loaning a File to Someone

On a server-based LAN, people share files by copying them to the file server or by creating them on the file server. The file server directory that contains a file must be accessible to the people who want to share the file; this involves setting up the proper rights and permissions for those people.

On a peer LAN, where every workstation is also a server, sharing files is somewhat easier than on a server-based LAN. The files can be shared without first being copied to a central file server. As on a server-based LAN, the appropriate rights and permissions must exist in order for the files to be shared.

DOS Was Not Designed for File Sharing

DOS was designed more than 10 years ago as a single-user, single-task operating system. From the outset, DOS was designed to work well with floppy disks. When hard disks came along, the programmers at Microsoft simply extended the floppy disk format to apply to hard disks.

Most peer LAN products are DOS-based. A workstation that is also a server is doing much more than DOS was ever designed to do. When you run an application on a workstation/server on a peer LAN, your application and the network operating system compete for the attention of DOS. Depending on the application, you may keep other people in the office from accessing their files on your computer. Or, if the NOS wins the competition, other people in the office can keep you from accessing *your* files.

The simplest example of such a conflict happens when you use a pop-up TSR program, such as Borland's SideKick, at your peer LAN workstation/server. Without meaning to, you can preempt the peer LAN NOS with this type of TSR. The other people in the office will not be happy as they try to deal with the error messages that appear on their monitors.

Worse yet, you may need to reboot your computer while it is a server on the LAN. The application you are running may have crashed, and the entire network may be disrupted. And, if you forget that your machine is a server and use the power switch to turn off your computer when you are not using it, the other people in the office will quickly remind you that your computer is a server.

DOS uses what is called a *file allocation table* (*FAT*) to locate files on a floppy disk. DOS treats hard disks in the same way it treats floppy disks. Unfortunately, the file allocation table scheme is excruciatingly slow for large files. And DOS is very slow at locating files in a directory that contains more than about 100 files. A DOS-based peer LAN server depends on and cannot operate any faster than DOS. If you and another person access your hard disk at the same time, one of you will have to wait for the other to finish.

Sharing a Printer

On a peer LAN, your locally attached printer also may be a shared, officewide LAN printer. In this case, you may find yourself the unwitting printer operator for the entire office. Your workload may not permit you the time it takes to attend to the printer.

Managing Your Files

You can, of course, see and access all the files on your computer—even the ones that belong to other people on a peer LAN. You can easily see that security on a peer LAN should be administered differently. At the very least, the people on a peer LAN should be cautioned to store private files on their own hard disks and not share the directories containing those files with other people on the LAN.

You will need to be careful about rebooting your computer on a peer LAN. If no one is writing files to your workstation/server at the time you reboot, the other people will simply see a notification message telling them that your computer is no longer available as a server. If someone *is* writing a file to your hard disk when you reach for the power switch, you probably will need to run CHKDSK before you can use the hard disk again, and the other person's file probably will be incomplete or corrupted.

Understanding Client/Server Architecture

If you operate your LAN in the simplest of ways, you share disk space on the file server, and you share files by making those files available to other people in publicly accessible directories. You can make your LAN work harder, how-ever. With *client/server architecture*, you integrate the LAN with one or more of the applications you run. You may designate one of the workstations on the LAN as a database server, for example, and use a product such as Microsoft's SQL Server to store your records.

Understanding Database Servers

Beyond treating a file server as just another drive letter lies a whole area of software technology—that of database servers. A *database server* is an unat-tended computer on the LAN that serves up records to the application(s) running on the other workstations. One of the goals of a database server is to take some of the workload away from the file server and the workstations.

An ordinary application that stores or retrieves records on a file server by using a file-indexing method causes a flurry of LAN traffic during each file access. To retrieve a record, the file I/O portion of the application reads through the index to find the desired key. Each read operation becomes a separate request message to the server and, a moment later, a response mes-sage back from the server. The network operating system performs this mes-sage passing, completely outside the application's control. The application is at the mercy of the NOS and the file server.

Looking at Database Server Advantages

The number of requests and responses depends, of course, on the size of the index file. You can get an idea of the number of LAN I/O messages, however, by multiplying the typical number of read operations to locate a key by the number of workstations on the LAN. The traffic adds up fast. Adding or deleting records causes even more traffic. The workstation has to rebalance or coalesce the index by manipulating the file indirectly, piece by piece. The file I/O activity takes place through the network operating system and the LAN cable.

In a database server environment, the application's file access logic (not the network operating system) controls the message passing. The application retrieves a record by sending the desired key as a LAN message to the database server. The database server sends back the desired record (or a record-doesn't-exist indication). This process greatly reduces LAN message traffic. More important, it puts the indexed file I/O burden on a separate machine.

On a busy LAN, a database server helps distribute the processing evenly and fairly. You can select a computer and operating system for the database server based on criteria that may be different from the criteria you used to pick the file server machine. You may even go so far as to use Macintoshes for user workstations and a high-powered superserver as the database server computer. Because the workstation no longer has to contain the actual file I/O logic, the application can be smaller by saving whatever memory those file I/O routines consume. If the application is DOS-based and needs to run within the infamous 640K of conventional memory (minus what DOS and the network use), you will find database server technology tempting for the RAM it saves.

Looking at Database Server Disadvantages

When you need to ensure good performance and control the LAN environment more closely than a particular network operating system allows, you can build a database server into your LAN architecture. Unfortunately, you almost certainly will need the services of a programmer (or a staff of programmers) to implement a database server. You will incur the cost of programming (or reprogramming) the primary application on the LAN to use the database server. Simply installing a database server product on your LAN is not enough. You must somehow connect the application to your new database server.

Using an Uninterruptible Power Supply (UPS)

You know that rebooting a peer LAN workstation/server can affect other people's work. With a server-based LAN, when the power in your building fails, everyone's work is affected. People writing files to the server at the time of the failure may find their files incomplete or corrupted when power comes back. You may have to use your latest backup to restore some of the files on the file server after a power failure. An uninterruptible power supply (UPS) helps you avoid this problem.

Defining an Uninterruptible Power Supply (UPS)

An uninterruptible power supply (UPS) runs your computer off batteries all the time. UPSs cost from about $1,000 to $3,500. When power fails, the file server computer just keeps on running, using electricity provided by the UPS batteries. The UPS contains an *inverter* that turns the direct current (DC) power from the batteries into a pure alternating current (AC) sine wave for your computer. The batteries are continuously charged from the AC power. If commercial power fails, the batteries last from a few minutes up to several hours before running down. Note that you shouldn't try to connect all the computers on the LAN to a single UPS. Connecting just the file server should be sufficient. Because they consume so much power, laser printers are generally not good candidates for UPS power protection.

A UPS is simpler than a *standby power system (SPS)*. Because a UPS runs continuously, however, it must be much more sturdily built than an equivalently rated SPS. A UPS costs about twice as much as an SPS. Because your file server computer sees only smooth battery power, the server is immune to nearly all forms of AC power problems, such as sags and spikes. A UPS unit may end up costing more than the computer it protects, though.

Caution

Some companies advertise SPS products as UPS systems. Watch out for the term *transfer time*. An SPS must transfer from the AC power to batteries at the time of power failure. A true UPS always runs your computer off the batteries. If the sales literature mentions a transfer time (1 to 18 milliseconds is typical), the literature describes an SPS, not a true UPS.

Understanding How the UPS and Server Work Together

Some network operating systems recognize the presence of a UPS. The UPS may come with a special adapter card you install in the server computer, or the UPS may attach to the server's COM1 or COM2 serial port. The network operating system monitors the information flowing from the UPS. If power to the server fails, the network operating system notifies people on the LAN (if their computers are still operational) of the failure. When the batteries in the

II

Building a Network

UPS begin to run down, the network operating system gracefully closes all files, makes sure that all the data is stored on the hard disk, and quietly shuts itself down.

Summary

You now have an excellent understanding of the heart of your LAN—the file server. You know what a file server does, and you know what makes a good file server. In this chapter, you examined both the hardware and the software components of file servers. You recognize the important roles played by the server's hard disk drive and the server's CPU chip. And you understand why installing more memory (RAM) chips in a server can result in better performance.

The network operating system in your file server may be a peer LAN product or it may be server-based. You learned to distinguish between the two, and you know the reasons why a server-based LAN can sometimes be a better choice than a peer LAN. You learned how file servers share their files and printers. You know what happens when you perform the login sequence on a LAN. You understand the considerations for security and administration on both peer and server-based LANs. And you realize the importance of using an uninterruptible power supply to protect the data stored on the LAN.

In the next chapter, you explore the LAN substrata. You discover how the workstations and the file server use a *protocol* to communicate with one another through the network adapters and LAN cables.

Chapter 5

Using Protocols, Cables, and Adapters

Earlier chapters described how workstations and file servers communicate with one another, with the file servers honoring requests submitted by the workstations for file operations (such as print, open, read, write, and close). This chapter explains exactly how the LAN supports these PC-to-PC communications. After exploring the general concepts of protocols and message frames, you become familiar with the OSI model, and you discover how the different manufacturers' products compare to the OSI standard. In particular, you get an in-depth look at these low-level protocols: Ethernet, Token Ring, ARCnet, and Fiber Distributed Data Interface (FDDI).

The midlevel protocols that operate on top of these low-level protocols are NetBIOS, IPX/SPX, and TCP/IP. And at yet a higher level, the file redirection you learned about in Chapter 4, "Using File Servers," occurs through protocols such as IBM's Server Message Blocks (SMB) standard or Novell's NetWare Core Protocol (NCP). This chapter covers all these layers of protocols.

After you understand what information your LAN sends from computer to computer, you turn to a discussion of the different types of LAN cables that carry the information. You learn the differences in twisted pair, coaxial, fiber optic, and other types of cables.

The network adapter enables each computer to send and receive message frames. In this chapter, you find out how network adapters support the various protocols and how each type of network adapter works.

Examining Protocols, Frames, and Communications

The network adapter sends and receives messages among the LAN computers, and the cable carries the messages. The layer of protocols in each computer, however, turns the computers into a local area network.

At the lowest level, networked PCs communicate with one another and with the file server by using message packets, often called *frames*. These frames are the foundation on which all LAN activity is based. The network adapter, along with its support software, sends and receives these frames. Each computer has a unique address on the LAN to which frames can be sent.

You can send frames for various purposes, including the following:

- To open a communications session with another adapter

- To send data (perhaps a record from a file) to a PC

- To acknowledge the receipt of a data frame

- To broadcast a message to all other adapters

- To close a communications session

Figure 5.1 shows what a typical frame looks like. Different network implementations define frames in different ways, but the following data items are common to all implementations:

- The sender's unique network address

- The destination's unique network address

- An identification of the contents of the frame

- A data record or message

- A checksum or CRC for error-detection purposes

Using Frames That Contain Other Frames

The layering of protocols is a powerful concept. The lowest layer knows how to tell the network adapter to send a message, but that layer is ignorant of file servers and file redirection. The highest layer understands file servers and redirection but knows nothing about Ethernet or Token Ring. Together, though, the layers give you a local area network. Frames are always layered (see fig. 5.2).

SENDER ID	DEST ID	FRAME TYPE	DATA/MESSAGE	CRC

Fig. 5.1
The basic layout of
a frame.

When the higher-level file redirection protocol gives a message to a midlevel
protocol (such as NetBIOS, for example) and asks that the message be sent to
another PC on the network (probably a file server), the midlevel protocol puts
an *envelope* around the message packet and hands it to the lowest-level protocol, implemented as the network support software and network adapter card.
This lowest layer in turn wraps the NetBIOS envelope in an envelope of its
own and sends it out across the network. In figure 5.2, you see each envelope
labeled *header* and *trailer*. On receipt, the network support software on the
receiving computer removes the outer envelope and hands the result upward
to the next higher-level protocol. The midlevel protocol running on the
receiver's computer removes its envelope and gives the message—now an
exact copy of the sender's message—to the receiving computer's highest-level
protocol.

You learn much more about each layer (including NetBIOS) later in the chapter. For now, you need to remember that lower-level frames can contain
higher-level frames and that different protocols exist to deal with each layer.

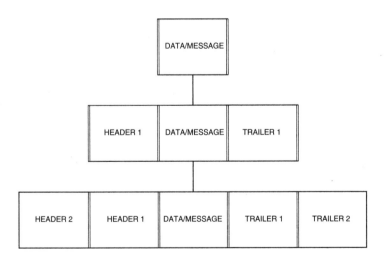

Fig. 5.2
Frame layers.

Using Frames and Files

Figure 5.3 illustrates how file redirection works. When an application wants
to read or write a file located on the file server, the portion of the network

operating system at the workstation intercepts the file I/O operation. The workstation NOS software, often implemented as a TSR program, turns the read or write operation into a LAN message (a frame). The workstation NOS software gives the frame to the LAN support software layer, which adds its own information to the frame and hands the result to the network adapter. The network adapter adds yet more information to the frame and sends it to the file server. The response from the file server travels the opposite route back to the requesting workstation.

Fig. 5.3

The redirection of DOS file requests.

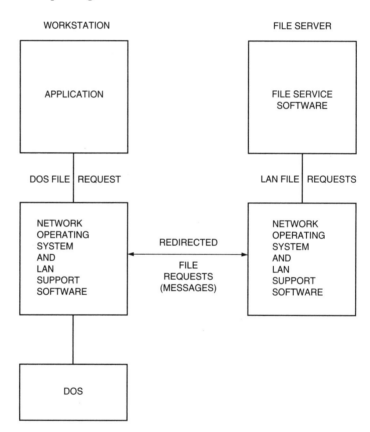

Different vendors split the LAN communications functions in different ways, but they all compare themselves to the OSI model.

Using the OSI Model

ISO, the International Standards Organization, has published a standard called the Open System Interconnection (OSI) model. Most vendors of LAN products endorse the OSI standard but have not yet implemented OSI fully. The OSI model divides LAN communications into seven layers. Most network operating system vendors use three or four layers of protocols.

The OSI model describes how communications between two computers should occur. Sometime in this decade, this theoretical standard will become a practical one as more and more vendors switch to OSI. The OSI model declares seven layers and specifies that each layer be insulated from the others by a well-defined interface. Figure 5.4 shows the seven layers.

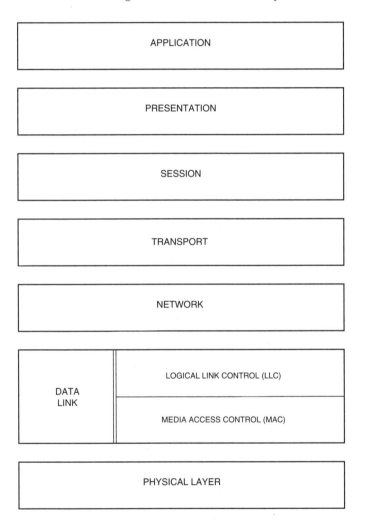

Fig. 5.4
The OSI model.

Following are descriptions of the seven layers:

- *Physical*. This part of the OSI model specifies the physical and electrical characteristics of the connections that make up the network (twisted pair cables, fiber optic cables, coaxial cables, connectors, repeaters, and so on). You can think of this layer as the hardware layer. Although the rest of the layers may be implemented as chip-level functions rather than as actual software, the other layers are software in relation to this first layer.

■ *Data Link.* At this stage of processing, the electrical impulses enter or leave the network cable. The network's electrical representation of your data (bit patterns, encoding methods, and tokens) is known to this layer, and only to this layer. It is at this point that errors are detected and corrected (by requesting retransmissions of corrupted packets). Because of its complexity, the Data Link layer often is subdivided into a Media Access Control (MAC) layer and a Logical Link Control (LLC) layer. The MAC layer deals with network access (either token-passing or collision-sensing) and network control. The LLC layer, operating at a higher level than the MAC layer, is concerned with sending and receiving the user data messages.

■ *Network.* This layer switches and routes the packets as necessary to get them to their destination. This layer is responsible for addressing and delivering message packets.

■ *Transport.* When more than one packet is in process at any time, the Transport layer controls the sequencing of the message components and regulates inbound traffic flow. If a duplicate packet arrives, this layer recognizes it as a duplicate and discards it.

■ *Session.* The functions in this layer enable applications running at two workstations to coordinate their communications into a single session (which you can think of in terms of a highly structured dialog). The Session layer supports the creation of the session, the management of the packets sent back and forth during the session, and the termination of the session.

■ *Presentation.* When IBM, Apple, DEC, NeXT, and Burroughs computers want to talk to one another, obviously a certain amount of translation and byte reordering needs to be done. The Presentation layer converts data into (or from) a machine's native internal numeric format.

■ *Application.* This is the layer of the OSI model seen by an application program. A message to be sent across the network enters the OSI model at this point, travels downward toward layer 1 (the Physical layer), zips across to the other workstation, and then travels back up the layers until the message reaches the application on the other computer through its own Application layer.

You can use the United States Postal Service as an analogy to explain the functions of these layers. The Application layer would be a plain sheet of paper, folded to fit in an envelope. The Presentation layer is an envelope with windows for the addresses to show through. The Session layer is the envelope with the names of the sender and recipient showing through the windows. The Transport layer is the post office. The Network layer is the mail carrier. The Data Link layer is your mailbox. And the Physical layer is, of course, the mail truck.

One of the factors that makes the network operating system of each vendor proprietary (as opposed to having an *open architecture*) is the vendor's non-compliance with the OSI model.

Using Low-Level Protocols

Local area networks work in one of two basic ways: *collision-sensing* or *token-passing*. Ethernet is an example of a collision-sensing network; Token Ring is an example of a token-passing network.

The Institute of Electrical and Electronic Engineers (IEEE) has defined and documented a set of standards for the physical characteristics of both collision-sensing and token-passing networks. These standards are known as IEEE 802.3 (Ethernet) and IEEE 802.5 (Token Ring). Be aware, though, that there are minor differences between the frame definitions for true Ethernet and for true IEEE 802.3. In terms of the standards, IBM's 16-mbps Token Ring adapter card is an 802.5 Token Ring extension. You learn the definitions and layout of Ethernet and Token Ring frames in the sections "Using Ethernet" and "Using Token Ring" in this chapter.

Some LANs don't conform to either IEEE 802.3 or IEEE 802.5, of course. The most popular of these is ARCnet, available from such vendors as Datapoint Corporation, Standard Microsystems, and Thomas-Conrad. Other types of LANs include StarLan (from AT&T), VistaLan (from Allen-Bradley), LANtastic (from Artisoft), Omninet (from Corvus), PC Net (from IBM), and ProNet (from Proteon).

Fiber Distributed Data Interface (FDDI) is a new physical-layer LAN standard. FDDI uses fiber optic cable and a token-passing scheme similar to IEEE 802.5 to transmit data frames at a snappy 100 mbps.

II

Building a Network

Using Ethernet

In the collision-sensing environment, often referred to by the abbreviation CSMA/CD (carrier sense, multiple access, with collision detection), the network adapter card listens to the network when it has a frame to send. If the adapter hears that another card is sending a frame at that moment, the card waits a moment and tries again. Even with this approach, collisions (two workstations attempting to transmit at exactly the same moment) can and do occur. It is the nature of CSMA/CD networks to expect collisions and to handle them by retransmitting frames as necessary. These retransmissions are handled by the adapter card and are not seen or managed by you or your applications. Collisions generally happen and are handled in less than a microsecond.

> **Caution**
>
> Although many people blame poor CSMA/CD (Ethernet) network performance on the number of users currently on the network who are sending and receiving message traffic, the truth is that more than 90 percent of transmission problems on an Ethernet network are the result of faulty cables or malfunctioning adapter cards.

On an Ethernet network, data is broadcast throughout the network in all directions at the rate of 10 mbps. All machines receive every frame, but only those meant to receive a frame (by virtue of the frame's destination network address) respond with an acknowledgment. Figure 5.5 illustrates an Ethernet network.

Fig. 5.5
An Ethernet network.

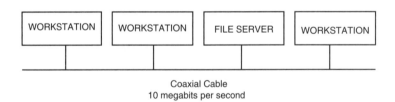

Digital Equipment Corporation and 3Com Corporation are major suppliers of Ethernet hardware. Other companies that offer Ethernet equipment include AST Research, Data General, Excelan, Gateway Communications, Micom-Interlan, Proteon, RAD Data Communications, Thomas-Conrad, Ungermann-Bass, Western Digital, and Zenith.

Ethernet is a LAN standard that is based on the Experimental Ethernet network designed and built in 1975 by Xerox at the Palo Alto Research Center (PARC). Ethernet operates at 10 mbps over 50-ohm coaxial cable; the current version is 2.0, established in November, 1982.

IEEE 802.3 is a LAN standard similar to Ethernet. The first edition of IEEE 802.3 was published in 1985. The differences between the two Ethernet standards are in the areas of network architecture and frame formats.

In terms of network architecture, IEEE 802.3 distinguishes between MAC and LLC layers; true Ethernet lumps these layers together into a single Data Link layer. Ethernet also defines an Ethernet Configuration Test Protocol (ECTP) that is absent from the IEEE 802.3 standard. Note, however, that the important differences between the two are in the types and lengths of the fields that make up a frame. These differences can cause the two protocols to be incompatible. The Ethernet and IEEE 802.3 frames are discussed in the following sections.

Using Ethernet Frames

Figure 5.6 shows the layout and data field definitions for a true Ethernet frame (the original, non-IEEE Ethernet).

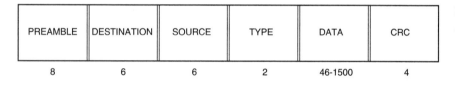

Fig. 5.6
An Ethernet frame.

Length of each field, in bytes

Following are descriptions of the original Ethernet frame:

- *Preamble.* This field, used for synchronization and framing, is 8 bytes long (the standard refers to a byte as an *octet*, or 8 *bits*; you can call them *bytes*). The Preamble always contains the bit pattern 10101010 in the first 7 bytes, with 10101011 in the last (8th) byte.

- *Destination address.* This field is 6 bytes in size and contains the address of the workstation that will receive this frame. The first (leftmost) bit of the first byte has a special meaning. If the leftmost bit is a 0, the destination address is a physical address that is unique throughout the

Ethernet universe. As a result of a naming scheme administered by Xerox Corporation, the first three bytes are a group address assigned by Xerox, and the last three are assigned locally. If the leftmost bit is a 1, it represents a broadcast frame. In this case, the rest of the destination address can refer to a group of logically related workstations or to all workstations on the network (all 1s).

■ *Source address*. This address field is also 6 bytes, and it identifies the workstation sending the frame. The leftmost bit of the first byte always is 0.

■ *Type*. This field contains 2 bytes of information that identify the type of the higher-level protocol that issued (or wants to receive) this frame. The Type field is assigned by Xerox and is not interpreted by Ethernet. It enables multiple high-level protocols (referred to as *client layers*) to share the network without running into one another's messages.

■ *Data portion*. This portion of the frame can contain 46 to 1,500 bytes. It is the data message that the frame is intended to carry to the destination.

■ *CRC*. Finally, the frame contains 4 bytes of *cyclic redundancy checksum remainder*, calculated via a CRC-32 polynomial. The workstation that receives this frame performs its own CRC-32 calculation on the frame and compares the calculated value to the CRC field in the frame to find out whether the frame arrived intact or was damaged in transit.

Disregarding the preamble for a moment, you can see that an entire Ethernet frame is between 64 and 1,518 bytes in size. You can see also that the minimum size of a data message is 46 bytes.

Using IEEE 802.3 Frames

Figure 5.7 shows an IEEE 802.3 frame, which contains the following fields:

■ *Preamble*. This field contains 7 bytes of synchronization data. Each byte is the same bit pattern: 10101010.

■ *Start Frame Delimiter (SFD)*. The SFD consists of a single byte that has the bit pattern 10101011. (The Preamble and SFD IEEE 802.3 fields match the single Ethernet Preamble field.)

■ *Destination address*. This field can contain 2 or 6 bytes, depending on which type of IEEE 802.3 network you install, and indicates the workstation for which the frame is intended. Note that all addresses on a particular network must be 2- or 6-byte addresses. The most popular type of IEEE 802.3, called 10BASE5, specifies 6-byte addresses. The first bit of the destination address is the individual/group bit. The I/G bit has a value of 0 if the address refers to a single workstation, or a 1 if it represents a group of workstations (a broadcast message). If the destination address is a 2-byte field, the rest of the bits form a 15-bit workstation address. If the destination address is a 6-byte field, however, the bit following the I/G bit is a universally/locally administered bit (the U/L bit). The U/L bit is a 0 for universally administered (global) addresses and is a 1 for locally administered addresses. The rest of the 6-byte field is a 46-bit workstation address.

■ *Source address*. This is the 2- or 6-byte address of the sending workstation. The I/G (first) bit is always 0.

■ *Length*. These two bytes express the length of the data portion of the frame.

■ *Data portion*. This field ranges from 0 to 1,500 bytes of data. If this field is less than 46 bytes long, the next field (Pad) is used to fatten the frame to an acceptable (minimum) size.

■ *Pad*. The Pad field contains enough bytes of filler to ensure that the frame has at least a certain overall size. If the data portion is large enough, the Pad field does not appear in the frame (Pad has zero length).

■ *CRC*. The *cyclic redundancy checksum remainder* has 4 bytes of remainder from the CRC-32 algorithm—the same as for Ethernet.

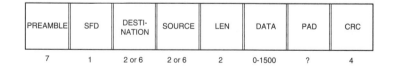

PREAMBLE	SFD	DESTI-NATION	SOURCE	LEN	DATA	PAD	CRC
7	1	2 or 6	2 or 6	2	0-1500	?	4

Length of each field, in bytes

Fig. 5.7
An IEEE 802.3 frame.

The size of a frame under both true Ethernet and IEEE 802.3 Ethernet (assuming Type 10BASE5), excluding the Preamble and SFD, is the same: from 64 to 1,518 bytes. Under IEEE 802.3, however, it is permissible for the application (or an upper-layer protocol) to send a data area that is less than 46 bytes, because the frame is padded automatically by the MAC layer. Under true Ethernet, data frames that are too small are considered to be error situations.

II

Building a Network

Using Token Ring

You can think of a token-passing network as a ring. Even though the network may be wired electrically as a star, data frames move around the network from workstation to workstation in ring fashion, as shown in figure 5.8. A workstation sends a frame to the MSAU (multistation access unit), which routes the frame to the next workstation.

Fig. 5.8

A token ring network.

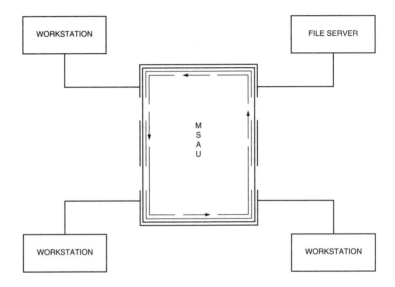

Each network adapter card receives a frame from its *upstream neighbor*, regenerates the electrical signals making up the frame, and passes the result along to the next (*downstream*) workstation. The frame may consist of some data that one computer is sending to another, or the frame may be a token. A *token* is a 3-byte message, indicating that the LAN is idle.

When a workstation wants to send a frame, the network adapter waits for the token. The adapter then turns the token into a data frame containing a protocol-layered message.

The frame travels along from adapter to adapter until it reaches its destination, which acknowledges reception of the frame by setting certain bits in the frame. The data frame continues its journey around the ring. When the sending station receives its own frame back, and if the frame was properly received, the sender relinquishes use of the LAN by putting a new token into circulation. A token-passing network is designed so that collisions never occur.

IBM currently offers Token Ring products that operate at either 4 or 16 mbps. Several other companies make equipment compatible with IBM Token Ring, including Thomas-Conrad, Gateway Communications, Western Digital, 3Com, General Instrument, Harris Data Communications, Madge Networks, NCR, Proteon, Pure Data, Racore, RAD Data Communications, DatAmerica, Siecor, and Ungermann-Bass. A few of these companies (including Proteon and Siecor) make Token Ring hardware that operates at different rates or that uses fiber optics.

Early Token Release

Early Token Release (ETR) is easily misunderstood; Token Ring itself is a fairly complex subject. On a momentarily idle Token Ring LAN, workstations circulate a token. The LAN becomes busy (carries information) when a workstation receives a token and turns it into a data frame targeted at the file server (or targeted back at a file-needy workstation if originated by a server that is answering a file I/O request). After receipt by its target node, the data frame continues circulating around the LAN until it reaches its source node. The source node turns the data frame back into a token that circulates until a downstream node needs it. So far, so good—these are just standard Token Ring concepts.

A workstation needs to send only a few bytes to tell the file server that it needs some part of a file. If the signal must go into and out of many workstations to circulate the ring, and if the data frame is small, latency occurs. *Latency* is the unproductive delay that occurs while the source node waits for its upstream neighbor to return its data frame.

The source node appends idle characters onto the LAN following the data frame until the data frame circulates the entire LAN and arrives back at the source node. The typical latency of a 4-mbps ring is about 50 to 100 idle characters. On a 16-mbps ring, latency may reach 400 or more bytes' worth of LAN time.

With Early Token Release, available only on 16-mbps networks, the originating work-station transmits a new token immediately after sending its data frame. Downstream nodes pass along the data frame and then receive an opportunity to transmit data themselves—the new token. If you had a token ring microscope, you would see tokens and other data frames (instead of a long trail of idle characters) chasing the data frame. You would also know that your 16-mbps token ring LAN is using ETR to keep itself busy.

II

Building a Network

Using Token Ring Frames

In 1985, Texas Instruments and IBM jointly developed the TMS380 chipset (IBM doesn't use the chipset; it builds its own proprietary chipset, which is mostly compatible with the TI/IBM set). The TMS380 chipset implements the IEEE 802.5 standards for the Physical and Data Link layers of the OSI model. The functions of both the MAC sublayer and the LLC sublayer of the Data Link layer are supported. Originally released as a set of five chips, the TI product now can be produced as a single chip.

Here are the TMS380 functions:

- *TMS38051 and 38052 chips.* These chips handle the lowest level, the ring interface itself. They perform the actual transmission/reception of data (frames), monitor cable integrity, and provide clocking functions.

- *TMS38020 chip.* This chip is the protocol handler. It controls and manages the 802.5 protocol functions.

- *ROM chip.* This chip has program code burned into it. The permanently stored software performs diagnostic and management functions.

- *TMS38010 chip.* This chip is a 16-bit dedicated microprocessor for handling communications; it executes the code in the ROM chip and has a 2.75K RAM buffer for temporary storage of transmitted and received data.

Although most people think of a token ring as a single piece of cable that all the workstations tap into, a token ring actually consists of individual point-to-point linkages. Joe's workstation sends the token (or a data frame) to your workstation, your workstation sends the token or frame downstream to the next workstation, and so on. Only the fact that one of your downstream neighbors also happens to be Joe's upstream neighbor makes it a ring. From a communications standpoint, the messages go directly from one PC to another.

Not all workstations on the ring are peers, although the differences are invisible to the outside world. One of the workstations is designated as the *active monitor*, which means that it assumes additional responsibilities for controlling the ring. The active monitor maintains timing control over the ring, issues new tokens (if necessary) to keep things going, and generates diagnostic frames under certain circumstances. The active monitor is chosen at the time the ring is initialized and can be any one of the workstations on the network. If the active monitor fails for some reason, there is a mechanism by which the other workstations (*standby monitors*) can decide which one becomes the new active monitor.

Three formats are defined for IEEE 802.5 token ring message packets: tokens, frames, and abort sequences. These formats are discussed in the following sections.

Using the Token

Figure 5.9 shows the first format of the IEEE 802.5 message packet: the token. In principle, the token is not a frame but simply a means by which each workstation can recognize when its turn to transmit has arrived.

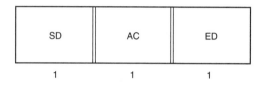

Fig. 5.9
A token.

Length of each field, in bytes

A token is 3 bytes long (24 bits) and contains the following three fields:

- Start Delimiter

- Access Control

- End Delimiter

The Start Delimiter (SD) field appears at the beginning of the token (as well as at the beginning of every message or frame that is sent across the network). The SD field consists not just of 0s and 1s, but of a unique series of electrical impulses that cannot be mistaken for anything other than a Start Delimiter field. Because the SD field contains four nondata symbols (each 1 bit long) and four (normal) 0 bits in the field, the field totals 1 byte in size.

Next comes the Access Control (AC) field. This field is divided into four sub-fields:

P P P   T   M   R R R

P P P are the priority bits, T is the token bit, M is the monitor bit, and R R R are the reservation bits.

A network adapter can prioritize a token or frame by setting the priority bits to a value ranging from 0 to 7 (with 7 being the highest priority). A workstation can use the network (that is, change a token into a frame) only if it receives a token with a priority less than or equal to the workstation's own

II

Building a Network

priority. The workstation's network adapter sets the priority bits to indicate the priority of the current frame or token. Refer to the description of the reservation bits for more on how this works.

The token bit has a value of 1 for a token and has a value of 0 for a frame.

The monitor bit is set to 1 by the active monitor and set to 0 by any workstation transmitting a token or frame. If the active monitor sees a token or frame that contains a monitor bit of 1, it knows that this token or frame has been once around the ring without being processed by a workstation. Because a sending workstation is responsible for removing its own transmitted frames (by recirculating a new token), and because high-priority workstations are responsible for grabbing a token that they claimed previously, the active monitor detects that something is wrong if a frame or a prioritized token has circulated the ring without having been processed. The active monitor cancels the transmission and circulates a new token.

The reservation bits work hand in hand with the priority bits. A workstation can place its priority in the reservation bits (if its priority is higher than the current value of the reservation bits). The workstation then has reserved the next use of the network. When a workstation transmits a new token, the workstation sets the priority bits to the value that it found in the RRR field of the frame it just received. Unless preempted by an even higher-priority workstation, the workstation that originally set the reservation bits will be the next station to turn the token into a frame.

The final field of the token is the End Delimiter (ED) field. As with the Start Delimiter field, this field contains a unique combination of 1s and special nondata symbols that cannot be mistaken for anything else. The ED field appears at the end of each token. Besides marking the end of the token, the ED field contains two subfields: the Intermediate Frame bit and the Error-Detected bit. These fields are discussed in the next section; they pertain more to frames than to tokens.

Using the Data Frame

Figure 5.10 shows the second format of the IEEE 802.5 message packet: the true data frame. Data frames can, of course, contain messages that a network operating system or an application sends to another computer on the ring. Data frames also sometimes contain internal messages used privately among the Token Ring network adapter cards for ring-management purposes.

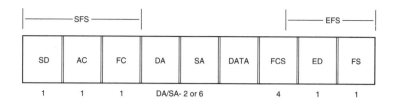

Fig. 5.10
A token ring data frame.

Length of each field, in bytes

A frame consists of several groups of fields: the Start Frame Sequence (SFS), the Destination Address (DA), the Source Address (SA), the data itself (DATA), the Frame Check Sequence (FCS), and the End Frame Sequence (EFS). Together, these fields form a message record (envelope) that is used to carry either ring-management information (MAC data) or user data (LLC data). You already know about LLC data; these are the frames that contain application-oriented data, such as PC-to-PC messages or a portion of a disk file (from a file server) that is being shared through the network operating system. The network adapters use MAC frames internally, though, to control and manage the ring. The IEEE 802.5 standard defines six MAC control frames. The Frame Control field indicates the type of the frame (MAC or LLC); if it is a MAC frame, this field also indicates which of the six is represented by this particular frame.

Briefly, the six MAC frames are these:

- *Duplicate Address Test.* Sent by a workstation when it joins the ring to ensure that its address is unique.

- *Active Monitor Present.* Circulated every so often by the active monitor to let other workstations know that it is still alive.

- *Standby Monitor Present.* Sent by a monitor other than the active monitor.

- *Claim Token.* If a standby monitor thinks that the active monitor may have died, it starts sending claim token frames. The standby monitors then go through a process of negotiation with one another to determine which one becomes the new active monitor.

- *Beacon.* Sent in the event of a major network problem, such as a broken cable or a workstation that is transmitting without waiting for the token. By detecting which station is sending the beacon frame, diagnostic software can localize the problem.

II

Building a Network

■ *Purge.* Sent after ring initialization and after a new active monitor establishes itself.

Each frame (MAC or LLC) begins with a Start Frame Sequence, which contains three fields:

■ *Start Delimiter (SD).* The definition of SD is the same for frames as for tokens.

■ *Access Control (AC).* The definition is the same for frames as for tokens.

■ *Frame Control (FC).* This is a 1-byte field containing two subfields, Frame Type and MAC Control ID:

> F F C C C C C C

The two frame type bits (FF) have a value of 00 for MAC frames and 01 for LLC frames (11 and 10 are reserved).

The MAC control ID bits identify the type of ring-management frame:

CCCCCC	MAC Frame
000011	Claim Token
000000	Duplicate Address Test
000101	Active Monitor Present
000110	Standby Monitor Present
000010	Beacon
000100	Purge

The Destination Address (DA) follows the Start Frame Sequence fields. The DA field can be 2 or 6 bytes long. With 2-byte addresses, the first bit indicates whether the address is a group address or an individual address (just as in the collision-sensing IEEE 802.3 protocol). With 6-byte addresses, the first bit also is an I/G bit, and the second bit tells whether the address is locally assigned or globally assigned (the U/L bit, which again is the same as in the IEEE 802.3 protocol). The rest of the bits form the address of the workstation to which the frame is addressed.

The Source Address (SA) field is the same size and format as the Destination Address field.

The data portion of the frame (DATA) can contain a user data message record intended for (or received from) a midlevel protocol such as IPX, TCP/IP, or NetBIOS. Or the Data field can contain one of the MAC frames just discussed. The Data field has no specified maximum length, although there are practical limits on its size based on how long a single workstation may have control of the ring.

The Frame Check Sequence (FCS) field is 4 bytes of remainder from the CRC-32 cyclic redundancy checksum algorithm. It is used for error detection.

The End Frame Sequence (EFS) is composed of two fields: End Delimiter and Frame Status. Following are descriptions of these fields:

- *End Delimiter (ED)*. You read about this field in relation to tokens; in a frame, however, this field takes on additional meaning. Besides consisting of a unique pattern of electrical impulses, it contains two subfields, each 1 bit in size. The intermediate frame bit is set to 1 if this frame is part of a multiple-frame transmission, and the bit is set to 0 if the frame is the last (or only) frame. The error-detected bit starts as a 0 when a frame is sent originally. Each workstation's network adapter, as it passes the frame along, checks for errors (verifying that the CRC in the Frame Check Sequence field still corresponds to the contents of the frame, for example). An adapter sets the error-detected bit to 1 if the adapter finds something wrong. The intervening network adapters that see an already set error-detected bit pass the frame along. The originating adapter notices that a problem occurred and tries again by retransmitting the frame.

- *Frame Status (FS)*. This 1-byte field contains four reserved bits (R) and two subfields, the address-recognized bit (A) and the frame-copied bit (C):

      A   C   RR   A   C   RR

  Because the calculated CRC does not encompass the Frame Status field, each of the 1-bit subfields is duplicated within frame status to ensure data integrity. A transmitting workstation sets the address-recognized bit to 0 when it originates a frame; the receiving workstation sets this bit to 1 to signal that it has recognized its destination address. The frame-copied bit also starts out as 0 but is set to 1 by the receiving (destination) workstation when it copies the contents of the frame into its own memory (when it actually receives the data). The data is copied (and the bit set) only if the frame is received without error. If the originating (source) workstation gets its frame back with both of these bits set, it knows that a successful reception occurred.

If, however, the address-recognized bit is not set by the time the frame gets back to the originating workstation, the destination workstation is no longer on the network; the other workstation must have crashed or powered off suddenly.

Another situation occurs when the destination address is recognized but the frame copied bit is not set. This setting tells the originating workstation that the frame got damaged in transit (the error-detected bit in the end delimiter also will be set).

If the address-recognized bit and the frame-copied bit are both set, but the error-detected bit also is set, the originating workstation knows that the error occurred after the frame was correctly received.

Using the Abort Sequence

Figure 5.11 shows the third format of the IEEE 802.5 message packet: the abort sequence. An abort sequence can occur anywhere in the bit stream and is used to interrupt/terminate the current transmission.

Fig. 5.11
An abort
sequence.

Length of each field, in bytes

An abort sequence consists of a Start Delimiter followed by an End Delimiter. An abort sequence signals cancellation of the current frame or token transmission.

Using the Fiber Distributed Data Interface (FDDI)

The Fiber Distributed Data Interface (FDDI) is a much newer protocol than Ethernet or Token Ring. Designed by the X3T9.5 Task Group of ANSI (the American National Standards Institute), FDDI passes tokens and data frames around a ring of optical fiber at a rate of 100 mbps. FDDI was designed to be as much like the IEEE 802.5 Token Ring standard as possible. Differences occur only where necessary to support the faster speeds and longer transmission distances of FDDI.

If FDDI were to use the same bit-encoding scheme used by Token Ring, every bit would require two optical signals: a pulse of light and then a pause of darkness. This means that FDDI would need to send 200 million signals per second to have a 100-mbps transmission rate. Instead, the scheme used by FDDI—called 4B/5B—encodes 4 bits of data into 5 bits for transmission so that fewer signals are needed to send a byte of information. The 5-bit codes (symbols) were chosen carefully to ensure that network timing requirements are met. The 4B/5B scheme, at a 100-mbps transmission rate, actually causes 125 million signals per second to occur (this is 125 megabaud). Also, because each carefully selected light pattern symbol represents 4 bits (a half-byte, or *nibble*), FDDI hardware can operate at the nibble and byte level rather than at the bit level, making it easier to achieve the high data rate.

Two major differences in the way the token is managed by FDDI and IEEE 802.5 Token Ring exist. In Token Ring, a new token is circulated only after a sending workstation gets back the frame that it sent. In FDDI, a new token is circulated immediately by the sending workstation after it finishes transmitting a frame. FDDI doesn't use the Priority and Reservation subfields that Token Ring uses to allocate system resources. Instead, FDDI classifies attached workstations as *asynchronous* (workstations that are not rigid about the time periods that occur between network accesses) and *synchronous* (workstations having very stringent requirements regarding the timing between transmissions). FDDI uses a complex algorithm to allocate network access to the two classes of devices.

Figure 5.12 shows an FDDI token. The token consists of Preamble, Start Delimiter, Frame Control, End Delimiter, and Frame Status fields. These fields have the same definition for tokens as for frames.

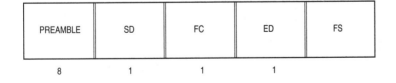

Length of each field, in bytes

Fig. 5.12
An FDDI token.

Figure 5.13 shows the layout of an FDDI frame. Notice the similarity to the IEEE 802.5 Token Ring frames just discussed. An FDDI frame, like its slower cousin, carries MAC control data or user data.

Fig. 5.13
An FDDI frame.

Length of each field, in bytes

Following are the fields in an FDDI frame:

- *Preamble*. This field is used for synchronization purposes. Although this field is initially 64 bits (16 symbol-encoded nibbles) in size, subsequent workstations can modify the Preamble's length dynamically according to their own clocking and synchronization requirements.

- *Start Delimiter (SD)*. A unique two-symbol (1-byte) field; its pattern identifies the start of the frame.

- *Frame Control (FC)*. A two-symbol (1-byte) field made up of the following subfields:

      C L FF T T T T

  The C subfield designates the frame class, which tells whether the frame is being used for synchronous or asynchronous service. The L bit is the frame address length and indicates whether 16- or 48-bit addresses are being used (unlike with Ethernet and Token Ring, both kinds of addresses are possible on the same FDDI network). The FF bits are the Frame Format subfield, which expresses whether the frame is a MAC frame carrying ring-management information or an LLC frame carrying user data. If it is a MAC frame, the T T T T bits specify the type of the MAC control frame contained in the Info field.

- *Destination Address (DA)*. This field can be 16 bits or 48 bits long and identifies the workstation to which this frame is being sent.

- *Source Address (SA)*. This field, which can be 16 or 48 bits, identifies the sending workstation.

- *Information (INFO)*. This field is the data portion of the frame. It contains a MAC control record or user data. This field can vary in length, but it cannot cause the overall length of the frame to exceed 4,500 bytes.

- *Frame Check Sequence (FCS)*. This field contains 4 bytes (eight symbols) of CRC data used for error-checking.

- *End Delimiter (ED).* In a frame, this field is 1 nibble (1 symbol) long. In a token, it is 1 byte (2 symbols) long. This field uniquely identifies the end of the frame or token.

- *Frame Status (FS).* Of arbitrary length, this field contains the error-detected bit, the address-recognized bit, and the frame-copied bit. These subfields do the same job on an FDDI network as on a Token Ring network.

NOS Control of Network Adapters

Open Datalink Interface (ODI) and Network Driver Interface Specification (NDIS) are two competing standards for how the network operating system controls the network adapter.

ODI

Novell and Apple Computer developed ODI jointly. A network adapter manufacturer can make its boards work with NetWare, the most popular network operating system, by supplying ODI-compliant software drivers with the boards.

NDIS

NDIS, developed jointly by 3Com Corporation and Microsoft, performs many of the same functions as ODI, but NDIS and ODI are incompatible. NDIS is a cornerstone of the LAN Server and LAN Manager network operating system products. A network adapter manufacturer can make its boards work with these network operating systems by supplying NDIS-compliant software drivers with the boards.

As you would expect, network adapter manufacturers supply both NDIS and ODI drivers with their products.

The PROTOCOL.INI File

ODI network drivers use a file named NET.CFG to configure themselves, whereas NDIS drivers use a file named PROTOCOL.INI. The format and content of the two files are quite distinct.

Most installation software for network products automatically creates PROTOCOL.INI (or NET.CFG) files for you. However, you'll often have the opportunity to inspect and perhaps modify the PROTOCOL.INI file on a workstation or at the file server. You might need to increase certain parameters to provide new connectivity for database management software products that you install (more NetBIOS sessions, for example), or you might need to tune the parameters to improve network performance.

II

Building a Network

If you've edited a Microsoft Windows INI file, you'll immediately be at home editing the PROTOCOL.INI file. As a simple text file, the PROTOCOL.INI file contains one or more named sections, with each section the module name of a protocol or MAC (Media Access Control) driver. Brackets ([and]) surround the section name. Underneath each section name and indented slightly (usually by three spaces), named configuration entries appear in the format *name = value*. The indentation is optional. Each entry identifies a configuration value or binding instruction for NDIS. For example, one section of the PROTOCOL.INI file might contain the following entries:

```
[XYZNetBIOS]
   Drivername = NetBIOS$
   Bindings = ETHERFAST
   MaxNCBs = 16
   MaxSessions = 32
   MaxNames = 16
```

NDIS understands PROTOCOL.INI file entries only with a particular syntax. If you follow the NDIS rules as you modify an INI file, you'll be assured that the NDIS Protocol Manager (PROTMAN) and the NDIS driver modules will be able at least to parse your changes. The specific keywords and values you use depend on the drivers you load. You'll need to check the documentation that came with your network adapter (for MAC drivers) or your network operating system (for protocol drivers).

How do you deal with products, though, whose documentation lacks a clear, complete description of driver parameters? One approach, of course, is to call the technical support telephone number supplied with the product. A less obvious but sometimes fruitful alternative involves using a file-browse utility, in hexadecimal display mode, to inspect the file containing the driver software. While viewing the contents of the executable file, you sometimes can recognize keyword names of parameters that have meaning inside the PROTOCOL.INI file. Also be aware that NDIS-compliant driver installation software typically uses NIFs (Network Installation Files) to indicate what entries can legally go into the PROTOCOL.INI file. The installation software reads and uses the NIF to know what configuration choices to present at installation time. You can also explore the NIF with a file-browse utility to better understand the parameters for a driver.

Following are the NDIS rules for constructing a PROTOCOL.INI file:

■ The name of each protocol or MAC module must appear in brackets ([XYZNetBIOS] in the earlier example), and the name must contain 15 or fewer characters. You can use uppercase or lowercase letters without worrying about case sensitivity; the Protocol Manager converts all entries to uppercase as PROTMAN reads the file into memory.

■ The entry *Drivername = <device driver name>* is required in sections that describe device driver modules. This entry defines the name of the the OS/2 or DOS device driver that contains the module. Each network device driver can ask Protocol Manager to let it view the in-memory version of the PROTOCOL.INI file, and the network device driver finds its module section by searching for the appropriate Drivername entry. NDIS also requires a Drivername entry for DOS dynamic modules such as TSRs. Even though the TSR doesn't represent a device driver, the Drivername entry enables the TSR to find pertinent sections of the PROTOCOL.INI file. Incidentally, it is possible for a single device driver name to appear multiple times in a PROTOCOL.INI file. Such mentions of the name occur if the device driver contains multiple logical modules.

■ Protocol modules (but never MAC modules) can optionally have a *Bindings = <module name>* entry in the INI file. When present, the Bindings entry tells the protocol module how to determine which MAC modules the protocol will bind to. You can use this characteristic to reconfigure a protocol to bind a different MAC module, if your protocol supports it. You don't need the Bindings entry if the protocol driver is preconfigured to bind to a particular MAC module or if the protocol stack will contain only one MAC module and one static protocol module.

■ The rest of the PROTOCOL.INI file consists of *keyword = value* pairs, with each keyword being 15 or fewer characters. As with the entries already mentioned, Protocol Manager is not case-sensitive. The *keyword = value* pairs pertain only to the named section in which they appear. Notice that you can put spaces on either side of the equal sign if you find that the white space makes the INI file more readable; Protocol Manager removes white space surrounding the equal sign as well as trailing white space on each line of text in the file. White-space characters are spaces, tabs, and formfeeds. A carriage return and linefeed mark the end of each line.

■ One or more parameters follow the equal sign on each line of text. If an entry has no parameters, the equal sign is optional. If there are multiple parameters, you separate the parameters with spaces, tabs, commas, or semicolons. Notice that the Protocol Manager doesn't interpret the parameters; only the protocol or MAC module looks at the values you specify. If a parameter is a number, the parameter is treated as a 32-bit signed quantity. You can express numbers in either decimal or hexadecimal format. To indicate a hexadecimal number, prefix the parameter with either 0X or 0x, as in 0x0400. String parameters can be any length. A string parameter begins with a nonnumeric first character or appears inside quotation marks ("").

■ Lines that have a semicolon in the first column are comment lines. (Few installation programs insert comment lines to explain what they've created for you, but you can add comments later, if you want.) Protocol Manager ignores comment lines and lines that are blank.

When Protocol Manager or one of the drivers detects a syntax error in the PROTOCOL.INI file, NDIS mandates that Protocol Manager or the software driver displays an error message detailing the exact syntax problem. If possible, the module that finds the error should assume a valid (nonfatal) value for the parameter and continue processing. (Notice that not all drivers written by all manufacturers of network adapters comply fully with this mandate. You sometimes find modules that die instantly when they discover errors in the PROTOCOL.INI file.)

Using the IBM PC LAN Support Program

The IBM PC LAN support program is an IBM software product for DOS-based Token Ring LANs. It implements the network adapter support software, as well as NetBIOS, in a set of device drivers (SYS files) that are loaded at boot time. Typically, you use three device driver files. Although memory usage depends on how the drivers are configured, typical memory usage ranges from 40K to 50K. The file DXMA0MOD.SYS is an interrupt arbitrator for the Token Ring card. The DXMA0MOD device driver acts as a clearinghouse, routing communication requests to the various software modules in the layers of network support software. The DXMC0MOD.SYS file is the layer of adapter support software that talks directly to the IEEE 802.5 chipset on the Token Ring card. The DXMT0MOD.SYS file implements the midlevel protocol, NetBIOS.

Using Midlevel Protocols

The protocols discussed so far operate at a low level on the LAN. Ethernet, Token Ring, and FDDI carry messages (frames) reliably from computer to computer but know nothing about file redirection and file servers. The low-level protocols do not even provide an easy-to-use scheme for ensuring that a set of messages arrive in the same order in which they were sent, or for identifying the applications that need to communicate with one another on the LAN.

The midlevel protocols NetBIOS, IPX/SPX, and TCP/IP—when contrasted with the OSI model—fall mostly into the Transport layer, with some characteristics of other layers (such as the Session layer). These protocols make computer-to-computer communications easier on a LAN.

The higher-level protocols that do understand file redirection and file servers use midlevel protocols to send message frames from workstation to file server and back again. Later sections of this chapter discuss the higher-level protocols.

Regardless of how each particular vendor's protocol is designed, all have certain common basic functions and features:

- *Initiating communications*. Each protocol provides the means to identify a workstation by name, by number, or by name and number. This identification scheme is made available to both the file redirection layer and to an application. Point-to-point communications are activated by one workstation, identifying a destination workstation (often a *file server*) with which it wants to carry on a dialog. The originating workstation also designates the type of dialog—either *datagram*, in which frames are addressed and sent to the destination without guarantee or verification of reception; or *session*, in which a connection (or pipe) is established and which guarantees delivery of message data.

- *Sending and receiving data*. Each protocol provides the means for originating and destination workstations to send and receive message data. A protocol-specific limit on the length of a given message is imposed, and each participant in a session-type dialog is given the means to determine the status of the dialog (for example, a workstation may inadvertently power down in the midst of a dialog—perhaps someone kicked the power cord—and the other participants are notified that an error has occurred).

- *Terminating communications*. The protocol provides the means for the participants to end a dialog gracefully.

The protocols discussed next are IPX, SPX, TCP/IP, and NetBIOS. The actual data messages that fly around the network come from your application software or from the file redirection software that shuttles DOS file-service requests to the file server and back.

II

Building a Network

Using Datagrams and Sessions

The two types of PC-to-PC or PC-to-server communications are datagrams and sessions. A *datagram* is a message that is never acknowledged by the receiver; if verification of message delivery is required, it must be supplied by the receiver in the form of a return message. In other words, the sender and receiver must agree on a protocol of their own so that they can use datagrams safely. Each datagram message stands on its own; if more than one datagram is outstanding, the order in which they're delivered is not guaranteed. In some cases, the maximum size of a datagram is much smaller than that of a session-related message. Most networks can send and receive datagrams faster than session-related messages.

In contrast to datagrams, a *session* is a logical connection between two workstations in which message reception is guaranteed. Datagrams can be sent at will. For messages to be sent during a session, however, more work must be done: the session must be established, data messages must be sent and received, and the session must be closed at the end of the dialog.

Using NetBIOS

NetBIOS accepts communications requests from the file-redirection portion of the network operating system or from an application program (such as an electronic mail product). NetBIOS requests fall into four categories:

- *Name support.* Each workstation on the network is identified by one or more names. These names are maintained by NetBIOS in a table; the first item in the table automatically is the unique, permanently assigned name of the network adapter. Optional user names (such as BARRY) can be added to the table for the sake of convenient identification of each workstation. The user-assigned names can be unique or, in a special case, can refer to a group of users.

- *Session support.* A point-to-point connection between two names (workstations) on the network can be opened, managed, and closed under NetBIOS control. One workstation begins by listening for a call; the other workstation calls the first. The computers are peers; both can send and receive message data concurrently during the session. At the end, both workstations hang up on each other.

- *Datagram support.* Message data can be sent to a name, a group of names, or to all names on the network. A point-to-point connection is not established, and there is no guarantee that the message data will be received.

■ *Adapter/session status*. Information about the local network adapter card, other network adapter cards, and any currently active sessions is available to application software that uses NetBIOS.

IBM used to offer NetBIOS as a separate program product; it was implemented as a terminate-and-stay-resident (TSR) file named NETBEUI.COM. This file is now obsolete. If you have an older Token Ring network that uses NETBEUI, you should consider replacing the low-level network support software on each workstation, including NETBEUI, with the later IBM PC LAN support program's device drivers.

Using IPX/SPX

Novell implements a datagram-oriented protocol, IPX, on its NetWare LANs. Novell implements also a session-oriented protocol, SPX.

Using IPX

IPX, which stands for the *internetwork packet exchange*, is the underlying protocol used by NetWare's file-redirection modules. IPX is an adaptation of a protocol developed by Xerox Corporation called XNS—Xerox Network Standard. IPX supports only datagram messages (it is said to be connectionless). IPX corresponds to the Network layer of the OSI model; IPX performs addressing, routing, and switching to deliver a message (packet) to its destination. This protocol is speedier than the session-oriented SPX protocol. Although delivery is not guaranteed, Novell indicates that IPX packets are correctly received about 95 percent of the time.

NetWare's file-redirection modules use the IPX protocol (not the session-oriented SPX protocol) to send and receive file-service packets to and from the file server. This method is safe and reliable because every such request from a workstation requires a response from the file server. The file-redirection modules never assume that a file-service packet (to write data to a file, for example) has been processed by the file server until the proper acknowledgment response is returned.

If you use NetWare, you obviously already have IPX. Depending on the version of NetWare you have, you may have SPX as well.

Using SPX

SPX, which stands for *sequenced packet exchange*, is a session-level, connection-oriented protocol. Before SPX packets are sent or received, a connection must be established between the two sides that want to exchange information. Once established, messages within a session can be sent in either direction with the guarantee that they will be delivered. SPX also guarantees that packets will arrive in the correct order (if multiple packets are sent at one time). SPX operates at one layer above the Transport layer of the OSI model, the Network layer. SPX also has some of the characteristics of the Session layer. NetWare uses IPX to send and receive file-service packets, but NetWare uses SPX to allow access to its internal diagnostic and network management functions.

SPX "sits on top of" IPX and uses IPX to actually send or receive message packets. If you have NetWare, you know that IPX exists on your LAN. This is not necessarily true for SPX; early versions of NetWare did not support SPX. If you have Version 2.0a of NetWare, you have SPX only if the version of the file-redirection program (ANET3.COM) is 2.01 to 2.04. SPX is present in all later versions of NetWare (2.1 and later).

Using TCP/IP

TCP/IP is like NetBIOS, IPX, and SPX in several ways. TCP/IP stands for *Transmission Control Protocol/Internet Protocol*. The Department of Defense designed TCP/IP for ARPANET, a geographically large network (not a LAN) that connects the various sites of the DoD Advanced Research Projects Agency. TCP/IP is a layer of protocols, not a LAN operating system. IP provides datagram communications between nodes on a network (like Novell's IPX). TCP is like NetBIOS in that it provides point-to-point, guaranteed-delivery communications between nodes. A set of fairly standard utilities exists for transferring files (FTP), doing simple remote program execution (TELNET), and sending electronic mail (SMTP) over TCP/IP networks. These utilities do not perform file redirection. You need a product such as Sun Microsystems' NFS (Network File System) or Locus Computing's PC Interface (sold by IBM under the name AIX Access for DOS Users) to do file redirection on a TCP/IP-based network.

Because TCP/IP is a public, not proprietary, protocol, it has become extremely popular as the basis for interconnecting LANs from different vendors. However, this popularity may gradually wane. The federal government decreed that all major federal computer/network acquisitions after August, 1990, must comply with GOSIP, the Government OSI Profile. The government planned that OSI protocols would replace TCP/IP by the late 1990s, but the planners did not take TCP/IP's immense popularity into account. Few OSI-compliant network software products exist, and programmers continue to base their products on TCP/IP.

Using Named Pipes

A *pipe* is a stream of data between two programs. One program opens the pipe and writes data into it; the other program opens the pipe and reads the data from the first program. If this sounds easy and simple to program, that's because it is. A *named pipe* is a file whose name has a particular format:

\PIPE*path**name.ext*

OS/2 provides a set of functions for opening, using, and closing named pipes. The application that creates the pipe (called the *server*, but don't confuse this with a file server) starts the communication session, and another application (called the *client*) joins in. An application can treat named pipes as simple data streams or, if the programmer of the application prefers, as message pipes. In the latter case, each read operation fetches one message at a time from the pipe.

Because named pipes do so much work, yet require only a programmer to code a few simple program statements, named pipes are extremely popular on OS/2 LANs.

Using File-Redirection Protocols

The file-redirection portions of the various network operating systems use proprietary high-level protocols to accomplish their file redirection. In the LAN Server and LAN Manager products, IBM and Microsoft use server message blocks (SMBs). In NetWare, Novell uses its NetWare Core Protocol (NCP). Peer LANs sometimes use SMBs but often implement their own high-level protocols for file redirection.

Using Server Message Blocks (SMBs)

At the workstation, LAN Server or LAN Manager intercepts an application's file I/O operations and shunts them across the network to the file server. The workstation software modules that accomplish this redirection are called DOS LAN Requester (DLR), and DLR uses a Server Message Block (SMB) protocol to accomplish this redirection. DOS LAN Requester, running on a workstation, opens NetBIOS sessions with the LAN Server or LAN Manager software running on the file server. DLR then uses NetBIOS to send SMBs to the server; LAN Server or LAN Manager responds with SMB protocol messages. IBM defines four categories of SMBs: session control, file access, print service, and messages.

Using NetWare Core Protocol (NCP)

On a NetWare LAN, the workstation software module that performs file redirection is called the *shell*. Until recently, you needed a different version of the shell program for each different version of DOS. The shell program for DOS 3 was NET3.COM. NET4.COM was for DOS 4, and NET5.COM was for DOS 5. Currently, Novell offers a DOS-version independent shell program, NETX.COM.

All the versions of NETX.COM use the NetWare Core Protocol (NCP) to send and receive file-service message packets. The inner workings of NCP are considered a trade secret by Novell. Although IBM has published the SMB protocol for programmers and network administrators to understand, Novell offers the NCP protocol only to developers for a hefty license fee.

Using LAN Cables

Cabling systems for LANs vary widely in their appearance, characteristics, intended purpose, and cost. This chapter discusses the three most popular ways to tie computers together on a LAN: the IBM cabling system, the AT&T premises distribution system, and the Digital Equipment Corporation cabling concept called DECconnect.

Generally speaking, the cabling systems described in the next few sections use one of three distinct cable types. These are twisted pair (shielded and unshielded), coaxial cable (thin and thick), and fiber optic cable.

Using Twisted Pair Cable

Twisted pair cable is just what its name implies: insulated wires with a minimum number of twists per foot. Twisting the wires reduces electrical interference (*attenuation*). *Shielded twisted pair* refers to the amount of insulation around the wire and, therefore, its noise immunity. You are already familiar with unshielded twisted pair; it is often used by the telephone company. Shielded twisted pair, however, is entirely different in appearance. Shielded twisted pair looks somewhat like the wire used to carry house current (110 volts) throughout your home or apartment. Appearances are deceiving, because shielded twisted pair actually carries a relatively low voltage signal. The heavy insulation is for noise reduction, not safety.

Figure 5.14 shows unshielded twisted pair cable; figure 5.15 illustrates shielded twisted pair cable.

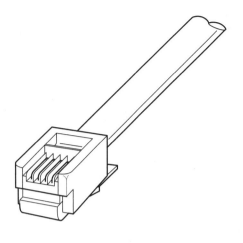

Fig. 5.14
An unshielded
twisted pair cable.

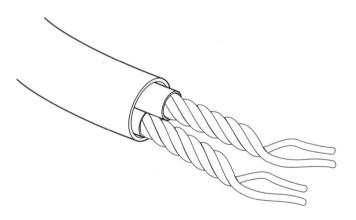

Fig. 5.15
A shielded twisted
pair cable.

II

Building a Network

Using Coaxial Cable

Coaxial cable is fairly prevalent in your everyday life; you often find it connected to the backs of television sets and audio equipment. *Thin* and *thick*, of course, refer to the diameter of the coaxial cable. Standard Ethernet cable (thick Ethernet) is as thick as your thumb. The newer Thinnet (sometimes called CheaperNet) cable is about the size of your little finger. The thick cable has a greater degree of noise immunity, is more difficult to damage, and requires a *vampire tap* (a piercing connector) and a drop cable to connect to a LAN. Although thin cable carries the signal over shorter distances than the thick cable, Thinnet uses a simple BNC connector (a bayonet-locking connector for thin coaxial cables), is lower in cost, and has become a standard in office coaxial cable.

Figure 5.16 is a picture of an Ethernet BNC coaxial connector, and figure 5.17 illustrates the design of coaxial cable.

Fig. 5.16
An Ethernet coaxial cable connector.

Fig. 5.17
Coaxial cable.

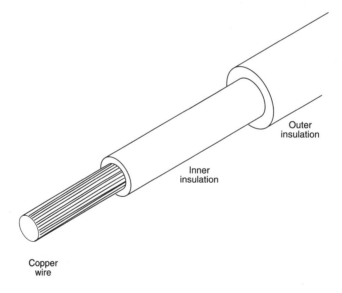

Using Fiber Optic Cable

Fiber optic cable, as its name suggests, uses light rather than electricity to carry information. Fiber can send data over huge distances at high speeds, but it is expensive and difficult to work with. Splicing the cable, installing connectors, and using the few available diagnostic tools for finding cable faults are skills that very few people have.

Fiber optic cable is simply designed but unforgiving of bad connections. Fiber cable usually consists of a core of glass thread, whose diameter is measured in microns, surrounded by a solid glass *cladding*. This, in turn, is covered by a protective sheath. The first fiber optic cables were made of glass, but plastic fibers also have been developed. The light source for fiber optic cable is a light-emitting diode (LED); information usually is encoded by varying the intensity of the light. A detector at the other end of the cable converts the received signal back into electrical impulses. Two types of fiber cable exist: single mode and multimode. Single mode has a smaller diameter, is more expensive, and can carry signals for a greater distance.

Figure 5.18 illustrates fiber optic cables and their connectors.

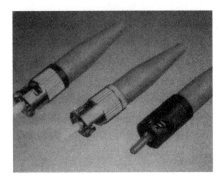

Fig. 5.18
Fiber optic cables use light to carry LAN messages. The ST connector is commonly used with fiber optic cables.

II

Building a Network

Using the IBM Cabling System

The IBM cabling system, ironically, is not manufactured or sold by IBM. This cabling system consists of a published IBM standard for wiring systems in office buildings that defines cabling system components and different cable types. When it was introduced in 1984, IBM described the IBM cabling system as the intended backbone of its Token Ring network. The first such cables to be manufactured by third-party companies were tested by IBM, verified to IBM specifications, and actually given IBM part numbers. At present, however, cable manufacturers have to rely on the ETL or UL independent testing laboratories or on industry-standard manufacturers (such as AMP) to verify compliance with the specifications published by IBM.

The IBM specification defines workstation faceplates, adapters/connectors, access units, and wiring-closet termination methods. The standard also defines the following cable types:

- *Type 1 data cable.* Copper-based, for data connections only. Available in nonplenum, plenum, and outdoor varieties. It consists of two twisted pairs of 22-gauge solid conductors, shielded with both foil and braid, and covered with a polyvinyl-chloride (PVC) sheath. Type 1 data cable is used for connecting terminal devices located in work areas to distribution panels located in wiring closets and for connecting between wiring closets. The plenum cable is installed in plenums, ducts, and spaces used for environmental air; in case of fire, it gives off less toxic fumes than nonplenum cable. The outdoor cable is protected in a corrugated metallic shield with a polyethylene sheath, and the core is filled with a jellylike compound to prevent moisture from entering.

- *Type 2 data and telephone cable.* For both data and voice (telephone) applications. This cable is similar to Type 1 but has four additional twisted pairs (22-gauge). Type 2 cable comes in plenum and non-plenum varieties.

- *Type 3 telephone twisted pair cable.* Consists of four-pair, 24-gauge wire in polyvinyl-chloride plastic. This cable is equivalent to the IBM Rolm specification and is available in plenum. This cable is unshielded and not as immune to noise as Type 1 cable when used for data.

- *Type 5 fiber optic cable.* Contains two 100/140-micron multimode optical fibers (100-micron core surrounded by 140-micron cladding layer). This cable is not defined by IBM.

- *Type 6 patch panel cable.* For connecting a workstation to a wall faceplate or making connections within a wiring closet. This cable is more flexible than Type 1 cable (hence, its use as patch cable). This cable consists of two twisted pairs of 26-gauge stranded conductors.

- *Type 8 undercarpet cable.* An undercarpet cable useful for open office or workstation areas where there are no permanent walls. Type 8 cable consists of two pairs of 26-gauge solid conductors in a flat sheath.

- *Type 9 low-cost plenum cable.* An economy version of Type 1 plenum cable, with a maximum transmission distance about two-thirds that of Type 1 cable. Type 9 cable consists of two twisted pairs of 26-gauge stranded conductors. This cable is not defined by IBM.

Using the AT&T Premises Distribution System

The AT&T premises distribution system (PDS) is similar in many ways to the IBM cabling system but relies more heavily on unshielded telephone twisted pair. PDS also integrates voice and data wiring. Connections are based on modular jacks/plugs and the cross-connect techniques originally designed for voice PBX to telephone-set wiring, which uses multipair cable. With its strong roots in the telephone company's existing wiring systems, PDS obviously builds on the huge installed base of telephone cable. Generally, the AT&T PDS is lower in parts cost than the IBM system but is more labor-intensive to install.

Using DECconnect

The DECconnect cabling concept is based on the use of Thinnet 50-ohm thin coaxial cable, commonly used in Ethernet networks. The DECconnect system has standardized much of the connecting hardware used in major DEC installations of VAX systems. DECconnect also defines a line of protocol converters, line drivers, and satellite closet rack and termination hardware. A *satellite closet* is a small room in your office that you set aside just for communications equipment. Many DECconnect installations consist of an Ethernet *backbone* (a central cable to which all other cables connect) wired throughout a building, with *taps* (connection points) provided at VAX computer sites and the satellite closets.

Connecting the Cables

In a token-passing network, the cables from the workstations (or from the wall faceplates) connect centrally to a multistation access unit (abbreviated MSAU, or sometimes just MAU). The MSAU keeps track of which workstations on the LAN are neighbors and which neighbor is upstream or downstream. It is an easy job; the MSAU usually does not even need to be plugged into a electrical power outlet. The exceptions to this need for external power are an MSAU that supports longer cable distances, or the use of unshielded twisted pair (Type 3) cable in high-speed LANs. The externally powered MSAU helps the signal along by regenerating it.

An IBM MSAU has eight ports for connecting one to eight Token Ring devices. Each connection is made with a genderless data connector (as specified in the IBM cabling system). The MSAU has two additional ports, labeled RI (Ring-In) and RO (Ring-Out), that daisy-chain several MSAUs together when you have more than eight workstations on the LAN.

It takes several seconds to open the adapter connection on a Token Ring LAN (something you may have noticed). During this time, the MSAU and your Token Ring adapter card perform a small diagnostic check, after which the MSAU establishes you as a new neighbor on the ring. After being established as an active workstation, your computer is linked on both sides to your up-stream and downstream neighbors (as defined by your position on the MSAU). In its turn, your Token Ring adapter card accepts the token or frame, regenerates its electrical signals, and gives the token or frame a swift kick to send it through the MSAU in the direction of your downstream neighbor.

In an Ethernet network, the number of connections (taps) and their interven-ing distances are limiting factors. Repeaters regenerate the signal every 500 meters or so. If repeaters were not used, *standing waves* (additive signal reflec-tions) would distort the signal and cause errors. Because collision detection depends partly on timing, only five 500-meter segments and four repeaters can be placed in a series before the propagation delay becomes longer than the maximum allowed period for the detection of a collision. Otherwise, the workstations farthest from the sender would be unable to determine whether a collision had occurred.

The people who design computer systems love to find ways to circumvent limitations. Manufacturers of Ethernet products have made it possible to create Ethernet networks in star, branch, and tree designs that overcome the basic limitations mentioned. You can have thousands of workstations on a complex Ethernet network.

Local area networks are local because the network adapters and other hard-ware components cannot send LAN messages more than about a few hundred feet. Table 5.1 reveals the distance limitations of different kinds of LAN cable. In addition to the limitations shown in the table, keep in mind that you can't connect more than 30 computers on a Thinnet Ethernet segment, more than 100 computers on a ThickNet Ethernet segment, more than 72 computers on unshielded twisted pair Token Ring cable, or more than 260 computers on shielded twisted pair Token Ring cable.

Table 5.1 Network Distance Limitations			
Network Adapter	**Cable Type**	**Maximum**	**Minimum**
Ethernet	Thin	607 ft.	20 in.
	Thick (drop cable)	164 ft.	8 ft.

Network Adapter	Cable Type	Maximum	Minimum
	Thick (backbone)	1,640 ft.	8 ft.
	UTP	328 ft.	8 ft.
Token Ring	STP	328 ft.	8 ft.
	UTP	148 ft.	8 ft.
ARCnet (passive hub)		393 ft.	depends on cable
ARCnet (active hub)		1,988 ft.	depends on cable

Using Network Adapters

As mentioned earlier in this chapter, network adapters generally are collision-sensing or token-passing. A network adapter's design ties it to one of the low-level protocols—Ethernet, Token Ring, FDDI, ARCnet, or some other protocol. Figure 5.19 is a photograph of ARCnet network adapters.

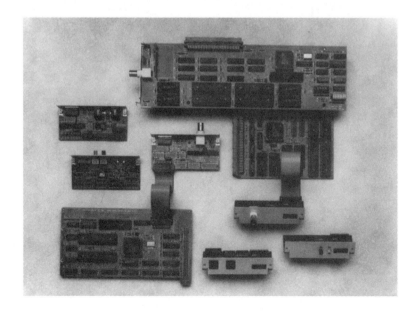

Fig. 5.19
ARCnet network adapter cards.

If you have fast workstations and a fast file server, you want a fast network. Even 16 mbps may be too slow if your applications are data-intensive. TCNS, from Thomas-Conrad, operates at 100 mbps and doesn't cost a lot more than Token Ring. Figure 5.20 shows the TCNS network adapters and hub. TCNS gives you all the advantages of FDDI without FDDI's high price tag. NetWare, LAN Manager, POWERLan, LANtastic, and other ARCnet-compatible network operating systems work well with TCNS. The only catch is that you have to use fast computers to realize performance gains with TCNS.

Fig. 5.20
The high-speed TCNS network adapters and hub.

You can use the same shielded twisted pair (IBM Type 1) or coaxial (RG62A/ U) cabling already in place for Token Ring or ARCnet, or you can install 62.5-micron fiber optic cable. You can mix and match cable types by using a TCNS Smart Hub with different connectors. You wire a TCNS network in a distributed star fashion, just as you would with ARCnet or Token Ring. TCNS adapters and hubs use ST connectors for fiber optic cable, BNC connectors for coaxial, and DB-9 connectors for STP.

Imagine ARCnet running at 100 mbps, and you have a good picture of TCNS. A TCNS network adapter is register-compatible with an ARCnet adapter, which enables TCNSs to use industry-standard ARCnet software drivers. Thomas-Conrad also supplies "Accelerated Drivers" for an even greater performance boost. TCNS consists of network adapters with STP, coaxial, or fiber optic connectors, one or more Thomas-Conrad Smart Hubs, and software drivers. The adapters come in 16- and 32-bit, and ISA- and EISA-bus varieties. You can put up to 255 TCNS workstations on a single LAN segment, and you can span significant distances: 2,950 feet (hub to workstation) with fiber optic cable, 492 feet with shielded twisted pair cable, and 338 feet with RG62A/U coaxial cable.

Chips & Technologies makes a network adapter that works on both Ethernet and Token Ring LANs, but you should be aware that Ethernet and Token Ring cards cannot operate together on the same LAN cable. You may have a dual-purpose network adapter, but your LAN can use only one type of low-level protocol. To mix two LANs that use different low-level protocols, you must install a bridge between them.

A *bridge* connects different LANs, enabling communication between devices on separate LANs. Bridges are protocol-independent but hardware-specific. Bridges connect LANs with different hardware and different protocols. An example is a device that connects an Ethernet network to a Token Ring network. With this bridge, it is possible to send signals between the two networks. Figure 5.21 shows some typical Ethernet network adapters.

Fig. 5.21
Popular Ethernet adapters.

Collision-sensing and token-passing adapters contain sufficient on-board logic to know when it is permissible to send a frame and to recognize frames intended for themselves. With the adapter support software, both types of cards perform seven major steps during the process of sending or receiving a frame. Outbound, when data is being sent, the steps are performed in the order presented in the following list. Inbound, as data is received, however, the steps are reversed.

1. *Data transfer*. Data is transferred from PC memory (RAM) to the adapter card or from the adapter card to PC memory via DMA, shared memory, or programmed I/O.

2. *Buffering*. While being processed by the network adapter card, data is held in a buffer. The buffer gives the card access to an entire frame at once, and the buffer enables the card to manage the difference between the data rate of the network and the rate at which the PC can process data.

3. *Frame formation*. The network adapter has to break up the data into manageable chunks (or, on reception, reassemble it). On an Ethernet network, these chunks are about 1,500 bytes. Token Ring networks generally use a frame size of about 4K. The adapter prefixes the data packet with a frame header and appends a frame trailer to it. The header and trailer are the Physical layer's envelope, which you learned about earlier in this chapter. At this point, a complete, ready-for-transmission frame exists. (Inbound, on reception, the adapter removes the header and trailer at this stage.)

4. *Cable access*. In a CSMA/CD network such as Ethernet, the network adapter ensures that the line is quiet before sending its data (or retransmits its data if a collision occurs). In a token-passing network, the adapter waits until it gets a token it can claim. (These steps are not significant to receiving a message, of course.)

5. *Parallel/serial conversion*. The bytes of data in the buffer are sent or received through the cables in serial fashion, with one bit following the next. The adapter card does this conversion in the split second before transmission (or after reception).

6. *Encoding/decoding*. The electrical signals that represent the data being sent or received are formed. Most network adapters use *Manchester encoding*. This technique has the advantage of incorporating timing information into the data through the use of *bit periods*. Instead of representing a 0 as the absence of electricity and a 1 as its presence, the 0s and 1s are represented by changes in polarity as they occur in relation to very small time periods.

7. *Sending/receiving impulses*. The electrically encoded impulses making up the data (frame) are amplified and sent through the wire. (On reception, the impulses are handed up to the decoding step.)

Of course, the execution of all of these steps takes only a fraction of a second. While you were reading about these steps, thousands of frames could have been sent across the LAN.

Network adapter cards and the support software recognize and handle errors, which occur when electrical interference, collisions (in CSMA/CD networks), or malfunctioning equipment cause some portion of a frame to be corrupted. Errors generally are detected through the use of a cyclic redundancy checksum (CRC) data item in the frame. The CRC is checked by the receiver; if its own calculated CRC doesn't match the value of the CRC in the frame, the receiver tells the sender about the error and requests retransmission of the frame in error. Several products exist that perform network diagnostic and analysis functions on the different types of LANs, should you find yourself in need of such troubleshooting. Chapter 12, "Managing Your Network," covers these tools in detail.

The different types of network adapters vary not only in access method and protocol, but also in the following elements:

- Transmission speed

- Amount of on-board memory for buffering frames and data

- Bus design (8-bit, 16-bit, or MicroChannel)

- Bus speed (some fail when run at high speeds)

- Compatibility with various CPU chipsets

- DMA usage

- IRQ and I/O port addressing

- Intelligence (some use an on-board CPU, such as the 80186)

- Connector design

Most network adapters are installed in one of the slots on the motherboard of your personal computer. In support of the rapidly growing number of laptop and notebook computers that do not have slots, however, some companies offer network adapters that you simply plug into the parallel printer port of your computer. These devices are called *pocket network adapters*. Xircom makes the most popular pocket network adapters, offering models for Ethernet, Token Ring, and ARCnet LANs. Figure 5.22 shows the Xircom Pocket Ethernet Adapter.

Fig. 5.22
The Xircom
Pocket Ethernet
Adapter connects
to the computer's
parallel (printer)
port.

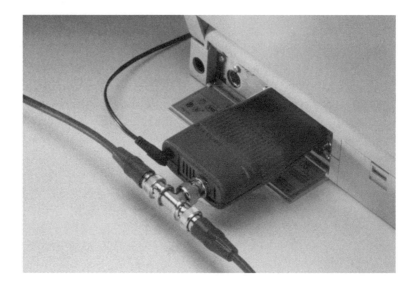

Xircom's address follows:

Xircom
26025 Mureau Road
Calabasas, CA 91302
(818) 878-7600

Summary

In this chapter, you took a detailed look at the inner workings of a LAN. You learned about the OSI model. You explored the Ethernet, Token Ring, and FDDI low-level protocols, and you learned how these protocols carry information from computer to computer on a network. This chapter discussed how the IPX, SPX, NetBIOS, and TCP/IP midlevel protocols work and how they relate to the OSI model. You learned that each network operating system vendor uses a file-redirection protocol that makes one vendor's products generally incompatible with other network operating systems. This chapter also explained the different types of LAN cable and how they carry information. Finally, you looked at how network adapter cards (or pocket adapters) work.

In Chapter 6, "Using Workstations," you learn about the role that your own personal computer plays on the LAN: that of a workstation.

Chapter 6

Using Workstations

If local area networks were perfect, you would not need this book. You could use a computer as a workstation without having to know that the LAN is present. An administrator would set up the file server, and people using their computers would not need to know that anything had changed. However, local area networks have a long way to go before they are as easy to use as this.

AppleTalk LANs come the closest to making workstations seem like stand-alone computers with enhanced capabilities. Other LANs come close, but with any LAN, you need to be aware of certain differences between your computer as a stand-alone tool and your computer as a workstation on the LAN.

DOS-based computers constitute the majority of workstations on local area networks. Most of the LAN designers' efforts have gone into making DOS-based access of file servers as transparent as possible. However, if you use Microsoft Windows on your DOS-based computer, for example, your view of the LAN will be different. If you use OS/2's capability to give you both multiple DOS and multiple OS/2 sessions, your view also will be different.

Your computer may boot from a local hard drive (or floppy disk), or your PC may get a copy of the operating system from a file server. If you have the latter type of PC, you likely have a *diskless workstation*, and your computer will behave differently (or not at all) when the computer's LAN connection or the file server fails.

If you use a Macintosh, your view of the LAN also will be different. Or, if your computer uses the UNIX operating system, you will see the LAN in yet a different way.

This chapter is divided into sections that address each of these types of computers and operating systems. Each section discusses the practical aspects of how your particular combination of computer, operating system, and operating environment behaves on a LAN, with particular emphasis on what you need to know when your computer is a LAN workstation.

Using DOS-Based Computers

When you connect a DOS-based computer to a LAN, your workstation benefits from several advantages of DOS. For example, your DOS-based computer can access extra drive letters and provides you with additional commands and utilities that you can run, although some of the DOS commands behave differently on a LAN. If you have a LAN printer, you can send output to it from the DOS-based PC. In addition to providing these benefits, however, attaching a DOS-based computer to a LAN also imposes some changes to your computer. Your applications may have less memory in which to run. Your computer's DOS PATH statement almost certainly will change after you connect your PC to the LAN. You may have to change entries in your CONFIG.SYS file. And, unless you have a diskless workstation, new network-related files are stored on your computer.

The next sections of this chapter address these issues for DOS-based computers.

Drive Letters

At boot time, DOS assigns drive letters whose values depend on the number of floppy disk drives, number of hard disk drives, and number of DOS-formatted partitions on those hard disk drives. DOS always reserves drives A and B for floppies, even if you do not have a drive B. DOS assigns drive C to your first hard disk. DOS uses drives D and E and other drive letters to refer to your second hard disk, your additional DOS partitions, and your additional floppy disk drives.

The network operating system (NOS) also assigns drive letters, but usually not until you perform the login sequence. With many network operating systems, you can choose which drive letters you want the NOS to assign. By default, NetWare assigns drive F as the file server hard disk. You can use the NetWare MAP utility to assign other server hard disks, if they exist, or to change the drive letter assignment. An example of the NetWare MAP utility follows:

    MAP G:=SYSTEMPRO\SYS:

This example tells NetWare that you want to refer to the SYS: volume (hard disk) on the server named SYSTEMPRO as drive G.

The LASTDRIVE parameter, which you can place in your CONFIG.SYS file, influences how some network operating systems assign drive letters. Usually, the NOS assigns drive letters that follow LASTDRIVE. For LAN Manager and LAN Server, however, LASTDRIVE encompasses local and network drives. You may see an entry such as the following in the CONFIG.SYS file of a workstation on a LAN Manager network:

    LASTDRIVE=Z

You may have applications that write to the root directory of the current drive. On a LAN, you may not have sufficient rights to the root directory of the file server's disk to run such applications. (If the application put such files in the root directory for every user on the LAN, confusion would reign.) In such a case, you can use NetWare's MAP ROOT feature. With MAP ROOT, you set up a drive letter for which the root directory is really another directory on the file server; G:\, for example, may refer to the directory SYS:\USERS\BARRY. The application thinks it is writing files in the root directory of drive G, when, in fact, it is writing them in \USERS\BARRY.

> **Note**
>
> With some network operating systems, you can assign a drive letter to a file server disk drive that is the same as that of a local disk drive. If you do this, your local disk drive becomes "invisible," and you cannot use the files on that disk drive until you undo the overlapped drive-letter mapping.

The LAN Printer

In Chapter 2, "Sharing Computer Resources," you learned the basics of LAN printer sharing, and you learned the etiquette you should use in a shared-printer environment. In Chapter 4, "Using File Servers," you looked at printer sharing from the file server's point of view. From your workstation's point of view, you print to the LAN printer in almost the same way that you print to a locally attached printer.

Your computer's printer ports are LPT1, LPT2, and LPT3. If you have a locally attached printer, it probably uses LPT1. In this case, you can assign (redirect) LPT2 to the LAN printer. If you do not have a locally attached printer, you can assign LPT1 to the LAN printer. With most network operating systems, you can assign all three printer ports to one or more LAN printers. You do not have to have a physical parallel printer port on your computer to use the LAN printer. The network operating system enables you to pretend that you have an LPT1 port.

With NetWare, you use the CAPTURE command to redirect your printouts. With LAN Server and LAN Manager, you use the NET USE command. NetWare's CAPTURE command has more options and capabilities than other network operating systems' printer redirection commands. However, all printer redirection commands provide the same basic function: making your applications think they are printing to a real printer. The application software does not know that the print data becomes LAN messages that transfer to the server, into the print queue, before the server's spooler modules print the data.

Here is an example of a NetWare CAPTURE command:

CAPTURE NT NFF NOTIFY TI=10 NB Q=LASERJET

Descriptions of the command elements follow:

Element	Function
NT	Tells the spooler module not to expand tabs into spaces
NFF	Tells the spooler not to add a formfeed to the end of the printout
NOTIFY	Tells the spooler to send a notification message to your workstation when the printout finishes
TI=10	Tells the print redirector portion of your workstation's network software to interpret a 10-second pause of silence as meaning that the application has completed printing
NB	Indicates not to print a banner page
Q=LASERJET	Indicates that you want your printout to go to the print queue named LASERJET

Here is an example of a LANtastic printer redirection command:

NET USE LPT1 \\SERVER1\@LASERJET

LPT1 is the printer port to assign, SERVER1 names the file server to which the printer is attached, and @LASERJET specifies the printer.

After you send a printout to the LAN printer, you do not lose control of the data. With most network operating systems, you can manipulate the print queue entry before it actually prints. You can delete (cancel) the entry, or you can hold it for later processing. You can modify some of the characteristics of the queue entry, such as how many copies you want to print. You cannot change the contents of the printout, however.

> **Note**
>
> Just as with drive letter assignments, you can tell the network operating system to override the printer port assignments that DOS uses. If you have a locally attached printer on LPT1 and you assign LPT1 to the LAN printer, you lose the use of your local printer until you undo the assignments.

Network Commands and Utilities

After you log in to the LAN, you have a new set of commands and utilities that you can use to manage your workstation's relationship with the network. Besides giving you a way to redirect printer output, the network commands enable you to turn off printer redirection and do several other useful things. Following is a list of many of the NetWare commands and their purposes:

Command	Function
CAPTURE/ENDCAP	Starts/stops printer redirection
CHKDIR, CHKVOL, VOLINFO	Displays file server disk data
FLAG	Manages file attributes
GRANT/REVOKE	Changes a user's rights
MAP	Assigns and redirects drive letters
NCOPY	Copies files
NETBIOS	Provides NetBIOS emulation
NPRINT	Prints files
NVER	Shows network version data
PCONSOLE	Manages print queues
SALVAGE	Undeletes a file
SLIST	Lists file servers
SMODE	Sets file-sharing mode
SYSCON, FILER, SESSION	Manages users, files, and sessions
USERLIST	Shows who is logged on

II

Building a Network

Other network operating systems offer similar commands and utilities, although not quite as many as NetWare. Three popular commands on a LANtastic network follow:

Command	Function
NET COPY	Copies a file
NET PRINT	Prints a file
NET WHO	Shows who is logged on

DOS Commands and Utilities

For the most part, your DOS commands and utilities operate on your LAN workstation just as they did on your stand-alone personal computer. Be careful, though, about sharing DOS commands through a public directory. If some of the people on the LAN use a version of DOS that is different from the one you put on the file server, they see the following message when they try to use a DOS command:

```
Incorrect DOS version
```

The DOS TSR program SHARE.EXE is especially important on a LAN. The SHARE command enables file sharing. You should run SHARE immediately after logging in. You probably will want to make SHARE part of the BAT file that loads the network software.

The following DOS commands do not work on a file server hard disk across the LAN:

ASSIGN
CHKDSK
DISKCOMP
DISKCOPY
FDISK
FORMAT
LABEL
RECOVER
SYS
UNDELETE
UNFORMAT

Furthermore, most third-party disk diagnostic and maintenance utilities do not work on a file server hard disk. These utilities include such products as Norton Utilities and PC Tools.

The following DOS commands, however, operate on a file server disk just as well as they do on your local hard disk:

    ATTRIB
    BACKUP
    COMP
    COPY
    FC
    RESTORE
    SORT
    TREE
    XCOPY

Memory Constraints

The network software that loads at your workstation is usually a TSR (terminate-and-stay-ready) program or a combination of TSRs and device drivers (SYS files loaded by statements in the CONFIG.SYS file). If your workstation's CPU chip is an 8088, 8086, or 80286 model, the network software (such as NetWare's IPX.COM and NETX.COM) will probably consume part of your computer's 640K of conventional memory, leaving less memory in which you can run your application software.

Memory managers can help you reduce the network's use of conventional memory. If your workstation uses an 80386 or 80486 CPU chip and has more than 1M or 2M of RAM, you usually can use a memory manager to load some or all of the network software into upper memory. Note the following memory-management products and their manufacturers:

    386MAX and BlueMAX
    Qualitas
    7101 Wisconsin Avenue
    Suite 1386
    Bethesda, MD 20814
    (800) 733-1377

    Dynamic Memory Control
    Adlersparre & Associates
    501-1803 Douglas Street
    Victoria, BC Canada V8T 5C3
    (604) 384-1118

II

Building a Network

Maximizer
SoftNet Communication
11 Hillcrest Drive
Great Neck, NY 11021
(800) 627-7060

Memory Commander
V Communications
4320 Stevens Creek Boulevard
Suite 275
San Jose, CA 95129
(408) 296-4224

NetRoom
Helix Software
47-09 30th Street
Long Island City, NY 11101
(800) 451-0551

QEMM-386
Quarterdeck Office Systems
150 Pico Boulevard
Santa Monica, CA 90405
(213) 392-9851

QMAPS and UMB Pro
Quadtel Corporation
3190-J Airport Loop Drive
Costa Mesa, CA 92626
(714) 754-4422

In addition, if you use NetWare as your network operating system, Novell offers special versions of its shell (redirector) module. The plain version, NETX.COM, loads into and uses a portion of conventional memory. EMSNETX, however, loads into expanded memory, and XMSNETX loads into upper memory.

DOS Versions 5.0 and 6.x contain 80386/80486 memory-management capabilities. Depending on how much conventional memory you need for your applications, you may be able to use DOS without having to purchase a separate memory-management product.

The DOS PATH Statement

Naturally, you will want to extend your DOS PATH statement to enable you to load applications and utilities from network drives as well as from your local hard disk. The PATH statement functions the same on a network, but be aware that the maximum length of the PATH statement is 128 characters. On a large LAN, it is easy to make the mistake of trying to exceed this limit.

STACKS

With DOS Version 3.2 (released at the same time IBM began offering its Token Ring LAN products), it was necessary to insert in the CONFIG.SYS file a special statement that looked like this:

    STACKS=128,9

With DOS Version 3.3 and later, however, this entry is not necessary. You can save a small amount of conventional memory by inserting the following statement into your CONFIG.SYS file:

    STACKS=0,0

A DOS Memory-Management Dictionary

Conventional memory. This is the memory directly addressable by an Intel CPU in real mode. The upper boundary is normally the infamous 640K limit, but some memory managers raise that ceiling.

DOS Protected Mode Interface (DPMI). Developed by Microsoft, DPMI offers functions similar to Virtual Control Program Interface (VCPI) memory but enforces control over extended memory access.

Expanded memory. Developed jointly by Lotus, Intel, and Microsoft, expanded memory enables an application to bank-switch RAM, in 16K blocks, from EMS memory into conventional or upper memory. (*Bank-switching* is the mapping of a given page of memory into an address space the application can reach.) The specification is the Lotus/Intel/Microsoft (LIM) Expanded Memory Specification (EMS). Version 4.0 of the EMS is the most recent. On 80386 and 80486 machines, memory managers can transform extended memory into expanded memory.

Extended memory. This is the memory above the 1M threshold, addressable only in protected mode.

Extended Memory Specification (XMS). Also developed by Lotus/Intel/Microsoft, this standard provides a rudimentary means for DOS applications to use portions of extended memory.

(continues)

(continued)

High memory area (HMA). The first 64K of extended memory, minus 16 bytes, beginning at the 1M threshold. Because of a quirk in the design of the 80286, 80386, and 80486 CPU chips, you can address these 65,520 bytes in real mode.

Protected mode. The 80286, 80386, and 80486 CPU chips can operate in protected mode or real mode. In protected mode, the CPU can address more than 1M of memory.

Real mode. The default for Intel CPU chips, real mode is the only mode available for 8088 and 8086 CPU chips. In real mode, the CPU can address only up to 1M of memory.

Upper memory. This is the memory between 640K and 1M. Video adapters, ROM BIOS chips, hard disk controller ROMs, and network adapters use RAM in this region, but there are *holes*—upper memory blocks—that some memory managers can map as regular memory.

Virtual Control Program Interface (VCPI) memory. Quarterdeck Office Systems and Phar Lap Software developed the VCPI standard to enable DOS applications to share extended memory without conflict. However, VCPI does not prevent software from sometimes accessing portions of RAM that belong to other computer programs.

New Files

On a NetWare LAN, you may have one or more device drivers (SYS files that you load with statements in the CONFIG.SYS file) to help turn your computer into a workstation. You definitely will have the two TSRs: IPX.COM and NETX.COM (or EMSNETX or XMSNETX). For NetWare, these files are all you need to gain access to the LAN. You may have a NET.CFG or SHELL.CFG file to help configure IPX and NETX at login time. All told, these files take a little over 100K of space on your local hard disk.

Many of the peer LAN products take from 200K to 2M of new files on your workstation's hard disk after you install a product. For LAN Server and LAN Manager, the installation procedure puts about 3M of files on your computer.

Using Diskless Workstations

Imagine a PC that consists of just a keyboard, a network adapter, and a monitor—no floppy drives or hard disk. You turn the computer on, and it attaches itself immediately to the network. Such a computer is fairly inexpensive. Sounds like a great way to save money on LAN workstations, doesn't it? Don't be fooled; it isn't. A diskless workstation must rely completely on the file server's hard disk and, therefore, increases network message traffic dramatically. Furthermore, a diskless workstation is a single-purpose computer that you will not be able to upgrade later. Such a machine cannot run OS/2 or be used as a stand-alone computer. So diskless workstations will not save money in the long run. However, there is a reason for using them: security. If you have a LAN environment in which it is important that its users cannot copy files to disk and transport them, diskless workstations may give you just the security you need.

If you use a diskless workstation, you probably want to know how the workstation appears to run DOS just like all the other workstations that have their own disk drives. The network adapter in a diskless workstation contains a special boot ROM chip. When you start up the computer, this chip automatically receives control at the end of the power-on self test. The chip contains software that knows how to find a file server, look for a special copy of DOS on the server, and load DOS across the LAN cable.

Using DOS and Microsoft Windows

When installed on an individual computer, Microsoft Windows Version 3.1 occupies from 5M to 15M of disk space of the computer's hard disk. On a large LAN with many Windows users, the total disk space that Windows files consume is considerable. However, if you configure things properly, you can share certain Windows files from one or more file servers.

You can use Windows' built-in menuing facilities to create application menus for individuals and groups. The object-oriented Windows menus can, of course, use file server search paths. However, if a user logs in to the network from a computer that has a different kind of monitor, keyboard, or mouse, he or she may run into problems running Windows. When you design your login scripts, take this situation into account.

> **Note**
>
> A special version of Windows, called Windows for Workgroups, has networking software built into it. Windows for Workgroups combines Microsoft Windows with a network operating system. Chapter 9, "Using Peer LANs," discusses Windows for Workgroups in detail.

Installing Windows on a File Server

Installed in stand-alone mode on a personal computer, all Windows software—including program files, fonts, initialization files, customization files, and dynamic link libraries (DLLs)—resides entirely on your local hard disk.

II

Building a Network

Windows cannot actually run on the server, but you can store some of its files there. Through the network operating system, Windows transfers these files into local workstation memory as needed. On a LAN, you can store the files that Windows reads (but not the ones that it writes to) in a central, public directory on the file server. These files include program files, fonts, DLLs, and help files. You should store each user's initialization and customization files (the INI files, for example) on the personal computer's local hard disk or perhaps in a private server directory for each user.

If your LAN has diskless PCs that need to run Windows, you definitely should create private, user-specific server directories to hold the Windows initialization and customization files.

Sharing Windows files from a file server has several advantages. For the LAN's users, the most important advantages are the access and management of LAN resources through the Windows interface. You can connect and disconnect remote printers with the Control Panel, view and manage remote files with the File Manager, and view or change the status of print jobs on LAN printers with the Print Manager. Probably the next most important advantage is the savings in disk space that you can achieve. The savings become even more significant if the LAN workstations consist of personal computers with relatively small hard disks.

As you contemplate storing Windows files on your LAN, study carefully the mix of software applications, users, and hardware configurations that make up your LAN. If only a few people in your office use Windows, putting Windows on the file server may not be cost-effective. Installing Windows on a network is usually difficult and tedious. The effort is worthwhile only if Windows is a popular operating environment in your office. You also need to choose whether to have Windows begin running automatically on the workstations, or whether to make it an option for the LAN's users. You should study how people in the office use Windows, and whether most of the applications that they use are DOS or Windows applications.

If you have used Microsoft Windows, you know that it requires computers and adapter cards that are extremely compatible with the IBM PC standard. You know also that Windows requires a computer with a certain amount of speed and internal memory. These requirements become key issues if you want to integrate Windows with your network.

Keep in mind that Windows executes in the workstation, not in the server. You cannot improve the performance of Windows on a slower personal computer by installing Windows on a high-performance file server. The server acts only as a place to store the files that make up the Windows environment.

Sharing Windows from a Server

While running, Windows frequently reads and writes each user's initialization and customization files. You can save some hard disk space on a local workstation by putting these files on the file server, but performance will suffer. When Windows accesses files on the server, the Windows file requests must be redirected across the LAN like all other file requests. A diskless workstation usually does not provide a speedy Windows environment.

As the LAN becomes easier for people to use, the network administrator's job gets harder. This is doubly true for Microsoft Windows on a LAN. If you are (or become) a network administrator, you should document and keep detailed records of the Windows configurations on the LAN.

If you plan to install and run Windows from a shared directory on the LAN, be sure to give all files in this directory a read-only attribute so that every user can access but not write to the files. You can do this with the Windows File Manager, with the ATTRIB command at a DOS command-line prompt, or with a network utility such as NetWare's FLAG command. Most Windows applications' program files must have read-only status before they can be shared.

Printing with Windows on a LAN

With Windows Version 3.1, you can access network queues directly from within the Windows Print Manager. You can see which print jobs are in the queue, delete print jobs, and reselect printers easily. You should set your LAN printer defaults by running the printer redirection command (CAPTURE, for example) before starting Windows.

A large LAN usually offers several LAN printers that users share. When printing from within Windows, they choose a printer from the list of configured printer devices. Such lists can sometimes be unwieldy. You should set up and configure Windows for those printers that are used most often. Most people do not like to scroll through multiple printer selections to find the one they want to use.

Configuring Windows on a LAN

You should create a different SYSTEM.INI file for each Windows user, putting the file in a personal Windows directory unique to that user. This means that when you modify configuration settings, you have to change many separate files, but Windows will not operate properly otherwise. To save time and effort, you can first create a template SYSTEM.INI file and then customize this file for each user.

As you create the template file, you need to know the configuration parameters that the network uses. Descriptions of these network-related parameters are provided here (if you want further information about these parameters, refer to your Microsoft Windows documentation):

■ *AllVMsExclusive=*. This Boolean setting controls whether a DOS application can run in a window or must run in exclusive full-screen mode, regardless of the settings in the program information file. The default setting is FALSE. If the setting is TRUE, the network will complete its Windows sessions more slowly.

■ *[Boot] Section Network.drv=*. This setting specifies the network driver file name that you are using. The default setting is None. When you use SETUP, most network driver choices are available. To change your network driver setting, choose the SETUP icon located in the Main group window and then modify your network choice. If you want to install a network driver that Windows does not provide, you must run SETUP again.

■ *FileSysChange=*. This Boolean setting controls whether the File Manager automatically receives messages from non-Windows applications when those applications create, delete, or rename files. If the setting is FALSE, a virtual machine can perform file manipulation while running independently of the File Manager. If it is TRUE, all messages automatically go to the File Manager, and system performance is degraded.

■ *InDOSPolling=*. This Boolean setting determines whether other applications can run when memory-resident software has the InDOS flag set. The default setting is No. You must change the setting to Yes if your memory-resident software needs to be in a critical section to perform operations. When the setting is Yes, system performance is degraded.

■ *INT28Critical=*. This Boolean setting specifies whether a critical section is required to handle INT28h interrupts for a memory-resident software application. The default setting is TRUE. If you do not need a critical section, change this setting to FALSE; this should improve Windows' task switching.

■ *INT28Filter=*. This numeric setting determines the number of INT28 (hexadecimal) interrupts that software loaded before Windows can use while your system is idle. The default value is 10. Increasing the value improves Windows' performance but can cause conflicts with memory-resident software such as network shells. Changing the setting to 0 eliminates the interrupts. Users of communication applications on a network should be aware that the lower the value of INT28Filter, the higher the system overhead, which can cause conflicts with the communication application.

- *NetAsynchSwitching=.* This setting controls whether Windows provides the capability to switch away from an application after it has made an asynchronous NetBIOS call. The default value of 0 indicates that task switching is not available. With a value of 1, task switching is available. Network users should determine whether any of their applications will receive network messages while switched to other applications; if an application does receive messages and you have a setting of 1, your system may fail.

- *NetHeapSize=.* This numeric setting determines the size (in kilobytes) of the buffer pool allocated in conventional memory (640K bytes) for moving data over a network. The default value is 8, but many networks require a larger buffer size. The larger the buffer size, the smaller the amount of memory provided to applications.

- *NetAsynchFallback=.* This Boolean setting can require Windows to try to save a NetBIOS request if it is failing. The default setting is FALSE. Windows has a global network buffer that handles data; if sufficient space is not available in this buffer when an application makes a NetBIOS request, Windows fails the request. If you change this setting to TRUE, Windows tries to save the request by creating a buffer in local memory and preventing all virtual machines from processing until the data has been received properly and the timeout period has passed. The setting NetAsynchTimeout controls the timeout period.

- *NetAsynchTimeout=.* This setting determines the length (in seconds, to one decimal place) of a timeout period when Windows is attempting to save a failing NetBIOS request. The default, 5.0 seconds, applies only if NetAsynchFallback is set to TRUE.

- *NetDMASize=.* This setting determines the buffer size (in kilobytes) for NetBIOS transport software. The buffer size always represents the largest value established by this setting or the DMABuffersize setting.

II

Building a Network

- *Network=*. This setting represents the 386 Enhanced-mode synonym for Device. The default is None and is controlled by SETUP.

- *PSPIncrement=*. This setting tells Windows to reserve, in 16-byte increments (from 2 to 64), additional memory for each successive virtual machine if the UniqueDOSPSP setting is TRUE.

- *ReflectDOSINT2A=*. This Boolean setting tells Windows to hide or reflect DOS INT 2A signals. The default is FALSE, which instructs Windows to hide this type of signal from software running in the Windows environment, providing more efficiency. If you have memory-resident software that requires knowledge of INT2A messages, change this setting to TRUE.

- *TimerCriticalSection=*. This setting (in milliseconds) tells Windows to go into a critical section around any timer interrupt code and use the timeout period specified. A value greater than 0 guarantees that only one virtual machine at a time will receive time interrupts. Some network memory-resident software will fail if you do not specify a value greater than 0. If you use this setting, system performance slows.

- *TokenRingSearch=*. This Boolean setting can instruct Windows to look for a Token Ring network adapter on machines with the IBM AT architecture. The default is TRUE. This search can interfere with another device.

- *UniqueDOSPSP=*. This Boolean setting can instruct Windows to start every application at a unique memory address (PSP). The default setting is FALSE. If the setting is TRUE, each time that Windows creates a new virtual machine to start a new application, a unique amount of memory below the application is reserved. Another INI file parameter, PSPIncrement, controls the amount of memory that is reserved. This approach guarantees that applications in different virtual machines will start at different addresses. Some networks use the load address of the application to identify each process on the network.

Identifying Problems with Windows on a LAN

When you load network operating system software into upper memory, Windows sometimes fails to start or behaves strangely. If this happens, try loading the network software in conventional memory (the first 640K bytes).

The Windows SETUP program modifies the PATH statement in your AUTOEXEC.BAT file. You should review SETUP's modifications to make sure that the PATH statement appears before the statements that load the network software. Make sure also that your network drives are mapped properly for your Windows environment. To change the drive letter mappings, you may have to make changes to the Windows customization and initialization files for each LAN user.

If SETUP has problems running on a workstation, try specifying SETUP /I when you run SETUP. The /I parameter disables SETUP's hardware detection. You may need to specify this command on an ARCnet LAN, for example. The SETUP program tries to detect an IBM 8514 video adapter by using certain machine instructions. Because these instructions use addresses that also exist on an ARCnet network adapter, SETUP becomes confused.

If you get incorrect page breaks, incorrect fonts, or extra blank lines when printing to the LAN printer, you may need to change the LAN print job configuration. Under NetWare, for example, use the PRINTCON utility to choose the No option for the Auto Endcap and Enable Timeout settings. Chapter 7, "Using NetWare," provides more on printing with NetWare.

If any of the Windows INI files seem to become corrupted when users access Windows from the file server, make sure that each person uses a unique, user-specific directory (or local hard disk) to store his or her customization and initialization files.

While you are at a DOS prompt in a Windows Enhanced mode DOS session, you should never attempt to log in, log out, or attach to the network server. Doing so will crash your workstation. Always perform these functions before you start Windows, or while you are in Windows, from the Windows Control Panel.

If you see file-error messages on a NetWare LAN, you most likely need to increase your maximum number of file handles from the NetWare default of 40 files to 60 files. You can do this by adding the following line to the SHELL.CFG file:

    FILE HANDLES = 60

II

Building a Network

Identifying Networks Recognized by Windows SETUP

At SETUP (installation) time, Windows lets you choose from several network operating systems:

- 3Com 3+Open LAN Manager (XNS only)

- 3Com 3+Share

- Banyan Vines 4.0

- IBM PC LAN Program

- LAN Manager 1.x (or 100 percent compatible)

- LAN Manager 2.x Basic (or 100 percent compatible)

- LAN Manager 2.x Enhanced (or 100 percent compatible)

- Microsoft Network (or 100 percent compatible)

- NetWare 2.10 or later, or NetWare 386

Microsoft Windows operates a bit differently for each of these network operating systems, so choose your network carefully.

NetWare Considerations

On a NetWare LAN, make sure that you use recent versions of the NetWare shell and the NetWare utilities. The NetWare shell must be Version 3.01 or later.

In Enhanced mode, Windows can do some additional adjusting of your NetWare drive mappings. In Standard mode, all drive mappings that are changed while you are inside Windows are reset to the original mappings when you exit Windows. For example, if you change drive G from USER USER1 so that it represents PUBLICWINAPPS, it is reset to USER USER1 when you exit. In Enhanced mode, you can make all drive mappings stay in place even after you leave Windows. Simply add the following line in the [NETWARE] section of your SYSTEM.INI file:

RESTOREDRIVE=FALSE

The default for each virtual machine in Enhanced mode is to have its own (local) set of drive mappings. Thus, changing the mapping in one machine does not affect the other. If you want to have mapping (or any mapping change) affect all virtual machines (global), use the following setting in the [NETWARE] section of SYSTEM.INI:

NWSHAREHANDLES=TRUE

Microsoft LAN Manager Considerations

Windows is incompatible with early versions of LAN Manager 1.x. If you want to use Microsoft Windows, you may have to upgrade your LAN Manager software. Also, LAN Manager 1.x includes pop-up services that enable you to see incoming broadcast messages. This feature causes problems with the Windows graphical user interface.

You cannot load the LAN Manager workstation software into upper memory (with one of the memory-management products mentioned earlier) if you want to run Microsoft Windows.

If you want to have pop-up services, you should use the LAN Manager WinPopup utility, which is designed to work with Windows. You can find this utility in the LAN Manager NETPROG directory. You should include the utility in your DOS PATH statement.

To have the utility start automatically with Windows, you use the LOAD option in the [WINDOWS] section of WIN.INI, as shown in the following entry:

```
LOAD=WINPOPUP.EXE
```

For LAN Manager 2.0 Enhanced, Windows must have the two DLLs NETAPI.DLL and PMSPL.DLL in the LAN Manager NETPROG directory and in your PATH statement.

Other Network Operating Systems

For networks that support MS-NET and NetBIOS, be aware that the Print Manager cannot handle multiple print queues, so print jobs may be listed incorrectly.

To run Banyan Vines 4.0 with Windows in Enhanced mode, you need to obtain the software update that Banyan refers to as *patch OH*. When running Windows in Enhanced mode, you can run only one application at a time that makes use of NetBIOS. If, for example, you are printing to a LAN printer from a Windows application or you are running an application that uses NetBIOS, be sure to close all other virtual DOS sessions. Also keep in mind that if you want to use Windows printing functions and run non-Windows applications with VINES, you must load NetBIOS.

For 3Com networks, be aware that 3+Share and 3+Open LAN Manager use completely different software driver modules.

II

Building a Network

Using OS/2 Computers

IBM's newest edition of OS/2, Version 2.x, includes several features not found in DOS, earlier versions of OS/2, or Windows. Because IBM designed and developed OS/2 2.x after networks became popular, this latest version of OS/2 understands networks and does not need as much tweaking and fine-tuning as other environments.

When you use NetWare Requester for OS/2 2.x to turn your OS/2 computer into a workstation on a NetWare LAN, you will notice the extra drive letters, the capability to print to the LAN printer, and many of the other differences noted earlier for DOS-based workstations. The network software, however, does not use conventional memory under OS/2. You do not have to deal with the same memory issues, and you do not need a memory-management product to reclaim usable memory.

Multiple OS/2 and DOS Sessions

OS/2 2.1 gives you several operating environments: multiple OS/2 sessions (full-screen or windowed), multiple DOS sessions (full-screen or windowed), Microsoft Windows sessions, and Presentation Manager sessions. You manage these operating environments from your OS/2 desktop, which is called the *Workplace Shell*. The Workplace Shell is LAN-aware, and you can manipulate *remote objects* (those that are LAN-attached rather than local to the workstation) in the same way you manipulate local objects.

After you log in to the network and map your file server drives as drive letters, each new DOS session or OS/2 session that you create has equal access to the file server drives. A CAPTURE command issued in one DOS or OS/2 session affects all the other sessions. You can print from any environment in OS/2 after issuing the printer redirection command.

Usually, you will want your workstation to attach itself to the LAN each time you boot your computer. Under OS/2, you do this with batch file statements that you place in the file STARTUP.CMD. For example, you can create a STARTUP.CMD file that contains statements similar to the following:

```
L:
CD OS2
LOGIN BARRY
PASSWORD: <type your password here>
MAP F:=SYSTEMPRO\SYS:
```

Multitasking

OS/2 is a multitasking operating system. You can start a long-running print job in one session under OS/2, and then switch your attention to another session to get other work done. The print job continues in the background while you work. If you start another print job in a different session, the OS/2 spooler and the network spooler work together to keep the printouts separate.

OS/2 and the LAN also work together to protect the integrity of your data files. If, for example, you edit a document with a word processor in one session and try to edit that same document from another session, you receive a Sharing Violation error message from OS/2. The same mechanism that protects multiple users on the LAN from editing the same file at the same time also protects your multiple OS/2 and DOS sessions from colliding.

Using Macintosh Computers

If you use a Macintosh as a workstation on the LAN, you probably have a NetWare LAN or an AppleTalk LAN. Both are good platforms for Macintosh connectivity. You will probably notice very few changes in your Mac's behavior when it is on the LAN. The current version of the Mac operating system, System 7, contains some significant networking enhancements.

System 7 and AppleTalk

System 7's new LAN-related capabilities include peer-to-peer file sharing, Ethernet and Token Ring drivers, Interapplication Communication (IAC), and Apple events messaging.

System 7 provides peer-to-peer-based file sharing. File transfers occur directly between computers, so you do not have to use a file server as an intermediary. You can easily share a Mac's folders, hard disk drives, CD-ROM drives, or any combination of all three resources.

From the Finder's File menu, you simply click the objects that you want to share, and then select Sharing. File sharing has little effect on your Mac's performance unless another LAN user copies files to or from a shared object, and then the slowdown lasts for only the duration of the transfer.

Three Macintosh Control Panels (CDEVs—Mac configuration utilities) enable you to start or stop file sharing, arrange access rights to your Mac and shared objects, and monitor user access. The Sharing Setup CDEV switches file sharing on or off. It also sets a network name and password for your Mac and determines whether other users can use the IAC function to link applications.

The Users & Groups CDEV enables you to configure access privileges for your Mac and the shared objects. Finally, a File Sharing Monitor CDEV shows the shared objects and a list of users who are currently accessing your Mac.

When file sharing is active, your Mac appears to other LAN users as an AppleShare file server. To connect to your Mac, they use the Chooser desk accessory. The Items window displays shared objects as volumes.

For the network administrator, configuring file sharing is similar to setting up an AppleShare server. AppleShare users access shared objects the same way they access other objects. Peer-to-peer file sharing makes it easy for Mac users to exchange or distribute files. However, security on a peer LAN can be difficult to enforce. To prevent unauthorized access to confidential or sensitive information, you must plan carefully. Be especially careful when you configure parameters in the Users & Groups CDEV.

You can share Apple's CD-ROM drive on a System 7-based LAN, but you must upgrade the CD-ROM software driver to Version 3.1. In addition, you must upgrade to AppleShare 3.0 to run System 7 client/server applications on your LAN. Electronic mail or group-scheduling software requires the later version of AppleShare to support System 7-specific features such as the IAC Publish/ Subscribe mechanism.

Interapplication Communication is a System 7 feature that enables applications to exchange information by forwarding document updates across the network or by exchanging commands and information with other LAN-aware applications. IAC links applications running on different AppleTalk workstations.

The simplest form of IAC is the Publish/Subscribe mechanism. One Mac user (the person who "owns" the information and who is responsible for updating it) tells an application to "publish" all or part of the information. IAC automatically makes this data available to another Mac user on the LAN, who "subscribes" to that data through the Standard File dialog box that appears when he or she chooses Subscribe from the Edit menu. Each time the information changes, System 7 passes the information to the subscribers through an edition file, which is created by the application that publishes the data.

In System 7, applications can share information with special messages called *Apple events*. With this feature, one Mac application can request the services of another Mac application on the LAN (or within the same computer, for that matter). Apple events are a form of client/server architecture.

System 7 comes with both Ethernet drivers and Token Ring drivers. AppleTalk itself operates at the relatively slow rate of 230 kbps and supports a recommended maximum of 32 networked computers. The new drivers enable you to connect your Mac to larger, faster Ethernet and Token Ring networks.

Macs on a NetWare LAN

Novell offers Macintosh connectivity, in the form of two distinct products, for the NetWare 2.x and NetWare 3.x server-based network operating systems. These products are NetWare for Macintosh Version 2.2 and NetWare for Macintosh Version 3.0. In addition, the Dayna, Asante, and Xircom companies also sell Macintosh hardware and software that enable Macs to access a NetWare LAN.

NetWare for Macintosh Version 2.2 consists of server software that enables Mac users to access NetWare 2.x file and print services. NetWare for Macintosh Version 2.2 is a value-added process (VAP) that loads each time a NetWare 2.x server starts. At your Mac workstation, you use the same AppleShare workstation software that is part of the System 7 Macintosh operating system. NetWare for Macintosh Version 2.2 comes bundled with the NetWare 2.x network operating system.

The server portion of NetWare for Macintosh Version 3.0, which runs on NetWare 3.x and 4.x servers, is a NetWare Loadable Module (NLM). The workstation portion is a desk accessory (DA) that you install on your Mac. The desk accessory enables you to manage the print queue, send messages, and perform administrative functions, such as granting file-access rights and adding new users. For file sharing and printing, you use your System 7 AppleShare workstation software. You must purchase NetWare for Macintosh Version 3.0 separately from the NetWare 3.x network operating system.

To access NetWare file servers, you use the Chooser. At your Mac workstation, with either product, you retrieve and update files in the same way that you did before you became part of the LAN. You also print in the same manner. You have the resources of the network at your disposal, however, and users at other workstations on the LAN (including DOS, OS/2, and UNIX computers) can share files with you on a NetWare LAN.

Some software makers offer versions of their applications that run on DOS and Mac computers yet use a common file format. These applications include WordPerfect, Aldus PageMaker, Microsoft Excel, and Microsoft Word. DOS and Mac users can share such files without first having to convert the files from one format to another.

II

Building a Network

Using UNIX Workstations

You can use a UNIX-based computer as a workstation on a LAN and share files with DOS and Mac users. A DOS user sees the file server as a drive letter, directories, and files. The Mac user sees objects and folders. On a UNIX workstation, you see additional file systems, directories, and files. If you use a graphical user interface like the X-Window System on your UNIX machine, you also see icons and folders. Your new commands and utilities include such tools as RLOGIN, RCOPY, and RWHO, which are network versions of their UNIX counterparts. You also get TELNET (for executing programs remotely on other computers), FTP (for transferring files), and SMTP (for sending electronic mail).

Most UNIX networks are based on the TCP/IP protocol, which Chapter 5, "Using Protocols, Cables, and Adapters," discusses. TCP/IP is not a network operating system. To be able to access a file server, you must get additional software.

Sun Microsystems' Network File System (NFS) product is a popular way to connect UNIX-based computers. Several other computer manufacturers, including IBM, have licensed NFS. Locus Computing offers PC Interface, a network operating system for UNIX environments. IBM sells PC Interface under a different name, AIX Access for DOS Users. PowerFusion and POWERserve, from Performance Technology, also turn a UNIX host computer into a file and print server. Chapter 10, "Using UNIX LANs," describes each of these products in detail.

The Santa Cruz Operation's SCO Open Desktop 1.1 is a UNIX operating system that is based on SCO UNIX System V Release 3.2 (and later versions) for 386 and 486 computers. Open Desktop includes ODTNet, which enables you to connect to other computers on your company's network, as well as an X client application called Desktop Manager, which provides an icon-based interface. Desktop Manager enables you to copy, move, execute, print, and delete your LAN files simply by moving your mouse. Open Desktop LAN Manager enables you to work with computers connected with Xenix-NET, OS/2 LAN Manager, or IBM PC LAN Program. For more information on Open Desktop, contact the Santa Cruz Operation:

> The Santa Cruz Operation, Inc.
> 400 Encinal Street
> P.O. Box 1900
> Santa Cruz, CA 95061
> (800) 626-8649
> (408) 425-7222

Summary

You now understand how your workstation views its role on the network. Your desktop computer may be based on the DOS, DOS-plus-Windows, OS/2, Macintosh System 7, or UNIX operating system. Whichever personal computer and operating system you use, this chapter explained how the network changes your computer into a workstation. You covered the practical aspects of how your workstation behaves on the LAN, and you know what to expect from your personal computer when you log on to the LAN.

In the next few chapters, you explore several specific network operating system products. Chapter 7 gives you a close look at NetWare.

II

Building a Network

Part III

Networking Software

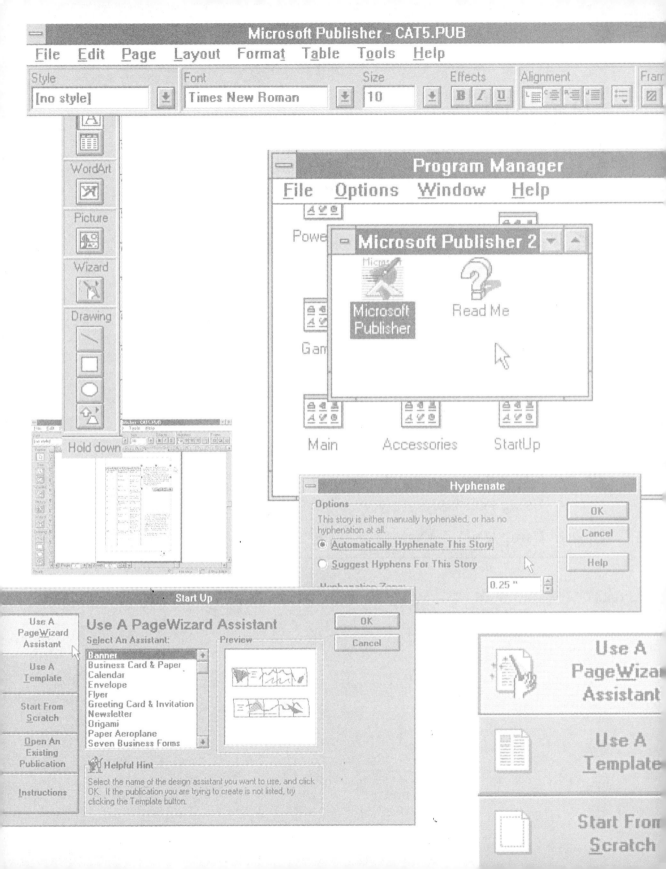

Chapter 7

Using NetWare

NetWare is the most popular network operating system in use today. More than half of all LAN installations run a version of NetWare. People like NetWare because it performs well, runs on several types of hardware, and offers a useful, comprehensive set of security features.

Novell offers several LAN-oriented products. Novell's flagship products are its three server-based network operating systems—enterprise (4.0), high-performance (3.12), and entry-level (2.2)—each of which are described in this chapter. In addition, Novell sells Personal NetWare and NetWare Lite, peer LAN products for smaller work groups. (See Chapter 9, "Using Peer LANs," for a discussion of Personal NetWare, NetWare Lite, and other peer LAN NOS products.)

In addition to its server-based and peer LAN network operating systems, Novell sells other network-oriented products. Novell's 3270 communications software package enables workstations to have 3270 terminal-emulation sessions with a host (mainframe) computer. Access Server is a communications hardware and software product that enables multiple remote workstations to dial up and log in to the file server. A Novell hardware and software product called LANalyzer diagnoses certain kinds of network problems. Chapter 12, "Managing Your Network," explains more about LANalyzer.

In this chapter, you learn about Novell's three server-based network operating systems. You survey each version of NetWare from a general perspective and gain an understanding of the utility software that Novell supplies with NetWare. After exploring many of NetWare's commands to see what they look like and what they do, you focus on NetWare's design objectives. You discover how a NetWare file server operates. You learn about NetWare security and fault tolerance. You look at NetWare's administrative functions and the software that turns a personal computer into a NetWare workstation. This chapter also discusses previous versions of NetWare, which many people still use. First, though, you should know a few things about Novell.

Understanding Novell's History

In 1982, in Orem, Utah, Ray Noorda, Judith Clarke, Craig Burton, and a talented set of programmers from a firm called Superset, Inc. started Novell, Inc. The company's first facilities consisted of a small office near the local steel plant. Novell began selling its first file server product in 1983. In its 10 or so years of operation, Novell has grown to more than 2,400 employees worldwide. In 1985, sales totaled $55 million; in 1990, sales soared to $497 million. Novell's mission statement is simple: accelerate the growth of network computing. Clearly, Novell is accomplishing its mission.

Novell was the first distributed-processing vendor to support heterogeneous, multiple types of computers. The company also was the first to support multiple topologies and to provide routing facilities between those topologies. Novell was the first to support OS/2 and all versions of DOS. The company provides connectivity options for IBM, Apple, UNIX, Digital Equipment Corporation (DEC), and other types of computers.

NetWare works with more than 200 network adapters and more than 100 disk storage subsystems, backup devices, and server computers. Novell maintains a certification laboratory to test its products with other vendors' hardware and software components. In one of its laboratories, Novell has 1,368 personal computer workstations to test its software.

Novell has contracts with some of the largest and most capable independent service organizations to provide support for NetWare. These organizations include Bell Atlantic, DEC, Hewlett-Packard, Intel, Prime, Unisys, and Xerox. Major system integrators and resellers of Novell products include Electronic Data Systems (EDS), Boeing Computer Services, NYNEX Business Centers, and Sears Business Centers. And, in 1990, the giant IBM became a reseller of NetWare.

Novell has sometimes encountered a rocky road in its quest for the high ground of networking. At one time, Novell sold file server computers along with its network operating system software. Novell also used to sell network adapter cards. Currently, the company has discontinued its hardware business so that it can concentrate on the software side of networking.

Reviewing NetWare Products

NetWare is the most popular network operating system for a good reason: its performance, reliability, and security appeal to almost everyone. However, NetWare is one of the more expensive network operating systems for small networks. In addition, installing and administering NetWare is sometimes complicated. And NetWare's TSR workstation components take up about 60K of RAM, leaving less of the workstation's 640K available for running applications. (On an 80386, 80486, or Pentium workstation with 1M or more of memory and a memory manager, such as DOS 5.0, DOS 6.x, QEMM, or 386MAX, you can usually locate Novell's TSR workstation components outside the lower 640K.)

A NetWare *file server* is a personal computer that uses the NetWare operating system to control the network. The file server coordinates the workstations and regulates the way they share network resources. The file server regulates who can access which files, who can make changes to data, and who can use the printer first. All network files are stored on a hard disk in (or attached to) the file server rather than on floppy or hard disks in individual workstations.

Novell offers three versions of NetWare. Version 2.2 works on 80286 (or later) server computers. You can buy licenses for 5, 10, 50, or 100 users. Which license you buy depends on the number of workstations that you want to be able to log on concurrently to the LAN. If you anticipate 7 users, you need to buy a 10-user license; if you anticipate 67 users, you need to buy a 100-user license. Version 3.12 and the new Version 4.0 run on 80386, 80486, or Pentium-based servers. Novell also has prepared special editions of NetWare 4.0 to run on UNIX-based computers and OS/2-based computers. On 80386 or later CPUs, Versions 3.12 and 4.0 of NetWare use 32-bit technology for extra speed. You can buy Version 3.12 for 20, 100, or 250 users. NetWare 4.0 supports up to 1,000 users.

You will not have a problem if you have NetWare 4.0, 3.12, and 2.2 servers on the same network; most of the NetWare utilities (the files in the PUBLIC directory) are the same for these versions. The utility programs are smart enough to recognize the NetWare versions and behave accordingly. NetWare 3.12, for example, has eight file-access rights that you can have; NetWare 2.2 has only seven. Both SYSCON and RIGHTS show the correct information, depending on which kind of server you are viewing. Later sections of this chapter cover SYSCON and RIGHTS.

The faster and more powerful NetWare 3.12 offers more connectivity options than NetWare 2.2. NetWare 4.0 extends the limits of NetWare 3.12 to enable more workstations and more servers to exist on the same LAN. NetWare 4.0 also makes it easier to administer logon accounts across multiple file servers. NetWare 2.2 is functionally comparable to SFT Advanced NetWare 286. Version 2.2 supports nondedicated file servers and is easier to install than previous versions of NetWare 286. Figure 7.1 shows the NetWare family of products.

III

Networking Software

Fig. 7.1
The NetWare
family.

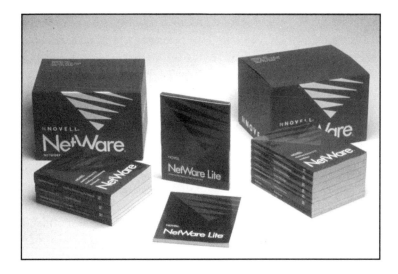

Using NetWare Utilities

You use NetWare utilities to perform network tasks. Two types of utilities are available: menu utilities and command-line utilities. Menu utilities enable you to perform network tasks by choosing options from menus. Command-line utilities enable you to perform tasks by typing commands at the DOS command line.

Using Menu Utilities

When you run a NetWare menu-based utility, such as FILER, you see the utility's main menu along with a screen header that shows the following information:

- The utility's full name

- The current date and time

- The directory path of your current directory (most utilities)

- Your user name on your file server (most utilities)

- Your connection number (most utilities)

To leave a NetWare menu utility, you can press Esc or the Exit key (usually Alt-F10). Pressing Esc saves your changes; the Exit key enables you to abandon any changes you have made.

The F1 (Help) key displays help screens. If you press F1, a help screen that applies to the task on which you are working appears. The help screen describes all the options on-screen. To get help on a specific option, highlight the option and press Enter.

If you press F1 twice, the menu utility lists your computer's function key assignments.

Using Command-Line Utilities

NetWare commands enable you to do single-purpose network tasks that do not require a menu. NetWare offers a multitude of such utilities. The installation process puts these program files into a standard NetWare directory named PUBLIC.

To show the similarity between NetWare and DOS commands, an explanation of two simple NetWare commands, NPRINT and TLIST, follows.

The NPRINT command is the NetWare equivalent of the DOS PRINT command. It sends a text file to a LAN printer. TLIST shows you the list of trustees for a directory. Examples of the command formats for the NPRINT and TLIST utilities follow:

NPRINT *path* [*option...*]

TLIST [*path* [USERS | GROUPS]]

The *path* parameter for NPRINT specifies the path and file name of the file you want to print. You use the *option* parameter to specify how you want the file treated as it prints. For TLIST, the *path* parameter specifies the directory for which you want trustee information. You can use USERS or GROUPS to tell TLIST whether you are looking for single user information or group information.

Using the NetWare LOGIN Command

To log in to your default server, you type the following:

LOGIN *servername/username*

LOGIN is a NetWare command. You replace *servername* with the name of the file server that you want to log in to. For *username*, you use your login name. The LOGIN command prompts you for your password. To log out of your default server, type **LOGOUT**.

III

Networking Software

If you have multiple NetWare servers on the same LAN, you use the ATTACH command to connect your workstation logically to each server after the first. You then log in to the attached servers.

You would attach to another file server if you wanted to do any of the following tasks:

■ Send messages to users on that file server

■ Map a drive to that file server

■ Copy a file or directory to (or from) that file server

You change your NetWare password with the SETPASS command. SETPASS asks you to type your old password and your new password.

Using Other NetWare Commands

To find out who is logged in to a workstation, you use the WHOAMI command. You see a response displayed, similar to the following:

```
You are user BARRY attached to server SERVER1, connection
12 Server SERVER1 is running NetWare v3.12. Login time:
Wednesday January 15, 1994 8:05 am
```

You can use the SLIST command to find out the names of the file servers on your network. To learn the user IDs of the other people who are logged in to the LAN, you use the USERLIST command. The USERLIST display looks something like the following:

```
User Information for Server SYSTEMPRO

Connection    User Name         Login Time

..........    ..............    ...................


1             THOMAS            1-06-1994 8:17 am

2             SUSAN             1-06-1994 8:19 am

4           * BARRY             1-07-1994 8:42 am
```

An asterisk (*) appears next to your user name.

Creating Your Login Script

Your *login script* is a program that sets up your workstation's environment each time you log in. The script performs tasks such as mapping network drives, executing programs and starting applications, and attaching you to different file servers. You cannot run terminate-and-stay-resident (TSR) programs (such as Borland's SideKick) from your login script, however. This section introduces you to some basic login script commands.

To edit your login script, you run the NetWare SYSCON menu utility. After choosing User Information, your user ID, and your login script from the menus, you are ready to configure your script. To execute your new login script, you must first log out of the network and then log in again.

Typically, the NetWare commands that you include in your login script are ATTACH, MAP, and SET. You can also use IF...THEN statements in your script. On a large LAN, you may put script commands into the system login script rather than your personal login script.

The MAP command can establish your network drive letters and augment the DOS PATH facility for locating executable files (applications and utilities). The latter type of mapped drive is called a *search drive*. The following is an example of a MAP command that you might place in your login script:

    MAP F:= SERVER1/SYS:

You learn more about drive mapping with the MAP command in the following section.

The # (pound sign) script command runs an executable file (a file with an EXE or COM extension). Note that you must be careful not to load TSRs within your login script. An example of the # script command follows:

    #SYSCON

This example runs the SYSCON NetWare utility each time you log in to the LAN.

The ATTACH command enables you to connect logically to other file servers while remaining logged in to your current file server.

The SET script command sets DOS variables. You might use SET as in the following example:

    SET user="jwilson"

In a login script, IF...THEN executes certain commands if a specified condition exists. An example follows:

    IF DAY_OF_WEEK = "Monday" THEN WRITE "AARGH... "

III

Networking Software

The WRITE login script command, as you can see, writes messages to your screen as the login script executes.

Mapping Network Drives

You can map an entire NetWare file server hard disk as a drive letter, and you can also map a subset of the hard disk (a directory and its subdirectories).

Mapped drives point to particular locations in the directory structure. In NetWare, three type of drives exist: *local drives*, *network drives*, and *search drives*. Local drives are physically attached to a workstation. Network drives are the disk drives in the file server (often referred to as *volumes*). Like the DOS PATH facility, a search drive enables you to execute programs (applications and utilities) that are in a directory other than the current directory.

To view the present status of your drive mappings, you type the MAP command with no parameters. You then see information similar to the following:

```
DRIVE A:  maps to a local drive
DRIVE B:  maps to a local drive
DRIVE F:= SERVER1/SYS:   /HOME/FRANK
DRIVE G:= SERVER1/SYS2:  /
DRIVE H:= SERVER2/SYS:   /APPS


SEARCH1:=Z:  [SERVER1/SYS:  /PUBLIC]
SEARCH2:=Y:  [SERVER1/SYS:  /PUBLIC/UTILS]
SEARCH3:=X:  [SERVER1/ACCT:  /APPS]
```

Suppose that you want to map a network drive to a directory in which you have files. To see which network drive letters are available, you type the MAP command. After choosing a drive letter that is not in use (such as J), you run MAP again. This time, you give MAP parameters that instruct the command to set up the new drive mapping. Suppose that your user name is FRANK and you want to map drive J to your home directory, which is on file server SERVER1 in volume SYS. You would type the following command:

    MAP J:= SERVER1/SYS:HOME\FRANK

Suppose that your search drives appear as follows:

```
SEARCH1:=Z:  [SERVER1/SYS:  /PUBLIC]
SEARCH2:=Y:  [SERVER1/SYS:  /PUBLIC/UTILS]
```

The next available search drive is SEARCH3 (S3). To map a search drive to directory APPS on volume SYS2:, type the following:

    MAP S3:=SERVER1/SYS2:APPS

When you type the MAP command again, the new search drive appears as follows:

```
SEARCH1:=Z:  [SERVER1/SYS:   /PUBLIC]
SEARCH2:=Y:  [SERVER1/SYS:   /PUBLIC/UTILS]
SEARCH3:=X:  [SERVER1/SYS2:  /APPS]
```

Sending Messages to Others

You can communicate with other users on your network by sending messages from your workstation command line. Suppose that you want to send the following message to users MARK and HOLLY:

Meeting at 1:30 today.

Suppose also that MARK and HOLLY are logged in to your default server. You would use the SEND command, as shown in the following example, to notify Mark and Holly of the meeting:

SEND "Meeting at 1:30 today." MARK, HOLLY

NetWare displays a confirmation message, telling you that it sent the message successfully to the two people.

If HOLLY is logged in to another file server called SERVER2, you would attach to that file server and type the following:

SEND "Meeting at 1:30 today." SERVER2/HOLLY

For another example of NetWare's simple, one-line messaging facility, suppose that you are your company's accountant (or president) and want to tell all employees that the paychecks are ready. Because the NetWare group EVERYONE includes all users, you could type this:

SEND "Paychecks are ready." EVERYONE

If you do not want to receive messages sent to you from any network stations, you can use the CASTOFF command. You see the following NetWare message:

```
Broadcasts from other stations will now be rejected.
```

To enable your workstation to receive messages again from other network users, you use the CASTON command.

III

Networking Software

Understanding Files, Directories, and Attributes

You can manage your files and directories in a variety of ways. You can copy, delete, rename, view, write to, share, and print them. NetWare's system of file and directory rights and file attributes ensures that only authorized network users can access and update LAN files.

Both files and directories can have attributes on a NetWare file server. These attributes override the rights granted to the users on the LAN. Suppose that you have the right to rename files (the Modify right). The file that you want to rename, however, is flagged with the Rename Inhibit attribute. The attribute prevents you from renaming the file, even though you have the right to do so.

Knowing Your Rights

To see what rights you have in the current directory, you use the RIGHTS command. If, for example, you have all rights in the directory, you see the following display:

```
SYSTEMPRO\SYS:BARRY

    Your Effective Rights for this directory are [SRWCEMFA]

    You have Supervisor Rights to Directory.        (S)
    * May Read from File.                           (R)
    * May Write to File.                            (W)
    May Create Subdirectories and Files.            (C)
    May Erase Directory.                            (E)
    May Modify Directory.                           (M)
    May Scan for Files.                             (F)
    May Change Access Control.                      (A)

    * Has no effect on directory.

    Entries in Directory May Inherit [SRWCEMFA] rights.

    You have ALL RIGHTS to Directory Entry.
```

Using the NCOPY Command

The DOS COPY command is an inefficient way to copy files on the LAN if the same file server is both the source and the target of the files. Because the DOS COPY command executes at your workstation and because of the way file redirection works, the source file must flow into your workstation as a series of LAN message packets, and then flow back to the server as yet another series of packets when you use COPY. The incoming packets represent the

COPY command's read-file operations. The outgoing packets are the write-file operations. Why not tell the file server to do the copy operation and avoid the LAN traffic?

The NetWare NCOPY command does exactly this. When NCOPY determines that a file server is both the source and target of a file copy, the command sends to the server a special message packet that instructs the server to copy the file. If the copy operation involves different file servers, or a file server and a workstation, NCOPY does its job exactly like the DOS COPY command.

Suppose that you want to copy a file called REPORT.DOC from your current, default directory on drive F to the MANAGERS directory. Both directories exist on volume SYS on the file server named SERVER1. You would type the following:

    NCOPY REPORT.DOC F:\MANAGERS\REPORT.DOC

Note that you can use the NetWare menu utility FILER to copy, delete, and rename files on the network.

Salvaging Deleted Files

You can undelete files on a NetWare LAN with the SALVAGE utility. From the utility's menu, you select View/Recover Deleted Files and specify whether you want to undelete a single file, multiple files that you select from a list, or multiple files based on wild cards you supply. You can give the resurrected file a new name during the salvage operation.

Using the NetWare NDIR Command

Like the DOS DIR command, the NetWare NDIR command lists files in a directory. NDIR is NetWare-aware and knows how to display the additional file information that NetWare stores for each file and directory. NDIR also can traverse the file server directory tree to look for a file. The NDIR utility searches all directories to which you have rights on the server to find a file that you have misplaced. A typical NDIR *.EXE display looks like the following:

```
SYSTEMPRO/SYS:BARRY

Files:          Size     Last Updated      Flags           Owner
- - - - - - - -   - - - - -  - - - - - - - - - -   - - - - - - - - -   - - - - - -
LANXPERT EXE   91,078  12-06-91  8:39p   [Rw-A----------]   BARRY
SHOW EXE        7,338   6-06-91  8:17p   [Rw-A----------]   BARRY

 98,416 bytes in  2 files
102,400 bytes in 25 blocks
```

III

Networking Software

Printing with NetWare

Printing on a NetWare workstation is similar to printing on a stand-alone personal computer. When you send a print job to a network printer, however, the job first is routed through the file server and then delivered to the printer by the print server. The file server and print server can be the same computer.

Using CAPTURE

After you issue a CAPTURE command to redirect printer output to the shared LAN printer, you can use that printer port just as if a local printer were attached to it. You can even use your PrtSc key to print screens to the LAN printer.

The following is a list of some of the most common CAPTURE options:

Option	Function
L=n	Indicates which of your workstation's LPT ports (local parallel printing ports) to capture. Replace n with 1, 2, or 3. The default is L=LPT1.
Q=queuename	Indicates the queue to which the print job should be sent. If multiple queues are mapped to a printer, you must include this option. Replace queuename with the name of the queue.
TI=n	Indicates the number of seconds between the last time that the application writes to the file and the time that it releases the file to the queue. You usually include this option when you want to print from an application without exiting the application. Replace n with a number of seconds (1-1,000). The default is TI=O (timeout disabled).

As an example, you can put the following CAPTURE command in a batch file that you run after you log in:

    CAPTURE TI=10 Q=laserjet

ENDCAP is a NetWare command that undoes the printer redirection of the CAPTURE command. If you have sent something to the printer, ENDCAP sends your print job to the print queue, without waiting for the timeout period to elapse. ENDCAP also ends the capture of your LPT port. You must then issue another CAPTURE command to reenable printing to the LAN printer.

Managing Your Print Jobs

A *print queue* is a special directory in which print files are stored while waiting for printer services. To see which jobs are waiting in a queue to be printed, you use the PCONSOLE NetWare menu utility. After selecting Print Queue Information and the name of the print queue, you select Current Print Job Entries from the Print Queue Information list. The print job entries are then displayed.

You can cancel your print job by deleting it from the print queue, even after the job has started printing. You can delete a print job only if you are the owner of the job or if you are the print queue operator. Print job removal is a function of the PCONSOLE utility supplied with NetWare. You highlight your print job in a menu displayed by PCONSOLE, press the Del key, and confirm the deletion of the print job.

Understanding NetWare's Design Objectives

NetWare was the first network operating system to enable users to share files instead of merely enabling multiple users to store private files on a central hard disk. As mentioned in the introduction to this book, Corvus Systems sold many hard disks to organizations such as local school boards. With Corvus software and network adapters, users could share space on a large, expensive hard disk. Each user's files were separate, however; no one could access the same file at the same time. Novell set a new standard for file sharing when it designed and developed NetWare.

Until Novell created NetWare, network operating systems were entirely proprietary. If you wanted a LAN, you had no choice but to purchase the vendor's hardware and software together. Novell designed NetWare to be hardware-independent, so you can run NetWare on several types of networks and with a variety of network adapters. Novell always has adhered to an open standard regarding its software products. An example of Novell's commitment to open architecture is its Open Datalink Interface (ODI) standard. Any network adapter manufacturer can make an adapter that works with NetWare simply by including a device driver that implements ODI.

NetWare's fault tolerance is another characteristic that sets it apart from other network operating systems. The basic design of the NetWare file system (the way data is written to the hard disk), the Transaction Tracking System

III

Networking Software

(TTS), disk mirroring, and disk duplexing all contribute to data integrity on a NetWare file server. You learn more about fault tolerance and the Transaction Tracking System in the section "Understanding NetWare Fault Tolerance" later in this chapter.

Using the NetWare Server and File System

A NetWare file server, although it looks like a regular IBM AT, IBM-compatible, or IBM PS/2 computer from the outside, is really a minicomputer in disguise. The hard disk (or disks) in the file server are formatted with a file system structure that is completely foreign to DOS. For example, you cannot boot a NetWare file server with a DOS disk and then access the hard disk with DOS commands. A user at a workstation, however, can view the file server as just another DOS disk drive. The magic that allows this, of course, is the redirection of DOS function calls that you learned about in Chapter 4, "Using File Servers." Novell has simply carried the principle a bit further than other NOS vendors.

The proprietary format of a NetWare file server disk contains more information about files and subdirectories than is possible under DOS. Not only can a file have the DOS attributes read-only, hidden, and modified-since-last-backup, but also the file can be marked as shareable or nonshareable (properties that enable or disable simultaneous access to the file by more than one user). NetWare also tags each file with its original creation date, the identification of the user who created the file (its owner), the date on which the file was last accessed, the date the file was last modified, and the date and time the file was last archived. Directories also have special properties, which the following section describes.

From this description of the file system that is used on a NetWare file server, you can tell that the operating system software running on the server is not DOS. NetWare operates the CPU in protected mode (something that OS/2 also does) and takes control of the entire computer. Protected mode enables the 80286 CPU chip to address 16M of memory, and protected mode allows an 80386, 80486, or Pentium CPU chip to address 4 gigabytes (billions of bytes). NetWare uses any extra memory that you install in the file server for file-caching purposes.

Understanding NetWare Security

Officewide (or companywide) information, consisting of data files and programs, resides on the same file server hard disk. Not all people in the office or company, however, should have access to all the information. Certain files (such as payroll files) contain confidential data and should be available only to certain users. In addition, applications that are not LAN-aware probably have data files that multiple users can update one person at a time. If two users access the same file at the same time, they may overwrite each other's work.

To prevent such problems, NetWare provides an extensive security system to protect the data on the network. NetWare security consists of a combination of the following:

- Login security, which includes creating user names and passwords and imposing workstation, time, and account restrictions on users.

- Trustee rights that control which directories and files a user can access and what the user is allowed to do with those directories and files, such as creating, reading, erasing, or writing to those files.

- Directory and file attributes that determine whether the directory or file can be deleted, copied, viewed, or written to. These attributes also mark a file as shareable or nonshareable.

Each directory has a *maximum rights mask* representing the highest level of privilege that can be granted to any of the directory's trustees. The eight rights that the rights mask can specify enable the user to do the following:

- Read from open files

- Write to open files

- Open existing files

- Create new files

- Delete existing files

- Act parentally—creating, renaming, or erasing subdirectories—and set trustee rights and directory rights in the directory and its subdirectories

- Search for files in the directory

- Modify file attributes

III

Networking Software

Understanding NetWare Fault Tolerance

Realizing that reliability is an important trait of a file server, the designers and programmers at Novell have tried to ensure the protection of the data stored on the server. NetWare 2.2, 3.12, and 4.0 incorporate Novell's System Fault Tolerant (SFT) technology. *Fault tolerance* refers to the file server's capability to continue functioning, without missing a beat. Both versions of NetWare employ basic strategies and techniques to minimize a failure of the disk surface to record data correctly; SFT goes a step further and provides *disk mirroring* and *disk duplexing*, which are software and hardware mechanisms for maintaining duplicate copies of disk data. Chapter 4, "Using File Servers," explains mirroring and duplexing.

The NetWare operating system recognizes signals from an uninterruptible power supply, through UPS monitoring. The operating system knows when the UPS is supplying power, and notifies users of how much time they have left before the UPS batteries run down. If commercial power is not restored within the time period, NetWare closes any open files and shuts itself down gracefully.

Finally, SFT NetWare offers the NetWare Transaction Tracking System (TTS). An application programmed to use TTS can treat a series of database updates as a single operation—either all the updates take place, or none of them do. A system failure in the middle of a multiple-file update does not cause inconsistencies between the files.

Assigning NetWare Users

You can assign four levels of responsibility to users on a NetWare LAN:

- Regular network users
- Operators (file-server console operators, print queue operators, and print server operators)
- Managers (work group managers and user account managers)
- Network supervisors

Regular network users are the people who work on the network. They can run applications and work with files according to the rights assigned to them.

Operators are regular network users who have been assigned additional privileges. A file-server console operator, for example, is a network user who is given specific rights to use FCONSOLE or the Remote Management Facility (RMF). The discussion of the specific features of NetWare 3.12, in the section "Using NetWare 3.12," covers RMF in more detail.

Managers are users who have been given responsibility for creating or managing other users. Work group managers can create and manage users. User account managers can manage, but not create, users. Managers function as supervisors over a particular group, but they do not have supervisor equivalence.

Network supervisors are responsible for the smooth operation of the whole network. They maintain the system, reconfiguring and updating the LAN as necessary.

Understanding a NetWare Workstation

Workstations use two pieces of software to communicate with the file server: the shell (redirector) and a protocol. Before any workstation can function on the network, you must load the shell into that workstation.

Two software components run on each NetWare workstation, both of which are terminate-and-stay-resident programs (TSRs). IPX manages the PC-to-PC and PC-to-file server communications by implementing Novell's IPX/SPX communications protocol. NETX (or perhaps NET2, NET3, NET4, or NET5, if you use the older, DOS-version-dependent programs) is the shell/redirector that shunts DOS file requests to and from the file server by issuing commands to IPX. Together, NETX and IPX make the file server's disks and printers look like DOS-managed peripherals. IPX takes about 19K of memory, and NET3 takes about 38K.

The NETX.COM NetWare shell directs workstation requests to DOS or NetWare. When software running at a workstation makes a file load, file save, or directory search request, the NetWare shell decides whether the request refers to the workstation's local disk drives (to be directed to DOS) or to the file server's drives (to be directed to NetWare). If the request refers to a local workstation drive (as would be true, for example, when you use the DOS DIR command to list the files on a floppy disk), NetWare lets DOS handle the

III

Networking Software

request. If the request is a network I/O task (such as printing a job on a LAN printer), NetWare handles the request. The shell sends the request to the appropriate operating system—DOS or NetWare—somewhat like a railroad track switcher that sends trains to the proper destination.

The workstation shell uses another file, IPX.COM, to send network messages to the file server and, in some cases, directly to other network stations. This IPX protocol is the language that the workstation uses to communicate with the file server.

You do not have to run NetBIOS on a NetWare workstation (unless, of course, you have applications that use its protocol), because the NetWare shell software uses IPX to communicate with the file server. Novell supplies a NetBIOS emulator that can be loaded on top of IPX and converts NetBIOS commands into IPX commands for transmission across the network, in case you want both protocols. This adds roughly 20K of memory to the resident portion of NetWare.

You can use the same IPX/NETX pair of programs on a NetWare 2.2 LAN as well as you can on a NetWare 3.12 LAN.

Reviewing Previous Versions of NetWare

Originally developed as the network operating system for the now obsolete Novell S-Net LAN, NetWare quickly migrated to the Intel 80x86 CPU chip. In 1985, Novell introduced Advanced NetWare 1.0; Version 1.2, released later that same year, was the first operating system to take advantage of the 80286 CPU chip's special protected mode operating environment.

Advanced NetWare 2.0

Version 2.0 of Advanced NetWare, released in 1986, brought increased LAN functionality, better performance, and an internetworking capability to NetWare. One of NetWare 2.0's milestones was its capability to connect up to four different networks with a single file server.

NetWare 2.1x, SFT NetWare, and NetWare 386

In 1987, Novell reworked NetWare yet again to provide significant levels of fault tolerance and data integrity in its SFT NetWare product. It introduced features that gave network managers more control of the LAN. For example, the FCONSOLE feature enables an administrator at a workstation to control the file server remotely across the LAN. Other new and enhanced features included new resource accounting and improved security.

To appeal to the cost-conscious, small-LAN market, Novell also created 5- and 10-user versions of NetWare, called NetWare ELS (Entry Level System) I and ELS II.

Version 2.15 of NetWare and NetWare for Macintosh made their debut in December, 1988. Providing Mac connectivity was an important step for NetWare, but customer complaints regarding the complexity of NetWare reached new heights during this time. One bitter complaint dealt with the COMPSURF utility, which ran automatically as part of the installation process. COMPSURF is a disk surface diagnostic program designed to reveal flaws in a hard disk. People complained that COMPSURF was too thorough—it typically would run for a full day or even two days before finishing. In addition to the amount of time that it took, the entire installation process required substantial expertise to accomplish correctly.

NetWare 386, a full 32-bit edition of the network operating system, shipped in September, 1989. Concentrating on data integrity and reliability, Novell significantly enhanced NetWare's security, performance, and flexibility in the NetWare 386 product.

In 1991, Novell released NetWare 2.2 and 3.11; in 1993, Novell enhanced Version 3.11 to become Version 3.12. Also in 1993, Novell released NetWare Version 4.0. These server-based LAN software products currently are Novell's flagship offerings.

Using NetWare 2.2

In NetWare Version 2.2, Novell consolidated all earlier versions of 80286-based NetWare (NetWare 2.15, SFT Advanced NetWare, ELS I, and ELS II) into a single product. Version 2.2 is quite similar to SFT Advanced NetWare. As with NetWare 3.12, price differences for NetWare 2.2 relate only to the number of users supported. All 2.2 editions provide exactly the same features; for example, a 5-workstation LAN has the same system fault tolerance (SFT) level as a 100-user LAN. Version 2.2 is available for 5, 10, 50, or 100 users. Prices vary from $895 for 5 users to $5,495 for 100 users. Later in this chapter, table 7.1 compares NetWare 2.2 with NetWare 3.12.

III

Networking Software

The installation process for NetWare 2.2 is almost as simple as that of NetWare 3.12. Novell responded to customers' feedback by redesigning the installation process for the two new products. In the basic installation mode, you answer just three questions about your file server and your local area network, wait a brief moment while the ZTEST disk test runs, and then insert several floppy disks. The product still includes the long-running COMPSURF program, but only as an optional step.

NetWare 2.2 also supports value-added processes (VAPs)—separate program modules linked with NetWare—which enable the file server to provide extra services. Novell's BTRIEVE file-access method is a good example of a VAP. Instead of using DOS redirection to ask the file server for various portions of a file, an application running on a workstation sends the key of the record that it wants directly to BTRIEVE, which looks up the record on the server and returns the appropriate record to the application.

Using NetWare 3.12

NetWare 3.12 takes advantage of the 80386, 80486, or Pentium CPU chip to extend the limits of NetWare. Version 3.12 supports up to 4 gigabytes of memory for caching. Up to 250 users can be logged in to a server, and up to 32 terabytes (32 trillion bytes) of disk storage can reside on a single server. Each file may be up to 4 gigabytes, and a file can span multiple physical drives. Up to 100,000 files can be open concurrently. NetWare 3.12 includes the features of SFT NetWare and adds enhanced security facilities. Also new is the concept of *NetWare loadable modules* (NLMs)—software modules that can be loaded into (or unloaded from) the file server even while the server is running. NLMs are much easier to use than VAPs.

NetWare 3.12 is not as good a client/server platform as the OS/2-based LAN Manager and LAN Server network operating systems (discussed in Chapter 8). However, Novell does offer a set of programmer-oriented tools for developing client/server applications. If you are a programmer, or if you have access to a staff of programmers, Novell offers several NetWare developer tools for writing applications that reside in both the file server and the client workstations, including a memory-protection NLM and several transport protocols that are relatively easy to program.

To help programmers manipulate this new environment more easily, Novell offers The Professional Developer's Program. Programmer tools from Novell consist of a C compiler, linker, symbolic debugger, libraries of LAN-related code, and NetWare RPC. RPC stands for *Remote Procedure Code*, a distributed processing concept in which different parts of an overall program or process are executed on different kinds of networked computers.

NetWare 3.12 runs on only 80386, 80486, or Pentium CPUs. You can buy NetWare 3.12 in 20-, 100-, or 250-user configurations. Prices range from $3,495 for 20 users to $12,495 for 250 users.

Version 3.12 of NetWare fulfills Novell's promise to support several workstation environments. The server can store files from DOS-, Macintosh-, OS/2-, UNIX-, and OSI-based client workstations transparently. To do this, NetWare 3.12 sets aside special name spaces on the server. You load optional server modules (NetWare loadable modules) to manage these name spaces. Each directory entry for a file holds a DOS-style name. The corresponding name space entry (two 128-byte areas) contains machine-specific name information. A file that originates on an OS/2 workstation, for example, can retain its extended attributes (long name, creation date, and so on). A Mac file uses the name space to hold the long name and Mac Finder (resource fork) information. An application running on a DOS workstation can access a file created by a Mac workstation, and vice versa.

The Mac, DOS, and OS/2 file-sharing features work well. After you load the NetWare for Macintosh NLM, you can create a Microsoft Word document on a Mac, revise the same file with Microsoft Word for Windows on a DOS-based computer, and perform a final revision under Word/PM on an OS/2 workstation. In each case, you would not know that the file originated on a different kind of computer. NetWare for Macintosh complies with Apple File Protocol (AFP) 2.0 and with AppleTalk Phases I and II.

NetWare's open architecture extends beyond its file system to include new transport layer interfaces, based on Novell's Open Datalink Interface (ODI). This interface provides a wide range of connectivity options, including IPX/SPX, NETBIOS, LU 6.2 (APPC), named pipes for DOS and OS/2 workstations, TCP/IP, a Berkeley 4.3 Sockets interface, and the AT&T UNIX System V Streams/Transport Layer Interface (TCI).

If you store files from many kinds of workstations on your server, you naturally are concerned about backing up these files. NetWare 3.12's SBACKUP utility enables you to back up and restore all server files, regardless of origin, to an internal server tape drive. The name space information goes onto the backup tape, too. You can back up and restore DOS, Macintosh, and OS/2 High Performance File System (HPFS) files, all in a single operation.

III

Networking Software

With the TCP/IP NLM included with NetWare 3.12, you can, for example, put a UNIX machine, such as the IBM AIX-based RS/6000, on a Token Ring segment of the LAN and use a NetWare 3.12 server with NetWare TCP/IP loaded to route IP packets internally from a DOS workstation to the separate RS/6000 segment. NetWare TCP/IP's IP tunneling feature enables NetWare 3.12 LANs to communicate across TCP/IP internetworks. To get IPX packets from one NetWare server to another across a TCP/IP link, NetWare wraps the IPX packets in an IP envelope and transfers them across the internetwork. In essence, the TCP/IP portion of the LAN becomes a natural extension of the IPX (NetWare) LAN.

To enable a UNIX workstation to use a NetWare file server, you load an NFS implementation on a UNIX machine (such as an RS/6000) and NetWare NFS on the NetWare file server. After you make the proper entries in the /ETC/HOSTS and other setup files on the UNIX computer, you create an empty directory and use the standard UNIX MOUNT command to turn the empty directory into a remote view of the NetWare 3.12 file server. You then access the NetWare file server from the UNIX workstation using ordinary UNIX commands, utilities, and application programs.

The NetWare FTAM NLM is a file-transfer facility that connects NetWare 3.12 servers to OSI-based networks. The facility is fully GOSIP 1.0-compliant; GOSIP workstations can use FTAM to share NetWare print services and send files back and forth.

NetWare 2.15's FCONSOLE workstation utility monitored server activity. The first few versions of NetWare 386 did away with FCONSOLE. Now it is back, thanks to the Remote Management Facility (RMF). You can use RMF to monitor a server or to upgrade NetWare at a second server. Remote installation works well, but you must follow the steps in the manual carefully.

NetWare 3.12 includes all the features and capacities of its NetWare 386 predecessors, including reliability, security, RAM usage, disk size, and file size. Installing NetWare 3.12 is easy.

The NetWare 3.12 on-line help system could use improvement. The data is there—all 1.7M of it—but the NFOLIO user interface is not intuitive and makes finding what you need difficult. You can move around the screen with cursor-movement keys and scroll the screen with the PgUp and PgDn keys. You press Tab to move the cursor to a subtopic name, and then press Enter to get help for that subtopic.

NetWare 3.12 performs well, partly due to the new Turbo file allocation table (FAT). Each volume contains a FAT—an index to one or more disk allocation blocks in which a file resides. NetWare keeps the entire FAT in server memory and creates a Turbo FAT for files larger than 64 entries, which provides faster access for larger files.

Another NetWare 3.12 feature, *dynamic memory allocation*, parcels out cache buffers for file buffering, NLM memory requests, FAT buffering, and directory table buffering. Because of its memory management, NetWare 3.12 can have more file service process (FSP) threads running concurrently than NetWare 2.2 can. This capability translates to faster workstation response times.

Table 7.1 compares the features of NetWare 2.2 and NetWare 3.12 so that you can see the similarities and differences between Novell's two most popular server-based network operating systems.

Table 7.1 A Comparison of Features: NetWare 2.2 and NetWare 3.12		
Feature	**NetWare 2.2**	**NetWare 3.12**
Operating system type	16-bit	32-bit
Minimum server CPU	80286	80386
Minimum server RAM (50 users)	2.5M	6M
Maximum memory supported	12M	4 gigabytes
Hard disk space required	5M	9M
Maximum server disk space	2 gigabytes	32 terabytes
Maximum disk volume size	255M	32 terabytes
Nondedicated server option	Yes	No
Server applications	VAPs	NLMs
Dynamic resource allocation	No	Yes
OS/2 clients	Yes[1]	Yes
Macintosh clients	Yes[2]	Optional
NFS clients	No	Optional
OSI clients	No	Optional
Network cards supported	8- or 16-bit	8-, 16- or 32-bit

[1]*NetWare 2.2 does not support long, HPFS-style names.*

[2]*Only Version 2.2 emulates AppleTalk, although Version 3.12 provides direct support for AppleTalk.*

Using NetWare 4.0

From your DOS, DOS/Windows, Macintosh, or OS/2 workstation, you may not notice your organization's upgrade to NetWare 4.0. Novell has carefully designed NetWare 4.0 to be completely compatible with Versions 2.2 and 3.12. If you are a network administrator, however, you'll notice a number of changes right away.

Novell began selling the core NetWare 4.0 product in March, 1993, after showing it at the Interop/Spring trade show in Washington, D.C. Also in 1993, Novell released NetWare System Fault Tolerance (SFT) III—a version of NetWare 4.0 that incorporates software techniques to ensure fail-safe operation of the LAN. Novell also offers NetWare 4.0 for UNIX and OS/2 2.x. The versions of NetWare 4.0 for UNIX and OS/2 are completely rewritten network operating systems, based more on the core NetWare 4.0 product than on the older Portable NetWare. NetWare for UNIX relies on technology provided by UNIX System Laboratories (USL), which Novell acquired from AT&T late in 1992. The version that runs on OS/2 was released late in 1993. No matter what OS platform you prefer, Novell wants to be the supplier of your network software.

You can install NetWare 4.0 from about 25 floppy disks (some of these are workstation disks) or from a CD-ROM drive. The CD-ROM installation method quickly and painlessly creates a NetWare 4.0 server. You may have to install a few more megabytes of RAM in a PC to give NetWare 4.0 room in which to work; NetWare 4.0 requires at least 6M of RAM and, depending on the features you install, 12 to 60M of disk space.

The 4.0 shell software that enables a DOS client to access a NetWare file server is smaller (53K rather than Version 3.12's 59K), but otherwise provides the same I/O redirection functions as the 3.12 shell software. Workstations can continue to use the older shell software; you don't have to upgrade all the workstations at once. Novell supplies the 4.0 DOS client software in modular form as virtual loadable modules, or VLMs. You can log in from within Windows just as you can from within OS/2 PM (see fig. 7.2). People who use the Windows or PM interface get new tools for managing their network sessions. NetWare 4.0 has built-in packet-burst support, enables you to back up DOS and OS/2 workstations, and uses less RAM on designated remote printer machines. *Packet-burst* is a LAN performance technique that helps workstations get faster responses from a file server.

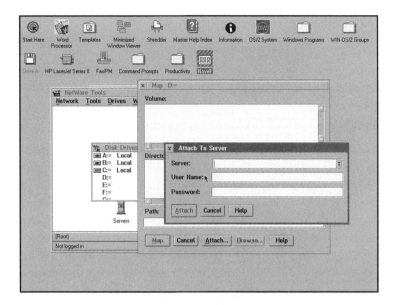

Fig. 7.2
The graphical
interface for using
NetWare.

The most significant feature of NetWare 4.0 is Novell's new NetWare Directory Services (NDS), a hierarchically organized database that replaces the old
bindery. Much 3.12-aware network utility software uses the Novell API to
access the bindery. By default, NetWare 4.0 turns on bindery emulation, so
you don't have to throw those utilities away. Version 4.0 includes a new
named directory service that Novell says will work with software written to
the X.500 specification. The new named service is the key that lets users log
on local servers in a single operation. Users also can easily access servers located in geographically dispersed LANs (called wide area networks, or WANs).

NetWare 4.0 supports up to 1,000 simultaneous connections (Version 3.12
supports only 250 connections to a server), and Novell sells licenses in strata
of 5, 10, 20, 50, 100, 250, 500, and 1,000 users. If you use the new shell,
NetWare 4.0 offers up to 54,000 server connections. (With Version 3.12, a
workstation can have only eight server connections.) You can run NetWare
4.0 in nondedicated mode with the UNIX and OS/2 versions, but the core 4.0
product remains a dedicated server environment.

NetWare 4.0 doesn't yet support multiprocessor machines. Version 4.0, in
answer to a frequent criticism of Version 3.12, does, however, distinguish
between ring 0 and ring 3 memory protection. These rings are protection
mechanisms that the CPU makes available to operating system software.
Software running in a particular ring has a specific privilege level, and the
CPU doesn't let software in one ring interfere with software running in a
different ring.

III

Networking Software

New in Version 4.0 is a read-ahead cache to help performance, along with two features to help you conserve server disk space: data block suballocation and data compression. You can configure the data compression to operate during off-hours, when most people have left the office, if you're afraid that on-the-fly compression will bog the server down. When you access a compressed file in the middle of the day, however, NetWare 4.0 must do extra work to fluff the file back to its uncompressed form.

NetWare Version 4.0 has the same limits as Version 3.12 on the number of volumes and total disk space. For better security, Version 4.0 offers RSA Public/Private Key cryptography, along with NDS and file system event-logging. You also get remote console session security and remote session modem callback. NetWare 4.0 can use a time server to synchronize the clocks of multiple servers (even in different time zones). Recent enhancements to Version 4.0 include Image Enabled NetWare, based on Kodak technology, and document-management services, based on content document architecture technology.

NetWare 4.0 is a logical, practical step up from previous versions. If you've outgrown the 250-user or 8-server limits of NetWare 3.12, or if you have several LANs connected in a WAN, you'll find that Version 4.0 injects new life into your network. However, if your network hasn't grown enough yet to need NetWare 4.0, you'll be glad to know that Novell will continue to sell and support the popular Version 3.12.

Summary

The server-based NetWare network operating systems come in enterprise (4.0), high-performance (3.12), and entry-level (2.2) versions. All three NetWare versions are easy to install and offer excellent security and reliability. NetWare 3.12 and 4.0 deliver long-awaited connectivity options to Novell customers who have DOS, OS/2, Macintosh, and UNIX computers.

NetWare 2.2 is an expensive solution if you are creating a small, entry-level LAN. However, this version is the right choice for small to medium-sized LANs in which data integrity is of paramount concern. A large LAN, or one that has a diverse mixture of workstation types, is a good candidate for NetWare 3.12. Version 3.12 is the first network operating system to support DOS, Macintosh, Windows, OS/2, and UNIX file and print services. NetWare 4.0 is appropriate for the largest of LANs—those with more than 250 workstations or more than 8 file servers.

The cost for NetWare 3.12 ranges from $3,495 to $12,495, depending on the number of concurrent users that your network must accommodate. The price of NetWare NFS is $4,995. NetWare for Macintosh 3.0 costs between $895 and $1,995. The price of NetWare FTAM is $995, and NetWare 2.2 runs from $895 to $5,495, depending on the number of concurrent users that you need.

For more information about NetWare, you can contact Novell at the following address:

> Novell, Inc.
> 122 East 1700 South
> Provo, Utah 84606
> (801) 429-5900
> (800) 346-7177

In Chapter 8, you learn about LAN Manager and LAN Server, the almost-twin network operating systems from Microsoft and IBM, as well as Microsoft's new Windows NT Advanced Server.

III

Networking Software

Chapter 8

Using LAN Manager, Windows NT, and LAN Server

Although NetWare is the most popular server-based network operating system at the present time, NetWare doesn't lend itself well to a relatively new software technology called client/server computing. Programming NetWare Loadable Modules (NLMs) is just too difficult a task. The server-based network operating system products from Microsoft and IBM, however, allow programmers to easily develop software that takes advantage of client/server technology. If all you need is the sharing of files and printers, NetWare may be the product you should buy. But if you are interested in going beyond the sharing of files and printers on your LAN, you'll want to be aware of what Microsoft and IBM have to offer.

This chapter focuses on Microsoft LAN Manager, Microsoft Windows NT, and IBM LAN Server. These products are growing in sales somewhat, but still lag behind NetWare by a wide margin. The network operating systems from Microsoft and IBM let people create client/server environments as well as share files and printers. As local area networks migrate in the direction of client/server technology, you may find that Microsoft and IBM someday sell more network software than Novell. However, the history of Microsoft and IBM working together to create their network software products is somewhat checkered. Both companies will have difficulty overcoming their past reputations in the networking software arena.

As Microsoft and IBM codeveloped the OS/2 operating system, they realized that OS/2 could form the basis for a new, full-featured network operating system. With OS/2 running as the file server, the software modules of the network operating system could service file and print requests in a multitasking, *threaded* environment. Threads are a software technique employed by some operating systems that enable different parts of the file server software to execute concurrently. (Threads enable the server to give the appearance of doing more than one thing at a time.) The workstations, which might be using DOS, OS/2, or some other operating system, would see the benefit of the new high-performance environment. OS/2 file servers and DOS workstations seemed like a natural, popular combination. Microsoft and IBM planned that customers would get an extra benefit, too. It is relatively easy to program an OS/2 computer, even one that is already running as a file server. If you have a staff of programmers, or if the application software you buy already supports it, client/server architecture becomes a possibility.

After developing OS/2 and the rather similar LAN Manager and LAN Server products, Microsoft and IBM stopped working together. Then, in 1993, Microsoft released yet another operating system (Windows NT) and a new network operating system based on Windows NT, called Windows NT Advanced Server. Microsoft still sells and supports LAN Manager, and the three products are, not surprisingly, somewhat similar.

It may seem odd to you that two companies would work together to create two virtually identical products with different names and slightly different sets of features. Therefore, the first subject covered in this chapter is the genesis of these OS/2-based network operating systems. You discover why OS/2 is such a rich environment for network operating systems in general and for client/server applications in particular. You get a detailed look at Microsoft's SQL Server, which is an excellent example of client/server architecture. You also learn how Windows NT provides networking services and a networking environment similar to those of LAN Manager and LAN Server.

You learn what LAN Manager, Windows NT Advanced Server, and LAN Server look like, how they operate, and what they offer in the way of functions and features. You explore, in depth, the procedures for logging in and mapping drives. You learn about OS/2 and Windows NT files, directories, and attributes. You see how your workstation behaves on an OS/2- or Windows NT-based LAN, and you find out how print redirection works with these products.

After you become familiar with print job management under LAN Manager, Windows NT, and LAN Server, you look critically at the levels of security offered by these network operating systems. If you are thinking of installing LAN Manager, Windows NT, LAN Server, and NetWare on the same LAN but on different file servers, you find out about the potential problems you face. You complete the chapter by covering a detailed list of the similarities and differences among LAN Manager, Windows NT Advanced Server, and LAN Server.

Exploring the IBM and Microsoft Team Effort

IBM and Microsoft have worked together on OS/2 since 1985. Each company markets its version of OS/2 differently, and each company has made slight changes to the operating system to customize it somewhat, but MS OS/2 and IBM OS/2 are essentially the same product. In 1985, the two companies added the writing of the OS/2 file server software to their Joint Development Agreement (JDA). IBM's product is called LAN Server, and Microsoft's is LAN Manager. Both share a common *codebase*, meaning that, like OS/2 itself, the network operating systems are the same software with only minor differences.

The first few versions of OS/2 were not greatly popular, despite the fact that OS/2 does not have a 640K limitation or many of the other problems associated with DOS. Microsoft and IBM envisioned that OS/2 would replace DOS, but this did not happen. Application developers did not rush to market an OS/2 version of every DOS application, as Microsoft and IBM expected they would. The emulation of DOS within the early versions of OS/2 was limited in significant ways, and not every DOS application would run in the DOS box under OS/2. People kept using their DOS applications, purchasing memory managers such as QEMM and 386MAX to give them more conventional memory in which to run their applications. Such purchases prolonged the life of the DOS applications, but people still complained when they ran out of room by bumping into the 640K DOS limitation.

The new version of OS/2, Version 2.x, rectifies the situation by giving you multiple concurrent DOS sessions, each with about 620K of conventional memory free for running your software. OS/2 2.x includes the Microsoft Windows environment, and of course, you can run OS/2 applications under OS/2 2.x. IBM calls OS/2 ". . . a better DOS than DOS, a better Windows than Windows, and a better OS/2 than ever before."

In the latter part of 1991, Microsoft and IBM split up and decided to go their own ways with OS/2 and their jointly developed network operating systems. Microsoft's LAN Manager still runs on OS/2, but in 1993 Microsoft began to

III

Networking Software

also sell a new operating system product, called Windows NT, and a complementary network operating system product called Windows NT Advanced Server. IBM, however, remains firmly committed to OS/2. IBM believes that, with its new features, OS/2 may yet replace DOS as the dominant operating system for personal computers. At the same time, Microsoft believes that Windows NT will someday dominate desktop computers.

In 1989 and again in 1990, Microsoft and IBM announced that the companies would merge LAN Manager and LAN Server into a single product. This has not happened, and the split between Microsoft and IBM makes it extremely unlikely that the merging of the products will ever take place.

With a history such as this, you begin to see why LAN Manager and LAN Server have not preempted NetWare as the most popular network operating system. Novell has always sharply focused on building a better network operating system. People perceive IBM and Microsoft as being not quite as focused. And OS/2 itself—the operating system—must sell better before people flock to LAN Manager, Windows NT, LAN Server, and client/server environments. The new OS/2 2.x may very well "conquer the desktop" and eclipse DOS as the operating system of choice at the workstation. But, at the file server, NetWare continues to give OS/2 strong competition. As you may expect, you can easily turn a computer running OS/2 2.x into a workstation on a NetWare LAN.

Looking at the History of OS/2

Software developers and end users had voiced complaints about DOS almost from Version 1. Through the late 1980s, DOS did not keep up with people's needs for personal computers that did more work and were more reliable. Specifically, people said they did not have enough memory in which to run their applications (the infamous 640K limitation), DOS did not support multiple concurrent applications, DOS was too fragile, DOS was too simple and rudimentary, and DOS was too slow when applications accessed large files. In short, DOS was not industrial-strength. The biggest complaint about DOS, however, was that each DOS application had its own user interface and required too much training to make the DOS environment truly productive.

Version 1.0 of OS/2 shipped in December, 1987. The first implementation of OS/2 had a single, small DOS *compatibility box*—a special version of DOS within OS/2—for running DOS applications along with OS/2 applications. This first version of OS/2 did not contain or support a graphical user interface. It did, however, offer up to 16M of memory to applications rewritten to run under OS/2 instead of DOS.

Version 1.1 of OS/2, essentially the 1.0 product with the addition of Presentation Manager, appeared in the last quarter of 1988. Still saddled with a small DOS compatibility box, OS/2 1.1 was nonetheless a technical marvel. OS/2 1.1 enabled software developers to transcend the limitations of DOS if they would rewrite their software. Unfortunately, few did.

At the same time that IBM and Microsoft released a Presentation Manager version of OS/2, IBM published a set of guidelines and standards, called *Systems Application Architecture* (SAA), to help the computer industry achieve some measure of consistency and coherence. IBM mentions its own products in the guidelines, but otherwise freely offers the guidelines as a set of suggested methods, interfaces, computer languages, and design techniques that software developers can follow. IBM reasons that consistency and coherence among software applications will encourage more people to use computers in more ways, more productively, and thus indirectly help IBM sell more hardware and software.

Microsoft and IBM also began offering an extended edition of OS/2. Called OS/2 EE 1.1, this special version contained a communications manager for computer-to-computer data transfer, a database manager based on IBM's *Structured Query Language* (SQL) standard for record keeping, and special support for local area networks. The regular version of OS/2 was called OS/2 Standard Edition (SE).

In December, 1990, IBM and Microsoft released Version 1.3 of OS/2. Slimmed down considerably from earlier versions, OS/2 1.3 got the nickname OS/2 Lite. You could run OS/2 1.3 on a computer with as little as 2M or 3M of memory (although you would need more RAM if you wanted to use the machine as a file server). Version 1.3 did many things well for applications rewritten for OS/2, but it still had only a single, small DOS compatibility box. Although not true for earlier versions, IBM did most of the development work for Version 1.3. OS/2 1.3 was small, fast, and reliable and had printing capabilities. Its only drawback was its small DOS box.

IBM released Version 2.0 of OS/2 in March, 1992. In late spring of 1993, Version 2.1 of OS/2 became available. OS/2 2.1 has the following key features:

- Simple, graphical-user-interface installation

- System integrity protection

- Virtual memory

- Preemptive multitasking and task scheduling

III

Networking Software

- Fast, 32-bit architecture

- Overlapped, fast disk file access

- DOS compatibility

- More available memory for DOS applications (typically about 620K of conventional memory)

- Capability to run concurrently OS/2, DOS, and Windows 2.1, 3.0, and 3.1 software

- Multiple concurrent DOS sessions

- High Performance File System (HPFS)

- Presentation Manager (PM) graphical user interface

- Object-oriented Work Place Shell (WPS)

- National Language Support (NLS)

- Interactive on-line documentation and help screens

- Capability to run OS/2 on IBM and IBM-compatible hardware

- Support for popular Super Video Graphics (SVGA) adapters

- Support for additional printers

- Support for popular SCSI CD-ROM drives

- Advanced Power Management (APM) support

- Personal Computer Memory Card International Association (PCMCIA) support

Almost all the items in this list help OS/2 to be a good file server platform.

Using an OS/2 File Server

Both LAN Manager (LM) and LAN Server (LS) run on top of OS/2. LAN Manager 2.2 from Microsoft needs OS/2 Version 1.21 or later, whereas LAN Server 3.0 from IBM needs OS/2 2.0 or later. Workstations can run DOS Version 3.3 or later or OS/2 Version 1.21 or later. You can use an OS/2 file server (LM or LS) as a workstation and a server—in a peer-to-peer arrangement—but you probably will want to keep the OS/2 file server isolated for security reasons. Practically speaking, no one uses LM/LS as the basis for a peer LAN.

Learning LAN Manager and LAN Server Basics

You install LAN Manager and LAN Server after first installing OS/2 on the file server computer. Microsoft bundles MS OS/2 Version 1.3 with LAN Manager 2.2; IBM's LAN Server 3.0 requires you to purchase OS/2 separately. You will want to disable OS/2's capability to emulate DOS when you install OS/2, because LAN Manager and LAN Server consist of pure OS/2 software. A DOS box would just take up memory; you can give the network operating system more memory by disabling DOS emulation. The installation documentation for LAN Manager or LAN Server will give you other configuration changes you can make in order to help the OS/2 computer provide a better file server environment.

On the OS/2 computer, LAN Manager or LAN Server runs in an OS/2 session. You can have multiple OS/2 sessions on the file server, if you want. The network operating system software (LM or LS) does most of its work in the background. The work, as you know from earlier chapters, is the sharing of files, disk space, and perhaps a LAN printer across the network. The network operating system also performs administrative tasks such as recognizing workstations as LAN users log in and forgetting about workstations when those users log out.

You can use command-line entries or menus to do administrative tasks on the network, including logging in and setting up your shared drive letters and printers.

When you set up a DOS-based personal computer to be a workstation on a LAN Manager or LAN Server network, you designate the workstation as having basic or enhanced capabilities. A basic workstation can use fewer commands, does not need to perform a login sequence to use the LAN, and cannot use menus. Even though you do not have to log in from a basic workstation, you must still provide a password to use each shared resource. An enhanced workstation does offer menus and requires a login sequence that includes an account name and a password.

Using the High Performance File System

When you install OS/2 on the file server computer, the installation process asks you whether you want to use the High Performance File System. Because the computer is going to become a file server and you want the server to be as efficient as possible, you probably should answer yes to the question. If you answer no, OS/2 uses the same type of file system that DOS uses, known as the FAT (file allocation table).

> **Note**
>
> The file allocation table scheme was really designed to work with the small-capacity floppy disks that were popular when DOS was first released. Performance suffers when applications access FAT files, especially large files. DOS and OS/2 have to read and process long chains of physical disk location information to satisfy application requests for files.

OS/2 offers a High Performance File System (HPFS) option especially designed for hard disks. OS/2 can access files in an HPFS partition much more rapidly than files in a FAT partition. The difference in performance is most dramatic for large files.

Outside of OS/2, DOS cannot recognize files on an HPFS partition. If you use the OS/2 System Editor to create a text file on an HPFS drive, and then reboot your computer with DOS (perhaps by using Dual Boot to switch from OS/2 to DOS, or by using a system-formatted floppy disk), DOS will not show you the HPFS disk drive. DOS will reassign your computer's drive letters, and the HPFS drive will be invisible. However, if you use the DOS that is built into OS/2, your DOS applications can use files on an HPFS partition. On a file server, though, you do not want to use DOS.

HPFS gives you the ability to use long file names (up to 254 characters) and to include spaces and several periods in such a name. OS/2-based computers— either the file server or OS/2 workstations—can see and use these files. DOS workstations cannot.

Using Client/Server Architecture

LAN Manager and LAN Server provide good environments for client/server applications. Chapter 4, "Using File Servers," explains client/server architecture and discusses why you may want to take advantage of it on your LAN.

Programmability is the biggest reason that people talk about client/server in connection with the two OS/2-based network operating systems, LAN Manager and LAN Server. OS/2 is easily programmed, perhaps even more so than DOS. Both LAN Manager and LAN Server can share the network adapter with other OS/2 application software running on the file server computer. OS/2 *multitasks*, which means that it runs several computer programs concurrently. One computer program is the network operating system, of course. Another may be a database server application. The workstations can see and use the extra drive letters provided by the network operating system. Your programming staff also may program the workstations to send and receive special requests and responses to and from the file server (or a separate computer, for that matter). These custom-programmed requests and responses may, for example, carry SQL statements and relational database records.

OS/2 provides *named pipes* to programmers. The programmer treats a named pipe almost exactly as he or she would a file, but the named pipe actually contains message records. These message records travel from the workstation to the file server. On the file server, a custom-written application may do some record handling and other processing before returning a response to the workstation through the named pipe.

SQL Server is a Microsoft product that enables programmers to create client/ server applications. SQL Server provides a relational database "engine" that you install on an OS/2 computer on the network. Programmers write workstation software that sends SQL statements to SQL Server. SQL Server honors each request by sending back the appropriate records from within its database. Some database management products, such as Microsoft's FoxPro and Access and Borland's Paradox, can work with SQL Server to give you the ability to update and query your data without hiring programmers or studying the syntax and commands of Structured Query Language.

Saros FileShare is another client/server product. You would use it in your office to keep close track of file creation and use. (If you have thousands of document files on your LAN, you need to have the computer keep a record of who created a file, when it was created, and who currently has the file charged out.) FileShare provides centralized file-access management, version control, and file backup.

Lotus Notes is yet another client/server application. Notes offers intelligent, group-oriented electronic mail services. Notes enables sophisticated storage and retrieval of messages; an index contains the subject, author, recipients, and other key data items related to the messages. Notes is particularly useful for large, geographically dispersed organizations in which people need to exchange information frequently but do not work in the same time zone or have conflicting schedules or work styles. Notes uses a centrally located personal computer on a LAN to store its data. Workstations on the LAN or on a remotely attached LAN, through a wide area network, can interact with the central Notes computer.

III

Networking Software

Working with LAN Manager and LAN Server

In the next few sections, you see how to operate LAN Manager or LAN Server and what these network operating systems look like. You first cover the menu interface these products offer, followed by the command-line interface. You learn what it means to log in on a LAN Manager or LAN Server network. You discover how to map drive letters, use files and directories, and print on the LAN. You explore how your computer behaves when it becomes a workstation on a LAN Manager or LAN Server network, and you find out about the security features of these products. You also get a comparison of the two network operating system products.

Using Menus

The LAN Manager or LAN Server menu interface appears when you use the NET command with no arguments. If you type something following the word NET, the network operating system assumes that you want to use the command-line interface. Figure 8.1 shows the initial menu screen you see when you run the NET program. Note, however, that on a DOS workstation designated as basic (rather than enhanced), menus are not available.

Fig. 8.1

The initial LAN Manager menu.

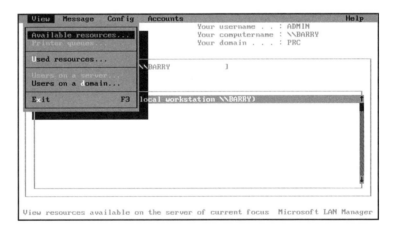

The LM/LS menu screens operate in text mode, not graphics mode; the screens are nonetheless CUA-compliant. This means that you use certain standard keystroke combinations or mouse actions to interact with the network operating system's menu. CUA stands for *Common User Access*, and CUA is part of IBM's recommended standards for information processing, SAA (Systems Application Architecture).

Where does the IBM standard for consistency and ease of use come from? An IBM team spent a number of years investigating user interfaces. The team's findings parallel the findings of the Xerox company at the Palo Alto Research Center (PARC) and of Apple, makers of the Macintosh computer. IBM published these findings in the form of suggested standards and called them Common User Access. The overall set of standards, Systems Application Architecture, covers communications, programming, database design, and user interfaces.

The menu interface of LAN Manager and LAN Server enables you to do anything with menus that you can do by typing commands at a DOS prompt. You can log in to the LAN, log out, map drive letters, and redirect your printer port to the LAN printer. You can change your password; send short messages to other logged-in network users; and see lists of the file servers, disk drives, and printers on the LAN. The manuals supplied with LAN Manager and LAN Server provide a thorough guide to the menu screens and the CUA keystrokes that you use to navigate and operate the menus.

Figure 8.2 illustrates a view of network resources you might see on your LAN Manager network if you use the Windows interface software. Figure 8.3 shows the status of individual disk drives through the same interface.

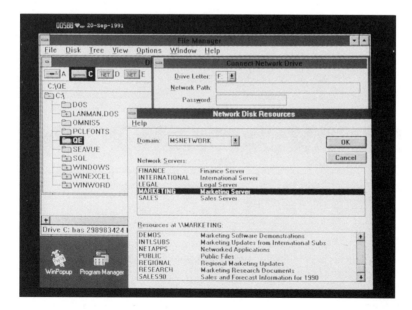

Fig. 8.2
Looking at network resources on a LAN Manager network through the Microsoft Windows interface.

Using the Command-Line Interface

Especially after you have gained some experience with LAN Manager or LAN Server, you may feel more comfortable issuing network commands at the DOS prompt of your workstation, or at the OS/2 prompt at the file server. You invoke the network commands by running the NET command, but you avoid the menu screens by typing parameters after the word NET. Table 8.1 describes the most important and most frequently used NET commands, with their parameters, that you use at a basic or enhanced workstation.

Fig. 8.3

The Microsoft Windows view of LAN Manager disk status.

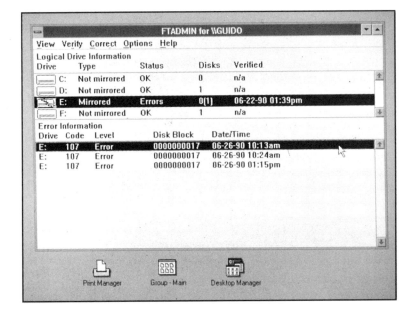

Table 8.1 The NET Commands and Their Parameters

Basic Command	Function
LOAD	Loads a different network protocol
NET CONTINUE	Continues a paused service
NET HELP	Gets help for a command
NET NAME	Assigns a computer name
NET PAUSE	Pauses a connection to a network service
NET PRINT	Displays the print queue or prints a file
NET START WORKSTATION	Starts the network

Basic Command	Function
NET USE	Displays shared resources or assigns a drive letter or device name to a new shared resource
UNLOAD	Unloads a network protocol

Enhanced Command	Function
LOAD	Loads a different network protocol
NET ACCESS	Views permissions
NET COPY	Copies network files
NET HELP	Gets help
NET LOGON	Logs on to the network
NET LOGOFF	Logs off the network
NET PASSWORD	Changes your password
NET PRINT	Controls print jobs and prints files
NET START	Starts a workstation or learns what workstation connections exist
NET TIME	Synchronizes the workstation's clock with the server's clock
NET USE	Displays shared resources or assigns a drive letter or device name to a new shared resource
NET VIEW	Displays a list of servers and server resources
NET WHO	Sees who is logged on
UNLOAD	Unloads a protocol

Using Utilities

The NET command performs most of the administrative duties you will perform on a LAN Manager or LAN Server network. However, the network operating system comes with additional utility programs that are helpful in some
instances. These computer programs enable you to schedule commands or
programs to run at a specified date and time, make backup copies of the
network's administrative files (passwords and permissions), restore these files,
verify a physical connection to a remote computer, and do other odd jobs on
the LAN.

III

Networking Software

Logging In

You use the NET LOGON command to log in to the network. This command establishes the user ID, password, and domain for a workstation. The user ID and password identify you in a particular domain and grant you access to shared resources. You can use shared resources in other domains after you have logged on. You need to perform the logon sequence only on an enhanced workstation. On a basic workstation, you supply a password to use a shared resource. You do not need to identify yourself on a basic workstation.

Forgetting your password can cause your account to be locked out. If you make repeated unsuccessful tries to enter your password, the system will disable your account. You will have to ask the network administrator to reenable your account. This security feature helps keep intruders from gaining access to the LAN.

Mapping Drives

You use NET USE, or the NET program's menus, to map drive letters. Depending on how the network administrator has set up the file server's shared resources, you may find that your workstation's new drive letter refers to an entire server disk drive or only a directory. The administrator decides the extent to which the file server's resources are shared. The distinction between sharing an entire disk drive and just a directory is invisible from a workstation.

The following is an example of a NET USE command that sets up drive F. The network administrator has published the shared resource with the name NORTHEAST on the server named \\SALES.

    NET USE F: \\SALES\NORTHEAST

If you use a basic workstation, you may supply a password after the resource name, or you may use an asterisk for a password. In the latter case, the system prompts you for a password. At the password prompt, what you type is not echoed to the screen.

You also issue a form of the NET USE command to delete, or cancel, the use of a drive letter. The same NET USE command that sets up your network drive letters also redirects your printed output to the LAN printer, as you will see later in the section "Printing with LAN Manager and LAN Server."

After you establish the network drive letters your workstation can use, you work with your applications as you ordinarily would. Files on the LAN are now available to the computer programs you run, as long as you have permission to use those files. If you do not have permission to even read a particular file, you cannot access that file at all. Be aware that you may have read permission but not write permission on some files. This means that you cannot save new data in that file. If you encounter strange error messages from the applications you run, you may want to visit your network administrator to make sure that your permissions are correct and appropriate.

Using Your Workstation

One of the biggest reasons that NetWare is more popular than LAN Manager or LAN Server is the disk space taken up by the LM or LS executable and configuration files. You generally need to use only from two to six relatively small files on a NetWare workstation to gain access to a file server. On a LAN Manager or LAN Server workstation, however, you need from 1M to 3M of workstation disk space. You can easily create a bootable floppy disk that gets you onto the network with NetWare. With LM or LS, you probably will not be able to create a bootable floppy disk to access the LAN. There are too many files.

The memory usage of the LAN Manager and LAN Server workstation software is also greater than that for a NetWare-based workstation. Memory requirements vary according to the type of network adapter card and associated software drivers, but you can expect that LM or LS workstation software will occupy about 90K of RAM. NetWare workstation software, however, usually occupies only 50K to 60K. On a workstation with an 80386, 80486, or Pentium CPU chip, you may be able to use a memory manager to load some or all of the network software into high memory. Chapter 6, "Using Workstations," discusses memory managers.

The workstation installation program will copy files to your computer's hard disk and put statements in your CONFIG.SYS and AUTOEXEC.BAT files to load the network software when you boot your computer. You can put your NET USE statements into a BAT file so that you do not have to retype them each time you reboot.

Printing with LAN Manager and LAN Server

Besides giving you network drive letters, the NET USE command also redirects your printed output to the shared LAN printer. The network administrator gives a name to the LAN printer in the same way that he or she gives names to the file servers and to the shared resources that become drive letters at your workstation. The administrator may set up a printer named HP_LASER on the SALES file server, for example. In this case, your NET USE statement for your printed output would look like the following:

    NET USE LPT1: \\SALES\HP_LASER

Then, when you copy a file to the LPT1 device or when you tell one of your applications to print, the network operating system creates a print job. The print job goes into the server's print queue, to be printed after other pending print jobs when the printer becomes available.

You can configure the network operating system to notify you when the print job is finished printing. If you are impatient and want to see where your job is in the queue, you can view the items in the print queue. You can hold, release, and delete print jobs in the queue (but only your own print jobs, of course).

Ensuring Security

You organize file servers and workstations into domains. A *domain* is a group of file servers and workstations with similar security needs. You can set up several domains on a large LAN Manager or LAN Server network. Domains provide a simple way for you to control user access to the network and the network's resources. A network user can have accounts in multiple domains, but he or she can log on in only one domain at a time.

User-level security on a LAN Manager or LAN Server network consists of logon security and permissions. Each user account has a password; the user specifies a user ID and the password to gain access to the network through a domain. A network administrator can limit a particular user's access to certain times of the day or to certain workstations. Permissions limit the extent to which a user can use shared resources. Figure 8.4 is an example of a screen in which you can designate these permissions. The network administrator, for example, can create a COMMON directory that everyone can use, and the administrator can create an UPDATE directory with files that only certain people can modify but everyone can read.

You can assign the following permissions for files and directories:

Permission	Description
Change Attributes	Flags a file as read-only or read/write.
Change Permissions	Grants or revokes access to other people.
Create	Creates files and directories.
Delete	Deletes files and removes directories (if the user has this permission).
Execute	Executes a program file (EXE, BAT, or COM file) but does not read or copy that file. Only workstations running DOS 5 or later or OS/2 recognize this permission, which is a restricted version of the read permission.

Permission	Description
Read	Enables you to read and copy files, run programs, change from one directory to another, and make use of OS/2's extended attributes for files.
Write	Enables you to write to a file.

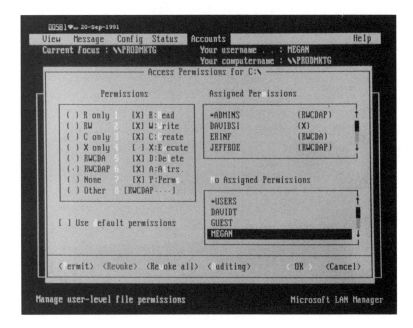

Fig. 8.4
The LAN Manager screen for managing directory permissions.

These OS/2-based network operating systems give you the ability to control access to the file server's keyboard and computer screen. In a special unattended mode, the file server enables people to view and manage print queues without enabling them to modify user accounts or other administrative data. You must specify a password in order to use other screens.

LAN Manager also provides share-level security, which you learn about in the section "Exploring the Differences among LM, NT, and LS" later in this chapter.

Windows NT Advanced Server

Microsoft surprised the industry by releasing NT Advanced Server at the same time as NT itself, in early August of 1993. Microsoft had previously said Advanced Server would lag behind NT by about 30 days. Windows NT Advanced Server extends the features and advantages of LAN Manager in several ways.

III

Networking Software

Like LAN Server 3.0, Advanced Server is a 32-bit network operating system. Unlike LAN Server, you can run NT Advanced Server on Intel, MIPS R4000, or DEC Alpha platforms. While CPU speed is rarely a bottleneck on file servers, you might choose to run Advanced Server on a symmetric multiprocessing (multiple CPU) computer. The extra CPU processing power might let you use the file server for additional client/server applications.

Advanced Server offers C2-level security, which means that the network operating system has a secure logon procedure, memory protection, auditing, and discretionary access control (the owner of a shared resource can monitor who is using the shared resource). Some corporate and military LANs require C-2 or higher security. In the area of reliability, Advanced Server uses a transaction-based file system that can back out file updates if a series of related updates don't finish successfully. Advanced Server supports RAID level 5 (Redundant Array of Inexpensive Disks—disk striping with parity), recognizes signals from a UPS, and comes with tape backup software.

NT Advanced Server adds an interesting dimension, called Trusted Domains, to the way domains work in LAN Server and LAN Manager. Suppose, for instance, that your LAN has separate domains for Engineering and Marketing. People in Engineering have developed a new product and want to allow product managers in the Marketing department to see the specifications for the new product. Engineering can authorize access to the files by making the Marketing domain "trusted" and giving read-only permissions to the Product Manager group. The product managers don't have to separately log in to the Engineering domain to view the files. When the file server holding the documents senses a request from a Marketing domain product manager, the file server verifies access permission, through the Engineering domain controller, with the "trusted" Marketing domain controller. However, if you want to use the Trusted Domains feature on a LAN with existing LAN Manager or LAN Server file servers, you need to add a Windows NT AS file server to each domain on your LAN.

A Performance Monitor utility helps administrators manage NT Advanced Server, and the NOS is also SNMP- and NetView-aware. Desktop and LAN management products such as OpenView, LANlord, LANDesk, and Frye's Utilities should soon support Advanced Server. (You cover LAN management concepts in Chapter 12, "Managing Your Network.") Microsoft says that Advanced Server will comply with the Desktop Management Task Force (DMTF) specification for the management of LAN-connected desktop computers as soon as the DMTF finalizes its specification. Other utilities you get with Advanced Server include User Manager, Disk Administrator, Event Viewer, and an enhanced Control Panel.

If you prefer not to establish permanent drive letter mappings for each work-station, but rather let each workstation browse lists of shared resources to create new connections to shared directories and printers, you'll like NT AS's BrowseMaster feature. Each PC with resources to share periodically reports a list of those resources to the BrowseMaster server. When a person at a workstation clicks the Browse pushbutton (for example, in Windows for Workgroups File Manager or Print Manager), the workstation gets the list of available resources from the central BrowseMaster computer. This technique keeps LAN traffic down because servers and workstations don't have to con-tinually broadcast resource lists to each other.

Advanced Server uses SMBs, on NetBIOS, to send and receive file I/O redirec-tion requests over the LAN cable (you learned about these protocols in Chap-ter 5, "Using Protocols, Cables, and Adapters"). This means that Advanced Server should interoperate with LAN Server, LAN Manager, Windows for Workgroups, and even the older PC LAN Program (PCLP). Advanced Server also supports TCP/IP and Novell's IPX/SPX transport layer protocols.

You get several other connectivity options with Windows NT Advanced Server: Windows Sockets, Named Pipes, Network Dynamic Data Exchange (NetDDE), IBM's data-link control (DLC) for host sessions, and Remote Proce-dure Calls (RPCs). This last interface is compatible with the Open Software Foundation Distributed Computing Environment (OSF/DCE) specification. Microsoft has announced that it will soon offer connectivity modules for SQL Server and SNA Server. The version of Remote Access Server for NT Advanced Server handles up to 64 concurrent connections over dial-up, leased, X.25, and ISDN lines.

Looking at LAN Manager and LAN Server Similarities

The Microsoft programmers in Redmond, Washington, and the IBM program-mers in Austin, Texas, worked closely together to create LAN Manager and LAN Server. The network operating systems use virtually the same computer software throughout. With a few limitations and restrictions, noted in the next section, you can install LAN Manager and LAN Server on file servers on the same LAN and have workstations connect to both kinds of servers.

Both network operating systems have basically the same user interface, perform about the same on equivalent hardware and under an equivalent workload, and offer many of the same features. These common features in-clude HPFS, ease of programming, and domains. Windows NT Advanced Server also has many of these same features.

LAN Manager, Windows NT, and LAN Server support Macintosh workstations as well as DOS workstations and OS/2 workstations.

III

Networking Software

Exploring the Differences in LM, NT, and LS

You tune LAN Server—make it work more efficiently for the type of information processing you do in your office—by using a text editor to modify the
computer's CONFIG.SYS and IBMLAN.INI files. LAN Manager features
autotuning, whereby the file server software monitors its own activity and
changes its initialization files automatically. To take advantage of autotuning,
you merely have to stop and restart a LAN Manager file server periodically.

Persistent net connections are another feature of LAN Manager. By default,
users get the same network connections they had in their last session each
time they log on. You can enable or disable persistent connections with the
/PERSISTENT= option on the NET USE command. You can also put entries in
a user's LANMAN.INI file to turn persistent net connections on or off, or to
freeze a certain set of network resources as shared by that user.

Demand Protocol Architecture (DPA) is a LAN Manager feature that Microsoft
got from 3Com. The 3Com company bought a LAN Manager license from
Microsoft and enhanced LM somewhat, but 3Com was never able to sell
many copies of its enhanced network operating system. Microsoft bought the
license back from 3Com when 3Com decided to get out of the business of
reselling LAN Manager. Basically, Demand Protocol Architecture enables you
to load and unload protocol stacks dynamically. You may use DPA to make
occasional reference to a NetWare file server; DPA would temporarily load the
NetWare IPX and NETX software at the workstation. After you close your
NetWare connection, DPA reclaims the memory used by IPX and NETX. In
everyday use, people with both LAN Manager and NetWare file servers need
more than temporary access to both kinds of file servers. DPA represents a
technical feat, but one you will find not entirely useful or practical. LAN
Manager comes with a special option called NetWare Connectivity to enable
you to easily access both LAN Manager and NetWare file servers at the same
time.

LAN Manager also offers remote administration. As long as you have administrative privileges, you can add users, delete users, and do other administrative
tasks from any OS/2 or LAN Manager Enhanced workstation. You do not
have to visit the file server to make your changes.

With share-level security, a feature of LAN Manager, you can set up a single
password to limit access to a shared resource or device. LAN Server does not
support share-level security.

Both LAN Manager and LAN Server use the concepts of domains and logon
security, but in slightly different ways. If you want to use LAN Manager and

LAN Server on the same physical network, you should set up separate domains for each network operating system. In one domain, all file servers should run LAN Manager, or all file servers should run LAN Server. You should ensure that workstations in a LAN Server domain log in to a LAN Server domain before trying to access LAN Manager file servers. Workstations in a LAN Manager domain, however, can log on in any domain.

LAN Server can use *aliases* (nicknames) for shared resources, but LAN Manager cannot. LAN Manager workstations must refer to the shared resources by their full name, not by the alias. Suppose that you have a LAN Server machine named PRODUCTION that shares a printer with an alias of REPORTS. The full name of the shared printer is \\PRODUCTION\PRINTER1. LAN Server workstations can share REPORTS, but LAN Manager workstations must use the full name \\PRODUCTION\PRINTER1 to access that printer.

LAN Manager and LAN Server interoperate well on a Token Ring LAN, but not on an Ethernet LAN. On Ethernet networks, you may need to modify both network operating systems' configurations. LAN Server supports both the Digital Intel Xerox (DIX) Version 2.0 protocol and the IEEE 802.3 protocol; LAN Manager does not support DIX. On Ethernet, you need to switch LM and LS to use IEEE 802.3 so that workstations can use both kinds of file servers.

LAN Manager is 16-bit software, whereas Windows NT AS and LAN Server are 32-bit software. As the numbers 16 and 32 imply, these last two products should theoretically do a better job of managing the 32-bit CPU chips that you find in the faster, more capable computers you can buy today. The LAN Server product is indeed a good performer, but Windows NT uses an operating system architecture that insulates the network software from the network adapter with many layers of intervening software. The result, according to benchmarks published by *PC Week* and *PC Magazine*, is that Windows NT AS is slower than either NetWare or LAN Server. Windows NT AS also takes up considerably more disk space and memory than either LAN Manager or LAN Server. Microsoft is working to make Windows NT AS a faster, smaller network operating system.

The Next Version of LAN Server

As this book went to press, IBM was working on a new version of LAN Server. IBM probably will release this new version of LAN Server, probably called LAN Server 4.0, late in 1994. IBM has not announced the availability of the software, nor has IBM made any claims about the features that will be in Version 4.0. However, IBM provided me with a list of features that you may see in the new version.

III

Networking Software

LAN Server Version 4.0 will likely have a graphical (point and click) interface to replace the text-mode interface of earlier versions. IBM would like LS 4.0 to have better security than earlier versions, and LAN administrators will probably be able to monitor and manage multiple domains of the network from one workstation. LS 4.0 will likely integrate the TCP/IP transport layer protocol as well as NetBIOS. IBM is rewriting the manuals that come with the product and will almost certainly provide those manuals in machine-readable form on a CD-ROM disk. In general, IBM plans to make LS 4.0 easier to install and use, and LS 4.0 will likely take up less disk space and use less memory than earlier versions. The DOS/Windows client memory utilization will be improved significantly.

In contrast to Windows NT AS, LAN Server 4.0 will probably not have a BrowseMaster feature. While Microsoft believes that people should be able to point and click to share and use network resources, IBM believes that a LAN administrator, for security reasons, should designate those disk drives and printers that are shared on the network, and that people should use just those designated shared resources. As mentioned earlier in this chapter, Microsoft's resource-browsing feature lets you point and click to create a new connection between your workstation and a shared disk or printer resource. Browsing for shared resources might seem like a handy and useful feature, but in reality the browsing can cause confusion when people forget which drive letter they've mapped to a file server directory. Browsing for resources can also result in a workstation exhausting the number of NetBIOS commands and NetBIOS sessions available to that workstation.

Pricing LAN Manager, Windows NT, and LAN Server

For more information about Microsoft's LAN Manager and Windows NT Advanced Server products, contact the following:

> Microsoft Corporation
> One Microsoft Way
> Redmond, WA 98052
> (800) 426-9400

For more information about IBM's LAN Server, contact the following:

> IBM
> Old Orchard Road
> Armonk, NY 10504
> (800) 426-2468

Summary

You looked at the almost-twins LAN Manager and LAN Server in this chapter. These two network operating systems from Microsoft and IBM look and behave alike but have subtle differences that you're now aware of. You understand why these products lend themselves to client/server architecture, you know why NetWare sells better, and you are familiar with the principles and concepts on which LAN Manager and LAN Server are based. You have also become acquainted with Windows NT Advanced Server. You have explored what these products look like, how they operate, and what they can offer in the way of advantages and benefits for your office.

In Chapter 9, you turn your attention to peer LAN products such as NetWare Lite Personal NetWare, Windows for Workgroups, POWERLan, and LANtastic.

Chapter 9

Using Peer LANs

Many more peer LAN network operating system products exist than server-based products. If you think that a peer LAN will meet your needs, you have a wide range of products to choose from. This chapter looks at five of the most popular of these products: Windows for Workgroups, a combination of Microsoft Windows and a peer LAN; Personal NetWare and NetWare Lite, Novell's low-cost peer-to-peer alternatives to its server-based high-end products; the peer LAN market-leading LANtastic from Artisoft; and the high-quality POWERLan software from Performance Technology. If you want to explore other peer LAN products, the list of peer LAN vendors in Chapter 2 is an excellent starting place.

A peer LAN enables every workstation to be a file server and vice versa. As Chapter 1, "A Networking Overview," explains, you don't need to dedicate a separate computer to be the file server on a peer LAN, which makes a peer LAN comparatively inexpensive. You will, however, notice slower performance if you have more than a few workstations or if the work consists of more than just word processing and light record keeping. Peer LANs are great for small workgroups that put only a light workload on the network. Naturally, some peer LAN network operating systems perform better than others.

Slow performance isn't the only problem you might encounter on a peer LAN. If someone runs an application on a PC that's acting as both server and workstation, and if that application locks up the PC, other people on the LAN (who are using that PC as a file server) may lose their work and will have to wait until the PC reboots before they resume using the network. Making backup copies of files in a peer LAN environment can be a problem, too. If files are scattered among several server/workstation PCs in a disorganized fashion, you run the risk of omitting important files from your daily backup procedures.

> ## Which Workstation Is Which?
>
> You can organize a peer LAN in myriad combinations of shared drives and printers. Keeping track of workstations, cable connections, and drive letters helps you avoid confusion on any LAN (peer or server-based). On a peer LAN, such good habits are especially important. You want your efforts and expense to be well spent. Organization is the key.
>
> Unfortunately, peer LANs are not completely self-documenting. In other words, the burden of knowing which drive letter denotes which workstation's hard disk is solely yours. You can help yourself by naming each workstation and attaching to each computer a label that shows its name. Because many peer LAN products enable you to refer to workstations by name, you can use the labels you attach to the workstations to remind you where your information resides.

Using Windows for Workgroups

Windows for Workgroups is a combination of Microsoft Windows 3.1, a peer-to-peer network operating system, an electronic mail application, and an appointment book application. The network operating system software is built into Windows. The electronic mail software is Microsoft Mail, and the appointment book software is Schedule+. The Windows SETUP program installs the latter two software products in the Main program group.

If you are part of a small team of people who are accustomed to using applications in a Windows 386 Enhanced mode environment, Windows for Workgroups can help the team share information. This means that the members of the team can store files in one or more common directories that everyone can access. A common directory might be on one of the team member's PCs or on a separate, unattended PC used just for file storage. With most applications, however, only one team member at a time can access a given file. To provide concurrent access to files, you need to purchase multiuser software.

People who use Windows for Workgroups can share printers as well as disk files. Through File Manager and Print Manager, you designate the PCs that should share disk directories and those that should share printers. When you share a disk directory or printer from a PC, you give the shared resource a name by which other team members can refer to that resource. Other members establish connections to shared resources by also using File Manager and Print Manager. Establishing the connection assigns a new drive letter (perhaps D:) to a shared directory and, for a shared printer, redirects the parallel printer port (LPT1) across the LAN to the shared printer. You can tell Windows for Workgroups to remember the connections you established. Windows for Workgroups automatically re-creates each connection when you start Windows.

With your new drive letter(s) and printer(s), you can work with files on other PCs as though those files existed on your PC's hard disk. When you print, the pages appear on the shared printer. You have access to shared directories and printers from within both Windows and the DOS applications you run in a Windows DOS session, through either the MS-DOS Prompt icon or a PIF file.

Windows for Workgroups is somewhat compatible with NetWare. You might use Windows for Workgroups to supplement an existing NetWare LAN. A small team of people, for example, can use Windows applications and Windows for Workgroups within the context of the team, yet retain access to the NetWare file server. You also can use Windows for Workgroups on a LAN that already is running Microsoft LAN Manager. On a server-based NetWare or LAN Manager network, Windows for Workgroups adds convenient peer-to-peer networking functions. Figure 9.1 shows the Windows for Workgroups screen you use to change your network settings and load support for a server-based network such as NetWare.

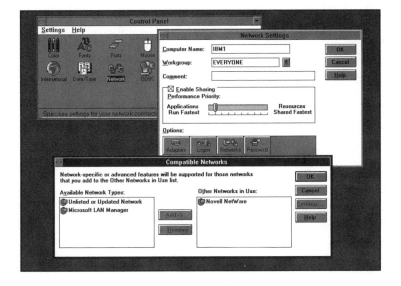

Fig. 9.1
Configuring Windows for Workgroups as part of a server-based network.

III

Networking Software

Windows for Workgroups runs best on an 80386-, 80486-, or Pentium (80586)-based computer with at least 8M of RAM. (Microsoft suggests at least 4M, but you'll see better performance with 8M or more.) On an earlier CPU chip or without sufficient memory, Windows for Workgroups executes in Standard mode instead of 386 Enhanced mode. You can share files only if Windows is running in Enhanced mode. In Standard mode or outside Windows, your computer cannot share its files with other people on your team.

Your PC needs MS-DOS or PC DOS Version 3.3 or later to run Windows for Workgroups. DOS Version 5.0 or 6.2 is best. You should have about 15M of free disk space to install Windows for Workgroups, plus 10M to 20M of free disk space that Windows can use for its swap file. To take advantage of Windows's graphical user interface, you need a VGA, SuperVGA, 8514/A, or XGA video adapter and an appropriate color monitor. And, of course, it's easier to use Windows if you have a mouse.

Microsoft offers a Windows for Workgroups Starter Kit that contains two Ethernet network adapter cards, 25 feet of LAN cabling, a videotape that explains how to install and use the Starter Kit, and a two-license copy of Windows for Workgroups software. You also can buy User Kits that provide additional licenses and network adapters.

The Workgroup Connection for DOS package consists of non-Windows, DOS-only software. Workgroup Connection for DOS permits PCs that can't or don't run Windows to access resources shared by computers that are running Windows for Workgroups. The converse isn't true, however; Workgroup Connection for DOS machines can't make their disk drives and printers available to other machines on the LAN.

Sharing and Using Files

On each of the computers that you designate as file servers, you tell Windows for Workgroups the name of the directory to be shared. You give each shared directory a share name. At a workstation that will use the shared directory resource, you connect to the resource by referring to its share name.

You use File Manager to share a directory on a PC running Windows for Workgroups in 386 Enhanced mode. Click the Main program group and then double-click File Manager. Choose Share As from the Disk menu to display the Share Directory dialog box, which you use to allow others to access the entire hard drive, a directory, a CD-ROM drive, or a floppy disk drive.

In the Share Directory dialog box, you enter a Share Name—the name by which a shared resource will be known on the LAN. The Path field specifies the drive letter and directory of the shared resource. If you want the resource to be shared automatically when Windows for Workgroups starts, check the Re-share at Startup check box. You have three options for setting up security for the resource: Read-Only, Full, and Depends on Password. Read-Only access grants people at other workstations the right to view files but not to delete or change them. Read-Only access also prevents anyone from creating directories below the shared resource directory name. Full access allows other people to view, edit, and delete files and to create or remove directories. If you use the Depends on Password option, you can give Read-Only access to some people and Full access to others. A person at another computer on the LAN obtains the appropriate level of access by entering a password that matches the Read-Only or Full access password you designate. The default Share Name is the current directory name. The default Path is the current drive and directory. By default, the Re-share at Startup and Read-Only options are selected.

The Connect Network Drive dialog box has a Drive field, a Path field, and a Reconnect at Startup check box. With these items, you can create new drive letters to use in your application software programs. This process is called *mapping* a network drive letter.

In the Drive field, you indicate the DOS drive letter you want to use. Normally, you should use the next available drive letter after those already assigned by DOS and those already mapped. You should not attempt to map a drive letter that is already assigned (or mapped). The range of drive letters extends from A: to the value of LASTDRIVE as specified in your CONFIG.SYS file. The DOS default for LASTDRIVE usually is E:, but the Windows for Workgroups SETUP program modifies the CONFIG.SYS file to contain the entry LASTDRIVE=Q. If you like, you can change your CONFIG.SYS file with a text editor to show LASTDRIVE=Z, but this means that you won't be able to map drives on a NetWare file server, if one is present. The Drive field shows File Manager's suggestion for a drive letter you can map. In the Path field, you specify both the computer name and the network name of the resource you want to map to a drive letter.

Printing with Windows for Workgroups

Just as File Manager is your tool for setting up shared file resources, Print Manager is your tool for both sharing and connecting to printers. When you installed Windows for Workgroups on PCs with printers attached, you identified the printer to the SETUP program. When you click Print Manager (in the Main group), Print Manager displays the list of attached printers. To share a printer in the list across the network, click the printer and choose Share Printer As from the Printer menu.

III

Networking Software

The resulting Share Printer dialog box contains the name of the printer, which you can change if you highlighted the wrong printer in the Print Manager list. This dialog box also contains a suggested network name in the Share As field, a Comment field, a Password field, and a Re-share at Startup check box. The available pushbuttons are OK, Cancel, and Help. You can change the network name, if you like, and the Comment field is a good place to describe the typical kinds of printouts the printer will produce. If you want the PC to be a dedicated print server, you should click the Re-share at Startup check box to cause Windows for Workgroups to make the printer available whenever Windows for Workgroups is running. Click OK to finish making the printer a LAN resource.

From a Windows for Workgroups workstation, you use Print Manager to create the connection to a shared printer. Choose Connect Network Printer from the Printer menu. Print Manager displays the Connect Network Printer dialog box.

The Connect Network Printer dialog box contains a Device Name field, a Path field, and a Reconnect at Startup check box. Also included is a list of workgroups and computers that currently share resources. As you click, from the first list, the name of a computer that is sharing a printer, the name of the printer appears in the second list. Clicking the name of the printer causes Print Manager to construct the network name of the printer in the Path field. If the printer is a resource that usually is available on the network, you'll likely want to check the Reconnect at Startup check box.

Learning Other Windows for Workgroups Features

Windows for Workgroups enables you to eliminate or reduce the hard-copy (paper-based) interoffice mail that you and other team members exchange. As Chapter 3, "Using Electronic Mail," explains, you can use Microsoft Mail to send and receive computer files that take the place of handwritten or typed notes. If you simply want to ask someone a question and you know that the person is currently using Windows on his or her computer, you can use the Chat program within Windows for Workgroups to get your answer.

The Schedule+ software included with Windows for Workgroups enables you to maintain an electronic appointment book. The software can display differ-ent views of your appointment book, including the appointments for a par-ticular day, general tasks (your to-do list), and the blocks of time represented by your scheduled activities. You can share your appointment book across the LAN. Sharing appointment books makes it possible for Schedule+ to coor-dinate the times when people on the team can get together for a meeting.

The Windows for Workgroups SETUP program installs Schedule+ in the Main program group. To begin using Schedule+, double-click the Schedule+ icon and, if you're not currently running the Mail program, sign in with your mail account name (mailbox name) and password.

The main Schedule+ screen is a computerized representation of a page in an appointment book. The page shows section tabs on the left side of the screen, a list of time slots containing entries for the day's scheduled activities in the center of the page, a calendar page in the top-right corner, and a place to write notes in the bottom-right corner.

You, or someone you designate, can use the displayed pages of the appointment book to maintain your daily schedule, jot notes about meetings, and request meetings with other people who also use Schedule+. An appointment (meeting) can be a single, recurring, or tentative event. You can allocate blocks of time for work you need to get done; other people who use Schedule+ won't be able to set up meetings with you during these blocked-off times.

In addition to the main Schedule+ screen—a day in your appointment book—the task list and planner views are available. You use the task list to make notes about work you are responsible for or are supposed to do. You categorize your work into projects and tasks, and you give the projects and their tasks priorities and due dates. As tasks are completed, change priority, or slip (become overdue), you can update the task list accordingly.

The planner view shows blocks of time for several days—a week or two, depending on the width of the planner screen. The easiest way to schedule a meeting with other people who use Schedule+ is through planner view. As you select the names of people you want to attend a meeting, information from their appointment books flows onto your planner view. You see at a glance when all the people are available for a meeting.

Windows for Workgroups also comes with WinMeter and NetWatcher. You use WinMeter to monitor how much of your computer's processing power other people are using. With NetWatcher, you can see who is connected to your PC and which of your files other people are accessing.

For more information about Microsoft Windows for Workgroups, contact the following:

> Microsoft Corporation
> One Microsoft Way
> Redmond, WA 98052
> (800) 426-9400

III

Networking Software

Using Personal NetWare and NetWare Lite

Novell's server-based LAN operating systems, NetWare 2.2 and NetWare 3.1x, have for several years outsold their competitors by a wide margin. Novell hasn't yet sold many copies of the newer NetWare Version 4.0. In the peer LAN arena, during the period in which Novell established market leadership with NetWare 2.2 and 3.1x, a group of smaller companies competed among themselves for market share—pricing, characterizing, and sizing their products to suit smaller groups for whom server-based NetWare was too expensive. In the fall of 1991, Novell introduced a peer LAN network operating system, NetWare Lite, to complement its server-based products and to compete in the growing market for peer LANs. Like the other companies' peer LAN products, NetWare Lite is DOS-based. You can turn your existing DOS computers into a network in which any PC can be both server and workstation. At your option, however, you can dedicate one of the computers on the LAN as a NetWare Lite file server.

Two years later, in the fall of 1993, Novell redesigned its peer LAN product and renamed it Personal NetWare. Novell continues to sell NetWare Lite to companies that already use Lite and need to add more PCs to an existing NetWare Lite LAN. But Novell doesn't plan to enhance NetWare Lite with additional features and functions; instead, Novell will focus on Personal NetWare.

Figure 9.2 shows the NetWare Lite product, and figure 9.3 shows the Personal NetWare utility that you use to map drive letters in the Windows environment. This section focuses on the newer Personal NetWare, but much of the discussion also applies to NetWare Lite.

Smaller workgroups can cost-justify a Personal NetWare LAN if the server-based NetWare 2.2 is not in the budget. NetWare Lite costs $99 per workstation for the software. Compare that product with NetWare 2.2, which costs $895 for five users and $1,995 for 10 users, plus the expense of a dedicated file-server computer.

Personal NetWare is copy-protected, but no laser holes are burned into the distribution disks. Instead, when you start Personal NetWare at a workstation, the software communicates with the other workstations to see whether the software is already running at another workstation. The same copy of Personal NetWare, from the same distribution disk, refuses to run on two workstations simultaneously. This network-based copy-protection scheme is the least intrusive and easiest to administer. As more software becomes LAN-aware, the old, annoying methods of copy protection will vanish; and interworkstation serial-number checks, such as those used by Personal NetWare, will become common.

Fig. 9.2
NetWare Lite from Novell, an easy-to-use peer LAN network operating system.

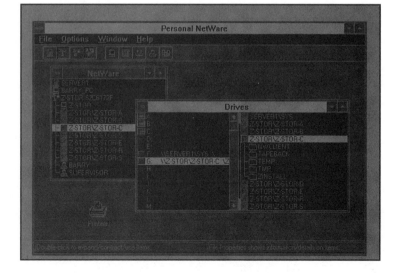

Fig. 9.3
Mapping drives with Personal NetWare in a Windows environment.

For Personal NetWare technical support, Novell offers several options:

- You can fax your inquires directly to Novell.

- You can use the NetWare forum on CompuServe. (You must purchase a CompuServe starter kit, own a modem and communication software, and pay connect-time fees to use CompuServe.)

- You can ask your dealer to answer your questions.

- You can pay for Novell technical support on a per-incident basis or purchase support for a specified number of incidents. Your first 30 days of technical support, starting with your initial telephone call, are free.

In the following sections, you learn how Personal NetWare compares in the categories of performance, ease of use, features, security, and memory usage. First, the chapter presents an overview of Personal NetWare so that you understand what the software can and cannot do.

Capabilities

To use Personal NetWare, you need a workgroup of 2 to 25 computers. Each computer that will serve as a file server must have a hard disk. Personal NetWare runs inside conventional memory (it is a terminate-and-stay-resident program) and does not require extended or expanded memory. If you have extended memory in your PC, however, you can load the Personal NetWare modules into high memory. Novell recommends that you have 640K of conventional memory in the workstations. You need to purchase a copy of Personal NetWare for each workstation.

You need one network adapter for each workstation, along with cables, connectors, and terminators. The documentation you get with the network adapters tells you how to configure and install the adapters and cables. Finally, you need the device driver software that enables Personal NetWare to communicate with the adapter. Novell supplies several such drivers with Personal NetWare, and network adapter manufacturers supply a disk containing third-party drivers with each adapter. Personal NetWare works with any drivers that comply with Novell's Open Datalink Interface (ODI) standard, as does NetWare Lite.

Personal NetWare and NetWare Lite interoperate with NetWare 2.2, 3.12, and 4.0. For Lite, you simply run NET*x*.COM in addition to the Lite software, and then you log on to the NetWare file server as usual. Lite comes with ODI (Novell's Open Datalink Interface) drivers for a variety of network adapters and works with any adapter that supplies an ODI driver. Personal NetWare uses Novell's VLM (virtual loadable module) software technology to manage the loading of the ODI drivers and redirector functions.

Before you install Personal NetWare, you should plan which computers will share what resources. You may, for example, want to designate only certain computers as file servers, and you may not want to share every printer in the office. Drawing a diagram that indicates which computers' hard disks and printers will become public resources is helpful. Label the file server comput- ers, indicating how their hard disks and directories are mapped, and label also the shared printers. Post the drawing in the office so that everyone can visu- alize the LAN's resources. Organizing your LAN and communicating that organization to the people who use the network will go a long way toward reducing confusion.

Installing Personal NetWare consists of running the INSTALL.EXE program on the first distribution floppy disk. As you perform the installation, you should label each distribution disk with the name of the computer on which you install that copy of the software. Later, if you have to reinstall Personal NetWare on a particular workstation, you will know what disk to use, thus averting trouble with Personal NetWare's built-in copy-protection scheme.

When you start (boot) a Personal NetWare workstation, you run a BAT file— STARTNET.BAT—to load the network software and initiate the login process. The installation process creates the STARTNET.BAT file for you. You can use a text editor to place the contents of the STARTNET.BAT file in your AUTOEXEC.BAT file, if you want. At the DOS prompt, you log on to the net- work by typing **NET LOGIN** and providing your user ID and password. You now are connected to the LAN, but you have not yet mapped drive letters or set up your printer redirections. You can use Personal NetWare's menu-based NET command to choose drives and printers from a series of menus, or you can use command-line parameters to issue a set of commands to set up your drives and printers. These commands can, of course, reside in a BAT file that you run after logging on.

Personal NetWare commands, menus, and command-line options enable you to perform the following tasks:

- Display the audit log
- Save the audit log to a file
- Turn auditing on or off

- Synchronize the system date and time of each computer on the LAN

- Create or modify network directories

- Map drive letters

- Display the error log

- Save the error log to a file

- Receive messages (one-line notes)

- Send messages

- Set your password

- Capture printer ports and control your print jobs

- Configure network printers

- Back up and restore system files

- Change file server configuration

- Display server status

- Create, modify, or delete user accounts (user IDs)

- Display your user account

The Personal NetWare manual explains each of these tasks in simple terms and tells you when you should perform each task. The manual also identifies the authorization level you must have to perform the task. For example, you must have server-management rights if you need to use the NET DOWN command to stop the SERVER program that is running on a PC.

Performance

The performance tests determine NetWare Lite's network file I/O performance and Personal NetWare's network file I/O performance by reading and writing files of random sizes. POWERLan (described in the section "Using POWERLan" later in this chapter) won the race by outdistancing both Personal NetWare and NetWare Lite (see table 9.1).

Table 9.1 Performance of POWERLan versus NetWare Lite and Personal NetWare		
POWERLan 3.0	**NetWare Lite 1.1**	**Personal NetWare**
Baseline, on workstation's local drive:		
Read 10.20	11.03	10.95
Write 8.60	8.95	8.15
Remotely with one workstation, treating the workstation as a server:		
Read 17.90	25.40	26.25
Write 12.05	15.43	15.00
Remotely, under load and with concurrent activity from four workstations:		
Read 29.10	41.09	38.85
Write 18.90	34.78	34.12

Note: Smaller numbers represent shorter times and faster performance.

These tests used a LAN based on Thomas-Conrad's 100-mbps, fiber-optic-based TCNS hardware, with 33 MHz 486 ALR PowerPro and 33 MHz 386 Gateway 2000 computers as peer servers and workstations. Certainly, with 100-mbps fiber optics and fast workstations such as these, the hardware was not a limiting factor. A 32K RAM cache was set up with SMARTDRV.SYS, which comes with DOS 5.0 and later. All the computers were rebooted before each test to make the tests as fair as possible.

When asked why NetWare Lite was slower, a Novell spokesperson said that Lite is designed for simple operation and ease of use, not speed.

The final tests performed PC-to-PC communications, using both NetBIOS and IPX programming techniques. Third-party LAN utilities, remote control, and some electronic mail packages use these protocols to talk PC to PC. Personal NetWare and NetWare Lite passed the tests in this category with flying colors, and these two products are the only peer LAN NOSs that provide both IPX and NetBIOS protocols.

Ease of Use

Easy installation, ease of use, and simplicity are hallmarks of Personal NetWare and NetWare Lite. The easy-to-read NetWare Lite manual uses metaphors based on how a railroad works to explain LAN basics, making difficult concepts clear through illustrations. Lite's on-line help facility also is clear and comprehensive. The Personal NetWare manual, by contrast, does not

III

Networking Software

include a simplistic metaphor to explain the operation of Personal NetWare. Instead, the manual contains an introductory discussion of local area networks and a large reference section detailing the operation of individual Personal NetWare commands and utilities.

You share directories and printers on each designated server by using simple commands or menus. The menus are clear, direct, and virtually foolproof. Lite is generally compatible with Microsoft Windows, although for Windows (and any applications you install), you must specify "no network" or "MS/Network compatible" instead of the usual "NetWare network" setup option. Personal NetWare integrates itself more completely into a Windows environment and can even coexist with Windows for Workgroups.

Features

Personal NetWare and Lite support up to 25 users—somewhat fewer than other peer LAN products. There is no technical reason why Personal NetWare and NetWare Lite could not support more users, but Novell reasons that you will switch to regular NetWare when your LAN grows to 25 users. Personal NetWare and NetWare Lite do not recognize an uninterruptible power supply. You can, however, share a CD-ROM drive across your network with both products. Each workstation must have a floppy or hard drive from which the Lite software will be run. Lite does not support remote boot, but you can use remote boot (with diskless workstations, for example) with Personal NetWare.

If you press Ctrl-Alt-Del at a server, Personal NetWare and NetWare Lite ask whether you are sure you want to reboot the computer. Afterward, you can reconnect NetWare Lite workstations to the rebooted server, but only by choosing Retry at this DOS message:

```
Abort, Retry, Ignore?
```

Personal NetWare handles disconnections in a friendlier, more foolproof manner. Personal NetWare automatically attempts to reestablish lost connections to a server that you rebooted.

Printing to a shared printer is easy with Personal NetWare and NetWare Lite. At a workstation, you use a NET CAPTURE command to redirect data to a remote printer. You can specify whether you want a banner page (job-separator page) printed, the number of copies to print, whether the network software should append a formfeed to the print stream, the amount of idle time Lite should use to detect the end of the print operation (in case the application does not actually close the LPTx file when it finishes printing), the setup string that the network software should use as a prefix to the print material, and other print parameters. You can view or change the print queue; Personal NetWare and NetWare Lite display job number, user, job name, and job status so that you can check the progress of your printout.

Security

Your data is as secure with Personal NetWare and NetWare Lite as with regular NetWare. For each user, you can enable or disable the account, grant or revoke supervisor (management) privileges, require passwords, set the minimum number of characters and expiration date of the password, and delete accounts. For each directory, you can specify default access rights and single out those users who should have nondefault access rights. In a Personal NetWare environment, you can choose to have no security at all. You do this by changing the STARTNET.BAT file to *not* load the security module. You save some workstation memory by not loading the security module, but then all workstations have full access to the shared resources of that server.

Memory Usage

Novell programmers tried to make Personal NetWare and NetWare Lite take up as little memory as possible. The various Lite modules take a total of 95.8K on a server machine—13.8K of adapter support software (including IPX), 13K of client software, 63K of server software, and 6K of SHARE.EXE. On a nonpeer, client-only workstation, Lite uses only 26.8K of RAM. You can load all the modules, including the server code, into upper memory on a 386 computer by using a memory manager, such as QEMM or 386Max. With DOS 5.0 (or later) also loaded into upper memory, Lite leaves 635K of conventional memory available for running applications, even while you are logged on to the Lite LAN.

Personal NetWare's virtual loadable modules consume 151K on a server—30K of adapter support and IPX, 71K of server software, and 50K of VLM and requester software. On a client-only machine, Personal NetWare uses 80K of RAM. You can load all the Personal NetWare modules in upper memory.

Summarizing Personal NetWare and NetWare Lite

Personal NetWare is not the cheapest or the fastest LAN operating system you can buy. (You should consider buying NetWare Lite only if you are adding workstations to an existing NetWare Lite LAN.) But Personal NetWare is easy to install, manage, and use. For a small first-time LAN or for peer access within a larger server-based NetWare LAN, Personal NetWare is an excellent choice.

III

Networking Software

Using LANtastic

Artisoft's LANtastic has been the peer LAN market leader for a long time in terms of sales and popularity. Novell, with its Personal NetWare product, and Microsoft, with Windows for Workgroups, obviously would like to penetrate the marketplace that Artisoft created. All these products are high-quality software, and it will be interesting to see which emerges as the most popular. POWERLan, discussed later in this chapter, also is a strong contender and may eclipse Personal NetWare, Windows for Workgroups, and LANtastic.

Artisoft endowed LANtastic with several convenient and useful features. LANtastic generally performs well, although it is not the fastest peer network operating system. LANtastic has excellent print-sharing capabilities. With optional hardware from Artisoft, you can even use voice mail on your LAN. You can share a CD-ROM drive on a LANtastic network. LANtastic uses very little (or none, in some cases) of the 640K of RAM. Artisoft sells Ethernet network adapters in addition to the network operating system; these adapters work especially well with LANtastic. You can connect Macintosh computers to a LANtastic-based LAN, and LANtastic also works well in a Microsoft Windows environment.

Technical support for LANtastic includes a bulletin board system you can dial into with your modem and the more customary telephone support from Artisoft's customer support department.

In the following sections, you learn how LANtastic compares in the categories of memory usage, performance, reliability, ease of use, security, and price. The discussion begins with an overview of LANtastic so that you understand what this peer LAN network operating system can and cannot do.

Capabilities

LANtastic has been a popular network operating system for several years. Version 4.0, released in July, 1991, added a true Windows application for managing your LANtastic network. If you are a Windows fan, LANtastic for Windows will appeal to you; it makes print-queue management, network management, electronic mail, and other tasks as simple as pointing and clicking.

Artisoft began selling Version 5.0 of LANtastic in March, 1993. This version adds compatibility with server-based NetWare LANs and the capability to share Windows applications' text and graphics data across the network. In April, 1994, Artisoft released Version 6.0 of LANtastic. The new version is slightly faster than previous versions of LANtastic and offers several Windows-based utilities for managing network resources. You even get a gateway to a digital text pager. Through paging devices that you buy separately, you can electronically page people who are away from their workstations.

Version 6.0 of LANtastic supports networkwide faxing of documents. You install a fax/modem (perhaps as an internal fax/modem adapter) in a server PC, load the optional LANtastic fax module, and let people on the LAN send and receive fax documents from their workstations. The new version of LANtastic offers more server-management tools, including the monitoring of RAM usage as you configure a server PC. The RAM-monitoring tool enables you to maximize the amount of memory that the server can use to respond to file service requests more quickly. Version 6.0 includes a built-in SHARE.EXE module (for enabling file sharing) that operates slightly faster than the SHARE.EXE that comes with DOS. A LANtastic server also will work with the DOS implementation of SHARE. LANtastic Version 6.0 works well in the presence of the server-based NetWare network operating system.

Previous versions of LANtastic were independent of network adapters. Beginning with Version 4.0, however, you need to buy special drivers (at $99 per workstation) if you want to use non-Artisoft network adapter cards with LANtastic. The list price of a LANtastic 16-bit Ethernet card is $299. If you are thinking of using a different card that costs less than $299 but more than $200, you will wind up paying more than if you had bought the Artisoft network adapter. The cost of the non-Artisoft network adapter plus the per-workstation cost of the "adapter independent" LANtastic driver would exceed the cost of an Artisoft adapter.

Artisoft markets LANtastic to companies with as few as two or as many as several hundred computers. Larger LANs, of course, suffer poorer performance because the underlying operating system on a LANtastic file server is DOS. Artisoft claims, however, that you can dedicate several computers on the LAN as LANtastic file servers and achieve reasonable performance.

LANtastic comes with many network utilities. You can use LANtastic's menu system to perform network tasks, or you can run these utilities from the DOS command line. You can chat with someone on the LAN through your keyboard, send electronic mail, start or stop the redirection of shared network devices, and perform administrative tasks. Artisoft also supplies a TSR module called LANPUP that enables you to use hot keys to access the network utility menu system.

III

Networking Software

Menus

When you run the LANtastic NET command without command-line parameters, you invoke the LANtastic menu system, and you see the NET Main Functions menu. The LANtastic menu offers the following options:

- Network Disk Drives and Printers

- Printer Queue Management

- Mail Services

- Chat with Another User

- Login or Logout

- User Account Management

- Display Server Activity

The first option, Network Disk Drives and Printers, enables you to select a file server and to enable or disable the sharing of a network drive or LAN printer. Figure 9.4 shows the list of devices redirected by LANtastic. The Printer Queue Management option displays print queue activity and enables you to control individual print jobs. If you have the appropriate network privileges, the display of print queue activity includes all print jobs from everyone on the LAN. Otherwise, you see only the print jobs you submitted.

Fig. 9.4

LANtastic's list of redirected devices.

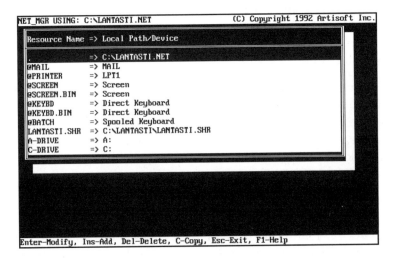

```
NET_MGR USING: C:\LANTASTI.NET              (C) Copyright 1992 Artisoft Inc.

 Resource Name => Local Path/Device

 .              => C:\LANTASTI.NET
 @MAIL          => MAIL
 @PRINTER       => LPT1
 @SCREEN        => Screen
 @SCREEN.BIN    => Screen
 @KEYBD         => Direct Keyboard
 @KEYBD.BIN     => Direct Keyboard
 @BATCH         => Spooled Keyboard
 LANTASTI.SHR   => C:\LANTASTI\LANTASTI.SHR
 A-DRIVE        => A:
 C-DRIVE        => C:




 Enter-Modify, Ins-Add, Del-Delete, C-Copy, Esc-Exit, F1-Help
```

Mail Services is the option you choose when you want to check a file server's mail queue for incoming electronic mail and send mail to other people.

You can send text files, and, if you have the necessary Artisoft hardware (a sound board at both the sending and receiving workstations), you can send voice mail files with your outgoing mail. The Chat with Another User option enables you and another person on the LAN to type messages to each other in real time.

You use the Login or Logout option to start and stop your sessions on the LAN. The User Account Management option enables you to change your password on a file server, disable your network account ID, or see the current status and configuration of your network account ID. You use the Display Server Activity option to find out who is logged on to a file server as well as what files those people are accessing. You can use this option to locate a file server that is less busy than the others.

Command-Line Utilities

You can run LANtastic's utilities at the DOS command-line prompt without using the menus. When you run the NET program with command-line parameters, NET performs the indicated network task without displaying a menu.

Table 9.2 lists the commands you can use on a LANtastic network. You precede each command with NET (by typing **NET ATTACH**, for example).

Table 9.2 LANtastic Network Commands	
Command	**Function**
ATTACH	Allocates all shared drives on the server.
AUDIT	Places an audit entry in the log file.
CHANGEPW	Changes your password.
CHAT	Enables you to type messages to another person.
CLOCK	Synchronizes your PC's clock with the server.
COPY	Tells the server to copy a file for you.
DETACH	Cancels disk drive redirection.
DIR	Like the DOS DIR command, but also displays non-DOS network file information and file attributes.
DISABLEA	Disables your account.

(continues)

Table 9.2 Continued	
Command	**Function**
EXPAND	Tells you the fully qualified path name for a file.
HELP	Provides on-line help.
INDIRECT	Enables you to create an *indirect file*, which contains a reference to a file in another directory. When you tell an application to use the indirect file, LANtastic, through redirection, actually gives the referenced file to the application. This command enables you to access files in other directories without changing the current directory.
LOGIN	Starts a network session.
LOGOUT	Ends a network session.
LPT TIMEOUT	Specifies the time LANtastic's print spooler should wait before assuming that an application has finished a printout.
MAIL	Sends electronic mail.
MESSAGE	Enables or disables notifications of incoming mail.
POSTBOX	Tells whether you have incoming mail.
PRINT	Like DOS PRINT, but sends the text file to the shared LAN printer.
QUEUE HALT	Stops the network print spooler.
QUEUE PAUSE	Temporarily stops the print spooler.
QUEUE RESTART	Resumes print spooler operation.
QUEUE STATUS	Shows print jobs in the print queue.
RECEIVE	Displays the most recent network message.
RUN	Executes a DOS program on a designated file-server computer.
SEND	Sends a one-line message to another person.
SHOW	Tells you the network configuration of your workstation, what servers (if any) you are logged on to, and the list of available servers.
SHUTDOWN	Schedules the stopping or rebooting of a file server.
UNUSE	Cancels disk drive or printer redirection.
USE	Redirects (maps) a drive letter to a server disk drive or sets up printer redirection.

Memory Usage

LANtastic needs only 34K in a workstation—3.2K for the driver software, 13.2K for NetBIOS, 5.1K for SHARE, and 12.5K for the redirector module. (The adapter support software downloads part of itself onto the LANtastic Ethernet network adapter.) The server module adds 26.5K, for a total of 60.5K. If you use LANtastic Ethernet network adapters and a memory manager to load LANtastic into upper memory on an 80386, 80486, or Pentium computer, use of conventional memory drops to zero; you can put all the LANtastic software modules in upper memory.

Performance

LANtastic is neither the fastest nor the slowest network operating system. LANcache, LANtastic's disk-caching program, can use conventional, expanded, or extended memory to help LANtastic file servers fill workstation requests more rapidly. You can tell LANcache how much memory it should use for file caching; the default setting uses all available expanded or extended memory. LANcache also has a delayed-write function that you can configure. With the delayed-write function, LANcache writes data to the disk drive several moments after receiving the data from a workstation. The file server, however, immediately tells the workstation that the data has been written. The person at the workstation can go back to work immediately after saving some data. If the office suffers a power failure or if the file server crashes, the person may lose some data and would have to reenter it later.

The older LANcache Version 3 had a nasty habit of corrupting hard disks, but Artisoft has fixed the problem in Version 4 and later versions.

Reliability

LANtastic correctly implements file sharing, record locking, NetBIOS connectivity, and other LAN functions. Applications that you run on a LANtastic network should work well especially if they are LAN-aware. LANtastic recognizes an uninterruptible power supply (UPS) and will gracefully shut down operations if the UPS batteries begin to fade before power is restored.

Version 6.0 of LANtastic has an automatic-reconnect feature that helps workstations reestablish connections to a server PC that you rebooted. Earlier versions of LANtastic often had trouble reconnecting workstations to the network.

Ease of Use

LANtastic is easy to install and administer. The documentation is clear and easy to follow, but finding things in the index sometimes is difficult. The

III

Networking Software

manual does not mention that you need to use LOADFIX to install LANtastic under DOS 5.0 or later. This problem is a small oversight on Artisoft's part, but one that may cause you some puzzlement and annoyance during installation.

As you can tell from the list of NET commands provided in table 9.2 earlier in this chapter, you can accomplish virtually every network task with LANtastic. With its on-line help feature, LANtastic makes network administration and day-to-day network use fairly simple and painless.

Security

You can set up as much or as little security on a LANtastic network as you need. After creating each network user, you can use the Windows interface to point and click as you grant permissions and rights on the LAN. Alternatively, you can use the NET_MGR command to administer security. Either way, you must have system administrator privileges to change LANtastic security.

The NET_MGR command requires a special password; this is LANtastic's first line of defense in its security system. Artisoft recommends that LAN users change their passwords at periodic intervals, and you can tell LANtastic to enforce this recommendation. You can allow or disallow access to various directory structures on the file server. You can use LANtastic's audit trail feature to monitor file server access. You can even set the days of the week and times of day during which each user account can log on to the network.

Price

Artisoft offers the Ethernet starter kit—two 16-bit Ethernet cards, a 25-foot coaxial cable, connectors, terminators, and software for up to 300 users—for $699. You pay $99 per workstation if you want to use the network-adapter-independent version of LANtastic.

Summarizing LANtastic

LANtastic is small, reasonably fast, and generally reliable. If you plan to use both DOS-based and Macintosh personal computers on your LAN, LANtastic is a good choice for your network operating system. For more information about LANtastic, contact the following:

Artisoft, Inc.
575 East River Road
Tucson, AZ 85704
(602) 293-6363

Using POWERLan

In 1985, a group of technical experts left Datapoint (creator of ARCnet) to form Performance Technology. These people designed and developed a range of networking products, including POWERLan.

The fastest peer-to-peer network operating system, POWERLan comes with many features, including a version of the Office Logic product for electronic mail. You buy a POWERLan license for 5, 15, or an unlimited number of connections, but the restriction applies to only the number of simultaneous connections to dedicated servers. For peer-to-peer (no dedicated file-server computer) LANs, the 5-user version ($795) supports the NetBIOS maximum of 255 nodes. POWERLan offers significant interoperability and connectivity if you have UNIX, LAN Manager, or LAN Server computers on your LAN. And POWERLan users within the larger context of a NetWare LAN can access a NetWare file server as well as a POWERLan server. Figure 9.5 shows the POWERLan product.

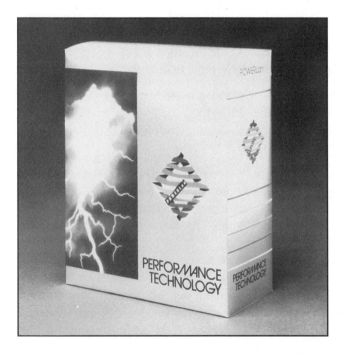

Fig. 9.5
POWERLan is a fast peer LAN network operating system that works with many other companies' network software products.

POWERLan achieves its performance through well-written software; the NetBIOS implementation is one of the best on the market. You can access shared disk drives and printers under Windows 3.x, and you can use POWERLan with Version 3.3 or later versions of DOS.

Technical support for POWERLan is available from Performance Technology's customer support department by telephone or through a modem-based bulletin board system.

In the following sections, you learn how POWERLan compares in the categories of memory usage, reliability, ease of use, security, performance, and price. First, the chapter presents an overview of POWERLan so that you understand what this network operating system can and cannot do.

Capabilities

POWERLan consists of a set of terminate-and-stay-resident (TSR) software modules. Depending on the peer LAN services you want a computer to have, you select the modules that provide the set of services you choose. These modules provide workstation connectivity (through NetBIOS), the capability to map a DOS drive letter to represent another computer's disk drive, printer redirection, printer sharing, and file sharing.

The POWERLan network operating system is both versatile and rich in features. A POWERLan file server recognizes signals from an uninterruptible power supply (UPS) and performs a graceful shutdown when the UPS batteries run out. You can share CD-ROM drives across the network, and POWERLan has an extensive on-line help system.

POWERLan's print-queue manager enables you to see what is in the print queue and tells you when the printer is off-line or out of paper. Queue-maintenance tasks, such as changing print job priorities and canceling print jobs, are easy.

The Performance Technology programmers decided to use the IBM-standard Server Message Block (SMB) protocol to transfer file I/O requests from the workstation to a file server and back. This means that POWERLan interoperates with a LAN Server, LAN Manager, or other SMB-based network. Users can access both networks simultaneously simply by mapping drive letters to the different kinds of servers. POWERLan comes with special redirector modules that enable POWERLan to coexist on a NetWare LAN. If you have UNIX computers on your network, you will be interested in Performance Technology's POWERfusion product (described in Chapter 10, "Using UNIX LANs").

One of the POWERLan utilities, Navigate, is an excellent tool for managing directories and files on the LAN (see fig. 9.6). With its sliding window interface, Navigate enables you to browse through an entire file server to locate and view shared files and resources. You also can use Navigate to manage your local hard disk.

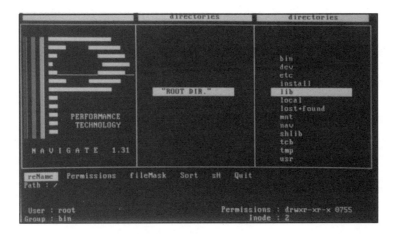

Fig. 9.6
POWERLan's Navigate utility helps you find your way around the directories and files on a file server.

POWERLan supports more than 45 Ethernet and ARCnet network adapters from 22 vendors. (The software device drivers are bundled with the product.) POWERLan is compatible with ODI and NDIS network adapter drivers, and you can run POWERLan on a Token Ring network. Figure 9.7 shows one of the POWERLan installation screens.

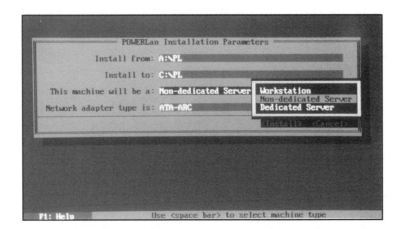

Fig. 9.7
POWERLan installation is simple and menu-driven.

Memory Usage

A POWERLan workstation requires NetBIOS, Redirector, Server, and the DOS SHARE programs. You select other modules at installation time for printer sharing, disk caching, and workstation remote control (POWERView). Without loading POWERLan into upper memory, you will have about 504K of

RAM free in which to run applications. The DOS program SHARE takes 5.1K, POWERLan NetBIOS takes 29K, the Redirector takes 15K, and the Server module takes 20K—for a total of 69.1K. On an 80386 computer, you can load all of POWERLan except NetBIOS in high memory. In this configuration, you can have about 597K free for DOS applications.

Reliability

POWERLan passes all LAN compatibility tests. It correctly implements DOS file sharing, record locking, machine-name retrieval, and remote-drive-detection functions. In tests, POWERLan's NetBIOS also behaves properly. You should have no trouble running LAN-aware applications with POWERLan.

Ease of Use

The brief user manuals lack screen illustrations but otherwise are helpful and to the point. The character-based POWERLan user interface complies with IBM's Systems Application Architecture/Common User Access (SAA/CUA) specifications, offering pull-down menus and dialog boxes to guide you through your network tasks. You can use POWERLan in command-line mode, if you prefer.

Security

POWERLan offers a range of security options. You can assign passwords to shared printers; grant users read, write, and create rights for disk drives and directories (but not for individual files); dole out privileges that allow or restrict multiple concurrent server logins; and otherwise protect your data. You designate one or several server PCs as logon servers; these specially designated machines authenticate the logon operations that each workstation performs. POWERLan encrypts the passwords as they flow through the LAN wire, making it difficult for an intruder to break into the network. On a dedicated file server, you can specify a password that a person must enter before he or she can type commands at that server. You can restrict a logon account to use the LAN only on certain days or at certain times, and you can set expiration dates on passwords to make sure that users change their passwords frequently.

Performance

The speediest of the peer LAN network operating systems, POWERLan consists of well-designed and well-written software. Performance Technology bundles with POWERLan a disk-caching program that you can install at dedicated file servers. The cache program can use up to 32M of expanded memory to make POWERLan perform even better.

You can use POWERLan in larger organizations to do more work in situations in which other peer LAN products would degrade the productivity of network users.

Price

The cost for unlimited peer-to-peer or up to 5 users of each dedicated server is $795. The cost for up to 15 users of each dedicated server is $1,790. For unlimited users of each dedicated server, the cost is $3,195.

Summarizing POWERLan

POWERLan has a wide array of features, a CUA-compliant user interface, and a level of performance unmatched by other peer LAN products. POWERLan is not as well known as Windows for Workgroups, LANtastic, or Personal NetWare, but you certainly do not want to overlook this network operating system if you are searching for the best system for your office.

For more information about POWERLan, contact the following:

Performance Technology, Inc.
800 Lincoln Center
7800 IH-10 West
San Antonio, TX 78230
(210) 349-2000

Summary

In this chapter, you learned about five specific peer LAN products: Windows for Workgroups, Personal NetWare, NetWare Lite, LANtastic, and POWERLan. If you want to research other peer LAN products, see Chapter 2, "Sharing Computer Resources," which provides a list of vendors, addresses, and telephone numbers.

The criteria and features presented here can form the basis of your evaluation of other products, but you should start your evaluation with one of the five peer LANs described in this chapter. All five offer good performance, features, reliability, and ease of use.

In Chapter 10, you learn about networks built around computers that use UNIX for an operating system. These networks are different from DOS-based peer LANs, NetWare, LAN Manager, and LAN Server networks.

III

Networking Software

Chapter 10

Using UNIX LANs

Networks built around computers that use UNIX for an operating system are somewhat different from DOS-based peer LANs. They are different from NetWare, LAN Manager, and LAN Server networks, too. In this chapter, you explore these differences.

Interestingly, if you were to take the best qualities of a peer network, a NetWare network, and a LAN Manager/LAN Server network, you would have most of the characteristics of a network based on a UNIX file server. The only thing holding UNIX back from being a predominant part of networks is UNIX itself. UNIX and the computers it runs on are sometimes expensive, and people think of UNIX as an operating system for engineers and scientists. UNIX commands are cryptic. Too many programmers, many of them college students, have had their hand in modifying and enhancing UNIX over the years. UNIX is large and bulky; it is a general-purpose operating system that is not specifically designed for networking. Nonetheless, UNIX can be an effective basis for a LAN. So-called RISC computers (such as the IBM RS/6000) perform extremely well and enable UNIX to be a good host for a network operating system.

UNIX is an old operating system, as operating systems go. It is a popular operating system for minicomputers, but not for PCs or mainframes. In this chapter, you learn the basics of UNIX, and you find out why UNIX is popular on minicomputers as you read the first few sections.

If you are unfamiliar with UNIX and want to learn more, you will find Que's *Introduction to UNIX* an invaluable tool to help you understand this arcane but useful operating system.

UNIX networks very often use what is called TCP/IP to send data among computers. Technically, TCP/IP refers to a pair of protocols. Unofficially, TCP/IP is a term people use generically for a set of protocols and utility software.

You cover TCP/IP early in this chapter, and you discover why TCP/IP is frequently used on UNIX networks. You soon will understand how TCP/IP works.

Several vendors offer network operating system products that enable you to treat a UNIX computer as a file server. This chapter gives you a detailed look at three of the best of these products: PC Interface (available from IBM as AIX Access for DOS Users, or AADU), POWERfusion and POWERserve, and Network File System (NFS).

Defining UNIX, the Operating System

UNIX is a general-purpose, multitasking, multiuser operating system. A computer running UNIX can support more than one computer program at a time, typically for more than one logged-in computer user. You may be using a database application at the same time your coworker is using a word processor, on the same computer. Both of you would be using terminals to access the central "host" UNIX machine. To use the computer, you first log in. UNIX supports the grouping of user accounts; the system administrator assigns your UNIX account to one of the groups.

The following sections explain the fundamentals of the UNIX environment.

Defining the Characteristics of UNIX

At Bell Laboratories in 1969, a group of AT&T employees created the first version of UNIX on a small DEC PDP-7 computer. In 1973, Ken Thompson and Dennis Ritchie rewrote the UNIX operating system in the C programming language. This made it somewhat easy to make UNIX run on different kinds of computers. The core of UNIX has not changed very much since 1973.

AT&T licensed UNIX to several universities for educational purposes beginning in 1974 and made the operating system a commercial product a few years later. AT&T now sells UNIX source code licenses to computer manufacturers.

When a computer manufacturer develops a new kind of minicomputer, that company wants its new computer to run the most application software possible. How can the computer manufacturer do this if the computer is a completely new design? By licensing UNIX from AT&T, the computer maker ensures that its new computer will run UNIX applications. And the company saves time and money by getting the already developed operating system from AT&T. The computer engineers can spend their time designing the computer hardware instead of worrying about developing a new operating system. A great number of minicomputers run UNIX, including some from IBM.

At its heart, UNIX is a time-sharing operating system *kernel*. The operating system software controls the resources of a computer and allocates them to the applications running on that computer. A shell program interacts with you, the human, to enable you to run programs, copy files, log in, log out, and do other tasks. The shell may display a simple command-line prompt or present a graphical user interface with icons and windows. In either case, the shell and the applications you run on UNIX make use of the kernel's services to manage files and peripheral devices.

As distributed by computer makers, UNIX includes much more than the shell. You will find tens of megabytes of utilities and other software on a UNIX computer. Running many of these utilities requires quite a bit of expertise; this is why UNIX got its reputation as a cryptic, difficult operating system.

Defining the UNIX File System

Everything in the UNIX system is a file. This principle guided the development of UNIX and helped make it simple yet all-encompassing. A *file* is a sequence of characters (bytes). The operating system imposes no special organization on files. The layout and meaning of the information in a file is strictly up to the software that accesses that file. Magnetic tapes, disk files, mail messages, keyboard characters, printer output—all of these *information containers* are a sequence of characters (a file) in the UNIX system. Even directories are just files that point to other files.

In most UNIX implementations, file names and directory names can contain up to 14 characters and are case-sensitive. The files named xmemo.doc and Memo.Doc are two distinct files in UNIX. Each file has a set of permissions that tells UNIX who may use the file and how. A file's permissions specify the rights of you, the others in your group of accounts, and those of anyone not in your group. The permissions express who may read from the file; who may write to it; and, if the file is a computer program, who may execute it. If the file is a directory, the permissions express who may see what is in that directory.

Defining Communications and UNIX

You would expect a multiuser, time-sharing operating system to have excellent communications capabilities. UNIX fulfills your expectations. A person typically uses UNIX by dialing in through a modem from his or her terminal, or through a direct connection. The communications link is usually an asynchronous, serial connection between the terminal's RS-232 port and a similar port on the UNIX computer. Sometimes the link is a LAN cable.

Defining UNIX-Based Networks

Turning a UNIX computer into a file server is relatively simple. You run software at the UNIX host computer that accepts requests from workstations, processes those requests, and returns the appropriate response to the workstations. The file server software is just another computer program for the multitasking UNIX to manage. If the computer is fast enough, you also can run UNIX applications alongside the file server software and thus get the most from the computer system. Chapter 8, "Using LAN Manager, Windows NT, and LAN Server," discusses why LM and LS are such good environments for client/server architecture. UNIX is also a natural environment for client/server architecture.

TCP/IP (explained in the following section) is a popular protocol for UNIX-based networks. Some software networking products, however, use NetBIOS to get information packets from computer to computer.

A workstation on a UNIX-based network sends file requests to the host computer and handles the responses as if they had come from the workstation's local hard disk. The workstation may run DOS, OS/2, UNIX, or System 7 (if the workstation is a Macintosh). File redirection enables the workstation to store and retrieve UNIX files as if they were DOS, OS/2, or Mac files. Sometimes, however, you must perform some level of file translation to make a file accessible to different kinds of workstation computers. DOS text files provide a simple example. By convention, DOS ends each line of a text file with two characters: a carriage return and a linefeed. UNIX text files use only a linefeed.

Mac files are more complicated. The UNIX host may store the file name but not the *resource fork* portion of the file's directory entry. (On a Mac, a resource fork is an extension of the file directory that enables the Mac operating system and applications to store more information about the file besides its name, date, and length.) In this latter case, the resource fork does not get stored on the server, and a Mac file may lose some of its attributes when retrieved by another workstation.

Using TCP/IP

As you learned in Chapter 5, "Using Protocols, Cables, and Adapters," TCP/IP stands for *Transmission Control Protocol/Internet Protocol*. The Department of Defense designed TCP/IP for ARPANET, a geographically large network (not a LAN) that connects the various sites of the DoD Advanced Research Projects Agency. TCP/IP is a layer of protocols, not a network operating system. IP provides datagram communications between nodes on a network (similar to Novell's IPX). TCP is similar to NetBIOS in that it provides point-to-point, guaranteed-delivery communications between nodes. TCP/IP usually comes with a set of standard utilities for transferring files (FTP), doing simple remote program execution (TELNET), and sending electronic mail (SMTP); these utilities are designed to work with TCP/IP. These utilities are not a PC DOS shell/redirector, of course; the remote computer is not a file server.

Because TCP/IP is a public, not a proprietary, protocol, it has become extremely popular as the basis for interconnecting LANs from different vendors. This popularity is bound to wane, however—the federal government already has decreed that all major computer/network acquisitions after August, 1990, must comply with GOSIP, the Government OSI Profile. By the late 1990s, OSI protocols will have replaced TCP/IP, at least for federal government work. For now, though, the number of vendors that support TCP/IP is actually increasing.

TCP/IP works on a peer networking concept. All computer systems connected by a TCP/IP network are peers from the network's viewpoint, although some computers will have more functions and capabilities than others, of course. The designers of TCP/IP based its architecture on a layer of protocols and the *Internet address*, a standard computer-identification scheme.

The physical transport protocol underneath TCP/IP can be Ethernet, Token Ring, a serial (modem) link, or another physical medium for sending and receiving packets of information.

FTP Software sells one of the best TCP/IP products for DOS computers connected to a UNIX-based LAN. Here is the company's address:

> FTP Software
> 26 Princess Street
> Wakefield, MA 01880
> (617) 246-0900
> Internet Address info@ftp.com

III

Networking Software

Using Internet Addresses

At the heart of TCP/IP is a scheme for routing messages that relies on unique, assigned addresses called Internet addresses. On a local or wide area basis, TCP/IP routes messages between networks and between computer systems on each network. Every TCP/IP host and every workstation has a unique Internet address, consisting of a centrally assigned network ID and a locally administered local host address. This scheme enables the routing of messages between, as well as within, local area networks. The part of TCP/IP that has the job of recognizing Internet addresses is the *Address Recognition Protocol* (ARP).

An Internet address has four parts, in the form AAA.BBB.CCC.DDD. Each part, or field, is usually a decimal number. Periods separate the fields. The *class* of the Internet address is A if the first field is from 0 to 127, B if the first field is from 128 to 191, or C if it is from 192 to 255. The first field should not exceed a value of 255. Here is an example of a class A Internet address:

    89.1.10.2

The interpretation of an Internet address depends on its class. For class A addresses, the *network portion* of the address is the first field of the Internet address. For class B, the network portion is the first two fields. Class C addresses use the first three fields as the network portion of the address. The computer systems on a single network should all use class A, B, or C Internet addresses.

The *host address* portion of an Internet address consists of the rest of the fields after the network portion. Each field in the host address portion can have a value less than 256. You should not use 0 in all the host address fields; this can cause host systems to get confused. TCP/IP software, by convention, assumes that at least one of the fields is nonzero.

As you can see, the size and range of the host address depend on the class. You may find the following Internet addresses already assigned on your network:

    192.10.100.1

    192.10.100.2

    192.10.100.3

These three Internet addresses are class C addresses, because the first field is 192. The network portion of the addresses in the example is 192.10.100, and the host address portion is 1, 2, or 3.

You would find these numbers difficult to associate with individual workstations on the network, and so the numbering scheme enables you to assign a *host name* to each Internet address. This host name is easier to remember than the pure Internet address. This higher-level naming method is called *domain naming.*

If you have access to a UNIX computer, you may want to display the list of host names on that computer. At a UNIX system prompt, type the *cat* command to reveal the contents of the hosts file in the /etc directory:

    cat /etc/hosts

This command displays the list of host names and their Internet addresses.

If you plan to use Internet addresses on a TCP/IP-based network only within your company, without communicating with other companies or universities over the TCP/IP networks collectively known as Internet, you can assign your own network and host IDs.

The DDN Network Information Center, a part of SRI International (333 Ravenswood Avenue, Menlo Park, CA 94025), assigns standard Internet network addresses and domain names. This ensures uniqueness and enables routing of TCP/IP messages among diverse companies and organizations. SRI imposes some structure on domain names as well as Internet addresses. IBM has several Internet addresses, for example. The domain name is ibm.com. The domain directory com includes all commercial users. The domain directories edu and gov include educational users and government users. Within IBM, different locations have different domain names. Two such domain names are austin.ibm.com and raleigh.ibm.com.

Using Protocols

TCP/IP technically consists of two protocols (IP and TCP, which you explore in a moment). Often, though, people use TCP/IP as a generic name for a collection of protocols and utility software programs.

TCP/IP does not specify the physical medium or protocol on which it runs. The most common TCP/IP physical protocols are Ethernet and serial (modem) connections, but you can use any physical transmission medium for TCP/IP as long as all devices that will communicate with each other use the same medium. Gateways can connect networks that use different physical protocols. Both local area networks and wide area networks can use TCP/IP to exchange information.

III

Networking Software

The *Internet Protocol* (IP) is the first, lowest layer of TCP/IP. The Transmission Control Protocol (TCP) and User Datagram Protocol (UDP) are two TCP/IP protocols that use IP. Another intermediate protocol that uses IP is the *Internet Control Message Protocol* (ICMP). ICMP enables the exchange of control and error messages between IP hosts. The Application layer occurs on top of TCP/IP and consists of utility programs and application software.

Using the Internet Protocol (IP)

The basic unit of information exchange is a *datagram packet*. The Internet Protocol portion of TCP/IP provides for the routing of packets from computer to computer, and this is the only job it does. Higher-level protocols and software do not concern themselves with the routing of packets. The IP protocol layer on a network can forward datagrams to their destinations without help from higher-level protocols.

You may run across the acronym SLIP at some point. SLIP stands for *Serial Line IP*, and it is an implementation of IP designed for serial communication links. You can connect a remote PC to a central UNIX LAN by using SLIP and a modem.

Like Novell's IPX protocol (discussed in Chapter 5, "Using Protocols, Cables, and Adapters"), IP does not guarantee delivery of packets.

Using the Transmission Control Protocol (TCP)

The Transmission Control Protocol uses IP to send and receive message packets. Like NetBIOS (discussed in Chapter 5), TCP provides the reliability factor—it guarantees successful reception of packets. TCP performs error checking to ensure that each packet's contents arrive intact, and TCP disassembles and reassembles packets to and from logical messages.

Using the User Data Protocol (UDP)

The User Datagram Protocol, like TCP, uses IP to send and receive messages. Unlike TCP, UDP (as a datagram-oriented protocol) does not provide for guaranteed delivery of messages. Computer programs that use UDP must implement their own checks for delivery, retransmission, and error recovery. However, UDP is faster than TCP. The programmer chooses TCP or UDP, depending on the requirements of the particular application.

Using Popular TCP/IP Utilities

Networking vendors almost always offer a suite of utility software programs with TCP/IP. These utilities enable you to send mail, receive mail, emulate a terminal across a TCP/IP link, transfer files, log on to a different UNIX-based computer, run software on another UNIX-based computer, and do other tasks.

Using Simple Mail Transfer Protocol (SMTP)

You can use the *Simple Mail Transfer Protocol* (SMTP) to send electronic mail on a TCP/IP network. You create your mail message with a text editor and use UNIX commands, such as sendmail, to format your outgoing mail. The addressee identification consists, naturally, of a domain name that TCP/IP converts for you to an Internet address. You can designate a mail relay host that will queue and forward your mail to remote destinations not directly connected to your LAN. SMTP is rudimentary, but it is simple to understand and use.

Using TELNET

The *TELNET* command enables you to access applications on another UNIX computer system as if you were directly attached to that system. TELNET behaves somewhat like a terminal emulator. Many implementations of TELNET are line-oriented and do not provide a full-screen mode of operation. You log on to the remote UNIX computer system through TELNET in much the same way you log on to your local UNIX computer system.

The TELNET command operates in two modes: command mode and input mode. When the TELNET command is issued without arguments, it enters command mode. You also can enter command mode by pressing Ctrl-T in input mode. In command mode, you can enter subcommands to manage the remote system. Some of these subcommands return you to the remote session on completion. If a subcommand does not return you to the remote session, press Enter.

When you issue the TELNET command with arguments, it performs an open subcommand with those arguments and then enters input mode. The type of input mode is either character-at-a-time mode or line-by-line mode, depending on what the remote system supports. In character-at-a-time mode, most text typed is immediately sent to the remote host for processing. In line-by-line mode, all text is echoed locally, and completed lines are sent to the remote host.

Table 10.1 describes some typical TELNET commands.

III

Networking Software

Table 10.1 Some TELNET Commands	
Command	**Function**
?	Prints help information
close	Closes current connection
display	Displays operating parameters
emulate	Emulates a VT100 or 3270 terminal
mode	Enters line-by-line mode or character-at-a-time mode
open	Connects to a site
quit	Exits TELNET
send	Transmits special characters
set	Sets operating parameters
status	Prints status information
toggle	Toggles operating parameters
z	Suspends TELNET

Using File Transfer Protocol (FTP)

The *ftp* command is the interface to the File Transfer Protocol (FTP). This command uses FTP to transfer files between the local host and a remote host or between two remote hosts. The FTP protocol is designed to enable hosts that use dissimilar file systems to transfer data between each other. Therefore, although the protocol provides a lot of flexibility for transferring data, it does not attempt to preserve file attributes that are specific to a particular file system (such as the file's protection mode or date and time). Additionally, the FTP protocol makes few assumptions about the overall structure of a file system and does not enable you to do such things as recursively copy subdirectories. If you are transferring files between UNIX systems and need to preserve file attributes or recursively copy subdirectories, you should use the rcp command.

The ftp command provides subcommands for tasks such as listing remote directories, changing the current local and remote directories, transferring multiple files in a single request, creating and removing directories, and escaping to the local shell to perform shell commands. The ftp command also provides for security by sending passwords to the remote host and enables you to perform automatic login, file transfers, and logoff.

Table 10.2 lists some typical ftp commands.

Table 10.2 Some ftp Commands	
Command	**Function**
account [Password]	Sends a supplemental password that a remote host may require before granting access to its resources.
append LocalFile [RemoteFile]	Appends a local file to a file on the remote host.
cd RemoteDirectory	Changes the working directory on the remote host to the specified directory.
cdup	Changes the working directory on the remote host to the parent of the current directory.
close	Ends the file transfer session but does not exit the ftp command.
delete RemoteFile	Deletes the specified remote file.
get RemoteFile [LocalFile]	Copies the remote file to the local host.
lcd [Directory]	Changes the working directory on the local host. If you do not specify a directory, the ftp command uses your home directory.
ls [RemoteDirectory] [LocalFile]	Writes an abbreviated file listing of a remote directory to a local file.
mkdir [RemoteDirectory]	Creates the directory, *RemoteDirectory*, on the remote host.
nlist	Prints a list of the files of a directory on the remote machine.
open HostName	Establishes a connection to the ftp server at the specified *HostName*.
pwd	Displays the name of the current directory on the remote host.
quit	Closes the connection and exits the ftp command.
rename FromName ToName	Renames a file on the remote host.
rmdir RemoteDirectory	Removes the directory, *RemoteDirectory*, at the remote host.
send LocalFile [RemoteFile]	Stores a local file on the remote host.

III

Networking Software

(continues)

Table 10.2 Continued	
Command	**Function**
size	Returns the size of *filename* on the remote machine in bytes.
status	Displays current status of the ftp command.
user User [Password]	Identifies the local user as *User* to the remote ftp server.

Using rlogin, rcp, rsh, and ping

The *rlogin* command logs you in to the remote host and connects your local terminal to the remote host. The remote terminal type is the same as that given in the local environment variable TERM. The terminal or window size is also the same, if the remote host supports these sizes. All echoing takes place at the remote host, so, except for delays, the terminal connection is transparent. You can press Ctrl-S and Ctrl-Q to stop and start the flow of information, and the input and output buffers are flushed on interrupts.

The *rcp* command copies files between a remote host and your local UNIX computer. You would use rcp after first logging in to the remote host with rlogin. By default, the mode and owner of an existing destination file are preserved. Normally, if a destination file does not exist, the mode of the destination file is equal to the mode of the source file as modified by the unmask command at the destination host. If the -p flag is used, the modification time and mode of source files are preserved at the destination host. If a remote host name is not specified for the source or the destination, the rcp command is equivalent to the cp command.

When copying files to or from a remote host, any remote file or directory name must be prefixed by the host of the remote host and a colon (:). Local file and directory names do not need to have a host specified. Because the rcp command assumes that a colon (:) terminates a host name, however, local file or directory names must have a backslash (\) inserted before any colons that are embedded in the name.

The user name entered for the remote host determines the file access privileges the rcp command uses at that host. Additionally, the user name given to a destination host determines the ownership and access modes of the resulting destination file or files.

The *rsh* command executes a command at a remote host or, if no command is specified, logs you in to the remote host. The rsh command sends standard input from the local command line to the remote command and receives standard output and standard error from the remote command.

Because any input to the remote command must be specified on the local command line, you cannot use the rsh command to execute an interactive command on a remote host. If you need to execute an interactive command on a remote host, use the rlogin command or the rsh command with no parameter specified. If you do not specify a command, the rsh command executes rlogin instead.

The *ping* command sends an ICMP ECHO_REQUEST to obtain an ICMP ECHO_RESPONSE from a host or gateway, and is useful for determining the status of the network and various foreign hosts. You also can use the ping command to track hardware and software problems, as well as in network testing, measurement, and management. Ping is also useful for problem isolation.

The Host parameter is either a valid host name or Internet address. If the host is operational and on the network, it responds to the echo. Each echo request contains an IP and ICMP header, followed by a timeval structure, and enough bytes to fill out the packet. The PacketSize parameter indicates the number of bytes in each datagram, with 64 bytes used as the default. The optional Count parameter specifies a number of echo requests to send. The default is to send echo requests continuously until an interrupt is received (Ctrl-C).

When trying to isolate a problem, first run the ping command on the local host to verify that the local interface to the network is up and running. Then use the ping command for hosts and gateways that are progressively more distant from the local host. The ping command sends one datagram per second and prints one line of output for every response received. Ping calculates round-trip times and packet-loss statistics and displays a brief summary on completion.

If you are accustomed to working with UNIX, the commands and utility programs you have just learned about probably seem like natural extensions of your current UNIX environment. But also notice that, with each command, you had to think of the remote computer as a separate environment. When you use rlogin, for example, you have to remind yourself that you are logged in to a remote UNIX machine, not your local one. And you have to consciously use commands like ftp or rcp to copy files from one computer to another.

III

Networking Software

On the other hand, if you use a DOS-based computer as a workstation, the UNIX commands and utilities seem somewhat alien and cryptic. Arcane commands such as the ones you just covered are the Achilles heel of UNIX. If you had a way to treat a remote UNIX computer as just another DOS drive letter, you would be much happier.

In the following sections, you explore products that solve these problems. You first look at Network File System, often called NFS. People use NFS to tie a collection of UNIX computers into a cohesive whole. You then move on to PC Interface and the POWERfusion/POWERserve combination, which enable DOS computers to see a networked UNIX computer as just another DOS drive letter.

Using Network File System (NFS)

Network File System (NFS) is a popular network operating system for sharing file systems and directories across TCP/IP-based networks. Developed by Sun Microsystems, NFS is an Application layer protocol that uses the lower-level transport protocol TCP/IP. All major vendors of UNIX-based systems offer NFS, and some vendors of non-UNIX computers offer software products that implement or work with NFS.

Understanding What NFS Does

The NFS protocol enables you to access a remote directory and its files as if that directory were on your local UNIX computer. Your UNIX applications use the files in the remote directory structure just as if the files were local. Through file redirection, NFS transparently makes the remote machine's UNIX file systems available to you. When you use the UNIX command *mount* to gain access to a remote computer's directories, your computer becomes a *client* host. A remote computer that enables its directories to be mounted by other computers is a *server* host. A host may be a server for one or more clients and may at the same time be a client of one or more other servers. You mount the remote directories over local directory *stubs*—empty directories that exist just to facilitate remote access.

Using Remote Procedure Calls (RPC)

Sun Microsystems based its design of NFS on the *remote procedure call* (RPC) concept, which enables software on different machines to communicate with each other. If you have ever written a computer program or done some batch file programming, you know you can modularize your program so that separate sections of the software do different jobs. With RPC, these separate sections can reside on different kinds of computers. The Network File System uses RPC to redirect file I/O operations across a network.

RPC and Client/Server Architecture

Remote procedure call (RPC) is a magic glue that enables programmers to treat a heterogeneous network of computers as if they were one big computer. With RPC, each part of an application can be targeted for the kind of computer it is best suited for. RPC is a good tool for building client/server systems.

What does a programmer have to do to use RPC? He or she codes each module in the C programming language, as usual. Each program module is designated as a *server* or *client*. Server modules typically are the back end of the application (calculations, report generation, and storage of permanent database records), while client modules manage the front-end user interface. The programmer creates an RPC compiler script that identifies the server and client modules. The programmer then runs the RPC compiler to generate the C source code that glues the modules together as if they were one executable program. Under the covers, the generated code creates a communications session between the client and server modules on the different computers. To the programmer, though, the server modules are called in the same way as any other subroutines the client code might call. The fact that the client and server modules execute on different computers becomes transparent to the programmer's application.

The computers that participate in an NFS network may be different brands and models, and they very likely represent data in different ways internally. NFS uses the *External Data Representation* (XDR) protocol to take care of these differences. With XDR, the information in the message packets is rearranged and translated to a computer-model-independent form.

NFS is a *stateless* protocol; servers and clients do not remember previous file operations. A workstation may open a file by sending the name of the file to the remote NFS server and getting back a response indicating that the file is now open. Later, when that workstation wants to read the file, the workstation sends a read-file request to the server. The read-file request contains the name of the file, as well as the current file position, so that the server does not have to remember the previous open-file operation it did on behalf of the workstation. One consequence of NFS's statelessness is that NFS is somewhat slower than other network operating environments. The slower performance is the result of the extra LAN traffic from the larger packets (each one carries all the information necessary for that packet to stand on its own) and from the extra processing that NFS has to do for each packet.

III

Networking Software

The statelessness of NFS avoids complicated crash-recovery handling on the part of the server and client. A client simply resends requests until a response is received from the server. A client cannot tell the difference between a slow server and a server that has crashed. In the same vein, a server that has just been rebooted can resume honoring client requests without each of the clients also rebooting. NFS uses the User Datagram Protocol (UDP) described earlier to send and receive file requests and responses.

Using Yellow Pages

The *Yellow Pages* (YP) service (which in networking has nothing to do with the telephone company) complements NFS by providing a distributed network lookup service. Yellow Pages servers store databases called *maps* that client computers can query. Generally, these maps contain information about users, groups, network addresses, gateways, and other entities on the network.

Yellow Pages comes with shell scripts to help you build the map files. One such script is *ypinit*, which can build Yellow Pages server maps from files already available on your UNIX computer, including the local password, group, and TCP/IP configuration files. As people share resources on a UNIX-based network, a Yellow Pages server resolves naming and addressing differences among the networked computers. You sometimes will see Yellow Pages referred to as *Network Information Services* (NIS).

You can see that NFS helps make the networking of UNIX computers easier for people by enabling them to treat remote file systems as local file systems. But what about people who use DOS-based computers? If your personal computer uses DOS and you have a UNIX minicomputer in the office, you will want to read the rest of this chapter.

Using PC Interface/AADU

PC Interface (PCI) is a software product from the following company:

> Locus Computing
> 9800 La Cienega Boulevard
> Inglewood, CA 90301
> (800) 955-6287

IBM thinks highly enough of PCI to offer it as an IBM product under the name AIX Access for DOS Users (AADU). PCI consists of UNIX (server) software and DOS (workstation) software. You also can get a Macintosh version of PCI from Locus for the Macs on your network. PCI uses TCP/IP to send and receive file requests, print requests, and administrative (internal to PCI) message packets.

PCI (or AADU, if you buy the product from IBM) turns a UNIX computer into a file server and print server. PCI enables your DOS PC to create and use files on the UNIX computer. You can share those files with other workstations and software running on the UNIX computer. If the UNIX computer has a printer, the DOS workstations can share the printer with the applications running on the UNIX machine. PCI is compatible with Microsoft Windows. PCI also comes with terminal emulator software that enables you to log in to the UNIX computer across the LAN, so that you can run UNIX applications or execute UNIX commands.

Using UNIX Software

On the UNIX computer, two PCI computer programs run in the background continuously. These programs start when you boot UNIX. The first program, *pcimapsvr*, simply maintains a list of the UNIX host computers running PCI. About every 30 seconds, the pcimapsvr program on each machine gets an updated list from the other machines. When a workstation logs on, pcimapsvr sends the current list of PCI hosts to that workstation.

The second program, *pciconsvr*, broadcasts "I'm here!" messages every 30 seconds to each UNIX host running pcimapsvr. The pcimapsvr module uses these broadcasts to update its list of available PCI file servers. Pciconsvr also receives login requests from workstations. On receiving a login request, pciconsvr goes through a standard UNIX login ritual to make sure that you are who you say you are. Pciconsvr then starts another background computer program, *pcidossvr*, that becomes your personal file server software. Your workstation and the "one per login" background program interact to give you file and print services for the duration of your network session.

This structure of UNIX *daemons* (background software) works well until a DOS user forgets to use the PCI logout program to end a session. If the DOS machine reboots during a session (or even if it suffers a power failure or lockup), the pcidossvr daemon remains running as a *zombie* UNIX process. It takes a supervisor-level UNIX login (*root*) to kill the zombie.

Using Files with PCI

At a DOS workstation, when you log in to a PCI host, you supply a user ID and password. After you have logged in, PCI establishes a new drive letter (E, for example) that you can use. This drive letter gives you access to all the file

III

Networking Software

systems currently mounted on the UNIX host. PCI supports standard PC DOS and MS-DOS file sharing and record locking so that you can run your multiuser applications.

Naming PCI Files

UNIX file names may contain up to 14 characters, they can have multiple periods in them, and they are case-sensitive. DOS file names, as you know, may contain up to eight characters in the base name and have an optional one- to three-character extension. A single period separates the base name from the extension. DOS file names are not case-sensitive.

You will not have a problem with the differences between UNIX and DOS file-naming conventions if you access only DOS files from your workstation. If you use the CHDIR command to change to the root directory of the file server and type a DIR command, however, you will see typical UNIX directories such as USR, TMP, and LOST'UND. This last directory name is PCI's way of representing the ubiquitous UNIX lost+found directory in terms of the more restrictive DOS rules for file names. PCI provides the utility undir to enable you to see both the full UNIX name and the "mapped" DOS name. When a UNIX name does not map directly to a DOS file name, PCI substitutes special characters, such as apostrophes, in the name to help you access the file from DOS.

Using DOS Files and UNIX Files

On the host computer, PCI stores files as UNIX files. File redirection makes the UNIX-file-versus-DOS-file difference completely transparent, however. The files you save from one DOS workstation can be accessed from other DOS workstations without your having to worry about the differences between the file-naming conventions of the DOS and UNIX operating systems.

The only difference you have to be aware of is the way that DOS and UNIX each treat text files. UNIX uses a single linefeed character to end a line of text in a text file. DOS uses two characters: a carriage return followed by a linefeed. If you plan to share text files between DOS applications and UNIX applications, Locus supplies a conversion utility you can use to add carriage returns to UNIX files or delete carriage returns from DOS files.

Using UNIX File Permissions

For security, PCI relies on standard UNIX protections. You use the PCI login program, which prompts you for a UNIX account ID and password, to gain access to the network drive. The network administrator must add each PCI user to the UNIX system. You can be denied read or write access to files and directories on the UNIX host through the use of standard UNIX file permission masks.

Printing with PCI

The PCI command *PRINTER* redirects your DOS workstation's printer port to the shared LAN printer. This redirection works for print operations you do in your DOS or Windows applications. It also works for Print Screen requests; the copying of files to LPT1, LPT2, LPT3, or PRN; and the DOS PRINT command.

Managing Your PCI Print Jobs

After you invoke PCI's PRINTER command, your printouts appear on the LAN printer. You can tell the PRINTER command which (or all) printer ports to redirect. If you have more than one UNIX host acting as a file server, you can tell the PRINTER command which file server should process your printouts.

PCI's print redirection collects print material into a print job, with each print job separated by what PCI calls a *print break*. A print break occurs when an application performs a close print file operation, when the application exits, or when your workstation has stopped sending printer output for a specified number of seconds. You can tell PCI how many seconds to use as a timeout parameter to the PRINTER command. You also use a form of the PRINTER command to end printer port redirection.

If you want to check on your printout to see how many print jobs are ahead of you in the queue, you can log on to the UNIX host and use UNIX commands to display the print queue.

Using UNIX Print Facilities

Unless you say otherwise, the UNIX file server uses its default print program to produce your printout. This is usually the UNIX *lp* command. Optionally, you can tell PCI to use a different print program on the UNIX host, such as qprt. You can include parameters and command-line options, as shown in the following example of the PRINTER command:

        PRINTER LPT2 HOST1 "lp -d hplaser -o raw"

Running Terminal Sessions with UNIX

In addition to treating the UNIX computer as a file server, through a DOS drive letter and shared LAN printer, you can turn your personal computer into a terminal and log on to UNIX directly. The EM2 terminal emulator

III

Networking Software

supplied with PCI operates across the LAN. You can emulate a VT220, VT100, or PC scancode terminal in your UNIX sessions. EM2 supports most of the characteristics of a standard Digital Equipment Corporation VT220 terminal, including multinational character sets, programmable function keys, numeric keypad cursor control, flow control, and the usual DEC control and escape sequences.

If you use Microsoft Windows in 386 Enhanced mode, you know that Windows can give you multiple concurrent DOS sessions. In one session, you may treat the UNIX computer as a file server, running applications that access files on the network drive letter. In another DOS session under Windows, you may run the EM2 program to have a UNIX session with the UNIX computer. You can have only one terminal emulation session active at a time, however.

Using PCI Remotely through a Modem

You can use PC Interface through a modem, if you are not within reach of one of your network's LAN cables. PCI uses SLIP, the Serial Line Internet Protocol, to manage your remote LAN session. You can run applications and do everything you would do if you were directly connected to the LAN. Depending on the speed (baud rate) of the modem, though, you will find that your remote session performs much more slowly than if you were using a LAN cable. Dial-up communication facilities through the telephone company are always much slower than regular LAN connections.

Using PCI Commands

Locus provides a set of commands and utilities with PCI that you will find useful. Table 10.3 lists these commands.

Table 10.3 PCI Commands and Utilities	
Command	**Function**
DOS2UNIX	Strips carriage returns from text files
DOSWHAT	Samples a file and tells you what kind of file it is
EM2	Provides VT220 emulation so that you can run UNIX applications
JOBS	Displays the list of jobs initiated with the ON command
KILL	Stops a UNIX computer program

Command	Function
ON	Starts a UNIX program or command on the host (server) computer
PCICONF	Configures PC Interface
PRINTER	Redirects your LPTx port to the shared LAN printer or stops redirection
UDIR	Lists the names of files in UNIX and DOS formats
UNIX2DOS	Adds carriage returns to text files

Summarizing PCI

PC Interface uses only about 70K of DOS workstation memory. On an 80386, 80486, or Pentium computer, you can load PCI into upper memory with DOS 5.0 (or later) or a memory manager. PCI performs well, works with a wide variety of network adapter cards, and does an excellent job of making the UNIX computer appear as just another set of DOS resources for file and printer sharing.

Using POWERfusion and POWERserve

Like PC Interface, POWERfusion and either POWERfusion Extras for DOS or POWERserve enable your DOS computer to treat a UNIX computer as a file server. POWERfusion, POWERfusion Extras for DOS, and POWERserve are software products of the following company:

> Performance Technology
> 800 Lincoln Center
> 7800 IH-10 West
> San Antonio, Texas 78230
> (800) 825-5267
> (512) 349-2000

You read about Performance Technology's POWERLan in Chapter 9's discussion of peer LANs.

POWERfusion supplies terminal emulation and file conversion utilities. POWERfusion Extras for DOS, POWERserve, or POWERLan (the products interoperate well) provide DOS drive letter redirection. POWERfusion consists

III

Networking Software

of UNIX (server) software and DOS (workstation) software. POWERfusion uses NetBIOS, not TCP/IP, to send and receive file requests, print requests, and administrative message packets.

Learning What POWERfusion and POWERserve Do

POWERfusion and POWERserve turn a UNIX computer into a file server and print server. You use DOS commands and your applications to create and use files on the UNIX computer, and you can share those files with the other people on the LAN. You can treat the UNIX computer's printer as a shared LAN printer. POWERfusion and POWERserve are compatible with Microsoft Windows. POWERfusion alone simply provides the connectivity between your workstation and the UNIX host, including terminal emulation across the LAN. You use POWERserve, POWERfusion Extras for DOS, or the POWERLan product to give your workstation a DOS drive letter that refers to the UNIX computer's hard disk. These redirector modules also provide LAN printer-sharing facilities.

Understanding the UNIX Side of Performance Technology's Products

The POWERdrivers software component consists of NetBIOS device drivers for the UNIX computer. While the other products mentioned in this chapter use TCP/IP to deliver message packets from workstation to file server and back, POWERfusion uses NetBIOS. Several other network operating systems use NetBIOS as a transport protocol. These include LAN Manager; LAN Server; and Performance Technology's peer LAN product, POWERLan. Using NetBIOS rather than TCP/IP enables POWERfusion to coexist and work with these other network operating systems.

The primary POWERdrivers module is called *unxnet*. A UNIX device driver, this module turns NetBIOS message packets into streams of data for the tty and print spooler portions of UNIX. Another driver module implements a NetBIOS STREAMS protocol for asynchronous network I/O. The STREAMS driver is called /dev/nbsa on the UNIX machine. You can use ARCnet or Ethernet cards with POWERserve and POWERfusion.

The POWERserve portion of the UNIX software performs the same file server operations as described for PC Interface—mapping server hosts and providing file I/O services. Because POWERserve, POWERLan, and POWERfusion Extras for DOS use the same SMB protocol as the LAN Manager and LAN Server network operating systems, you can use these Performance Technology products on the same LAN as these other network operating systems. From a workstation running POWERLan, for example, you can access a LAN Manager server and a UNIX server at the same time.

Using Files

Because POWERserve uses the same SMB protocol as POWERLan, LAN Manager, LAN Server, and the old IBM PC LAN Program, the files you share with a Performance Technology network operating system can reside on UNIX, OS/2, and DOS file servers. POWERserve does as well as PC Interface to hide the differences between UNIX file names and DOS file names. DOS files that you want to share among workstations pose no problem. But POWERserve represents 14-character, case-sensitive UNIX file names on your DOS workstation by truncating the names and ignoring upper- versus lowercase. POWERfusion comes with utility software for converting UNIX text files to or from DOS text files. POWERserve supports DOS file sharing and record locking to enable you to run your multiuser applications on your UNIX-based network.

For security, POWERfusion uses standard UNIX account IDs and passwords. POWERserve adheres to UNIX file-permission conventions to enable or disable file access by a DOS workstation. The network administrator can protect files and applications across the LAN in exactly the same way that he or she can control access on the UNIX computer.

Printing with POWERserve

The printer server module uses the UNIX lp printer command to route print jobs to the shared LAN printer attached to the UNIX computer. You can password-protect the LAN printer—a unique feature of POWERserve and POWERLan.

The network administrator gives the LAN printer a name, and you use this name to redirect the LPT1, LPT2, or LPT3 port on your DOS workstation. At the UNIX host, the administrator configures options for how the lp command should process each print job. These options include the number of copies that should be printed and whether your workstation should receive a notification message when the printout is finished.

The POWERfusion Extras for DOS product includes a print redirector that enables a printer attached to any DOS workstation to act as the shared LAN printer. This LAN printer is even available to applications running on the UNIX computer.

Understanding Terminal Sessions with UNIX

The POWERfusion product includes a VT220 terminal emulator that enables you to view the UNIX computer as a host machine. You can use a hot key to go between the terminal emulator software and DOS. This makes it easy to run UNIX applications at the same time you use DOS commands or DOS

III

Networking Software

applications. The terminal emulator supports most of the characteristics of a standard Digital Equipment Corporation VT220 terminal, including multinational character sets, programmable function keys, numeric keypad cursor control, flow control, and the usual DEC control and escape sequences.

Using POWERfusion through Menus

You use menus in POWERfusion and the other Performance Technology components, rather than commands. The menu options enable you to configure your workstation, enable the workstation's connection to the LAN, map drive letters, initiate terminal emulation, perform file transfers, and convert text files. Performance Technology also includes a file manager called Navigate that you use to manage and visually explore the directory trees on your local drive or on the file server.

Summarizing POWERfusion and POWERserve

The DOS workstation modules take varying amounts of memory. NetBIOS uses about 7K, the print redirector uses about 13.5K, and the file redirector uses about 15K. On an 80386, 80486, or Pentium computer, you can load all the POWERfusion Extras modules except NetBIOS into upper memory with DOS 5.0 (or later) or a memory manager. Performance Technology offers a collection of network operating system components that work with a great number of network adapter cards, and you can use them with UNIX, LAN Manager, and LAN Server file servers.

Summary

You have added an extra dimension to your knowledge of networking in this chapter. You now understand the basics of the UNIX operating system, and you know about the popular multivendor protocol TCP/IP. Network File System (NFS) is no longer a mystery to you. And you thoroughly covered the UNIX networking products PC Interface and POWERfusion, Powerfusion Extras for DOS, and POWERserve.

In the next chapter, you turn your attention to the applications you will use on your LAN.

Part IV

Expanding a Network

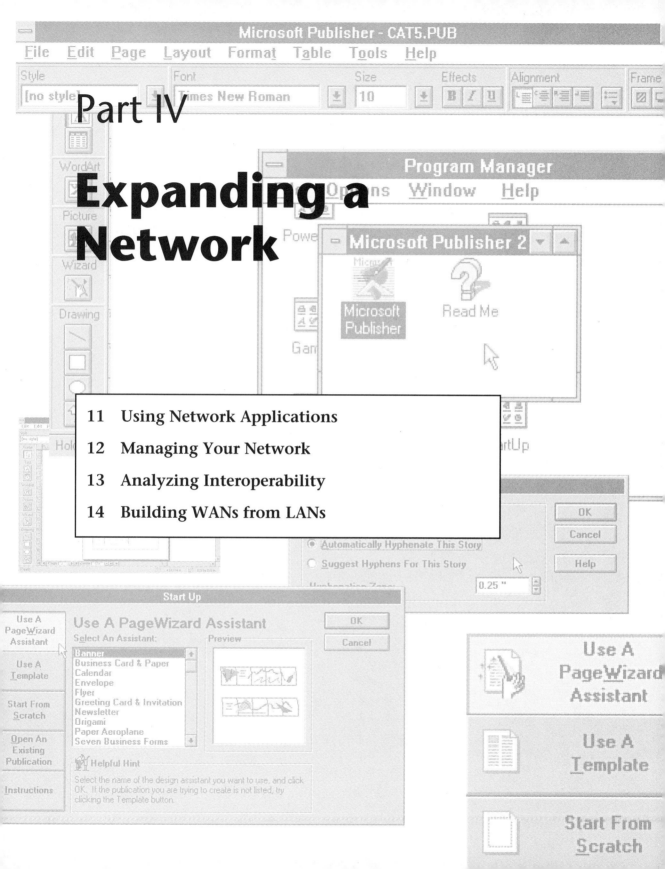

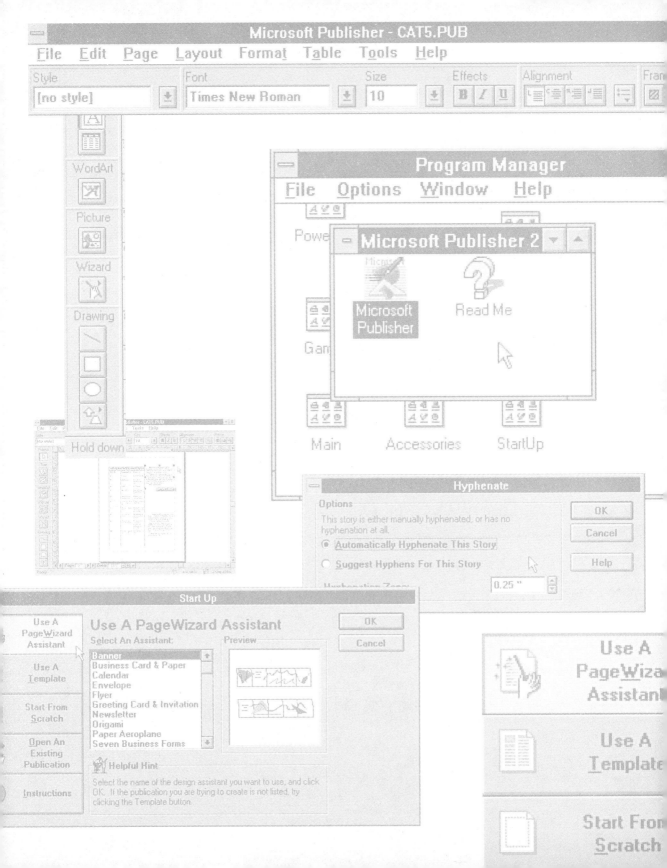

Chapter 11

Using Network Applications

Your individual personal computer exists to run software applications and help you get your job done. The network helps people in the office act as a team and get more work done. The network does this by enabling people to share information and computer resources. Your LAN makes the personal computers in your office part of the team.

Your favorite applications may be LAN-aware and allow multiple concurrent use by the people in the office, or they may be single-user, stand-alone applications. Even in the case of single-user software, you may be able to share each application's executable files and data files on the LAN. You may have to coordinate the sharing of specific files, however. This may involve telling others in your office that you have updated a particular spreadsheet file and that the file is now available for others to load and use at their workstations. On the other hand, your multiuser applications may help you share files in a way that makes it easy to know who updated a file last, why he or she updated the file, where the most recent file is located, and when the update took place.

A LAN-aware, multiuser application recognizes the presence of a network operating system and behaves accordingly. A single-user application treats the network drives the same as local drives and does not behave any differently when run on multiple, LAN-connected computers. This chapter shows you how to manage both multiuser software and single-user software on a LAN.

You start your exploration of LAN applications in this chapter by considering how DOS works on your computer when you are on the network. The various network operating systems implement rights and permissions for the sake of security, and this chapter shows how your applications behave differently according to how the network administrator grants or revokes these rights. You also learn about *deadlocks*—rare but data-damaging events in a multiuser environment.

You next look at the characteristics of a multiuser application. These characteristics include file sharing, record locking, user-specific configuration files, and multiuser printing. You cover the important issues of software licenses for multiple users. This chapter explains how to manage and use the different categories of application programs—word processing, desktop publishing, spreadsheets, and database managers—on a LAN. Because applications in the last category, database managers, lend themselves so well to multiuser operation, this chapter covers eight specific LAN-aware database manager products: Access, Alpha Four, DataEase, dBASE IV, FoxPro, Paradox, Paradox for Windows, and R:BASE.

Defining Single-User and Multiuser Operating Systems

DOS by itself is a single-user operating system. On a LAN, however, several users usually need to be able to run the same application on different workstations. A multiuser application, through DOS and the network operating system, coordinates the efforts of each user and workstation by understanding and manipulating the environment presented by the LAN. LAN-aware software extends DOS and adds an entirely new dimension to working with personal computers.

Using DOS

IBM, Microsoft, and Novell (in an independent sort of way) added functions to DOS to enable DOS computers to access a network. Microsoft and IBM, which own DOS and therefore control what goes into DOS, placed these new and extended functions directly inside DOS. Because Novell is not a partner in the maintenance and programming of the DOS operating system, Novell originally supported these capabilities with functions provided by the NetWare shell (NET*x*.COM). Besides offering its own proprietary set of multiuser functions and DOS extensions, Novell recognizes and supports the Microsoft/IBM functions.

Looking at Different Versions of DOS

Microsoft and IBM added LAN-related functions to versions of DOS starting with 3.0. Computer programs running under DOS 3.0 can exercise file-access control (exclusive or shared modes of opening files) and record locking. DOS 3.1 added the capability to obtain the identification of individual workstations, to determine which disk drives are remote (redirected/shared) and which are local, and to find out the network name of a remote disk drive. DOS 3.2 coincided with the release of IBM's Token Ring network adapter cards. DOS 3.3 added a function to enable programs to commit file data to disk (a sort of temporary close action). And DOS 4.0 made the loading of the SHARE.EXE program mandatory rather than optional. (The section "Using the DOS SHARE.EXE Program" later in this chapter describes the SHARE program.)

Several years ago, more people were using Version 2.1 of DOS than any other version of DOS. People do not necessarily upgrade to the next version of the operating system when each new version is released. Because of the approach Novell took to create a LAN environment based on a separate layer of software above DOS, DOS 2.1 users who have the appropriate NetWare shell software could have access to a LAN without upgrading to a new operating system. This is one of the reasons Novell got an early toehold in the LAN marketplace. Today, of course, this factor no longer is significant, because most users have a later (LAN-compatible) version of DOS.

Using DOS Commands

DOS is not immune to file-sharing problems; even something as simple as issuing a COPY command to DOS can cause problems on a network. The problems do not occur often, fortunately, but the DOS command processor COMMAND.COM is not particularly LAN-aware. For instance, a file collision occurs if you tell DOS to copy a file that currently is open at another workstation. It doesn't matter that the other workstation may be only reading from the file and the COPY command wants to share the file by also just reading from it. To perform the copy, COMMAND.COM opens the input (source) file in compatibility mode, which (unless the file's directory entry is marked with the read-only attribute) asks for exclusive access to the file. The COPY command should instead open the input file in a mode that prevents other workstations from writing to the file for the duration of the copy operation.

With NetWare, Novell supplies a file-copy utility of its own, called NCOPY. This utility not only is LAN-aware but also has a special feature for avoiding unnecessary message traffic across the LAN. If NCOPY detects that the source and destination files reside on the same file server, NCOPY performs the file copy directly at the file server instead of transmitting the file out to a workstation, which in turn would have to transmit the file back to the file server under the destination file name.

Configuring DOS on a Workstation

The installation software for your network operating system usually makes whatever changes are necessary to your CONFIG.SYS and AUTOEXEC.BAT files. If the software is well written, you will get a chance during the installation of the network to view, highlight, and perhaps modify the changes. The installation software also will put the workstation part of the network operating system on the hard disks of each of the personal computers in your office. The disk space required for these workstation files ranges from a few tens of kilobytes for NetWare to several megabytes for LAN Manager.

If you use an 80386, 80486, or Pentium personal computer and you have DOS 5 or later (or one of the memory manager products discussed in Chapter 6, "Using Workstations"), you can experiment with loading some or all of the network software into upper memory. Putting network driver software into upper memory usually is a trial-and-error process. If you are the analytical type, you can use the documentation that came with your network adapter card and the other adapter cards in your computer to select likely areas of upper memory to use for TSRs and device drivers. You probably will wind up rebooting your computer several times, making changes to your CONFIG.SYS and AUTOEXEC.BAT files each time, before you find a combination of TSR and device driver upper-memory usage that satisfies you. If you choose to go through this process, your reward is a much larger amount of memory in which to run your applications. You can free substantial amounts of the 640K of conventional memory with DOS 5 (or later) or a memory manager product.

Both Novell and the LAN Manager and LAN Server network operating systems can share an entire file server disk drive or, if you like, certain directories on the disk. The NetWare command MAP sets up drive mappings that specify the relationship between the drive letters and directories that a workstation sees on the network and the actual drive and directory structure on the file server. In a similar manner, for LAN Manager and LAN Server, the NET SHARE command (at the file server) and the NET USE command (at a workstation) specify drive and directory relationships.

Notice that the drive letters and the directory structures that are visible to your applications depend on how these commands are used. The installation section of the documentation for your application software may say a few words about how the application expects these drive mappings to be set up.

Using the DOS SHARE.EXE Program

SHARE.EXE enables file sharing on a LAN. SHARE, which is distributed on the DOS distribution disks, consists of a terminate-and-stay-resident (TSR) program that inserts hooks deep into DOS. These hooks are so deep that you cannot remove SHARE from memory without rebooting the computer.

If SHARE is not loaded, DOS ignores the special file-access modes that a LAN-aware application specifies at the time it opens a file (to acquire exclusive access to a file, for example). In fact, it is possible to corrupt a network disk quite thoroughly if file collisions occur and SHARE is not in effect. This is one of the reasons why beginning with DOS 4.0, SHARE is loaded automatically by DOS and no longer is something that you can forget to run. SHARE also is automatically in effect under OS/2. SHARE is built into the OS/2 operating system, and you do not have to load SHARE if you use OS/2.

The user guide or reference manual that came with your application software probably will remind you to run SHARE before accessing the application. The best time to run SHARE is after you have loaded the network software but before you do any work. It does not matter whether SHARE runs before the login process.

One interesting aspect of SHARE is that it enables file sharing even on a stand-alone, single-user PC. Because you can have several TSR-type programs loaded underneath an application program running in the foreground, DOS needs to keep separate track of the file I/O performed by each background or foreground program. If SHARE is loaded on a single-user computer, the same file-sharing that occurs across the network can occur between two TSRs, or between a TSR and a foreground application.

If you are a Microsoft Windows user on a LAN, you should make doubly certain to load SHARE before starting Windows. Windows does not enable you to run SHARE in one of its Enhanced mode DOS sessions. Windows prevents SHARE from running by pretending that SHARE is already loaded. Windows does this because you can use the DOS EXIT command to end a DOS session, which would remove SHARE from memory. Windows cannot enable this to happen, because SHARE hooks itself into DOS. As an unfortunate side effect, multiuser software that you run in a DOS session will think that file sharing is enabled, when in fact SHARE is not present. File damage and corruption can result.

Assigning Rights and Permissions

The concept of rights and permissions forms a significant part of the security offered by most network operating systems. These rights and permissions can protect data, but they can confuse application software (and you, too, when you run the applications).

An example of a situation that is unique to NetWare involves the shareable/nonshareable file attribute (covered in Chapter 7, "Using NetWare"). When a file is created on a NetWare file server, the network operating system gives the file a default attribute of readable, writeable, and nonshareable. This means that you or your application software will have to modify the attributes of the files that your applications expect to share among multiple users. If you have to modify the attributes manually, you can use the NetWare FLAG utility.

Searching Directories

Under NetWare, LAN Server, and LAN Manager, situations can happen that would never occur on a single-user computer. You will recall, for example, the discussion in Chapter 7 about the rights that can be associated with a directory on a NetWare server. A directory can be marked so that a program cannot even search it to see what files it contains. The files may actually exist (and may be visible to users who have different NetWare trustee rights), but users with insufficient rights may be restricted so that certain directories and files are invisible to the software they run and to the DOS commands they issue. Because of this, an application may appear to behave differently when run on different workstations on the LAN.

Reading and Writing Files

It is generally a misuse of rights and permissions to mark a directory as searchable but not readable. Most network operating systems support this combination of rights, but you will find it highly frustrating. You can see the files in the directory when you issue a DOS DIR command, but your application cannot open and read the files.

However, turning off file-write permission for all users but one (or a few) is useful. This security technique makes the person who can write a file responsible for that file. Other people can read the file but cannot replace the information it contains.

Encountering Deadlocks

Deadlock is a gruesome but appropriate word for a situation you very much want to avoid. Suppose that Workstation A and Workstation B are running different programs, but both programs need to update the same two files on the file server. Each program needs to lock the two files (file #1 and file #2) so that it can update the files with consistent data. At about the same moment, both programs reach the point in their processing at which they need to acquire the file locks. The sequence of events in a deadlock goes like this:

1. Program A locks file #1.

2. Program A writes to file #1 data that absolutely must be reflected in file #2.

3. Program B locks file #2.

4. Program B writes to file #2 data that absolutely must be reflected in file #1.

5. Program A tries to lock file #2. It fails.

6. Program B tries to lock file #1. It fails.

Another term for this situation is *deadly embrace*. This term is just as gruesome as *deadlock* and perhaps a bit more descriptive. Untangling the participants in a deadlock usually involves rebooting both workstations, which may leave inconsistent data in the files the applications were using.

If you encounter a situation that appears to be caused by a deadlock, you will want to notify the developer (or vendor) of the application software. It is up to the programmer to avoid deadlocks. You sometimes can verify that a deadlock has occurred by going to the file server and looking at the network operating system's display of currently open files and active record locks.

Defining Characteristics of a Multiuser Application

In the next few sections of this chapter, you will gain an understanding of what makes multiuser applications different from single-user applications. LAN-aware software behaves differently on a LAN and recognizes the need to support several application users at the same time. Such software uses file sharing and record locking to preserve the integrity of its files. Well-written applications enable each person to have individual files of configuration and preference information. Multiuser printing, properly done, ensures that each print job appears on the shared LAN printer with the right fonts and page orientation, without being affected by the preceding print job. And multiuser applications may have different licensing arrangements under which you purchase the software.

Learning How Software Behaves Differently on a LAN

You have seen how rights, permissions, and file attributes can cause an application to behave differently on a LAN. When an application does not handle the LAN environment very well, you have to shoulder part of the job of coordinating file updates yourself—for example, implementing an officewide strategy for notifying people when certain files can be accessed and updated. Some software cannot be run on a LAN at all. Utility programs that sort directories fall into this category.

Depending on the extent to which a multiuser application is LAN-aware, the application software may mesh smoothly with the work your office does. The software may recognize that it is running on a workstation, know which person is using the software, and configure itself for each person's use.

Identifying Users

The account ID (or user ID) that you use to log on to the LAN is available to application software. (Your password is not available, of course.) In some cases, the software may use a machine name to identify each workstation. The application can use either piece of information in a wide variety of ways. The software may produce an audit trail of application activity on a user-by-user basis or maintain separate configuration and preference files for each user.

The practice no longer is prevalent, but years ago some application software stored configuration information inside the executable program file itself. The computer program had built-in defaults for the configuration. When you changed the configuration, the software simply changed its internal defaults by treating part of the executable file as a data file. This is one of the most devastating things a programmer can do on a network. The scheme has two problems. First, the application software cannot store multiple individual user configurations for everyone on the LAN. Second, you cannot mark the executable file as shareable and read-only (a useful file attribute on a NetWare LAN).

Better-designed applications establish a configuration file for each user. The account ID, user ID, or machine name probably will be the basis for the name of the configuration file.

If the documentation for the application software tells you that you must set up a machine name for each workstation (or each user login account ID), and if the documentation suggests guidelines for constructing the name (for example, it must be unique, have one to eight characters, consist of alphabetic/

numeric characters, and otherwise conform to the requirements for a valid file name under DOS), you can bet that the application is using this technique. Examples of such names are BARRY.CFG, LINDA.CFG, and CHRIS.CFG.

Accessing Disk Sectors

You cannot run some utility programs on a network drive. The best example is CHKDSK. CHKDSK operates on disk sectors, and network operating systems do not provide the means for a program to lock a disk sector. Files may be locked during an update, but not sectors. In addition, CHKDSK understands only DOS-formatted disks. The file server disk drive may very well have an internal format that DOS does not understand.

Probably the most popular DOS-based hard disk utility product is Norton Utilities from Symantec Corporation. This set of computer programs enables you to set your screen colors, search for text strings in files, find files, set volume labels, test your system's performance, change file attributes, print text files, and do a number of other useful things. These "other things," however, do not work on a network drive. Norton Utilities contains computer programs for sorting directories, unerasing files, undeleting directories, and modifying the internal physical file-location tables (a process known as *defragmenting* your disk). These computer programs, while useful on a single-user DOS computer, are dangerous in a multiuser environment. If you were to sort a file server directory at one workstation while another workstation was using the same directory, you would in effect pull the rug out from under the other user.

Other popular hard disk utilities that do not work on a network disk drive include PC Tools Deluxe (Symantec), HDTest (Peter Fletcher), SpinRite (Gibson Research), OPTune (Gazelle Systems), and Mace Utilities (Symantec).

Using Root Directory Files

Some applications expect to be able to write files in the root directory of the current disk drive. The file may be a temporary file that holds work in progress while the software does its job. On a LAN, it is possible that you do not have sufficient permissions to write files in the network drive's root directory. For this reason, many network operating systems enable you to perform a special drive-letter mapping that makes your personal directory on the LAN look like a root directory to applications. This feature is called *map root*. As an example of how this works, suppose that your name is Chris and that your network administrator has created a personal network directory for you. The directory is F:\USERS\CHRIS. The network administrator may set up your drive letters so that F:\ really is F:\USERS\CHRIS. When your software thinks it is writing to the root directory of drive F, the files actually appear in F:\USERS\CHRIS.

Using File Sharing and Record Locking

Every open file on a file server is owned by the workstation that opened it. Ownership can range from possessive ("No one touches this file but me") to communal ("If we cooperate, we can all own this file"). There are gradations between these degrees of ownership. An application specifies how it wants to share a file when the computer program opens the file. Applications use file sharing and record locking to ensure that file updates occur on a consistent basis.

Examining the Need for File Sharing

What would happen if two workstations paid no attention to file-sharing concepts (did not load SHARE) and tried to change the contents of the same file? If the two workstations opened the same file and attempted to update it at the same time, the result could be messy, to say the least. Here is an example of what can happen:

> When workstation A reads a file or a portion of a file, the file server transfers the data from the file server hard disk into workstation A's memory for processing. Writing the data transfers it back to the file server. The same holds true, naturally, for workstation B. Suppose that workstation A reads a file and displays the file's data to person A. While person A is looking at the screen and keying in changes, workstation B also reads the file into B's memory and displays it to person B. Person B types faster than person A and saves his or her changes first. Person A, after pondering a few minutes, saves A's changes (by writing the data from workstation memory to the file server). Clearly, the changes that person B made are now lost; they've been overwritten by those of the slower typist, person A.

An even more complicated situation arises when several *interrelated* files need to be updated. Because the contents of one file are supposed to have a certain correspondence to the contents of the other files, a helter-skelter series of updates from multiple workstations would be disastrous. Any relationships that existed before the several updates took place would quickly be destroyed.

Using File Sharing

When an application opens a file located on the file server, the software informs the server of its intention simply to read from the file, or perhaps both to read and to write to the file. The software also can ask the server to deny other workstations access to the file.

If the application signals an intention only to read from the file, and if the file is flagged with a file attribute of read-only, the server enables the application to access the file. If you used the DOS ATTRIB command to mark a file as read-only and an application indicates that it wants to write to the file, the network operating system will prevent the application from using the file, causing the application to produce an error message.

An application uses *sharing mode* to control how other workstations can open a file concurrently. The application specifies sharing mode when it opens a file. Sharing mode works by enabling the application at one workstation to restrict (or not restrict) how other workstations use a file.

Applications express sharing mode in terms of denying certain capabilities to the other workstations that attempt to open the file. The restrictions that an application can specify (as defined in the *DOS Technical Reference* manual used by application programmers) are DENY_NONE, DENY_READ, DENY_WRITE, and DENY_READ_WRITE. In addition, there is a special mode called compatibility mode. With their capitalization and embedded underscores, the names of these modes may seem odd to you. However, these are the names that programmers actually use as they develop the software. When a programmer instructs the computer program to open a file, he or she considers the file-sharing requirements for that file and chooses an appropriate mode. If you are aware of these modes, you can recognize their behavior in the LAN-aware software that you buy and use.

DENY_NONE grants full access to the file by applications at other workstations. In essence, DENY_NONE defers the protection of the file's integrity until later, when the application updates individual records. If a workstation opens a file with a sharing mode of DENY_READ, the network operating system enables other workstations to write to the file but not read it. DENY_WRITE is the opposite; if a workstation opens a file with a sharing mode of DENY_WRITE, the network operating system does not enable other workstations to update the file. The other workstations can, however, read from the file.

DENY_READ_WRITE confers exclusive access to the workstation that opens the file. Attempts by other workstations to open the file (with any value of sharing mode) will fail.

Compatibility mode is the default sharing mode. If an application does not specify otherwise, the network operating system uses compatibility mode to determine how other workstations can open a file. In general, this mode grants exclusive access to an application. Compatibility mode also is in effect for new files that the application creates.

Using Record Locking

Because a file lock affects the entire file and extends from the time a file is opened until the time it is closed, the resulting *coarse granularity* (the systemwide effect on the group of people who are using the application at that moment) of the lock may be an inconvenience to the people in the office. A lock that lasts for the entire time that an application uses a file prevents others from accessing the file. A file lock does not enable file sharing.

A multiuser application uses record locking to protect the integrity of the data files. A record lock lasts only long enough to ensure that consistent data has been written to the file(s), and it usually affects only a small portion of the file.

A record lock specifies a certain region of a file by giving the region's location in the file (its offset) and its size (length). If the specified region cannot be locked successfully (another workstation opened the file in a mode other than DENY_NONE mode, or another workstation has locked the same record), the network operating system informs the application that the record is not available.

The locked region can encompass a portion of a data record, one data record, several adjacent data records, or the entire file. The choice is up to the application programmer. If each data record in a file is independent of the others, the application simply locks the affected data record. If relationships exist among the records in a file (perhaps one record contains a pointer to another record, or the updating of the file implies that several records may need to be moved in the file), the application may lock the entire file as if it were a single large record. In either case, the record lock usually lasts only a few milliseconds.

Using Multiuser Printing

You would think that sending print data to a shared network printer would be easy, painless, and not nearly as much trouble as trying to share files and records. Unfortunately, this isn't so.

Suppose that a person on the network is running Lotus 1-2-3 and needs to print a spreadsheet in condensed (small) print because it is several cells wide. The person sends control codes to the printer, prints the spreadsheet, and walks away from the network printer with a nicely formatted printout in hand. The next person on the LAN to print a report receives a printout with data tightly bunched on the left side of the page in small characters. The problem is that the preceding print job left the printer in condensed print mode.

For another example, assume that you tell your application to print a long, complex report. To your bewilderment, you find that other people's printouts are intermingled in the pages of your report. The page breaks occur nowhere near where they should. Yet the report prints correctly on a local (non-LAN-attached) printer. The problem is that the network software is inserting automatic page breaks that separate the printout into multiple print jobs. In this example, the application performs lengthy processing steps between sections of the report. The network operating system senses these pauses and, at each pause, thinks that the application has finished printing.

LAN Manager and LAN Server try to detect when an application finishes printing. The workstation can set a timeout value to help the network operating system know when a pause in printing really means the end of a print job. In addition, LAN Manager and LAN Server come with a PRTSC utility that enables you to press Ctrl-Alt-PrtSc to signal the end of a print job.

You can create a file that LAN Manager or LAN Server uses to print job-separator pages between printouts. The job-separator file supports a wide variety of printer control options, which you can use not only to specify what the separator page should look like but also to reset the printer to a default mode before each printout is produced. If you do not specify a job-separator file, LAN Manager uses its DEFAULT.SEP file. You use the NET SEPARATOR command to specify whether separator pages should be in effect and the name of the job-separator file.

NetWare offers somewhat more extensive control of the network printer through the use of the CAPTURE command (formerly the SPOOL command). You can control whether automatic formfeeds are added to the end of a file of print data, whether a job-separator page (Novell calls it a *banner page*) should be produced, whether tabs should be expanded into spaces and how many spaces to use, the number of copies that should be printed, the type of form that must be mounted in the printer, the variable text (user name or job name) that appears on the banner page, how NetWare detects the end of the print job (based on a timeout value or file-close operation), the lines per page, the width of each line, and some miscellaneous items. Current versions of NetWare also provide the means to reset the printer between print jobs.

Buying Software Licenses for Multiple Users

Whether or not the software you use contains any sort of copy protection, you know that legally, you must purchase a copy of the software for each person who will use it. You may interpret this to mean a single copy for everyone in the office, or you may interpret it to mean a copy for as many people as will use the software at one time. Either way, a LAN makes it easy—too easy—to share an application or utility from the file server's disk drive. Many companies buy too few copies of the software they use. Be aware that if you fall into this trap and are caught, the legal and financial penalties will be greater than the cost of the software.

Buying Software for Each User

Part of the problem of the multiuser license issue is that many software vendors have not come to grips with how to sell software to LAN users. These vendors insist that you purchase a single copy of the software for each LAN user. For one company in New York City, this means renting a small warehouse to store the unopened, shrink-wrapped copies of the software it purchases. The company buys a copy for each LAN user but continues to use the first copy (installed on the file server). The other copies go into the warehouse. A site license for each of these software products would go a long way toward helping this company administer its LAN, but the company is frustrated by the single-user-license agreements of many software vendors (see the section "Buying Site Licenses" later in this chapter).

Buying Network Packs

A few software vendors handle the multiuser license issue by selling network packs. You buy a license for simultaneous use of the software by 5, 10, or more people. The software resides on the file server, and you get the appropriate number of user manuals to supplement the software. Lotus Development offers a network version of 1-2-3 that takes this approach.

Buying Site Licenses

For more than 5 or 10 people, you really want a site license. This arrangement buys you the legal right for everyone in your office to use the software and perhaps to make photocopies of the user manual. Not many software vendors currently offer site licenses. If you are part of a large office, however, you should try to insist on a site license when you purchase software. If you can negotiate such an arrangement, both you and the software vendor come out winners. Eventually, site licenses will become more common.

Establishing Copy Protection on a LAN

You probably have run into copy-protection schemes before. With many of these schemes, you have to insert a key disk (which cannot be copied under ordinary circumstances) to activate the software. Some copy-protection schemes put hidden files on your hard disk. Some schemes rely on *dongles*— special hardware keys you attach to the printer port of your computer. Still other schemes mark the location on the hard disk where files reside, and prevent you from copying these files to other locations.

All these schemes have one objective: to prevent software *piracy* (the theft of software by making additional copies of the application's files). All these schemes also have one common characteristic: they annoy the purchasers of the software.

On a LAN, it is possible to enforce software license agreements unobtrusively and gracefully. The application running at one workstation can communicate with other workstations, through the LAN cable, to determine whether the same copy is being run at different workstations. NetWare Lite, for example, does exactly this to make sure that you purchase one copy for each workstation.

This chapter has explained what it means for software to be single-user or multiuser, and you have learned how a network operating system transforms single-user DOS into a multiuser environment on a LAN. You understand rights, permissions, file sharing, record locking, multiuser printing, and multiuser software licenses. The rest of the chapter focuses on the applications, beginning with word processing and desktop publishing applications. You explore the sharing of spreadsheet files on the LAN. And you look closely at the class of personal computer applications known as database managers. These applications are good candidates for multiuser access from LAN workstations because they usually involve large amounts of data entry.

Using Word Processing and Desktop Publishing Programs

You probably would not want another person's typing to mingle with your own as you prepare a memo, letter, or report with a word processing program. Perhaps groupware vendors someday will find a good reason to implement concurrent, multiuser file sharing for word processor files, but until then, you will want to restrict your file sharing to loaning copies of your files to others. If you and the other people in your office produce hundreds or thousands of document files, however, you definitely will want to find a way to organize and keep track of all the files.

Sharing Files

On a peer-to-peer LAN, where your workstation is a file server to the other people in the office (and vice versa), you can share files simply by telling another person the name of the file and the directory it is in. If the other person has permission from the network operating system to read files in that directory, you can share your document files with that person.

You may want to set up three directories for document files. You can mark the first directory with permissions that enable other people to read and write files. Such a directory enables everyone to update files, so you must coordinate the updates within your office. The second directory for document files may be flagged with read-only permissions for other people. Such a directory enforces ownership of the files; you are the only one who can update them. Other people can copy the files and make use of their contents, but the read-only directory is your repository of original copies of documents. If you need a place to put private document files that you do not want others to read or write, you may create a third directory and flag it with appropriate permissions to keep prying eyes from peering into your files.

A server-based LAN is slightly different. To share a file, you must create the file on the shared network drive or copy the file to the network drive after you create it. You may use a directory with read-only permissions (for other people) for serious communications and a second directory with read/write permissions for general correspondence.

Keeping Track of Documents

As document files proliferate in a single directory on the file server, the job of remembering what each one contains becomes monumental. You do not want your effectiveness to drop just because you cannot remember which file is which. When someone asks you for some information you have stored in a document file, you want to be able to find it quickly and easily.

The first thing you can do is clean house regularly. There is no substitute for periodically (perhaps once a week) going through your document files to decide which ones you no longer need. (If you happen to delete the wrong file, remember the backup copies your office makes each day. You can recover the file from the backup copy. Or, if you are on a NetWare LAN, you can use the SALVAGE command to restore the file.)

The next thing you want to do is create more directories. You can use the directories on the file server as an outline structure that matches the work you do. By filing your documents in an appropriately named directory, you can easily remind yourself where certain documents are.

You may want to go beyond manual methods for keeping track of files. To automate the indexing of your documents, you will want software that is LAN-aware and easy to use. A good place to start your research is a product called InfoSelect, developed by the following company:

> MicroLogic
> P.O. Box 70
> Hackensack, NJ 07602
> (800) 342-5930

InfoSelect comes in a LAN version that enables you to share an officewide card file, schedule meetings, send electronic mail, maintain an officewide electronic bulletin board, and (of course) index document files on the file server. Another resource is the list of groupware vendors in Chapter 3, "Using Electronic Mail." Magellan is a tool of which you will want to be aware. For more information on Magellan, contact the following:

> Lotus Development Corporation
> 55 Cambridge Parkway
> Cambridge, MA 02142
> (617) 577-8500

As you do your research, you will find other products to evaluate; there are several in this category.

Using Spreadsheets

You can manage the sharing of spreadsheet files in a manner similar to the one you use for document files. The contents of spreadsheet files, called *worksheets*, are somewhat more structured and organized than those of document files. You will want to implement well-known, consistent procedures within the office for sharing the information in spreadsheet files.

Worksheets lend themselves more to a multiuser, file-sharing environment than do document files. Although you still do not want other people's typing to mingle with yours as you enter data into a worksheet, it's easy to see that a useful set of spreadsheet files can be the product of a team rather than an individual.

Sharing Worksheets

You may find that you want to share specific cells and ranges within a worksheet. You may want to form the habit of inserting remarks somewhere within the spreadsheet file to let others know which parts of the file they should use. You have learned to document your worksheets so that you can understand them after being away from them for a while. On a network, you need to extend this documentation to include remarks that will help others understand the information encoded in the files.

Working with Multiuser Spreadsheets

In Release 4 of 1-2-3, Lotus Development Corporation has provided features that facilitate group usage of a spreadsheet. The Version Manager makes it remarkably easy for coworkers to share data. Different people can enter versions in the same range of a worksheet file without overwriting each other's data. Version Manager keeps track of who created or modified each version or scenario and provides a merge utility that combines versions and scenarios from one file into another file. You can use Version Manager to do the following:

- Create and display different versions of data in a named range

- Group versions together into scenarios

- Display information about versions and scenarios, including what you entered (data and its assigned name) as well as where you entered it (range in which the data is located), when you entered it (date and time stamp), and even why you entered it (comments entered for each version or scenario)

- Create reports about the data in the versions

- Merge versions and scenarios from one file into another file

Using Database Managers

A *database* is any collection of related information in the form of lists, tables, notes, or other organizations of data. A database manager (DBMS) is the generalized software that enables you to enter, store, retrieve, process, and report the data. You design an application by telling the DBMS what data you want to keep track of, how it is laid out, how it should be processed, and how the data should be reported. You subsequently use the DBMS by entering data and instructing the DBMS to process and report the data.

You can easily imagine a group of people entering data into the same database from many workstations. A database manager is a good candidate for LAN-awareness. With the proper file-sharing, record-locking, and workstation-identifying methods in place, the database manager becomes an essential tool for recording and processing information in your office. You will want to make sure that you get a LAN-aware version of the software; using a single-user version of a DBMS on a LAN can be disastrous. You will find errors and inconsistencies creeping into the data as multiple users try to access the same file-server files without the benefit of file sharing and record locking.

The following sections look at eight LAN-aware database managers: Access, Alpha Four, DataEase, dBASE IV, FoxPro, Paradox, Paradox for Windows, and R:BASE. All eight are reasonably priced, popular, capable, and reliable. Any database manager product you buy for your LAN should be available in a LAN version that uses file sharing and record locking; these products certainly qualify (unlike some other DBMS products, such as Nutshell Plus II).

As you evaluate these and other database managers, apply the criteria in the following checklist:

- *Installation.* You will want to discover how much memory the software uses, what types of memory it uses, and whether you can run the DBMS under Windows or OS/2.

- *User interface.* Decide whether you like the way the program is designed to interact with you.

- *On-line help and documentation.* Look for help screens and written documentation that seem useful. If you are new to the DBMS environment, ask whether the product comes with a tutorial.

- *Data types.* All DBMS programs enable you to define the data entry fields as numeric or text-based. Other data types you may use include memo/note, telephone number, Social Security, date, and time.

- *Query formation.* A DBMS should offer pick lists and other features that help you form queries.

IV

Expanding a Network

■ *Special reports.* A DBMS should enable you to design your reports with a report generator, and you should be able to design specially formatted reports without a great deal of programming effort.

■ *Import/export.* Look for the capability of the DBMS to import and export a variety of file formats. Make sure that the software can interface with the other applications you use.

■ *SQL usage.* Structured Query Language (SQL) is an IBM standard for dealing with databases. If you need to access databases on host computers, or from products such as Microsoft's SQL Server, IBM's DB2 for OS/2, or Gupta Technology's SQLBase, you will want your DBMS to use SQL in a way that is compatible with these other products.

■ *Application-code generator.* Unless you are a professional programmer, a menu-driven method of creating the procedural statements that make up the processing steps of the application is important.

■ *Distributable applications.* You may want other people to be able to use the applications you develop. Determine how you can do this with the DBMS you are thinking of buying, and whether you have to pay extra for the capability.

Using Access

Microsoft Access is a Windows-based database manager that offers several interfaces. You can use the product's Windows interface to query and update your data; you can use a computer language called Access Basic (similar to Visual Basic) to program your own applications; and you can use Microsoft's Open Database Connectivity (ODBC) driver to allow Access to interface with other ODBC-compliant database tools and SQL servers.

Like most SQL databases, Access maintains a single disk file per database, storing multiple tables within that file. It's not a database server, however. In a multiuser situation, each Access client must fetch records from shared storage and process the records locally. Access does not have FoxPro's blazing speed when querying single tables.

Access can attach to and work with Paradox, dBASE, FoxPro, and Btrieve files. Access includes engines that understand Paradox, dBASE, and Btrieve engines, and it will maintain foreign indexes in place. That means that Access and Paradox, for example, can enjoy concurrent multiuser access to the same shared files. Access's update capability also is a great enhancement to products such as Btrieve (a record-manager programming tool from Novell) and FoxPro.

For more information about Access, contact the following:

> Microsoft Corporation
> 1 Microsoft Way
> Redmond, WA 98052
> (800) 426-9400
> (206) 882-8080

Using Alpha Four

Alpha Four lacks the tools you would need to build complex applications with sophisticated interfaces. This DBMS does not offer a compiler or procedural language. You can use Alpha Four to quickly create simple applications in your office, however. You certainly do not need to be a programmer to use Alpha Four.

Alpha Four features well-thought-out menus that guide you through the steps of creating your application. Simplicity is Alpha Four's hallmark. The context-sensitive, on-line help is descriptive and contains several useful examples.

You designate whether the files you create with Alpha Four should be in dBASE III Plus or dBASE IV format. Although this DBMS product does not have a procedural language, it does come with a scripting facility that enables you to embed complex macros containing IF/THEN conditions and other expressions. The only printer font Alpha Four supports is Courier.

Alpha Four can have as many as two billion records per database. The product uses extended and expanded memory if present and supports up to 254 fields per record.

For more information about Alpha Four, contact the following:

> Alpha Software
> 1 North Avenue
> Burlington, MA 01803
> (617) 229-2924

Using DataEase

DataEase emphasizes the use of simple English questions and answers as you develop a database application or form queries. DataEase asks its questions in clear, nontechnical terms. You carry on a dialog with DataEase to accomplish virtually every task.

A well-liked database manager, DataEase shows the reason for its popularity in its straightforward approach to everything from creating the data input screen to forming queries and generating reports. The context-sensitive help system always seems to relate precisely to the task you want to perform. The help text makes liberal reference to the printed documentation so that you know exactly where to look for further information.

Whether you know something about computer programming or are a novice, DataEase makes using a database manager simple. You can use the procedural-language capability of DataEase, called *DataEase Query Language* (DQL), in either of two ways: you can write a program from scratch, or you can let DataEase prompt you for the query statements and processing logic that make up your application.

DataEase imports dBASE files but cannot export files in dBASE format.

The DataEase company offers a variety of SQL server modules that you can install on a LAN to complement the DBMS. These modules enable you to access an SQL database, such as Microsoft's SQL Server. If you are an advanced programmer, you can interface your Pascal, C, or assembler programs with DataEase. DataEase will run in a DOS session under Microsoft Windows, but this DBMS does not yet offer a graphical Windows interface.

DataEase can have as many as two billion records per database. It uses extended and/or expanded memory if present, and it supports up to 255 fields per record.

For more information about DataEase, contact the following:

DataEase International
7 Cambridge Drive
Trumbull, CT 06611
(800) 243-5123

Using dBASE IV

With Borland International's purchase of Ashton-Tate in 1991, the famous, best-selling dBASE won a new lease on life. When Ashton-Tate released the first version of dBASE IV two years behind schedule, dismayed developers found *bugs* (errors) in the product that made it virtually unusable. Later versions of dBASE IV contained fixes for the bugs as well as new features, but the product's reputation preceded it, and dBASE IV did not sell well. Other DBMS products offer more features and faster performance than dBASE IV. Application developers hope that Borland turns dBASE IV into a state-of-the-art DBMS.

For years, dBASE was a standard among database manager products; other DBMS products were measured by their capability to import or export dBASE-format files. To use dBASE IV to create such files, however, you must be a programmer, and you must know the dBASE programming language. Other products use menus and prompts to help you write programs. dBASE IV comes with a menuing system called Control Center, but this menuing system does not help you write programs. Furthermore, Control Center is not as easy to use as the menuing systems of Paradox or R:BASE.

dBASE IV does offer a helpful *query by example* (QBE) feature. With QBE, you build and store complex queries that help you find information in your database. The difficult task consists of designing and writing the database application.

The report-generator module of dBASE IV is similarly helpful, enabling you to quickly produce reports in several standard formats. Custom formats, however, require programming effort on your part.

dBASE IV can have as many as one billion records per database. The product uses extended and/or expanded memory if present, and it supports up to 256 fields per record.

For more information about dBASE IV, contact the following:

> Borland International
> 1800 Green Hills Road
> Scotts Valley, CA 95067
> (800) 331-0877

Using FoxPro

FoxPro, a database manager that Microsoft acquired in its purchase of the Fox Software company, is the fastest-performing DBMS—and also one of the fastest-selling. These attributes probably account for Microsoft's purchase of Fox Software early in 1992, just a few months after Borland acquired Ashton-Tate. In addition to selling a Windows-based version of FoxPro, Microsoft offers the Windows-based Access database manager product, described earlier in this chapter. It will be interesting to see how Microsoft positions Access and FoxPro in the marketplace.

The DOS-based FoxPro user interface is text-based rather than graphics-based. FoxPro uses character-mode windows to display data, however, and has a Windows-like set of pull-down and pop-up menus. You can use a mouse with FoxPro, and you can even move FoxPro's windows and click character-mode buttons on-screen to activate options. You can move database fields during a browse operation with click-and-drag mouse actions. Like FoxPro's file operations, the text-mode user interface is responsive and quick. The Windows version of FoxPro, however, doesn't have the same lively, fast user interface as the text-mode version.

Fast indexing of files is the heart of FoxPro's performance. The relational QBE feature lacks most SQL commands but is flexible enough for almost any database inquiry you may want to make. FoxPro offers a range of application design tools to make your job easier. The procedural language is sophisticated, and you can use the optional compiler module to turn your application into executable (EXE) files.

FoxPro is not a simple tool for creating simple databases. This DBMS is likely to stretch your programming skills a bit as you develop your first few applications. FoxPro's context-sensitive, on-line help is rich with examples and explanations, but you will find the help text oriented more to programmers than to novice computer users.

FoxPro can have as many as one billion records per database. It uses extended and/or expanded memory if present, and it supports up to 255 fields per record.

For more information about FoxPro, contact the following:

Microsoft Corporation
1 Microsoft Way
Redmond, WA 98052
(800) 426-9400
(206) 882-8080

Using Paradox

Paradox is so successful that many people wonder why Borland acquired Ashton-Tate and the dBASE products. Paradox is full-featured and easy to learn. You will find Paradox to be almost as fast as FoxPro, even on the largest databases.

Speed notwithstanding, the Paradox user interface is its strongest selling point. Borland paid a great deal of attention to the content and organization of the software's menus, help screens, and printed documentation. Borland also offers a Windows version of Paradox.

The product's straightforward, easy-to-understand approach to application development enables novices and experienced programmers to create sophisticated applications. You can let Paradox build a standard column-oriented report for you, or you can design a custom-formatted report. Paradox imports and exports a wide range of file types. Paradox also offers a graphing tool that can help you create 10 kinds of graphs, ranging from pie charts to 3-D bar graphs. The product contains a QBE module that enables you simply to check off the fields you want to include in a query. A separate SQL Link module for accessing SQL database servers is available from Borland.

The Paradox Applications Language (PAL) is not difficult to learn. You can even create a simple application by letting Paradox record your keystrokes; Paradox transforms your keystrokes into a script you can play back. Experienced PAL programmers can use the script to create a complete application. Object PAL, which is the version of PAL that comes with Paradox for Windows, is highly object-oriented.

Paradox can have as many as two billion records per database. It uses extended and/or expanded memory if present, and it supports up to 255 fields per record.

For more information about Paradox, contact the following:

Borland International
1800 Green Hills Road
Scotts Valley, CA 95067
(800) 331-0877

Using R:BASE

R:BASE has been around for almost as long as dBASE. The years of competing with the former Ashton-Tate product have honed its features, help screens, and printed documentation. You can create useful, complete applications just by following R:BASE's application-generator menus. You certainly do not have to be a programmer to use R:BASE.

R:BASE contains a menu-driven QBE module that quickly leads you through the formation of a database inquiry. You can convert a query into a new database table, if you want. Each R:BASE database can have up to 80 tables (files), and a query can use up to five databases.

R:BASE's menus help you build sophisticated applications. The application-code generator turns your data entry screens and file descriptions into a custom-programmed application that you can use in your office, even if you have never programmed before.

R:BASE comes with an easy-to-learn procedural language. You can add pull-down menus, help screens, and other features that make it easy to operate your application. The R:BASE programming language provides a full set of SQL commands. R:BASE can import and export dBASE-format files.

R:BASE files can have an unlimited number of records per database, depending on the amount of free disk space you have. R:BASE uses extended and/or expanded memory if present and supports up to 400 fields per record.

For more information about R:BASE, contact the following:

Microrim
15395 S.E. 30th Place
Bellevue, WA 98007
(800) 628-6990

Summary

This chapter brought you up-to-date on network applications and what makes them different from stand-alone software. You first learned how DOS behaves in a multiuser environment; you then learned how the network operating system implements rights and permissions. After exploring the characteristics of multiuser applications—sharing files, locking records, identifying each user or workstation, and printing correctly on a shared LAN printer—you considered the software licensing issues you face on a LAN.

You then turned your attention to the applications you use on a LAN. You looked at word processing, desktop publishing, and spreadsheets from a multiuser point of view. And you surveyed eight database manager products.

In the next chapter, you learn how to manage your LAN so that it stays healthy and efficient.

Chapter 12

Managing Your Network

Network management is more art than science. As networks grow to connect hundreds or even thousands of workstations, the job of keeping the system up and running requires considerable experience, in-depth knowledge, and thorough training. Novell started its Certified NetWare Engineer (CNE) program just to solve this problem. The appendix in this book discusses certification programs in detail.

You are likely to see a variety of LANs in medium-size and large businesses. One department may be running TCP/IP over Ethernet, with NFS on the departmental file server; another part of the company may run NetWare over Token Ring, while yet another runs POWERLan over ARCnet. Interconnecting LANs that use different cables and protocols is a big challenge in network management. When the network crashes, however, managing even a few nodes in a peer LAN can be a bigger job than you planned.

As you see in this chapter, the designers of networks offer two special protocols just for network management: Simple Network Management Protocol (SNMP) and the OSI-compliant Common Management Information Protocol (CMIP). The protocols discussed in Chapter 5, "Using Protocols, Cables, and Adapters," enable workstations and file servers to communicate. The SNMP and CMIP protocols supply data that shows the health of your network.

When problems occur on your LAN, you need to take a systematic approach to solving them. Diagnosing and identifying the problems are the most difficult steps. In this chapter, you learn how to recognize the causes of most LAN problems. You become familiar with the tools that help you pinpoint network errors.

The network management protocols SNMP and CMIP, along with new versions of the network operating system software, someday will enable you to see and control an entire network without leaving your workstation. Hardware and software from different vendors will adhere to the new standards; managing the LAN will be systematic and routine. Until then, however, you will need the information in this chapter to keep your LAN healthy.

Learning the Basics of Network Management

Networks are proliferating faster than people are gaining the necessary skills and training to manage them. The job of managing the network is growing in importance, yet not enough people can do the job. To understand what the job entails, you first have to look at the basics of network management.

Keeping a LAN up and running is complicated by the dynamic, distributed nature of networks. Many LAN environments intermix PCs, gateways, bridges, routers, minicomputers, and mainframes. The LAN may very well include software systems that were not designed for a large network, and to complicate the situation further, the LAN may contain components from many different vendors.

To manage a network, you need a plan. The system plan must change and grow as the network changes and grows. The plan must address such issues as cable diagrams, cable layout, network capacity, protocol and equipment standards, workstation growth, and new LAN technologies. The plan needs to stay abreast of new network management tools and products.

Examining Technical Issues

Most network operating systems keep track of LAN activity and enable you to see performance statistics, traffic volumes, error counts, and accounting information. You sometimes can control servers and bridges remotely. And many vendors are offering add-ons for existing systems. A simple upgrade of your network operating system may provide you with a wealth of information. Vendors of networking products are keenly aware of the need for management tools and information, and these vendors are working to address the technical issues of network management.

These vendors are working also on standards and conformance testing to ensure that their products will interoperate with the variety of hardware and software on today's heterogeneous LANs. The effort to provide management solutions that are compatible with the wide range of available LAN products, however, is not keeping up with the technological advances of the LAN industry.

You need some level of automated network management system if you are to view and control a large LAN. Such a system must consider several technical issues regarding how LANs fail.

Dealing with Common Mode Failures

Sometimes a failure in one LAN component affects other components. The on-board logic of a network adapter, for example, may garble the interior portion of a received message packet. The network adapter will hand the result to the network operating system, which may not detect the error. If the network operating system puts the garbled data into a file, the file will be corrupt. Cross-checks and consistency checks help prevent such failures. A network management system must implement these checks.

Managing Traffic

A hardware or software failure may bring the LAN to a quiet halt, or the failure may cause more message-packet traffic than the network is designed to handle. In the latter case, network adapters may detect the error and broadcast error message packets of their own, adding to the traffic. The overburdened network may give no outward sign of failure except for poor performance. A network management system must be able to detect and report such failures.

Determining Robustness

A LAN management system is likely to encounter unexpected or invalid (badly formed) message packets in its lifetime. How the system handles the unexpected message is important. The software must react properly to duplicate messages or to messages from unregistered, off-line nodes. A robust LAN management system carries on by ignoring the bad message (letting the lower-level protocols handle the problem by resending the message) or by notifying an operator of the error and then issuing reset commands to the failing nodes.

Testing the LAN

You need to be able to tell the LAN management system how and when to test the network. The product must include built-in test points that enable you to exercise the LAN interfaces, perform an inventory of LAN facilities, and trace LAN activities.

Extending the LAN

The LAN management system needs to adapt to the network's growth. The growth may involve adding nodes, connecting the LAN to other networks, or introducing new technology. Unless it can adapt, the LAN management system itself will limit the growth of the network.

The LAN management system should have a long life span. Its adaptability to system changes depends on its capability to add new features and technology easily, with minimal effect on the existing system.

Examining Administrative Issues

In addition to handling technical issues, a LAN management system must handle a number of administrative issues. These issues include software distribution and version control, error determination and correction, system-configuration management, and access control and security.

Managing Software Distribution

You need to manage software distribution to prevent the introduction of nonlicensed software and computer viruses into the network. One way to control software distribution is to handle it from a central location in the network. You copy software onto a file server from a single distribution point and then remotely copy it to local hard disks. IBM's LAN Distribution Utility (LDU) is a product that automates this process.

You also want to synchronize all the workstations to ensure that everyone is using the correct version of the software. In some applications, such as those in the banking industry, you also have to synchronize remote software versions with central transaction-processing software versions. The simplest way to handle this synchronization is to make sure that all transactions include version information and that the central software rejects any out-of-date versions it receives.

Helping the Administrator

On small networks, the LAN administrator's job falls by default to someone in the office, probably as a part-time position. On larger systems (20 or more workstations), the administrator's job may be a recognized full-time position. In either case, the administrator will need help finding and solving problems, making backups, keeping a vigilant eye on security, and monitoring performance. The LAN management software may report results to the administrator's workstation or, on LANs with hundreds of nodes, send the data up to a host system for further analysis and review.

Discovering Problems

The LAN management software records problems (events) related to network adapters, cables, and other LAN components. When an error such as a failed network adapter occurs, the software notifies the LAN administrator. If the management software is sophisticated enough, it may suggest alternative solutions to the administrator. The management software also should provide facilities for monitoring file server activity, print servers, and gateways. When a problem occurs, the software typically alerts the LAN manager with an audible alarm and a highlighted indication of the problem on the display.

On a LAN with hundreds of workstations, the management software may forward the alert report to a host computer. The central site can use the information to maintain a centralized problem-history file for each remote LAN. The alert log can contain vendor contacts for specific problems, generate trouble tickets, and include information about how the problem was resolved.

Logging and Reporting Events

The management software can log network events—such as peak network-utilization times, new network addresses observed on the network, and error conditions—to a disk file or a printer. The administrator may import the logged events into a database for further filtering, reporting, and statistics gathering. The LAN management software must be capable of writing a file in a format that can be imported into other applications. The software may offer its own facilities for reporting the data. Typically, you can generate reports from the information stored in the event log over a selected period. A network administrator, for example, often wants to review network utilization for the past 24 hours and will want the software to provide that information.

Determining Operator Control

An administrator will want to query the status of a device attached to the network, such as a workstation, bridge, or gateway. The LAN management software should offer this capability. If the network adapters maintain a history of error statistics and traffic activity, the administrator will want to routinely gather this information from all nodes or selected nodes on the LAN.

Another useful LAN-management software function tests the status of the path between two workstations. This function is especially handy when repeaters or bridges separate the workstations.

Managing the LAN's Configuration

Configuration management requires knowing what software is installed on which workstations and how those workstations are configured. For applications that your company developed internally and distributed automatically (subject to strict version control), this problem seldom occurs. But for off-the-shelf, shrink-wrapped software (spreadsheets and word processors), keeping track of which workstation accesses what version of a software product is a big job.

Large corporations most frequently take the approach of putting a certain collection of supported software packages on the network. Typically, the list includes one or two packages in each of the standard categories: word processing, database management, spreadsheets, and telecommunications.

If you use these packages, you can get help from the company's technical support personnel in the form of question answering and problem solving, tutorials and training, and data conversion utilities. If you prefer to use other packages to perform the same basic functions, the corporation may not offer technical support and may even remove the offending software from the file server.

In an environment of hundreds of workstations, such a corporate policy supports an organized, rational approach to managing the LAN. Version control, problem solving, training, and migration to new software can take place in an orderly, well-defined manner. The LAN management software may help enforce the corporate policy.

Typically, you can configure a workstation and its software to suit your preferences. In a large corporate environment, this arrangement may hinder technical support. A configuration change involving screen colors is not important, but other workstation-setup modifications may make the tasks of answering questions and fixing problems difficult. These modifications include unusual printer-control codes and nondefault directory structures.

An organization may have guidelines and rules that attempt to limit the customization and configuration of software products. Nonetheless, and perhaps in defiance of the rules, individuals sometimes like to express themselves by choosing different configuration options. For shrink-wrapped software products, the organization is usually helpless to prevent such modifications because the organization cannot reprogram the software.

If you have a technical support question and you've configured the software you use in nonstandard ways, the person who tries to answer your question may have difficulty understanding your configuration. The best approach for a LAN that encompasses hundreds or thousands of workstations is to have a prescribed standard configuration for each supported program. In the worst case, technical support personnel can return your workstation to the standard configuration as the first step in determining and correcting a problem.

Managing Access Control and Security

On a small LAN, the network operating system usually controls access. On a large network that connects many LANs and mainframe computers, controlling access becomes a function of a LAN management facility.

Your account and password will log you on to your LAN, but you may need to pass additional security checkpoints to access certain resources of the LAN. If your LAN is attached to a mainframe, this becomes especially true. You may find that certain applications contain their own security features. The network administrator has the job of setting up security at the various levels. A LAN management product will support the administrator's role as security chief and may even provide the application-level password control.

A diskless workstation does not save money because it lacks disk drives, but it can be a useful tool if security is important in your office. Such a workstation prevents people from copying information on the file server to a transportable floppy disk. A diskless workstation also prevents anyone from introducing foreign software and data files into the system.

Defining the Network Administrator's Role

Managing a LAN from a centralized location is a difficult task. As yet, vendors do not offer a complete set of tools for network administration, so the network administrator typically uses a mixed bag of partial-solution software and hardware tools. The administrator has to be an expert in using the available tools, often calling on his or her own creativity to solve unusual problems. To solve problems as they occur, the administrator must understand the network's configuration, performance, accounting, planning, security, and applications. The administrator will likely spend a great deal of time traveling to workstations, servers, and other network devices to solve problems.

Using the LAN Management Protocols: SNMP and CMIP

A large part of network management consists of keeping track of the devices on your networks, checking the network's performance, and diagnosing and correcting problems. Many of the LAN industry's efforts have been directed toward developing automated ways to accomplish these tasks. These efforts have resulted in two distinct yet similar protocols for managing a network. These two protocols were designed by committees, not by specific vendors. (You learn about IBM's SNA Management Services in an upcoming section, "Using IBM's Network Management Tools.")

The Simple Network Management Protocol (SNMP) is an outgrowth of TCP/IP communications needs. Jeff Case, president of SNMP Research of Knoxville, Tennessee (a company that supplies software to SNMP vendors), and a group of other people created SNMP to solve problems within such networks as the Internet (discussed in Chapter 10, "Using UNIX LANs").

The Common Management Information Protocol (CMIP), which is part of the Open Systems Interconnection (OSI) standard, is the product of an international standards committee.

Both protocols have their advantages, and vendors of networking products are developing LAN management systems that incorporate both protocols. In the next few sections of this chapter, you discover the similarities and differences between SNMP and CMIP.

Comparing CMIP and SNMP

CMIP and SNMP have a common goal: to bring network management details to the network administrator so that the administrator can make changes, find out where a fault lies, or just retrieve information from a node on the network. Both protocols help the administrator diagnose problems, plan capacity, and generate reports.

Both protocols use a Management Information Base (MIB). An MIB consists of a set of variables, test points, and controls that all devices on the network support and that a network administrator can control. Both protocols also support vendor-specific extensions to the MIB. These extensions enable network devices with more intelligence to report or accept greater amounts of information without requiring that all devices support the same intelligence.

As they develop network management products, vendors are merging the capabilities of SNMP and CMIP MIBs. By making SNMP and CMIP use compatible MIBs, vendors can create a network management product that can accept information from SNMP or CMIP but store the information in a common format.

Contrasting CMIP with SNMP

CMIP and SNMP differ in the ways they retrieve and report data across the network. The two protocols offer different functions, require different amounts of computer-processing power, and use different amounts of memory. Each protocol uses a different set of lower-level protocols to send and receive network management information on the network, and each protocol has the support of a different standards committee.

Data Access

SNMP and CMIP have data retrieval functions that require a different outlook on the part of the retriever. SNMP is better at accessing specific individual items of information, whereas CMIP is oriented toward retrieving collections of information. With SNMP, you ask for the particular item you want. With CMIP, you must make a general request and then qualify that request by specifying what you do *not* want. SNMP operates in a more focused manner, whereas CMIP deals with classes of data that you constrain with qualifications you have to state.

Both approaches have their advantages. For some problems, you know exactly what information you want; SNMP's approach would be quite satisfactory in such cases. At other times, you want the broadest possible answer to a query so that you can see all relevant information.

Polling Versus Reporting

SNMP works by *polling*, in which a central management processor (perhaps your workstation) regularly asks each device on the network for its current status. CMIP uses *reporting*, in which the device only informs your central management station about changes in the device's status.

With the SNMP approach, a large number of network devices will cause a great deal of message traffic and perhaps slow the network. SNMP does, however, allow you to have devices on the network that do not have to be intelligent enough to detect and report problems. SNMP makes it simpler to detect a failed device that cannot report its failure. The implementation of SNMP in the remote device only has to be large enough to answer Yes or No when it is polled.

Size and Performance

A network management system built on SNMP can be smaller, faster, and less expensive than a CMIP implementation. CMIP requires a faster computer and more memory to do its job. This is logical, because polling requires less intelligence from the devices being managed than reporting does.

In most cases, a vendor can easily implement SNMP in a TSR program on a DOS-based personal computer. It would be difficult to do this with CMIP.

CMIP is broader in scope and has more features and capabilities than SNMP. But as mentioned in the preceding section, you pay the price in terms of memory and speed to have CMIP's functions. You may not want or need all of CMIP's functions on your network.

Vendors of network management systems that are primarily SNMP-based will have to be more creative, but they can accomplish almost the same tasks as with CMIP.

Transport Layer Protocols

To send a network management request or response across the network, SNMP uses simple datagrams. As mentioned in Chapter 5, "Using Protocols, Cables, and Adapters," datagrams are connectionless, and there is no guarantee of delivery. The two communicating devices must consider the possibility that a datagram will not get to its destination. This means that the sender will retry the send operation several times before declaring that the receiver has died. SNMP can use simple communications protocols (such as IPX or IP and UDP) to route messages.

The difference between datagram- and session-oriented communications is best illustrated by comparing a letter and a phone call. The phone call sets up a two-way circuit, but the letter simply is sent. Letters require less equipment and overhead than phone calls require, and this is also true for datagrams.

Its use of connection-oriented communications sessions makes CMIP better at retrieving large amounts of data—but this feature also can make the network harder to manage when problems occur. If the network is failing and almost nonfunctional, SNMP will retry its network management requests until one of them gets through. The session-oriented connections on which CMIP depends may no longer exist as a result of the network failure.

Protocol Standards

CMIP, like other OSI protocols, is an international standard controlled by international standards bodies such as the International Standards Organization (ISO). Vendors can test their implementations against a conformance test suite from the Corporation for Open Systems (COS), which also performs conformance tests for other OSI protocols.

SNMP, by contrast, is not an international standard. Like TCP/IP, however, SNMP is controlled by the Internet Activities Board.

Assessing CMIP and SNMP Product Availability

If practicality is the most important principle to you, SNMP has one undeniable advantage: many more products support it than support CMIP. Despite the considerable interest in CMIP, it has not yet been implemented in as many network products. Products based on SNMP—routers, Ethernet hubs, fiber devices, and Ethernet devices—are common. Part of the reason is the difference in age between the two protocols; SNMP has been around longer. Many companies now are developing network management systems that use CMIP or a combination of CMIP and SNMP.

Choosing SNMP or CMIP for Your LAN

Should your network management system be based on SNMP or CMIP? SNMP is oriented more toward managing specific devices, whereas CMIP is better at communicating information between two or more network management systems. In this context, SNMP and CMIP play complementary roles. Depending on the size and complexity of your network, you may find that the best network management system for your office uses both CMIP and SNMP. The system may use SNMP to manage specific devices on a particular LAN. The same software may use CMIP to help a network administrator in New York manage a wide area network of LANs in Chicago, Los Angeles, and Dallas.

Using IBM's Network Management Tools

Large wide area networks are not uncommon among IBM customers, so it should come as no surprise to you that IBM offers network management products for such networks. Token Ring and IBM's own Systems Network Architecture (SNA) are the foundation on which LAN Network Manager and NetView are built.

Managing Token Ring LANs

Token Ring always has had special capabilities in the areas of internal diagnostics and ring management—capabilities that have gone largely untapped by network management software. Unlike ARCnet and Ethernet, Token Ring LANs circulate a constant stream of Medium Access Control (MAC) frames that provide a wealth of information regarding the network's status.

The network adapter cards use these MAC frames privately to keep the network running, but network management applications can intercept the frames to reveal the status and health of the network.

Few vendors offer software tools that capture these MAC frames for network management purposes. One vendor, IBM, augments the MAC frames with another protocol layer of management services as defined by Systems Network Architecture. In large companies, Token Ring LANs often are part of SNA networks. SNA is an IBM standard for networking that encompasses just about everything. Terminals, PCs, LANs, controllers, mainframes, and even remote printers come under the SNA umbrella. An SNA network node is characterized as an *entry point* or a *focal point*. An entry point can generate SNA statistics and status information; a focal point receives the data and presents it to an operator.

Within SNA, IBM has defined a Management Services standard that defines how network management products communicate with one another. The IBM standard, for example, says that an *alert* (a record of an error or other significant event) contains such data fields as the address of the node at which the error occurred, the date and time of the error, the ID of the management component reporting the error, the probable cause, and a recommended action. (Of course, the node that initiated the alert may not be able to supply all these items.) Although it was developed by IBM, SNA nonetheless is a well-known, fully documented standard to which many computer manufacturers adhere so that their hardware and software are IBM-compatible.

Not all Token Ring workstations are peers. One workstation is designated as the *active monitor*, which means that it assumes additional responsibilities for controlling the ring. The active monitor maintains the ring's timing control, issues new tokens (if necessary) to keep things going, and generates diagnostic frames under certain circumstances. The active monitor, which can be any workstation on the network, is chosen when the ring is initialized. If the active monitor fails, the other workstations (the standby monitors) automatically negotiate with one another to choose a new active monitor.

The IEEE 802.5 Token Ring standard defines six types of MAC frames. A workstation sends a Duplicate Address Test frame when it joins the ring to ensure that its address is unique. To tell other workstations that it is still alive, the active monitor sends an Active Monitor Present frame every so often. Other workstations periodically send a Standby Monitor Present frame. A standby monitor sends Claim Token frames when it suspects that the active monitor may have died. A workstation sends a Beacon frame in the event of a major network problem, such as a broken cable or a workstation transmitting without waiting for a token (for example, going out of turn). A Purge frame is sent after a ring initializes itself or after a new active monitor is established.

Network management software locates the active monitor on the LAN by looking for the Active Monitor Present MAC frames. Software watches for Beacon frames and uses them to trigger diagnostic actions. Using the standard ring-polling technique defined in the IEEE 802.5 Token Ring specification, the software also can determine the status of each network adapter card on the network. If an adapter is found to be disabled and the Token Ring LAN is part of an SNA network, an alert can be generated. When errors occur on a Token Ring workstation, the real culprit sometimes is a different workstation. The *nearest active upstream neighbor* (NAUN) workstation—the node responsible for passing a token or frame downstream to this workstation—may have malfunctioned and corrupted the data. Network management software can detect the NAUN relationship and use it to point you in the right direction.

Using SNA on Token Ring

Above the MAC layer, a focal point or an entry point that needs to perform management tasks can use SNA Management Services. If SNA-aware support software is loaded into a workstation, that workstation can be queried, tested, and diagnosed from a remote location. SNA is rich in management and maintenance functions. It defines services for performing traces, recording memory snapshots (even from a remote system), requesting or responding to tests, and generating and recording statistics.

To trace events on a particular segment of the network, for example, the focal point issues an Activate Link (ACTLINK) request. It follows up with an Activate Trace (ACTTRACE) request, records the resulting Record Trace Data (RECTRD) events, and finally issues a Deactivate Trace (DACTTRACE) request. The RECTRD messages contain the link address, the trace type, and the trace data. An ACTTRACE request may specify that the trace include data for an entire segment (transmission group) or for a specific link.

A Request Maintenance Statistics (REQMS) request asks an SNA node to report resource maintenance statistics and specifies whether those statistics counters should be reset after being reported. A Token Ring workstation on an SNA network can respond to this request with *adapter engineering change level data* (version information about the network adapter), network software version data, traffic counts, and error counts. If error counts exceed predetermined thresholds, the workstation can initiate the sending of these statistics even without receiving an REQMS message.

As you can see, SNA provides many services for network maintenance and management.

Using IBM's LAN Network Manager

IBM's LAN Network Manager is a network management product that helps network administrators manage Token Ring LANs, especially those that are part of larger SNA networks. The software provides a simple menu interface that works with NetView (a mainframe IBM product) or by itself on a single-segment or multisegment Token Ring network. Do not confuse IBM's LAN Network Manager with Microsoft's LAN Manager: the IBM offering is a true network management application, whereas Microsoft's product is a network operating system.

The IBM LAN Network Manager complies with Systems Application Architecture and runs under OS/2 Presentation Manager. It uses OS/2 Database Manager to store and retrieve network configuration data and network error-event histories (alerts).

Version 1.1 of LAN Network Manager incorporates 80 NetView commands and uses the CMIP and SNMP protocols; it can display a pictorial (graphic) representation of your LAN.

Running alone, LAN Network Manager acts as a focal point on a network. When used with NetView, though, it also is an entry point (an agent) to the mainframe product NetView. When used as an entry point, LAN Network Manager is, in SNA terms, a System Services Control Point node. It uses an SNA SSCP-Physical Unit communications session to talk to NetView. Usually, several SSCPs exist in an SNA network, and they provide essential management services: helping to activate or deactivate the network, allocating network resources, managing the recovery of the network from communications failures, collecting traffic data, interacting with network operations people, executing their commands, and coordinating the interconnection of the different segments of the network. NetView itself is an SSCP node that offers central management of a large, geographically diverse network.

What does this mean to you? You can initiate and control network management operations from any terminal or workstation on the network, whether or not the terminal or workstation is physically part of the Token Ring network being managed. This is especially useful to network administrators who are geographically remote from the LANs for which they care.

Using IBM's NetView

The mainframe-based product NetView incorporates and combines the features of several other IBM mainframe products. Network Communications Control Facility (NCCF) works across multiple-domain networks to record alerts, divide management responsibilities among several network operators, and run command-script programs. Network Logical Data Manager records session and routing information, including response-time data. Network Problem Determination Application analyzes network problems and presents the results at several levels of detail. At the lowest level, NPDA reveals the probable cause of an error or failure.

NetView integrates these and other functions into a simple menu-driven management application. A NetView operator can easily determine a particular SNA node's health, as well as analyze statistics or reconfigure (or reset) network devices. A LAN Network Manager or NetView operator, for example, can reconfigure a LAN bridge to have a different network address or a different *hopcount limit* (the maximum number of bridges through which a message frame can pass on its journey). From NetView or LAN Network Manager, you can collect performance and traffic statistics from LAN bridges (including a count of the frames that were discarded or not forwarded because of error conditions) and a count of broadcast frames intended for reception by all workstations.

You also can use NetView's NCCF to query or command LAN Network Manager without actually sitting down at a LAN Network Manager workstation. You can ask for the current status of a Token Ring node, remove the node from the network, perform a point-to-point test between two nodes, reset LAN Network Manager, and ask for a display of the current configuration of a LAN segment.

You can programmatically control NetView or obtain network-status and event-history information from it in two ways. First, NetView incorporates a script file processor that an administrator can use to automate the system's response to certain events. Programming the script language facility embedded in NetView is much like writing scripts for a PC communications program. You can easily write a program that wakes up when a particular kind of alert is received, for example. Your program may try to recover from the error automatically by sending a reset-device command to the problem node.

The application programming interface to NetView, however, is more compli-cated, but it enables custom-written programs in a high-level language to access NetView configuration data files and alert histories. An application program also can use the NetView API to trigger an alert of its own—perhaps to signal a problem with a database file. NetView records the resulting alert in its history file and takes an appropriate action (as you define it). This action may consist, for example, of a notification that operator intervention is required.

A recent aspect of the NetView API is an LU 6.2 (peer-to-peer communica-tions) facility. LU 6.2 is a dialog-oriented protocol within SNA. With simple verbs such as *allocate, receive-and-wait, send-data, confirm,* and *deallocate,* the LU 6.2 protocol makes it easy to query NetView or perform custom network management tasks (implemented by your company's programmers, of course).

Another IBM product, NetView/PC, provides an API to NetView that other vendors can use to interface with their equipment. Such companies as Synoptics, AT&T, Paradyne, and Codex have products that work with NetView and are based on the NetView/PC interface. The devices that use this interface include Ethernet adapters, modem-management hardware, and T-1 network resources.

Auditing Your IBM LAN

LAN Network Manager works with other IBM products to control access to the network. It enables you to set up rules defining when certain worksta-tions can log on. With the IBM LAN Station Manager and 8230 Token Ring Controlled Access Unit, LAN Network Manager can detect intruder logins, generate an alert, and automatically remove the offender from the network by reprogramming or resetting the 8230 CAU. LAN Network Manager itself is password-protected, of course.

Do you know exactly where all your company's PCs are located? LAN Net-work Manager, LAN Station Manager, and the CAU work together to help you map your LANs as they change over time.

The CAU incorporates a data-reporting function that notifies LAN Network Manager of adapter, lobe, and segment identifications for the workstations on the LAN. LAN Station Manager, available in DOS and OS/2 versions, col-lects device information from each workstation and then sends the informa-tion to LAN Network Manager. LAN Station Manager maintains a station database that contains user-specific information, such as room number, serial number, and a symbolic machine name. IBM suggests that you install LAN Station Manager on each workstation. LAN Network Manager (or NetView) can trigger the CAU or LAN Station Manager to report what they know and thus correlate a particular workstation with a particular building location. You can use the resulting information to track down all the PCs in your company.

IBM uses CMIP in its network management products, but use of IBM's CMIP and SNMP is fairly limited. One of the few places CMIP comes into the picture is between the new CAU device and LAN Network Manager. Other diagnostic and management functions within the network generally will not be CMIP-compliant. The primary protocol that IBM uses in its network management products is defined in SNA's Management Services, and this will remain true for years to come. An IBM spokesperson has said that future CMIP support will be added as the definition of CMIP becomes clearer.

Using IBM's Network Management Applications

Token Ring has hidden strengths, and you soon will see more network management applications that take advantage of these strengths. In the meantime, though, the IBM products discussed in this chapter can give you an inside look at the health of your network. LAN Network Manager and NetView are sophisticated yet simple. They also are somewhat expensive. You will not want to purchase these tools for a small-office LAN. If you have at least a medium-size Token Ring LAN, however, you may want to consider getting LAN Network Manager. Budgets notwithstanding, when you need tools like these, you need them badly.

Using General LAN Management Tools

In the following sections of this chapter, you learn about specific tools you can use to manage your network. These tools range from time-domain reflectometers (TDRs) to integrated management systems. Some of these tools can be quite expensive. If your network is important to your business, however, you may find these tools a wise investment.

Estimating the Cost of Downtime

In recent studies, major corporations reported sizable financial losses when problems occurred on their networks. One study calculated the lost productivity resulting from network problems to be more than $3 million per year, on average. The same study found that the average network is completely or partly disabled about twice a month and that the average downtime is more than half a business day.

Network *downtime*—the time that the network is down or degraded—can be expensive. This is particularly true for a business that runs its day-to-day operations on a network. As companies recognize the increased importance of their networks, they demand better and better tools from vendors to help keep the networks up and running. The biggest network applications of the 1990s may well turn out to be network management products.

Setting Network Management Goals

Network management has two goals. First, proper LAN management tries to reduce the number of network problems. If problems do occur, the second goal is to minimize inconvenience and localize the damage.

With these goals in mind, the International Standards Organization (ISO) identified five management categories a LAN management system should include: accounting, configuration, fault, performance, and security. Following are descriptions of these management categories:

Category	Description
Accounting management	Records and reports network resource-utilization data
Configuration management	Understands and controls the parameters that define the state of the network
Fault management	Detects, isolates, and controls problems on the network
Performance management	Analyzes and controls the rate at which the network can process data
Security management	Controls access to network resources

Four types of network management products exist to deal with the five ISO categories: physical-layer tools, network monitors, network analyzers, and integrated network management systems. Each kind of product offers different benefits to the people who manage today's heterogeneous networks.

Defining the Types of Tools

Physical-layer tools include time-domain reflectometers (TDRs), oscilloscopes, breakout boxes, power meters, and similar products that find problems such as cable breaks, short circuits, unterminated cables, and bad connections.

Using the Time-Domain Reflectometer

Years ago, cable testers were bulky, awkward devices. Microminiaturization, however, has produced relatively inexpensive hand-held devices that you can carry around the office to check individual cables. Some of these small devices even come with portable printers that you can use to produce a report on the health of each cable in your cabling system. All such devices are battery-powered, and a few use rechargeable NiCad batteries. Figure 12.1 shows popular LAN diagnostic products from the Microtest company.

Fig. 12.1
The family of LAN-cable and LAN-connection diagnostic products from Microtest.

A cable tester contains a time-domain reflectometer (TDR) and perhaps additional test circuits. A TDR works by sending sonarlike pulses through the LAN cable. The TDR detects the reflections, analyzes them, and displays the result.

Typically, a cable tester can tell you the length of a cable, whether the cable is correctly wired internally (pin-to-pin wire mapping), whether the cable contains a short circuit (wires touching each other through damaged or missing insulation), whether the cable contains a broken wire (an "open"), and whether the cable suffers from electrical crosstalk (interference). Any of these problems can bring down a network.

The Future of Cable Testers

Manufacturers of cable testers are pushing the technology of cable analysis to greater heights. New devices extend cable testing into the realm of protocol analysis. The Fluke 670 LANMeter and Scope Communications FrameScope units go beyond the Physical layer of the OSI reference model (the usual domain of cable testers) into layers 2, 3, and even 4. The Fluke 670 costs about $6,000, and the FrameScope costs about $4,000—both quite a bit below the price of a protocol analyzer.

Different models of both devices attach to a live Ethernet or Token Ring LAN. The devices accumulate and display statistics on the health and performance of your network. Generally, the statistics show message frame counts, either total or by type of frame, in relation to elapsed time. For Ethernet LANs, the devices reveal excess collisions (indicating a jabbering network adapter), late collisions (indicating that your cables are too long), and error frame counts (resulting from faulty connections). On a Token Ring LAN, each device can recognize and count Media Access Control (MAC) layer frames.

These frames show neighbor relationships (in terms of MAU connections), receiver congestion errors (network adapters whose buffers can't handle incoming traffic), line errors, CRC errors, and the dreaded beaconing LAN. Even when your LAN is beaconing, you can insert these new cable testers onto the ring and determine the network addresses of the affected nodes. When an MAU port gets "stuck," the tester informs you of the condition and lets you reset the port remotely from the enhanced cable tester. You also can determine whether a Token Ring cable is experiencing phase jitter (a difficult-to-sense noise condition that often indicates a bad MAU).

These devices don't decode and display particular LAN message frames. Instead, the devices "snapshot" each frame as it goes by, determine the type and meaning of the frame, and increment appropriate counters in the cable tester's memory. Both units incorporate flash ROM and have more than 256K of RAM for frame buffers and statistics.

You can choose to monitor overall network traffic, certain kinds of error situations, or traffic to and from a given node. You can determine which node is sending or receiving the most LAN traffic. You can *ping* (send a short message to) a file server or other LAN node to determine the active presence of that node. If you determine that a particular cable or network adapter is hurting the LAN, you can cause that network node to remove itself from the ring. You can also monitor the status of bridges and routers, and even determine token rotation time on a ring.

The units enable you to associate workstation names or individuals' names with network addresses, making it easy to see who is active on the LAN and whose connections are healthy. You won't have to know somehow that node 10005A123456 is Sue's PC. The units have serial ports through which you can download upgrades into the flash ROM chips. And, of course, these new devices can perform the more mundane cable tests you'd expect of a TDR device.

These enhanced cable testers, which have sizable LCD displays, remind you at first glance of a Nintendo Game Boy. Don't be fooled, though; these new hand-held cable testers are just what the doctor ordered for ailing networks. One such tester may find its way into your bag of network tools someday.

Short circuits and open connections can occur months or years after installation, especially if cheap insulation dries out, becomes brittle, and cracks. Conversely, a water-soaked cable won't carry LAN traffic very well. During installation, a person may pull a wire around a corner, and part of the insulation will scrape off (a condition called a *shiner*). This cable problem might not immediately manifest itself, but it could cause a network outage months later.

Some wiring problems occur during cable manufacturing and connection. Once in a great while, the factory or the installer puts connectors on the cable with the wrong wire leading to the wrong pin, and the new cable won't work at all. Or the person may mix up the wire pairs by attaching connectors in a way that causes one of the wires to carry a signal that the other wire pair should carry (a condition known as *reversed pairs*). Even with perfectly manufactured, carefully connected wire, you might inadvertently cause a cable problem. In planning a network installation or enhancement, you might overlook the published limitations of the wiring specification; the result is a LAN segment with cables that are too long or have too many nodes in a segment. It's easy to overlook distance and number-of-nodes limitations when you are concentrating on giving people access to the network.

Before you attach the cable tester to your LAN, you absolutely must know the type of cable your LAN uses. Electricity travels at different speeds in different types of cable. The testing device must know the nominal velocity of propagation (NVP) for your cable before the tester can make accurate distance determinations. NVP, expressed as a fraction or sometimes as a percentage of the speed of light in a vacuum, can vary from .60 to .90. For example, Level 3 UTP cable has an NVP of .62, Level 5 UTP has an NVP of .72, RG-58 has an NVP of .80, RG-62 has an NVP of .84, and Type 1 has an NVP of .78. The cable tester will display incorrect results if you don't supply the tester with the right information about the cable type. Even the difference between foam and nonfoam insulation in the cable can throw off the tester's results.

The first thing that you do with a new cable tester is calibrate the unit in relation to the type of cable you use. The cable tester often comes with a chart or table that provides the NVP for popular cable types. But you'll want to calibrate the tester anyway, in relation to the exact type of cable in your LAN. Calibration is a matter of trying different NVP values until the tester displays the correct cable length for a cable whose length you know because you've measured it.

You also need an up-to-date, accurate diagram of the *topology* (layout) of your LAN. When you think you've found a wiring fault, you will want to pinpoint the bad cable on your diagram to make sure that you understand how the symptoms of the problem (a particular group of workstations being dropped from the LAN, for example) relate to the wiring fault you've identified.

The basic procedure for using a cable tester is simple. After you detach both ends of the cable from the network, you connect the cable tester to one end and, for unshielded twisted pair (UTP), you connect a loopback device to the other end. The genderless data connector that you usually find on shielded twisted pair (STP) is its own loopback device. You then run through the tester's diagnostic steps to see whether the cable is healthy.

You can—and should—use a cable tester to check a new LAN cable installation. When you build a new LAN or add a new cable segment to an existing LAN, you'll want to know that the new wires can carry noise-free LAN signals before you try to log on to a file server. If you have a contractor install and maintain your LAN wiring, insist that the contractor perform cable tests during the installation. If you install your own wiring, use a cable tester to check your work.

Using Network Monitors

A *network monitor* is a computer device that attaches to a network and monitors all, or a selected portion, of network traffic. By examining frame-level information in each packet, network monitors can compile statistics on network utilization, packet type, number of packets sent and received by each network node, packet errors, and other significant information.

Network monitors are relatively inexpensive, and you can use several on a large LAN—one for each network segment. You generally would let your network monitors run continuously, allowing them to collect data and search for problems. A network monitor does a reasonably good job of detecting errors, and such tools can be part of an overall integrated management system.

The price of network monitors ranges from several hundred dollars (for software-only products) to about $10,000. Figure 12.2 shows the relatively inexpensive TXD product from Thomas-Conrad ($195 for a site license). TXD reveals statistical and diagnostic information about NetWare LANs.

Fig. 12.2
Thomas-Conrad's TXD is a diagnostic software product for NetWare LAN.

Using Network Analyzers

Although network monitors can detect network problems, *network analyzers* (sometimes called *protocol analyzers*) can help you track down and fix those problems. Network analyzers contain sophisticated features for real-time traffic analysis, packet capture and decoding, and packet transmission. Some even include troubleshooting expertise in the form of test suites. Network analyzers sometimes feature a built-in TDR. The most sophisticated network analyzers use special-purpose hardware to detect problems that are not visible to standard network controllers. Recently, manufacturers of network analyzers have begun adding artificial intelligence (AI) to their products.

Network analyzers are complicated, expensive tools for detecting certain kinds of LAN problems. You would use an analyzer to identify a failing device, configuration error, or LAN bottleneck. These tools are more sophisticated than cable testers or software-only network utilities. When you face a problem that requires you to examine the detailed contents of your data frames, you are like a doctor who reaches for a microscope to view cells in a blood sample; as a doctor, you have to know what normal cells look like and how many cells of each type you should see. On a LAN, the analyzer is like the microscope.

Network analyzers listen to all the frames flowing across the LAN and give you a picture of their health. The analyzer selects those frames that meet the filtering criteria you set up, captures them in a file, and summarizes the frames or decodes them to show their contents. You can tell a network analyzer to show only error frames, frames from (or to) a certain workstation or server, frames of a certain type or that contain a given pattern of data, or frames that exceed the size and frequency thresholds you establish. Some analyzers enable you to inject extra traffic into the LAN, enabling you to simulate adding more nodes.

When you know what to look for, a network analyzer can show exactly which network adapter is causing a broadcast storm, help identify a misconfigured gateway that is causing routing errors, or show the interpacket arrival rate of the frames involved in a performance problem. The network analyzer, however, does not substitute for experience and knowledge; you need to be a networking expert to use a network analyzer well.

Prices for network analyzers start at about $10,000; analyzers that support multiple physical media and protocol decoding can cost more than $30,000. Analyzers are sold as kits or complete products. The kit consists of a network adapter and software that you install in one of your PCs. If you buy the complete product, you get the adapter and software preinstalled in a PC of the vendor's choice. The Sniffer, from Network General, is a popular network analyzer. Figure 12.3 shows a typical Sniffer PC. Figure 12.4 illustrates the Sniffer family of products.

Fig. 12.3

The Network General Sniffer typically consists of a laptop computer with the Sniffer software preinstalled.

Fig. 12.4
The Sniffer family
of products.

Looking at the Hewlett-Packard Network Advisor. The HP Network Advisor is a 386-based PC with a monochrome or color LCD screen and a LAN interface designed for data acquisition. The HP software runs on top of DOS. Its graphical user interface is different from that of Windows or Presentation Manager, but it is not hard to get used to. The AI portion, Fault Finder, is written in Prolog and contains more than 100 rules.

When you invoke Fault Finder on a Token Ring LAN, it offers these categories:

- Monitor for Station Insertion Failures

- Monitor for Hard Errors

- Monitor for Beacon MAC Frames

- Monitor for Congested Station Receivers

- Monitor for Ring Beaconing

The Network Advisor then asks which fault(s) to investigate. You can ask Fault Finder to explain itself. If you ask for a definition of the last category, for example, Fault Finder responds with `The ring is considered to be beaconing if a station has transmitted 8 consecutive Beacon MAC frames.`

You can see from the simple nature of the categories and the explanation that Fault Finder is not yet a genius at finding problems on your LAN. HP started at the lowest layer (the Physical layer) of the LAN with its AI product and expects to move up the protocol ladder into more complicated scenarios as time goes on. The list of symptoms you can give Fault Finder eventually will grow from "Can't Connect" to such problems as "Sporadic Slowdowns," "Can't Access Server 3," and "Corrupted Server Files."

Beyond its Fault Finder component, the Network Advisor sports the same features and functions as other network analyzers. You can capture frames for a specified period, using filters you set up. The Advisor decodes MAC-layer frames, AppleTalk frames, IBM PC LAN Program frames (NetBIOS and SMBs, or System Message Blocks), NetWare frames (IPX, SPX, and NCP, or NetWare Core Protocol), IBM System Network Architecture (SNA) frames, and TCP/IP frames. To get more information on the Network Advisor, contact the following:

> Network Advisor
> Hewlett-Packard Company
> 5070 Centennial Boulevard
> Colorado Springs, CO 80919
> (719) 531-4497
> Fax: (719) 531-4505

Looking at the Network General Sniffer. The Sniffer can decode and interpret frames from more protocols on more networks than other products, but it does not offer as many ways to categorize network activity on a NetWare LAN as does Novell's LANalyzer, nor is it as easy to use. If you want to know how many directory search requests a workstation issued, for example, you first must tell the Sniffer what data pattern to look for—that is, which bytes in which frame locations identify a directory search frame. The information is easy to pick out of the Sniffer display, but you must describe the search pattern in terms of bytes and byte offsets. With the LANalyzer, you simply select the Directory Search category.

Sniffer can show statistics on LAN traffic to help you understand the current health of your LAN. To give you an idea of what these statistics look like, figure 12.5 shows absolute-traffic statistics on a Sniffer screen. Figure 12.6 shows a Sniffer server-status screen.

On a Token Ring LAN, a failing network adapter often passes garbled data to the next node on the token ring, which in turn begins beaconing an alarm on the network. All activity stops on the LAN until you find and replace the faulty card. The Sniffer can notify you that the network is beaconing and can report the address of the faulty node.

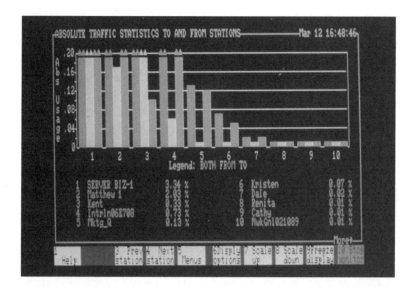

Fig. 12.5
Absolute-traffic
statistics, as shown
by a Network
General Sniffer.

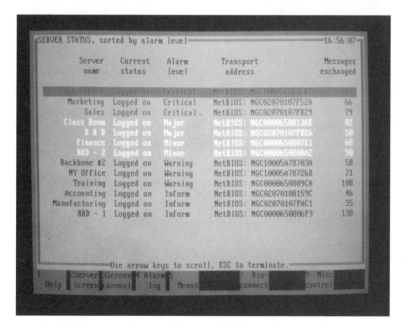

Fig. 12.6
Server status,
displayed by a
Sniffer.

Finding hardware errors and frame errors in the lower layers of the LAN is
one job for a network analyzer. But you also can isolate performance bottlenecks. Sniffer can capture frames between specific nodes (a workstation and a
server, for example) and display network utilization, frame counts, and total
number of bytes captured. During later analysis of this data, Sniffer shows
you when each frame appeared on the network and what that frame contained.

If you kept notes describing what the workstation operator did during the capture, you can correlate the work being done to the timings of the different kinds of frames. Suppose that the workstation loaded a 250K executable file from the file server. Sniffer would show 250 requests from the workstation interspersed with the 250 responses (assuming 1K packets) from the server. Unfortunately, Sniffer cannot explicitly tell you that the server hard disk, CPU, or disk controller is too slow; Sniffer looks only at the message traffic as the traffic appears on the LAN. You have to perform controlled experiments—varying the number of active workstations, the type of workstations, and other parameters—to get clear implications on which to base your conclusions.

For more information on Sniffer, contact the following:

Sniffer
Network General Corporation
4200 Bohannon Drive
Menlo Park, CA 94025
(415) 688-2700
(800) 952-6300
Fax: (415) 321-0855

Looking at the Novell LANalyzer. It goes without saying that Novell knows NetWare better than anyone else. LANalyzer does many of the same tasks as Sniffer, but on fewer networks and for fewer protocols. One of those protocols is, of course, NetWare. If you are a NetWare user, you'll find that LANalyzer characterizes your LAN activity in highly useful ways.

LANalyzer comes with preset templates, called *applications*, that you use to filter, interpret, and display the frames on your LAN. The applications for the Token Ring Physical layer, for example, include Devices, ErrMon, Map, Priority, RingChng, and RingMon. These applications, especially ErrMon and RingMon, help you determine the health of your network adapters and cabling system. At a higher level, the applications called BridgeVu, FileView, NodeView, OverView, and ServerVu show you the LAN traffic in terms of server, workstation, and bridge functions. If you want to see, for example, whether someone's PATH statement is causing too many wrong directories to be searched for an executable file, you can tell LANalyzer that you want to see file-open activity, directory-search activity, or both.

LANalyzer is a PC board and software that you install in one of your own PCs. The text-mode user interface looks and feels like the other NetWare utilities (SYSCON, FILER, and so on) with which NetWare users are familiar.

To get more information on LANalyzer, contact the following:

> Novell, Inc.
> LANalyzer Products Division
> 2180 Fortune Drive
> San Jose, CA 95131
> (408) 434-2300
> (800) 243-8526

Using the Integrated Network Management System

The fourth and final type of product available for managing a network is the *Integrated Network Management System* (INMS). Using an INMS, you can monitor and control your entire network from a central location. An INMS addresses all five ISO network management categories: fault, performance, configuration, security, and accounting.

You use an INMS through a console device that provides a graphical user interface. The console device is integrated with a network management station that communicates with network agents (special workstation software, for example) on remote computer devices to determine the state of the network. Agents collect interesting information—such as the number of packets the device has received—and make it available to the INMS on query. When a problem occurs, agents also can send alarms to the console to alert the network manager immediately. INMSs are the most expensive network management products.

Using the Tools

You learned at the beginning of this chapter that network management is both a science and an art. You must be a logical scientist and a creative artist to use these tools. As a scientist, you must understand how networks function, and you must know the relationships between the symptoms of a problem and the list of possible causes. As an artist, you must think your way through the diagnostic process, drawing on your experiences with similar problems to solve a problem. The diagnostic process consists of four steps that you repeat until you find and fix the problem: observing the symptoms, developing a list of possible causes, performing tests to isolate the cause, and analyzing the results.

Knowing What Is Normal

You have to sift through the observed symptoms and facts, looking for the cause of a problem. To recognize the symptoms, however, you must know what is normal and what is not normal on your network. The process of determining the normal characteristics of an individual network is called *baselining*.

Baselining is not one of the four steps in the diagnostic process; you must perform the baselining before the problem occurs. When the network is in a problem state, of course, it is too late to determine the normal behavior of the network. But if you have a clear, complete picture of the normal behavior of your LAN, you can answer the following questions:

- What is the average network utilization? How does it vary during the business day?

- What are the primary applications on the network?

- What protocols are running on the network? What are the performance characteristics of these protocols?

- Who manufactured the network interface controllers, media attachment units, hubs, and other network connection hardware? What are their performance characteristics?

- Who manufactured the repeaters, bridges, routers, and gateways on the network? What versions of software and firmware are they running? What are their performance characteristics?

Observing Symptoms

You first observe the symptoms of the problem. You may be tempted, in the rush to fix the problem, to begin experimenting with solutions before you finish a thorough examination of the symptoms. If you give in to temptation, you probably will wind up spending more time and money to fix the problem than if you had considered all the symptoms and their ramifications.

The most obvious symptoms are not always the key to understanding the problem. To know why this is true, you have to understand one of the primary characteristics of network protocols: network protocols are designed to hide network problems, not expose them. Most network protocols incorporate retry logic and other techniques to support automatic recovery from problems. This feature causes most network problems to display a single obvious symptom: slow response from the network. Although the network's attempts to retry a failing operation increase network reliability, the retries also make network troubleshooting more difficult because you see a common symptom for many problems.

In your analysis of the symptoms, you need to go beyond the slow-response symptom by asking yourself questions that help you focus on the behavior of the LAN:

- Does this problem affect everyone, everyone in a given area, or random individuals?

- What percentage of time does the problem occur? Is the problem continuous or intermittent? Does it occur regularly?

- What has changed recently? Has a computer device been added to the network? Have any internetworking devices been reconfigured?

- Which vendor's products may have failed to produce these symptoms? What are the vendor and version numbers of the computer systems, network adapter cards, hubs, routers, bridges, application software, and network operating system software?

After you gather this information, you can begin the second step in the diagnostic process: developing a list of possible causes for the symptoms you have observed.

Making a List of Possible Causes

With the baseline information at your fingertips, you can begin to ask how the observed symptoms relate to the normal operation of the network. You can distinguish unusual behavior and look for its cause. Experience and knowledge are your tools in this step.

To develop your list of possible causes, you must know how each network component can fail and what that failure can do to the entire network. As you make your list, visualize the dynamic nature of the LAN. Imagine how each component (network adapter, network operating system, cabling, or other unit) interacts with the rest of the network. Use your knowledge of protocols and network software to see how a network component's failure may cause the problem at hand. Excessive traffic, for example, can cause high collision counts on an Ethernet LAN, but a cable segment that is too long or a malfunctioning transceiver also can cause frequent collisions.

Isolating the Cause and Analyzing Results

In the third step, you test the LAN to see which of the items in your list is the culprit. You will use any and perhaps all of the tools covered earlier in this chapter, but you may find that the tool you use most frequently is the network analyzer. The analyzer enables you to monitor the network's behavior interactively, and the analyzer gives you more views of what is happening.

When you think you have found the failing component, you test your hypothesis. You simply may remove the failing component from the network to see whether the problem disappears, or you may reconfigure or reset the component. Because diagnosis usually requires 80 percent of the problem-solving effort and implementing a solution requires only 20 percent, you probably will find this last step to be the most straightforward.

Dealing with Common Problems

A typical network administrator spends a great deal of time solving problems and trying to understand the network's performance. Different parts of a network experience various kinds of problems and exhibit different symptoms.

Dealing with Network Hardware Problems

Network problems occur most frequently in the Physical layer—the lowest layer of the Open Systems Interconnection model. Because hardware is subject to physical stress, electrical connectivity problems are the most common fault type. These problems include cable breaks, cable shorts, breaks elsewhere in the circuit, and malfunctions in the actual network adapter circuitry.

Dealing with Cabling Problems

You can isolate cable problems with a network analyzer or TDR. You often can find problems with hardware circuitry by using a network analyzer to examine error traffic on the network. At other times, you must attack these problems by using process of elimination to isolate the cause. A cable management system also may help you locate the problem; for details, see the section "Managing Cables" later in this chapter.

Practicing Performance Tuning

Network monitors and analyzers enable you to compile statistics on your LAN's message traffic. You can use these figures to understand your LAN's performance as it relates to the traffic. You can view the daily network-utilization patterns, identify the heaviest users, determine the various percentages of different protocol traffic, see where network bottlenecks exist, and perhaps even recognize why those bottlenecks exist.

This analysis may suggest to you that you need to partition the network into multiple segments, add file servers, or upgrade your network adapters to obtain better performance. The performance-tuning task is not a small one, however; you need to spend a significant amount of time gathering statistics and relating those statistics to the particular components of your LAN.

Performance Tuning Your LAN

Network management is both an art and a science, but finding a bottleneck on a LAN can require the skills of a magician who has a Ph.D. in electrical engineering. You may get such advice as "Put a faster hard drive in the server," "Switch to Token Ring," "Switch to Ethernet," "Switch to NetWare," or "Switch to OS/2 LAN Manager." What if you take the advice and discover that performance does not change? The part you replaced was not the bottleneck; something else is.

You can use the following information to make your LAN faster, spending your budget dollars wisely in the process.

Performance Factors

When you run an application that resides on the file server and that in turn reads and writes files on the server, a flurry of activity takes place. First, COMMAND.COM looks in each of your PATH directories for the executable file. This searching of server directories causes a dialog of LAN messages. For each directory, your workstation sends a "Find File" request message, and the server sends back a response. The executable file loads into your workstation's memory by way of another series of LAN messages, usually in 512- or 1,024-byte packets (LAN packets have size limits). When the file is loaded, the application program issues open, read, write, and close requests that become LAN messages sent to the server. The server responds to each request by sending back an "OK" or a "Here's the data" message. On NetBIOS-based networks, the receiver acknowledges each message separately. On NetWare networks, however, the acknowledgment and the response message are the same.

The server has to manage a queue of requests from the many workstations on the LAN, and the queue can get quite long at times. If you use the server for remote printing, two problems can occur. Multiple print jobs may keep the file server busy reading and writing spool files, thus delaying other file-service requests. The file server also has to devote some time and effort to managing the shared printer. In addition, workstation and server messages (both for file service and print spooling) may have to cross one or more bridges, creating another delay.

The upper layers of the network software (such as NetWare's NETx.COM) filter each file and print request, and create one or more message records, handing the messages to a lower layer (IPX.COM). This layer in turn gives the request message to the network device drivers. Through an 8-, 16-, or 32-bit slot, these drivers tell the network adapter to send the request to the server. When it can use the LAN cable, the

(continues)

(continued)

network card sends the request. At the server, the network support software hands the request up through more layers of support code before the network operating system finally processes it. If the request cannot be satisfied from server memory (the RAM cache), the server waits for the hard disk to rotate into position to access the data. The response travels back to the workstation, through the support software, server network adapter, LAN cable, workstation network adapter, and workstation support software. A 250K program file, using 512-byte message packets, requires the interchange of more than 500 requests and 500 responses just to load the program. (Larger packets cause less server overhead.) When many people try to use the file server at the same time, the server is Grand Central Station for LAN traffic and file requests.

Locating a Bottleneck

The network bottleneck may be at the workstation, in the network drivers, in the network TSRs, or in the network adapter. Or the transmission rate of the LAN may be the bottleneck. At the server, you have several suspects. The server CPU may not be executing the network operating system software quickly enough. The network software may not be efficiently coded. Too little RAM in the server for file-caching purposes means that the server frequently must take the time to access the hard disk drive. The server may spend an inordinate amount of time acting as a print server. Perhaps your server's overhead would be less if you could configure it to use larger packets. Could the speed of the bus be holding you back? Or perhaps the server and the network adapter have trouble communicating through a confining 8-bit slot. The network adapter may not contain enough RAM to buffer all the LAN messages. Are your bridges slowing the network? The list of potential bottlenecks is a long one, and the picture is further complicated by the interactions that can occur between the components. As you look for performance bottlenecks on your LAN, you will need to keep these factors in mind.

Managing Cables

As a recent addition to the tools of the network administrator, the cable management system documents and displays the physical layout of your network. For a small LAN, your first documentation efforts may be a pencil-drawn map of the office that shows LAN cables and other components. A large LAN requires more sophisticated documentation. You can use a cable management system to track and locate cables and other *network assets*—a term made popular by vendors of cable management software.

Cable management systems offer a range of features that track the complete physical infrastructure of a network. The system stores data about each component (including its location) in a database. On demand, the system displays a graphical picture of the network. A typical cable management system also can produce reports on the network assets.

You can view the entire network, or you can zoom in on part of the network. By clicking an icon that represents a network component, you can quickly locate specific information such as cable routes, the available outlets on a given floor, or all items on a given circuit.

The database contains detailed information on the network assets, from the location of cables to the administrative information associated with each piece of equipment, cable, and cableway. The cable management database also stores information such as the brand of equipment, cost, model number, location within the facility, and connectivity and wiring schemes.

In addition to using a cable management system to document your LAN, you can use it to generate work orders for equipment moves and changes as well as repair orders for failed components. The system also keeps a history of changes made to the network.

Using the Resource Guide

Several companies offer products that can help you manage a network. The following list is a good place to start your evaluation of network management products:

AT&T Computer Systems
1776 On the Green
Ninth Floor
Morristown, NJ 07960
(800) 247-1212
(904) 636-2314
Fax: (904) 636-3078

Automated Design Systems
375 Northridge Road
Suite 270
Atlanta, GA 30350
(404) 394-2552

Banyan Systems, Inc.
115 Flanders Road
Westborough, MA 01581
(508) 898-1000

BICC Data Networks, Inc.
1800 West Park Drive
Westborough, MA 01581
(800) 447-6526
(508) 898-2422
Fax: (508) 898-3739

Blue Lance, Inc.
1700 West Loop S
Suite 700
Houston, TX 77027
(713) 680-1187
Fax: (713) 622-1370

Brightwork Development
P.O. Box 8728
Red Bank, NJ 07701
(800) 552-9876
(201) 530-0440
Fax: (201) 530-0622

Bytex
120 Turnpike Road
Southborough, MA 01772
(508) 480-0840

Cabletron Systems, Inc.
35 Industrial Way
Rochester, NH 03867
(603) 332-9400
Fax: (603) 332-4616

Certus International Corporation
13110 Shaker Square
Cleveland, OH 44120
(800) 722-8737
(216) 752-8181
Fax: (216) 752-8188

Cheyenne Software
55 Bryant Avenue
Roslyn, NY 11576
(800) 243-9462
(516) 484-5110
Fax: (516) 484-5110

IV

Chipcom Corporation
118 Turnpike Road
Southborough, MA 01772
(800) 228-9930
(508) 460-8900
Fax: (508) 460-8950

Computer Tyme, Inc.
411 North Sherman
Suite 300
Springfield, MO 65802
(800) 548-5353
(417) 866-1222
Fax: (417) 866-0135

Connect Computer Company
9855 West 78th Street
Eden Prairie, MN 55344
(612) 944-0181
Fax: (612) 944-9298

Data General Corporation
4400 Computer Drive
Westborough, MA 01580
(508) 366-8911

Daystrom Data Products
15 Sunrise Hill Road
Fishkill, NY 12524
(914) 896-7378

Digilog, Inc.
1370 Welsh Road
Montgomeryville, PA 18936
(215) 628-4530
Fax: (215) 628-3935

Digital Equipment Corporation
30 Proter Road
Littleton, MA 01460
(508) 562-4521

Dolphin Software
6050 Peachtree Parkway
Suite 340-208
Norcross, GA 30092
(404) 339-7877
Fax: (404) 339-7905

ETI Software, Inc.
2930 Prospect Avenue
Cleveland, OH 44115
(800) 336-2014
(216) 241-1140
Fax: (216) 241-2319

Fresh Technology Group
1478 North Tech Boulevard
Suite 101
Gilbert, AZ 85234
(602) 497-4200
Fax: (602) 497-4242

Frye Computer Systems, Inc.
19 Temple Place
Boston, MA 02111
(617) 247-2300
Fax: (617) 451-6711

Gazelle Systems
42 North University Avenue
Suite 10
Provo, UT 84601
(800) 233-0383
(801) 377-1288
Fax: (801) 373-6933

Hewlett-Packard Company
Vancouver Division
18110 Southeast 34th Street
Camas, WA 98607
(206) 254-8110

Horizons Technology, Inc.
3990 Ruffin Road
San Diego, CA 92123
(619) 292-8331
Fax: (619) 292-7321

Hughes LAN Systems
1225 Charleston Road
Mountain View, CA 94043
(415) 966-7300

IBM Corporation
1000 Northwest 51st Street
Boca Raton, FL 33432
(407) 443-2000

International Data Science
7 Wellington Road
Lincoln, RI 02865
(401) 333-6200
Fax: (401) 333-3584

Internetix, Inc.
8903 Presidential Parkway
Suite 210
Upper Marlborough, MD 20772
(301) 420-7900
Fax: (301) 420-4395

Isicad, Inc.
1920 West Corporate Way
P.O. Box 61022
Anaheim, CA 92803
(714) 533-8910

J.A. Lomax Associates
659 Adrienne Street
Suite 101
Novato, CA 94945
(800) 225-6629
(415) 892-9606
Fax: (415) 898-0867

LAN Support Group, Inc.
P.O. Box 460269
Houston, TX 77056
(800) 749-8439
(713) 622-4900

Microcom, Inc.
500 River Ridge Drive
Norwood, MA 02062
(617) 551-1000
Fax: (617) 551-1898

Microtest, Inc.
3519 East Shea Boulevard
Suite 134
Phoenix, AZ 85028
(800) 526-9675
Fax: (602) 971-6963

Network & Communication Technology, Inc.
24 Wampum Road
Park Ridge, NJ 07656
(201) 307-9000
Fax: (201) 307-9404

Network Computing, Inc.
1950 Stemmons
Suite 3016
Dallas, TX 75207
(214) 746-4949

Network General Corporation
4200 Bohannon Drive
Menlo Park, CA 94025
(415) 688-2700

Network Interface Corporation
15019 West 95th Street
Lenexa, KS 66215
(913) 894-2277
Fax: (913) 894-0226

Network Management, Inc.
19 Rector Street
15th Floor
New York, NY 10006
(212) 797-3800
Fax: (212) 797-3817

Novell, Inc.
122 East 1700
South Provo, UT 84606
(801) 429-5900
Fax: (801) 377-9353

Optical Data Systems
1101 East Arapaho
Richardson, TX 75081
(214) 234-6400
Fax: (214) 234-1467

Palindrome Corporation
850 East Diehl Road
Naperville, IL 60653
(708) 505-3300

Proteon, Inc.
Two Technology Drive
Westborough, MA 01581
(508) 898-2800
Fax: (508) 898-2118

ProTools, Inc.
14976 Northwest Greenbrier Parkway
Beaverton, OR 97006
(503) 645-5400
Fax: (503) 645-3577

Retix
2644 30th Street
Santa Monica, CA 90405
(213) 399-2200
Fax: (213) 458-2685

Saber Software Corporation
5944 Luther Lane
Suite 1007
Dallas, TX 75225
(800) 338-8754
(214) 361-8086
Fax: (214) 361-1882

SoftShell Systems
1163 Triton Drive
Foster City, CA 94404
(800) 322-7638
(415) 571-9000
Fax: (415) 571-0622

Spider Systems, Inc.
12 New England Executive Park
Burlington, MA 01803
(800) 447-7807
(617) 270-3510
Fax: (617) 270-9818

Standard Microsystems Corporation
35 Marcus Boulevard
Hauppauge, NY 11788
(516) 273-3100
Fax: (516) 273-2136

StarTek, Inc.
100 Otis Street
Northborough, MA 01532
(508) 393-9393
Fax: (508) 393-6934

SynOptics Communications, Inc.
4401 Great American Parkway
P.O. Box 58185
Santa Clara, CA 95952
(800) 776-8023
(408) 988-2400
Fax: (408) 988-5525

IV

Expanding a Network

Technology Dynamics, Inc.
145 15th Street NE
Suite 624
Atlanta, GA 30361
(800) 226-0428
(404) 874-0428

Telebit Corporation
1315 Chesapeake Terrace
Sunnyvale, CA 94089
(800) 835-3248
(408) 734-4333
Fax: (408) 734-3333

TGR Software, Inc.
2 Ravinia Drive
Suite 330
Atlanta, GA 30346
(404) 390-7450
Fax: (404) 390-7455

Thomas-Conrad Corporation
1908-R Kramer Lane
Austin, TX 78758
(800) 332-8683
(512) 836-1935
Fax: (512) 836-2840

3Com Corporation
5400 Bayfront Plaza
Santa Clara, CA 95052
(800) 638-3266
(408) 764-5000
Fax: (408) 764-5001

Ungermann-Bass, Inc.
3900 Freedom Circle
Santa Clara, CA 95052
(408) 496-0111
Fax: (408) 970-7343

Unisys Corporation
2700 North First Street
P.O. Box 6685
San Jose, CA 95150
(408) 434-2848
Fax: (408) 434-2131

Vitalink Communications Corporation
6607 Kaiser Drive
Fremont, CA 94555
(800) 523-9550
(415) 794-1100
Fax: (415) 795-1085

Wang Laboratories, Inc.
One Industrial Avenue
Lowell, MA 01851
(800) 225-0654
(508) 459-5000

Wollongong Group, Inc.
1129 San Antonio Road
Palo Alto, CA 94303
(800) 872-8649
(415) 962-7100
Fax: (415) 969-5547

Summary

In this chapter, you rounded out your exploration of local area networks by considering the issues, techniques, and tools of network management. After covering the basics, you learned about the Simple Network Management Protocol (SNMP) and the Common Management Information Protocol (CMIP).

You then turned your attention to the network management products that IBM offers, concentrating on the special capabilities of Token Ring. You now understand the purpose and use of general tools such as time-domain reflectometers, network monitors, network analyzers, and integrated management systems. You learned about cable management. Finally, you found a resource guide that you can use to research specific products and companies.

In the next chapter, you look at the issues you will face when vendors offer you additional LAN products, claiming that those products will *interoperate* with your existing network.

Chapter 13

Analyzing Interoperability

Vendors of LAN products like to claim that their products work on many types of networks. Both hardware and software vendors use the word *interoperability* to describe the degree to which a product can be used on different networks, in different situations, and for different purposes. However, you will find that you have to take these claims with a grain of salt if you try to treat the products as building blocks on your LAN.

Have you ever stared at a printed word a little too long and watched it turn into a strange, foreign-looking object? In the LAN industry, everyone seems to have stared at *interoperability* for too long. In this chapter, you take an analytical look at the word to see what *interoperability* really means. The word has been overworked and misused—it is time to put some meaning and substance back into interoperability, so that you can use the word constructively and productively in discussions of which LAN products actually work well together.

Interoperability pertains to nearly everything in your day-to-day life, to one degree or another. As you may imagine, most of the examples in this chapter deal with local area networks, but you also touch on other ways of making computer equipment components talk to one another. Modems, serial ports, printers, printer ports, application software, E-mail links, musical instruments, telephones, and even fax machines exemplify degrees of interoperability.

Learning What Interoperates

The more you hear or read about interoperability, the more skeptical you need to be. This is a cynical observation, but one you can use as a useful guide. You learn why in this chapter.

The first thing to notice about interoperability is that people stop using the word to refer to things that actually do interoperate. You probably have gone down to the store, bought a telephone and some phone cord with RJ-11 jacks (or a modular plug) at either end, plugged the phone into a wall jack in your house, and immediately picked up the handset to make a phone call from your handsome new telephone. You did not once use the word *interoperability* when you described the job to your friends. Here is an even better example: you had a few extra dollars while you were at the store, so you bought a small electrical appliance (a toaster, perhaps). You plugged it into a wall outlet and used it as soon as you got home, without thinking once of the word *interoperable*. The degree of interoperability with telephone companies and utility companies is exceedingly high.

Have you ever tried, though, to merge several LANs into one? Suppose that you have a mixture of networks, each using different network operating systems—IBM's LAN Server, NetWare (perhaps with some Macintosh workstations), LANtastic, and Network File System (NFS). You want to set things up so that all the LAN users get to share the same resources and files on all the servers. You will quickly begin using *interoperable* as an expletive while you try to make it work.

If you buy all your hardware and software from a single manufacturer, your concern for interoperability is eased somewhat. IBM, for example, produces charts and tables to show you which of its products work together and which do not. You still may run into products that do not work well together, however.

You could say that IBM is just another computer manufacturer. IBM is large enough, though, that its specifications and guidelines often become industry standards. This affects interoperability. Looking at things from the other direction, you can buy IBM modems that use the Hayes command set, which itself is a standard. Interoperability is closely linked to the existence of adhered-to standards.

Examining the OSI Protocol Stack

To impose some organization on the subject, you can use the Open Systems Interconnection (OSI) model as a guide. You can work your way up the OSI model protocol stack as you explore interoperability. Note that the OSI model is only a guide because many products are still not OSI-compliant. Nevertheless, the OSI model is an important reference point for discussions about LANs. As you analyze interoperability at the different layers of the OSI model, one of the things you will discover is that the degree of interoperability among products gets fuzzier and fuzzier as you get near the top of the stack. Vendor claims notwithstanding, interoperability is not always easily achieved, especially at the higher layers of the OSI model.

The OSI model defines seven protocol layers and specifies that each layer is insulated from the others by a well-defined interface. Figure 13.1 shows the seven layers.

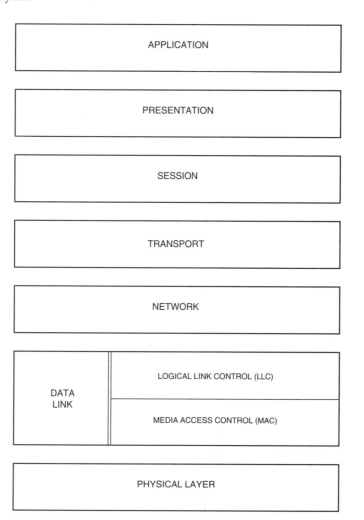

Fig. 13.1
The OSI model.

The OSI reference model organizes local area network connectivity into seven independent pieces, or layers. The following list explains these layers:

- *Application.* The Application layer is the highest level. It interfaces with users, retrieves information from databases, and transfers whole files. This layer is the part of the OSI model visible to you. The Application layer turns your LAN accesses into work requests that it passes to the next level down, the Presentation layer. The Application layer does not do any real work itself but delegates all tasks to the lower layers. A work request to be sent across the network enters the OSI model protocol stack at the Application layer, travels downward toward the first layer (the Physical layer), zips across to the other workstation or server, and then travels back up the protocol stack until the work request message reaches the application on the other computer through its own Application layer.

- *Presentation.* The Presentation layer receives work requests from the Application layer or delivers responses to the Application layer. The Presentation layer exists to hide differences between different kinds of computers. When IBM, Apple, DEC, NeXT, and Burroughs computers all want to talk to each other, some translation and byte-reordering is necessary. This layer converts data into (or from) a machine's native internal numeric format. The Presentation layer also compresses the messages into an encrypted form, for security purposes. (When delivering messages, the Presentation layer de-encrypts the messages.) When its job is finished, the Presentation layer submits its results to the next layer.

- *Session.* Computers on local area networks use names or numbers to identify each other. The Session layer uses each computer's identification to call another computer, in the same way you use telephone numbers to make telephone calls. The Session layer makes the initial contact and manages the progress of the call. The call itself is a *session*— an exchange of messages (a dialog) between two workstations. The functions in this layer enable applications running at two workstations to coordinate their communications into a single session. The Session layer, like a telephone company, does not say anything during the dialog.

- *Transport.* The Transport layer is the only layer that concerns itself with making sure that the information sent by one computer on the network is received properly by another computer. The Transport layer knows the maximum size of each LAN packet and breaks up a work request message (or response) into smaller packets as necessary. When more than one packet is in process at any one time, this layer controls the sequencing of the message packets and also regulates inbound traffic flow. If a duplicate packet arrives (perhaps the result of a retransmission), this layer recognizes and discards it. The Transport layer delegates the work of routing packets to the next lower layer.

■ *Network.* The Network layer plans the routing of the packets. The message packets may need to travel through several LAN segments to get to their final destinations. The Network layer keeps track of the different routes that a message packet may need to travel. The Network layer inserts this routing information into each message packet to help the intermediate computers and devices forward the message packet to its destination. This layer takes responsibility for addressing and delivering messages, end to end, from source computer to final destination.

■ *Data Link.* The Data Link layer is the most complex. It encompasses the sending of the characters that make up a message packet on a character-by-character basis. Because of its complexity, the Data Link layer is broken into a Media Access Control (MAC) layer and a Logical Link Control (LLC) layer. The MAC layer manages network access (token passing or collision sensing, for example) and network control. The LLC layer, operating at a higher level than the MAC layer, sends and receives the user data messages and packets (typically file service requests and responses). If the Data Link layer detects an error, it arranges for the sending computer to retransmit the message packet. The error detection is only point to point; the sending computer may be only forwarding a message from the originating computer. (The Transport layer has control and responsibility for end-to-end delivery.)

■ *Physical.* The Physical layer just needs to turn the characters making up a message packet into electrical signals. This layer does not need to process routing information, computer names, or the other contents of a message packet. Because the other layers already have done their supervisory work, the Physical layer merely has to send or receive the electrical signals through the LAN cable. This part of the OSI model specifies the physical and electrical characteristics of the connections that make up the network. It encompasses twisted pair cables, fiber optic cables, coaxial cables, connectors, repeaters, and so on. You can think of this layer as the hardware layer.

Interoperability—the degree to which LAN hardware and software products from different vendors work well with each other—varies greatly as you consider each of the layers of the OSI model. In the next few sections, using the OSI model as a guide, you look at the criteria and the obstacles for interoperability on local area networks.

The Physical and Data Link Layers

Within each type of cable, physical interoperability is pretty well defined. If you tell someone that you have connected some computers with an RG-58 A/U coaxial cable, there is a good chance that he or she will immediately think of thin Ethernet (Thinnet). If you mention shielded twisted pair (IBM Type 1) cable, Token Ring will likely come to mind. Unshielded twisted pair may be Token Ring or Ethernet's relatively new 10BASET. Fiber optics? FDDI (Fiber Distributed Data Interface) is new enough that you may just get puzzled looks. In each case, though, the simple mention of the type of cable is nearly enough to define the entire physical appearance of the network components, and to specify what will connect to what (interoperability). If your computer has a Token Ring card and you want to connect to a Token Ring LAN, you can ask two questions to find out whether it is possible: "Does the LAN operate at 4 or 16 megabits per second?" and "Does the LAN use shielded or unshielded twisted pair cable?" Once you know that your Token Ring adapter is using the right speed and can connect to the LAN's cabling system, you can reliably proceed to join the ring. This level of interoperability is made possible by the Institute of Electrical and Electronic Engineers (IEEE). The 802.3 (Ethernet) and 802.5 (Token Ring) standards specify *exactly* how the Physical layer of the network should behave, and these standards extend their reach into the Data Link layer.

Other physical standards are highly interoperable. The best example is a parallel printer cable (the Centronics Interface). If you buy a printer with a parallel interface and the printer does not work with a computer and cable that are known to be good, it is certain that the printer is not working.

The standard for serial cables, RS-232, is equally as rigorous and exacting as the Centronics parallel printer interface. This standard defines Data Terminal Equipment (DTE) and Data Communications Equipment (DCE), and it specifies exactly how to connect DTE and DCE to make them work (interoperate). You can buy a modem with an RS-232 interface, connect it to your RS-232 serial port with an RS-232 serial cable, and know that things are going to work.

Suppose that you get out some spare chips and a soldering iron and somehow manage to connect your Token-Ring-equipped computer to your Ethernet

LAN so that the Ethernet message packets (frames) successfully enter the Token Ring card. Can you "interoperate" your new network adapter on your LAN? Of course not.

First of all, your Token Ring adapter needs to see a three-byte token that it can claim before the adapter can send data on the network. The adapters in the other workstations rely on collision sensing to get their message across. But, even forgetting about tokens and collision sensing, the basic format of the data is different.

Pascal programmers call the data format of a message packet a *record*. In C, it is a *struct*. Assembler programmers may use a struc <> notation to define the data format. COBOL programmers think of it in terms of a record description. Basically, the data format is the layout of the data in memory—the organization of the data bytes into fields within a data record. Not only is an Ethernet data record (frame) laid out differently from a Token Ring frame, but IEEE 802.3 Ethernet is slightly different from what people term true Ethernet (fig. 13.2 shows the differences). Within each standard (IEEE 802.3 Ethernet or IEEE 802.5 Token Ring), though, the degree of interoperability is quite high.

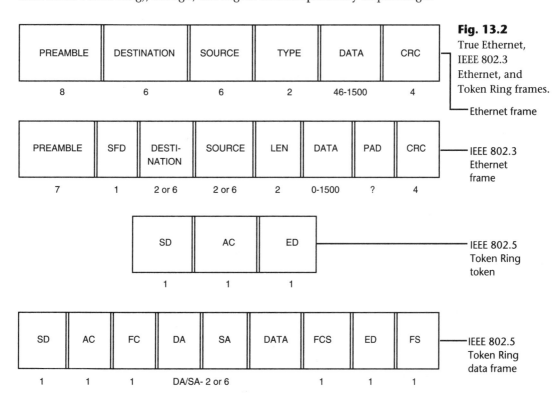

Fig. 13.2
True Ethernet, IEEE 802.3 Ethernet, and Token Ring frames.

ARCnet data records (frames), FDDI frames, and StarLAN frames are laid out differently, too—just as you would expect. The essential point, though, is that your hybrid, jury-rigged Token Ring card will not work with your Ethernet LAN because these record layouts are understood by the ROM program code burned into each adapter. If you did manage to modify the Token Ring card enough to make it work, you would not have a Token Ring card anymore—you would have built the world's most expensive Ethernet adapter.

In figure 13.2, the following parameters are used:

AC	Access control
CRC	Cyclic redundancy checksum
DA	Destination address
ED	End delimiter
FC	Frame control
FCS	Frame check sequence
FS	Frame status
PAD	Filler bytes to bring the frame to a minimum length
SA	Source address
SD	Start delimiter
SFD	Start frame delimiter

What about non-LAN examples? If interoperability is such a slippery thing, why can you use your fax machine to send documents and pictures to someone as if the two of you had picked your equipment from the same assembly line? The answer, of course, is standards. Group III FAX is a standard that is understood around the world.

Now quite popular, 9600-baud modems took a while to catch on, mostly because the standard for data representation was still evolving. Today you can buy CCITT V.32 modems from different manufacturers that reliably reach out and touch each other. Some modems, made just as the CCITT standard became official, do not always speak clearly to other 9600-baud modems. An example is the U.S. Robotics Courier HST modem; before USR's Dual Standard, its modems did not interoperate well with other 9600-baud modems, however. (The original HST used a proprietary modulation scheme that provides a 9,600-bps forward channel and a back channel running at 1,200 bps.)

IV

The Network and Transport Layers

People talk a lot about interoperability at the Network and Transport layers. If this chapter's earlier cynical observation is true (that the more people talk about interoperability, the more skeptical you have to be), this means that interoperability is sporadic and elusive at these levels.

IPX.COM implements the IPX protocol. IPX is the layer of NetWare workstation protocol software that exists between NET*x*.COM (above) and network adapter software (below). IPX (internetwork packet exchange) has its own API, and application software on one NetWare workstation can talk through this interface to other NetWare workstations. The workstation dialog takes place in a unique dialect of network languages, however; other workstations may use the same cables and network adapters, but they cannot participate if they do not speak the IPX language.

If you are getting confused by this talk of layers, protocol stacks, and interfaces, just look back at figure 13.2 for a moment. Look at the field labeled DATA in the Ethernet and Token Ring frames. The data field is yet another whole record layout. The fields in this encapsulated data record are defined by the software in the Network and Transport layers. If you send your NetWare workstation an Ethernet frame with a data field (record) containing bytes laid out a certain way, your IPX-based workstation will recognize the frame. If you put wrong values in those bytes, your workstation will not know what to do with the frame, even if the Ethernet portion is filled in correctly. At the Network and Transport layers, interoperability is defined mostly in terms of the definition of the data within the message packet.

IPX is a close adaptation of a protocol developed by Xerox, the Xerox Network Standard (XNS). Novell uses it, of course, but there are no other "major players" whose LAN products implement IPX directly. One way around this stumbling block to interoperability is to use the Clarkson Packet Drivers. Supported by Novell, FTP Software of Wakefield, Massachusetts, much of the academic community, and other groups, the Clarkson Packet Drivers enable multiple protocols to use the same network adapter. IPX data packets are routed to IPX, NetBIOS packets to NetBIOS, TCP/IP packets to TCP/IP, Network File System (NFS) packets to NFS, and so on. These drivers take up a little extra RAM, but they do a good job of providing interoperability at the Network and Transport layers—if, of course, you have multiple upper layers that all need to use the same network adapter.

TCP/IP, which stands for Transmission Control Protocol/Internet Protocol, is in the public domain because it was developed by the federal government. (In general, the government cannot have copyrights.) This is one big reason for the popularity of TCP/IP. TCP can be considered a Session layer definition, which is covered next. IP fits more into the Transport layer. TCP/IP is yet another piece to the interoperability puzzle. If everyone used TCP/IP (or IPX or NetBIOS), you would have a much easier time making networks interoperate. The different Transport layer definitions (record layouts and data field meanings) are the biggest obstacles to interoperability.

Another term that people use at the level of the Transport layer is *transport independence*. This is another way of saying *interoperability*. Suppose that you are a programmer and you want to develop an application where some modules run under OS/2 on an IBM PS/2, some on an Apple Macintosh (a Mac would be a good place to put the application's user interface component), and some modules run on a UNIX computer. You would like to design the modules so that the *calling interface*—one module passing parameters and control to another—is completely transparent to you and the other programmers on your team. You need special glue to put these pieces together. The glue is called *remote procedure calls*, or RPC.

RPC, because it enables different kinds of computers to process different parts of the same application, is a magic glue, like cynoacrylate (Crazy Glue). Companies like SunSoft (a subsidiary of Sun Microsystems), NetWise, Novell, Hewlett-Packard, and Momentum Software are doing amazing things with RPC. American Airlines, for example, is using Xipc from Momentum Software to develop a new cargo-routing system that runs on a variety of computers.

Transport independence means that all the machines making up the entire application system are using the same Transport layer definition—IPX, NetBIOS, TCP/IP, or something else. RPC works well when the same Transport layer is available for all the kinds of computers you want to use. You segregate your application program modules by target machine, and voilà— you have taken the best characteristics of each kind of computer and incorporated them into one system.

Thus far, you have concentrated on IPX and TCP/IP. Where does NetBIOS fit into the picture? Because much of NetBIOS works at the Session layer, you learn about NetBIOS next as you work your way up the OSI model.

The Session Layer

IPX.COM actually contains two protocols: IPX and SPX (sequenced packet exchange). As you would expect, SPX is a layer on top of IPX and uses IPX to send and receive its data messages. SPX is session-oriented, like NetBIOS, but the similarity ends there. The degree of interoperability between IPX/SPX and NetBIOS is exceedingly low.

Novell supplies a NetBIOS.EXE program with NetWare that you would think would solve the problem. It does not, however. If the various implementations of NetBIOS were interoperable, you could construct a protocol stack consisting of network adapter support software, IPX.COM, NetBIOS, and different redirector modules from Novell (NetWare NETx.COM), Artisoft (LANtastic), Performance Technology (POWERLan), IBM (DOS LAN Requester), and other vendors. And you would be able to access just about any file server ever created. (You learn about redirector software in the next section.)

Even if you had enough RAM to hold this protocol stack, you still could not use it to access anything. Each vendor expects its LAN software to work with the NetBIOS *it* implemented. You have climbed only five sevenths of the way up the OSI model, and already interoperability is out of focus and getting fuzzier by the minute.

While there are some differences in the programming interfaces of each of the implementations from various vendors, a bigger problem is the different data record layouts used to shuttle NetBIOS packets across the network. On a DOS-based workstation, IBM's NetBIOS module is the device driver DXMT0MOD.SYS (part of the IBM LAN support program). Novell's NetBIOS module is NETBIOS.EXE. Artisoft's NetBIOS for LANtastic is AILANBIOS. Performance Technology's POWERLan NetBIOS module is named for the adapter it supports. For each of these NetBIOS modules, the format and content of the data record (encapsulated inside the data field of the Ethernet or Token Ring frame) are different.

The Presentation and Application Layers

The software on your LAN that gives you access to the file server is the network shell, or redirector. On a NetWare network, this is NETx.COM, where the *x* denotes the version of DOS you run. Or you may use the DOS-version-independent NETX.COM. On an OS/2-based IBM LAN Server network, this layer is represented by DOS LAN Requester at DOS-based workstations. Other vendors' redirector software is usually called REDIR or simply NET.

You also can talk about electronic mail interoperability and the software mechanisms for sharing data in the OS/2 Presentation Manager and Microsoft Windows environments in a discussion about the Presentation and Application layers.

It goes without saying that NetWare LANs, OS/2 LANs, Banyan LANs, and peer-to-peer LANs are not easily interoperable at the Presentation and Application layers. Just as you would suspect from the discussion of lower layers of the protocol stack, the lack of communication among different vendors' redirector software modules is mostly a matter of data definition.

NetWare workstations use the NetWare Core Protocol (NCP) to request file services; servers respond in kind. NCP was highly proprietary until early in 1991, when Novell announced that it would license the NCP specification for a fee. It is uncertain how the Network General people managed to decode the NCP data packets some years ago. Network General's Sniffer is a protocol analyzer capable of interpreting and displaying the interior of LAN packets on a variety of networks. Perhaps Network General reverse-engineered the NCP protocol. If this is true, you can admire the Network General programmers. It is a huge, tedious job to make sense of streams of data bytes flying back and forth across a LAN.

IBM created the Server Message Block (SMB) protocol for use with the PC LAN Program. One of the best documents for understanding the SMB protocol is Volume 2, Number 8-1 of the *IBM Personal Computer Seminar Proceedings*. Printed in 1985, it is nonetheless a useful introduction to how SMBs work.

IBM currently uses the SMB protocol between OS/2 LAN Server and DOS LAN Requester workstations; a few vendors of peer-to-peer products (such as Performance Technology) also support SMBs.

Examining Interprocess Communications

Beyond the OSI model, new products and new standards for application-level interprocess communications come into being so often that it is hard to get a handle on the current state of affairs. *Interoperable* is used to describe each new product and standard. As this chapter suggests, the frequent use of the word is significant, but not in the way the vendor intends. A vendor's claims regarding interoperability should always be taken with a grain of salt.

Microsoft designed *dynamic data exchange (DDE)*, an application-to-application protocol for use in the Windows environment, in the spreadsheet program Excel. DDE is described in the Windows SDK (Software Developer's Kit) and is available to applications that have data to share with other applications. In addition, Microsoft now also offers *object linking and embedding (OLE)* for applications to use under Windows 3.1. DDE has five mechanisms that applications can take advantage of:

- *Execute.* One application controls the execution of another.

- *Hot link.* A server application sends data to a client application whenever data changes.

- *Poke.* Applications establish a back-channel transfer.

- *Request.* The client and server perform a copy-and-paste operation, without the need for the intermediate Clipboard.

- *Warm link.* The server notifies the client that data has changed, and the client can then request it.

In order for two applications to use DDE, they must agree on the format of the data to be exchanged. If the applications are from different vendors, the vendors must publish detailed specifications.

OLE is a layer on top of DDE that insulates the application programmer from some of DDE's tedious detail. One application puts data into a container located in the other application. The second application needs to know only how to display the data. If changes to the data are required, the second application invokes the first through a special interface.

Hewlett-Packard's New Wave is object-oriented. New Wave uses the concept of agents, and it contains an intelligent link manager that resolves object names into file system names. Version 3.1 of New Wave incorporates OLE.

Interoperability among the various providers of interprocess communications facilities probably will not happen for a long time. Even within a single protocol like DDE, interoperability will be highly application-dependent.

Examining Electronic Mail Interoperability

Commercial electronic mail products often adhere to the Message Handling System (MHS) or the X.400 standard. MHS messages, for example, have a header, a body of text, and perhaps an attached file. The header contains a destination address, a return address, a postmark, and other information. Both addresses have a particular format: <username>@<workgroupname>. Applications that define data in this same format can interoperate with MHS. Similarly, applications that use X.400 conventions can interoperate with other X.400 applications and users.

Of course, many electronic mail standards exist. Western Union has EasyLink, Telenet offers Telemail, and a rather popular one is PROFS from IBM. Interoperability among these systems is mostly a matter of reformatting data to look the way the other system expects.

Summary

Interoperability is such a big issue that an annual trade show—Interop—is devoted to it. Run by the Advanced Computing Environment people, Interop has one overriding criterion for its exhibitors: products must successfully connect (interoperate) with other products on a network. Interop is one of the best shows, with little fluff, good seminars, and good access to the technical people who sweat bullets to turn *interoperable* into a word you will not have to hear much of anymore.

In the next chapter, you widen your horizons to discover how you can connect multiple LANs to form a wide area network—a WAN.

Chapter 14

Building WANs from LANs

You learned in Chapter 1, "A Networking Overview," that a local area network can encompass a small geographic area, such as a department-size office or small building. Table 5.1 in Chapter 5, "Using Protocols, Cables, and Adapters," revealed the distance limitations of popular local area networks (Ethernet, Token Ring, and ARCnet). Your organization someday may need to exceed these distance limitations so that people in different locations can share files. In this chapter, you learn how to connect several local area networks (LANs) into one wide area network (WAN).

The chapter first covers the basics of wide area networks. You learn how to connect geographically dispersed LANs, and you find out what bridges, routers, and gateways are. You consider the differences between sharing files on a LAN and sharing files through a WAN. You discover the factors that influence where you should place shared files in a WAN. You learn how to print remotely across a WAN, and you gain an understanding of how WAN connectivity affects the administrative tasks you perform on WAN-connected LANs.

You then find a detailed description of the protocols you can use as you build your WAN. You learn the advantages and disadvantages of each protocol, and you discover that state and federal regulations sometimes dictate which protocol you choose.

Exploring WAN Basics

Within your own office space, you own your LAN. You purchase new workstations, cables, repeaters, and hubs, and you add these components to the LAN. You diagnose and correct the problems that occur on your LAN. With a WAN, however, the situation is different. You contract with a provider of communications services (your telephone company, for example) to connect two LANs that are across the street or across the country from one another. The telephone company will lease a special kind of phone line to you. You probably will purchase the WAN hardware that connects your LANs to the phone line, but you'll rely on the phone company to make sure that the special phone line is continuously available and noise-free.

WAN hardware consists of routers, bridges, and gateways. The section "Using Bridges, Routers, Brouters, and Gateways" later in this chapter describes this hardware in detail. Basically, the WAN hardware provides a path between LANs over which two or more LANs can share frames and packets. This communication of frames and packets between LANs enables a workstation on one LAN to access a file server or print server located on another LAN.

WANs don't use Ethernet, Token Ring, or ARCnet. At the Physical layer, WANs use protocols that typically encapsulate the Ethernet, Token Ring, or ARCnet frames. An encapsulated frame travels across the WAN link to the other LAN, where the WAN turns the frame back into a LAN packet. The WAN hardware decides which frames need to travel to another LAN, and the type and configuration of the WAN hardware determine which WAN protocol is used.

Different WAN protocols carry information at different speeds (and at different costs). You explore these protocols in detail in the section "Learning WAN Protocols" later in this chapter. In general, the WAN equipment (router, bridge, or gateway) uses one or more of these protocols to transport frames and packets between LANs. Because these WAN protocols typically operate more slowly than the LAN protocols described in Chapter 5, "Using Protocols, Cables, and Adapters," accessing files across a WAN takes more time than accessing the same files on your local area network. The difference in speed is usually one or two orders of magnitude; what takes 10 seconds to transfer across a LAN cable might take 100 or even 1,000 seconds across a WAN link. Although some newer WAN protocols operate at speeds equal to or greater than LAN protocols, most WANs in existence today provide relatively slow communications between LANs.

Connecting Distant LANs

You must do two things to connect different LANs into one network. First, you must create a physical path between the LANs: you must interconnect their topologies. Second, you must enable the flow of information between the LANs. This means that you establish a common protocol that the LANs can use to exchange information. Most vendor products for connecting LANs use a common high-level protocol such as TCP/IP, IPX, or NetBIOS. At a layer below the high-level protocol, the WAN uses a protocol designed for use over high-speed telephone lines to transport the TCP/IP, IPX, or NetBIOS packets.

You can think of interconnected LANs in terms of layers connected by these common protocols. The bottom layer consists of individual LANs, each with its own file servers and workstations. The common protocol ties the bottom layers together through special communications devices. Such a device does not change the individual LANs; the device simply transports message packets between the LANs.

If communications devices connect two LANs that are geographically distant from one another, you probably will use services and equipment offered by your telephone company to make the connection. Depending on the states and area codes in which the two LANs are located, you may very well find that federal or state regulations limit your choice of vendors, communications equipment, and available protocols. For example, Southern New England Telephone (SNET), at least through 1994, offers what are called T1 lines and SMDS lines, but it does not offer ATM or Frame Relay (you learn about these WAN protocols later in this chapter). Between two LANs that are within the 203 (Connecticut) area code, only SNET can provide private telephone-line services. These kinds of restrictions may greatly affect how you set up WAN connections between your LANs.

If you must connect two LANs, the job will be easier if the two LANs already use the same topology and network operating system. If the topologies or network operating systems are different, you must look for products that specialize in connecting those particular topologies or network operating systems. Interconnecting LANs is easier if your organization has adhered to widely accepted standards instead of proprietary topologies and protocols. If your organization has LANs that are not compatible, you can leave the LANs unconnected, or you can replace one or the other LAN with hardware and software that does enable interconnecting LANs.

Using Bridges, Routers, Brouters, and Gateways

Bridges, routers, brouters, and gateways enable you to connect different LANs into a single heterogeneous system. The following sections describe each of these connectivity devices.

Bridges

Bridges operate at a high level and enable you to link LANs you could not otherwise link, regardless of distance limitations. Bridges can interconnect network segments that use different physical media. It is not uncommon, for example, to see a bridge that uses both fiber optic cable and coaxial cable; such a bridge has a fiber optic connector at one end and a coaxial connector at the other end. Internally, the bridge translates between the two cabling schemes. In addition, bridges can tie together dissimilar low-level (Physical and Data-Link layers) protocols. You can use bridges to connect similar LAN segments, such as two Ethernet segments, or to mix dissimilar segments, such as a Token Ring segment and an Ethernet segment.

Bridges often feature high-level protocol transparency. Bridges can move traffic between two segments over a third segment in the middle that cannot understand the data passing through it. As far as the bridge is concerned, the intermediate segment exists for routing purposes only. Finally, bridges enable devices and segments using the same high-level protocol (TCP/IP or NetBIOS, for example) to communicate, regardless of the Physical layer that each LAN uses.

Bridges are intelligent. They learn the destination addresses of traffic passing through them and direct the traffic to its proper destination. This explains the importance of bridges in network partitioning. When you find that a physical network segment has excessive traffic and that its performance is beginning to degrade, you can use a bridge to break it into two physical segments. The bridge directs the traffic to its destination on the other LAN segment, limiting traffic that is not intended for a given segment. Bridges use a process of learning, filtering, and forwarding to keep traffic within the physical segment in which it belongs.

Because bridges must learn addresses, examine packets, and make forwarding decisions, they often are slow. Bridges, however, offer special connectivity advantages and options that make them useful in mixed-protocol environments.

Routers

Routers are, in some respects, more intelligent than bridges. Routers do not have the same capability to learn that bridges do, but they can make routing decisions that determine the most efficient data path between two network segments.

Routers do not care what topologies or access-level protocols the network segments use. Because routers operate at the layer above bridges (the Network layer of the OSI model), routers are not affected by medium or access protocols. Routers often are used between network segments that use the same high-level protocol. The most popular transport-layer protocol that routers handle is Novell's IPX.

Bridges make a forward or discard decision on each packet of data, depending on whether the packet is destined for an address on the other side of the bridge. Routers choose the best route for the packet by checking a routing table. They see only the packets addressed to them by the preceding router, whereas bridges must examine all packets passing through the network.

Most large internetworks can make good use of routers. You should remember, however, that routers need to have the same high-level protocol in all the network segments they connect. If you are connecting networks in a multiprotocol environment, you probably are better off using bridges. The same is true if you want to segment an existing network to control traffic loads.

Brouters

Brouters are a kind of hybrid of bridges and routers. Often referred to as *multiprotocol routers*, brouters provide many of the advantages of bridges and routers for very complex networks. True multiprotocol routers do not contain the bridging advantages of brouters; they simply enable the router to do what basic routers do with more than one protocol. Brouters actually make a decision on whether a packet uses a protocol that is routable. Brouters then route the packets they can, and bridge the rest.

Brouters are complex, expensive, and difficult to install, but for very complicated heterogeneous networks, they often provide the best internetworking solution.

Gateways

Gateways operate at the top layers of the OSI model. They provide the most sophisticated method of connecting network segments and networks to hosts. You use a gateway when you have to interconnect systems built on totally different communications architectures. You would use a gateway, for example, to interconnect a TCP/IP LAN to an SNA mainframe. The two architectures have no commonalities, so the gateway must completely translate the data passing between the two systems.

The Spanning Tree

Using a technique called the *spanning tree algorithm* (part of the IEEE 802.1 internetworking standard), you can place bridges between distant LANs. *Spanning tree* is another term for a switchable path between two devices on a network.

Under the spanning tree algorithm, the bridges that make up the alternative routes between Chicago and Dallas, for example, conduct a series of bridge-to-bridge negotiations. The result is that one bridge (the one that sees the best path) is in a *forwarding* state. The other bridge is *blocked* and will not forward packets. If the open path degrades, the other bridge opens and the first one closes, maintaining optimum traffic rates across the internetwork. This technique is not reserved for wide area networks; you also can use it to provide traffic-flow management locally or within a large office building.

Sharing Distant Resources

The WAN hardware creates an environment that enables a network operating system (NetWare, for example) to function the same across the WAN link as the NOS does on the LAN. You can copy files, share files, run network utility software, and print through the WAN link just as you can on your LAN. However, the WAN can't transport data between workstations and remote file servers as fast as the LAN does. Accessing data on a remote (WAN-linked) file server takes longer than accessing data on a local file server. Your application software, utilities, and operating system commands (such as COPY and DIR) will work over the WAN, but the difference in performance will be apparent to you.

Transferring and Sharing Files

A high-speed WAN connection to a remote file server can give you access that's faster than the floppy disk drive in your computer. Depending on how many other people are using a high-speed WAN link at the same time you are, you may even find that remote file-server access is nearly as fast as your local hard disk. A slow, less expensive WAN connection will provide access that's slower than your floppy disk drive.

You should analyze the different kinds of file operations that occur on your LAN and decide which of these file operations you will allow across the WAN link. Electronic mail is a good candidate for WAN connectivity, but copying large files across the WAN may not be.

Deciding Where Files Should Go

Each LAN in a wide area network will need to have its own file server (or servers). You'll want to make the WAN link as efficient as possible by grouping files on each file server in a way that puts the most frequently used files on a local file server, thus minimizing WAN traffic. Shared multiuser files naturally will have to exist in a central location, but you can prevent the WAN link from becoming overburdened by intelligently locating files near the people who use them most often. You might even consider, where appropriate, putting duplicate files on the file servers at both sites. You can run a batch file program after hours to synchronize the data between the WAN-linked file servers.

Printing Remotely

Even a few pages of printed output can represent a considerable amount of data. Although connecting to a shared printer across a WAN link is possible, the stream of print data might consume the entire capacity of the WAN link for several minutes (or longer). Streams of print data containing downloadable fonts, PCL commands (for Hewlett-Packard LaserJet printers), or PostScript commands are the worst culprits. You should carefully limit printing across the WAN link to printouts that absolutely must be produced at the remote site. Instead of printing through the WAN link, you might consider changing the work-flow procedures at each site so that related files are copied through the WAN link and then printed on the local area network to which the printer is attached.

Administering the Remote LAN

You manage a wide area network in much the same way you administer one of the LANs, except that you must take into account the different network topologies and protocols the LANs use. You also have to manage a few new devices that create the special communications links.

A heterogeneous network contains several network segments that differ in topology, protocol, or network operating system. The network may contain PCs operating on Ethernet or Token Ring, UNIX workstations running TCP/IP, and mainframes using IBM's Systems Network Architecture (SNA). The bridges, routers, and gateways create a heterogeneous, interconnected network. From an administrative perspective, you probably will find that you need to have a LAN administrator at each remote site. If two WAN-connected LANs are in the same building (or perhaps across the street from one another), you may not need to hire additional LAN administrators. In this case, though, the LAN administrator will want to assemble a toolbox of transportable tools, such as diagnostic disks, boot disks, cable testers, screwdrivers, and perhaps a protocol analyzer.

You can use remote-access and remote-control software products like those mentioned in Chapter 2, "Sharing Computer Resources," to administer a remote LAN from a central site. And some versions of the LAN management products described in Chapter 12, "Managing Your Network," are intended for use on WANs.

A large network, connecting many LANs in a wide area network, contains additional components that can cause network problems and failure. Because these products exist at intersections within the network traffic pattern, they can cause significant problems when they malfunction. Complex products such as routers, brouters, and gateways are subject to hard-to-locate configuration errors (refer to the section "Using Bridges, Routers, Brouters, and Gateways" earlier in this chapter). To isolate the problem, you may determine whether nodes on only one side of an internetworking product are affected. If this is the case, you can start the search with that product. Ask yourself what has changed recently and whether that change may have had unplanned side effects.

Learning WAN Protocols

You learned about the Ethernet, Token Ring, and FDDI physical-layer protocols in Chapter 5, "Using Protocols, Cables, and Adapters," and you learned also about the transport-layer protocols IPX and NetBIOS. Wide area networks use protocols designed especially for high-speed telephone lines, and these protocols are quite different from those covered in Chapter 5.

When you select the WAN hardware and type of telephone line that will link your local area networks, you can choose among a variety of protocols. Connecting two LANs located in different area codes may give you access to a wider variety of options, depending on the regulatory agencies that control the telephone company with which you've decided to do business. You need to consult the telephone companies that offer services in your area to find out which protocols you can select.

The following sections describe several ways to create wide area networks. Not all services or products are available from all telephone companies.

Using Dial-Up Modems

The least expensive and slowest type of WAN link uses dial-up modems over a voice-grade telephone line. The NetWare Asynchronous Remote Router from Novell is an example of a product in this category. You can create one or several connections between LANs with the Asynchronous Router. Through a regular voice-grade, dial-up telephone line, the router enables two NetWare LANs to share file and print services. You install the software on a PC at each location. Both PCs contain network adapters and serial (COM) ports. You might use the serial ports built into the PCs, or you might purchase special serial communications adapters from Novell; these adapters are called Wide Area Network Interface Modules (WNIM) boards. You connect the PCs' serial ports to modems and the network adapters to each LAN. After you have one modem dial the other modem's telephone number, the router software in each PC uses the connection to send and receive NetWare IPX packets. You typically use 9600-baud modems with the Asynchronous Router software.

Using X.25

An X.25 network consists of a number of components, called *packet switches*, that switch and route packets to forward them to their destination. The network breaks the transmitted data into a collection of small packets, transmits the packets through one or more data paths between the source and destination nodes, and then reassembles the data at the destination. The path between the nodes is a *virtual circuit*. To higher layers of software, the virtual circuit appears to be a single continuous logical connection. The X.25 protocol, however, enables the packets to travel different paths between the source node and the destination node.

The equipment that breaks up or reassembles the packets is a Packet Assembler/Disassembler (PAD). X.25 packets usually are 128 bytes, but the source and destination nodes can negotiate a different packet size when they establish the virtual circuit. The X.25 protocol can support a theoretical maximum of 4,095 concurrent virtual circuits across a physical link between a node and the X.25 network itself. In practice, the network will have fewer virtual circuits because most physical links can't send or receive data fast enough to have a large number of virtual circuits. An X.25 network typically uses a data transmission speed of 64 kbps.

Using Frame Relay

Engineers developed Frame Relay to support Broadband Integrated Services Digital Network (B-ISDN). B-ISDN is a high-speed protocol intended primarily for several kinds of information: voice, video, and data (including LAN data). Frame Relay typically offers higher data-transmission rates than X.25 networks by avoiding much of the overhead inherent in an X.25 network. A Frame Relay environment switches and routes packets, but at the lower Data Link layer. X.25 switching occurs at the higher Network layer. Frame Relay doesn't provide the flow-control and error-correction components that exist in an X.25 network; it instead relies on the higher layers of protocol software to verify and retransmit data as necessary. Frame Relay assumes that the Physical layer of the network is a reliable link between nodes. Frame Relay operates at transmission rates up to 2 mbps—slower than a LAN, but not much slower.

Using T1 Circuits

A T1 circuit, or link, is a point-to-point, full-duplex digital circuit originally designed to carry digitized voice signals. T1 circuits use a variety of media, including copper wire, coaxial cable, fiber optic cable, infrared, microwave, and satellite links. Almost every telephone company offers T1 circuits to its customers. Each T1 link operates at a data transmission rate of 1.544 mbps. You might lease several T1 links from the telephone company and use additional equipment to combine the links to support several concurrent voice and data sessions.

Using Synchronous Optical Network (SONET)

Bellcore, a telephone company subsidiary, first proposed the data transmission characteristics of SONET. SONET (which stands for Synchronous Optical Network) now is an international standard accepted by ANSI and the CCITT. SONET provides a point-to-point link over fiber optic cable and operates at a multiple of 51.84 mbps. The different rates are identified as OC-1, OC-8, OC-48, and so on. The OC portion of the designation stands for Optical Carrier, and the number is the multiple of 51.84 mbps at which the network transmits data. OC-8, for example, operates at a rate of 2,488.32 mbps. Frames within SONET consist of Synchronous Transport Signals (STS). An STS-1 frame is 810 bytes represented in matrix form. The matrix has 90 columns and 9 rows, with each cell of the matrix representing a byte. Twenty-seven bytes of the STS-1 frame contain network overhead, and the remaining 87 columns (minus 9 bytes for row-level transport overhead) contain the data. An STS-1 frame thus can carry 774 bytes of information. SONET sends an STS-1 frame every 125 microseconds, which is equivalent to 8,000 frames per second.

IV

Using Asynchronous Transfer Mode (ATM)

Asynchronous Transfer Mode (ATM) is a technology built on top of SONET. Each packet, called a cell, is 48 bytes and is the fundamental unit of ATM data transfer. Because each cell has a 5-byte header, the total cell size is 53 bytes. The 5-byte header contains destination address information. In the case of LAN message traffic, ATM uses LAN Terminal Adapters to break the LAN messages into ATM cells at the source node and reassemble them at the destination node. The packet-switching services of ATM can be used to support Frame Relay as well as other wide area network transport services. The multiplexing of cells in an ATM network provides good utilization of the available bandwidth. The network allocates cells on demand in times of high network traffic. The network flexibly responds to the needs of the LANs as the LANs send and receive LAN messages.

Comparing WANs and MANs

Metropolitan area networks (MANs) are similar to WANs. A citywide network is a MAN if that network adheres to a standard being promoted by the IEEE 802.6 committee. The standard provides for data transfer rates up to 155 mbps; MANs use fiber optic technology to achieve the high data-communication rate. The protocol used in a MAN, called Dual Queue Dual Bus (DQDB), consists of two loops of fiber optic cable to which the network nodes connect. A DQDB-based network forms a ring so that a central node or station can provide clocking and synchronization information to control and manage the proper transmission of frames. DQDB uses two loops of fiber to enable nodes to put transmission requests in a distributed queue; this technique helps the network provide consistent response rates regardless of the physical size of the network.

Using Switched Multi-Megabit Data Service (SMDS)

In addition to inventing SONET, Bellcore developed a WAN protocol called Switched Multi-Megabit Data Service (SMDS). SMDS uses a three-layer approach to interface to LANs. These layers are the SMDS Interface Protocol. The top layer, level 3, provides a datagram service whose packets are up to 9,188 bytes. At level 2, SMDS breaks the data into 53-byte ATM cells. Level 1 usually consists of a MAN link.

Talking to the Phone Company

You should consider the foregoing discussion of WAN protocols to be pure theory; some of the protocols represent relatively new technology and may not be available in your area yet. You'll need to talk to one or more phone companies to find out which of these services and products are available.

Prices vary widely from vendor to vendor, but achieving the most important goal—creating a reliable, effective link between LANs—will depend on getting compatible components. In addition to talking to telephone-company sales representatives, you'll want to discuss your needs with vendors of high-speed communications equipment, such as Cisco, Wellfleet, Microcom, and Andrew.

Looking at Special Kinds of Phone Lines

Leased-line service can be expensive, but renting a private telephone line from a phone company often is the only way to connect remote locations if you have a great deal of data to send and receive. WANs typically use leased lines to connect two or more LANs. Almost every telephone company—including AT&T, Sprint, MCI, and Cable and Wireless—offers leased-line services.

The following descriptions of some AT&T services give you a general idea of the available services. Other companies provide similar services, but costs vary widely among the different telephone companies. Be sure to check with different long-distance-service providers to investigate the services and current prices specific to each company. Notice particularly that the rates and services described in this chapter may have changed since this book was printed. Notice also that although this chapter uses AT&T services as examples, this book doesn't endorse any particular phone company.

AT&T's ACCUNET Spectrum of Digital Services is a digital private-line service for data, video, and voice at 9.6, 56, 64, 128, 256, 384, 512, and 768 kbps. Called *fractional T1*, the service offers transmission speeds slower than 1.5 mbps but faster than 56 kbps. AT&T customers can pay for the exact transmission speed they need.

AT&T typically charges a fixed fee of $270 per month, plus 32 cents per mile, for 9.6-, 56-, and 64-kbps lines. For higher speeds, AT&T monthly charges are similar to the following:

Speed (kbps)	Cost	Plus
128	$495	$0.57 per mile
256	$930	$1.08 per mile
384	$1,315	$1.53 per mile
512	$1,640	$1.92 per mile
768	$2,130	$2.52 per mile

Another AT&T service, ACCUNET T1.5 Service, is a digital private-line service that transmits high volumes of data, video, and voice transmissions at 1.544 mbps. The monthly rate for this service typically is $2,500, plus $3.50 per mile. For example, AT&T's suggested list price for a 200-mile, 1.544-mbps line is $3,200 per month.

ACCUNET T45 Service is a digital private-line service that transmits data, video, and voice at 45 mbps. This line service is AT&T's highest-capacity network service. If you need it, this service typically costs $16,000, plus $45 per mile, each month.

AT&T offers yet another service, one that is highly reliable. The DATAPHONE Digital Service rarely is unavailable or unusable. The service offers line speeds of 2,400, 4,800, 9,600, 19,200 and 56,000 bps. Monthly, the service typically costs $295 plus 35 cents per mile for the lower speeds, and $340 plus 40 cents per mile for a 19,200-bps line.

Summary

You learned how to build wide area networks (WANs) in this chapter. You explored the basic principles of wide area networking, and you looked at WAN hardware (bridges, routers, brouters, and gateways). You now understand that most WANs are slower than the LANs they connect, and you know to modify your usage of the LANs accordingly. You also understand the different WAN protocols that vendors offer.

Before you put this book on a shelf, for future reference, consider for a moment how much you've learned. From Chapter 1's gentle introduction to the basics of local area networking through this chapter's coverage of wide area networking, you've explored LANs from top to bottom. You learned what LANs can do for an organization (Chapter 2) and how LANs facilitate electronic mail (Chapter 3). You understand the components of a LAN—the file server (Chapter 4); the network adapters, cables, and protocols (Chapter 5); and the workstations (Chapter 6). You looked at several networking products, including NetWare (Chapter 7); LAN Manager, Windows NT, and LAN Server (Chapter 8); and Personal NetWare, Windows for Workgroups, and LANtastic (Chapter 9). You discovered how UNIX LANs work (Chapter 10), and you surveyed LAN-aware application software (Chapter 11). You delved into the intricacies of LAN management (Chapter 12), and you evaluated vendors' claims of interoperability (Chapter 13).

You've gained a solid foundation in networking technology that will serve you well no matter what brand of cable, network adapter, network operating system, or other LAN component you may someday encounter. If you feel your interest in LANs is above average, you'll want to continue reading through the appendix of this book. You'll learn how to take courses and pass tests that will certify your expertise in local area networking.

Understanding LAN Certification

Novell and IBM have programs, consisting of training courses and knowledge-verification tests, that you can use to gain professional recognition of your LAN skills. These programs give you greater status and might help you increase your salary. Employers in the computer industry are well aware of these certification programs and often look specifically for people who have achieved one of the levels of certification from these programs.

Getting Certified by Novell

The Novell program offers three levels of certification. You can become a Certified NetWare Engineer (CNE), an Enterprise Certified NetWare Engineer (ECNE), or a Certified NetWare Administrator (CNA). Additionally, Novell offers a special level of certification for the people who teach courses leading to one of the other levels. People in this last category are Certified NetWare Instructors, or CNIs.

Novell created the Certified NetWare Engineer designation to help Novell's customers know that a person is qualified to install and maintain a NetWare LAN. You become a CNE by passing a series of rigorous tests. Novell designed these tests to reveal your knowledge of local area networking and the NetWare products in particular. CNEs enjoy a special relationship—one not available to the general public—with Novell's technical support staff. If you are familiar with PCs, PC networks, and NetWare, you may want to undergo the tests to become recognized as a CNE.

You can take the CNE tests in any order, and the certification process begins when you take your first test. You have one year from the date that you first take a CNE test to complete the program.

The tests cover your skills and knowledge in several areas. These areas include the inner workings of personal computers; the configuration and use of DOS; and the use and configuration of NetWare Versions 2.2, 3.12, and 4.0. CNE candidates plan their own curriculum, within Novell guidelines. The Drake Authorized Testing Centers (DATC) administer the tests. Novell itself offers many training courses you can take; the courses are designed specifically to give you the knowledge needed to pass the CNE tests. You can call (800) 233-3382 to find out more about the Novell Authorized Education Centers near you. To contact Drake, call (800) RED-EXAM. You take the test at a computer; the testing software accepts your responses and scores the result. Each Drake Authorized Testing Center downloads the test before the test session and then uploads the results to a central Drake location after you finish the test. Novell receives the score results within 48 hours from Drake; you receive your test results before you leave the test center.

A problem you might encounter during the CNE test is "Describe the tables, performance features, blocks, and buffers important to the workings of file server memory." Another problem might be "Identify the NetWare 3.12 memory pools and describe the features, content, resource use, and effect of each."

In addition to the recognition that the CNE designation will bring, you get other benefits from your CNE status. Novell supplies CNEs with a free CD-ROM disk containing the Network Support Encyclopedia. This resource is a database of technical information regarding Novell products. The information in the database includes the following:

- Installation, maintenance, and troubleshooting techniques
- Technical bulletins and manuals
- Patches, fixes, and driver software
- Technical notes from manufacturers of PC hardware and software

Novell also gives each CNE two free "support incidents," which is Novell's term for telephone technical support to help you solve a problem. CNEs can purchase additional support incidents at half the regular rate. You also get to use the CNE logo on your business card and stationery. Novell encourages CNEs to join CNEPA, the CNE Professional Association. CNEPA is a nonprofit organization devoted to helping CNEs keep up with new hardware and software technologies.

The Enterprise Certified NetWare Engineer (ECNE) designation is for CNEs who want to achieve an even higher level of certification. To become an ECNE, you must first be a CNE. A person certified as an ECNE possesses an in-depth knowledge of many areas of networking, including TCP/IP, trouble-shooting difficult LAN problems, and communications technologies and theories.

A Certified NetWare Administrator (CNA) is an expert in managing NetWare LANs. A CNA doesn't require the technical skills of a CNE or ECNE, but a CNA must be familiar with the administration, configuration, and tuning of NetWare. The test a CNA candidate takes reveals knowledge in the following areas:

- Adding, changing, and deleting account IDs and groups

- Configuring printers

- Writing login scripts

- Setting up NetWare security

- Managing workstation network software

- Troubleshooting

- Making backup copies of server files

Getting Certified by IBM

IBM has a certification program similar to the one Novell offers, and the Drake Authorized Testing Centers also administer the tests you take in the IBM program. The IBM program leads to three different designations for people interested in local area networking: Certified LAN Server Administrator, Certified LAN Server Engineer, and Certified LAN Server Instructor. Whereas Novell's program emphasizes knowledge relating to NetWare, the IBM program focuses on the LAN Server network operating system. To find out more about the IBM certification program, call (800) IBM-TEACH or (800) 959-EXAM.

Like a Novell CNA, a Certified LAN Server Administrator is an expert in the day-to-day support of a local area network. This person knows how to manage logon accounts, make backup copies of server files, maintain security, and perform other network tasks.

A Certified LAN Server Engineer knows how to design, install, maintain, troubleshoot, and tune a local area network based on LAN Server.

A person who has achieved Certified LAN Server Instructor status is proficient both in local area network technology and in explaining that technology to other people.

People certified through the IBM program receive special recognition in the computer industry and attain a special status. If you are one of these people, IBM will (with your permission) list you in the Professional Certification Program Directory, which IBM supplies to its customers. IBM gives certified professionals priority status when they call for technical support. IBM distributes the Technical Library/Personal Systems CD-ROM disk to certified engineers as well as free subscriptions to newsletters and magazines that help the professional keep his or her skills current. The certified professional is also entitled to use a special certification logo on business cards and stationery.

The tests, administered by Drake, are similar to those in Novell's program. In fact, IBM will give you credit in the IBM program for some of the CNE, ECNE, or CNA tests you have already passed. IBM offers educational courses through its Skill Dynamics subsidiary, and those courses are available on a self-study basis.

Glossary

access method   A way to determine which workstation or personal computer will be next to use the LAN. Also a set of rules used by network hardware to direct traffic over the network, and one of the main methods used to distinguish various LAN hardware components. How a LAN governs users' physical (electrical) access to the cable significantly affects its features and performance. Examples of access methods are token passing and carrier sense multiple access with collision detection (CSMA/CD). See also *CSMA/CD*.

address   A set of numbers that uniquely identifies something: a workstation on a LAN, a location in computer memory, or a packet of data traveling through a network.

ANSI   An acronym for *American National Standards Institute*, a volunteer organization that helps set standards and also represents the United States in the International Standards Organization (ISO).

AppleTalk   Apple Computer's proprietary LAN for linking Macintosh computers and peripherals. AppleTalk is a CSMA/CD network that operates at 115 kilobits per second and accommodates up to 32 devices.

Application layer   The seventh and highest layer of the Open Systems Interconnection data communications model of the International Standards Organization. The Application layer supplies functions to applications or nodes, enabling them to communicate with other applications or nodes. File transfer and electronic mail work at this layer. See also *OSI model*.

ARCnet   Abbreviation for *attached resource computer network*. One of the earliest and most popular LANs, a 2.5-megabits-per-second LAN that uses a modified token-passing protocol. Developed by Datapoint, ARCnet adapter cards now are manufactured by many vendors, including Standard Microsystems, Thomas-Conrad, and Pure Data, Ltd.

backup server   A program or device that copies files so that at least two up-to-date copies always exist.

balun   An impedance-matching transformer. Baluns are small, passive devices that convert the impedance of coaxial cable so that its signal can run on twisted pair wiring. Baluns often are used so that IBM 3270 terminals can use twisted pair wiring. Baluns work for some types of protocols and not for others. Such devices can be bottlenecks that slow your network.

bandwidth   The difference between the highest and lowest frequencies of a transmission channel. A measure of the information capacity of the transmission channel. Bandwidth often is expressed in hertz (cycles per second) but sometimes in bits per second.

BNC   An acronym for *Bayonet-Neill-Concelnan*. A bayonet-locking connector for thin coaxial cables, such as those used with Ethernet.

bridge   Equipment that connects LANs, enabling communication between devices on separate LANs. Bridges are protocol-independent but hardware-specific. Bridges connect LANs with different hardware components and different protocols. A device that connects an Ethernet network to a Token Ring network is an example of a bridge. With this bridge, you can send signals between the two networks. A bridge differs from a gateway or a router. Routers connect LANs with the same protocols but different hardware. Gateways connect two LANs with different protocols by translating between them, enabling them to talk to each other. The bridge does no translation. Bridges are best used to break a large network into smaller networks while enabling the individual networks to share resources.

broadcast message   A message sent from one user to all users. On LANs, all workstations and devices receive the message.

brouter   A combination of a bridge and a router. The brouter acts as a bridge for some packets, a router for others.

bus network   A one-cable LAN in which all workstations are connected to a single cable. On a bus network, all workstations hear all transmissions on the cable. Each workstation selects those transmissions addressed to it based on the address information contained in the transmission. A bus network is the simplest and most common LAN topology.

cabling   The medium by which nodes on a LAN are connected. Cabling can be twisted pair, coaxial, twinaxial (cable used to connect 5250 terminals to System/36, System/38, or AS/400 IBM computers), or fiber optic.

coaxial cable   A type of electrical cable in which a solid piece of metal wire is surrounded by insulation, which in turn is surrounded by a metal tube. The axis of curvature of this metal tube coincides with the center of a piece of wire—hence, the term *coaxial*. Coaxial cables have wide bandwidths and can carry many data, voice, and video signals simultaneously. See also *bandwidth*.

collision   The result of two workstations trying to use a shared transmission medium (cable) simultaneously. The electrical signals "bump into" each other, corrupting both signals. Both parties then have to retransmit their information. In most systems, a built-in delay ensures that the collision does not occur again. The entire process takes a fraction of a second.

collision detection   The process of detecting simultaneous (and therefore damaging) transmissions. Typically, each transmitting workstation that detects the collision waits for some period before trying again. Collision detection is an essential part of the CSMA/CD access method. Workstations can tell that a collision has taken place if they do not receive an acknowledgment from the receiving station within a certain amount of time (usually fractions of a second).

communications server   Also called an *asynchronous server* or *asynchronous gateway*. A communications server handles different asynchronous protocols and enables nodes on a LAN to share modems or host connections. Usually, one machine on a LAN acts as a gateway. People on the LAN can go through this machine to access modems or a host.

contention   A way to determine how separate workstations can access the same cable, which is a shared transmission medium on a LAN. Each workstation tries to access the network at will. If the network is busy, the workstation must wait to try again.

CSMA/CD   Abbreviation for *carrier sense, multiple access, with collision detection*. A method of having multiple workstations access a transmission medium (multiple access) by listening until no signals are detected (carrier sense) and then transmitting and checking to see whether more than one signal is present (collision detection). Each workstation attempts to transmit when it thinks the network is free. If a collision occurs, each workstation attempts to retransmit after a preset delay, which is different for each workstation. CSMA/CD is one of the most popular access methods for PC-based LANs. Ethernet-based LANs use CSMA/CD.

cyclic redundancy check   A method of detecting errors in a message by performing a mathematical calculation on the bits in the message and then sending the result of the calculation along with the message. The receiving workstation performs the same calculation on the message data as it is received and then checks the result against the one transmitted at the end of the message. If the results don't match, the receiver asks the sender to send again.

database server   A specialized computer that serves database data to PCs on a LAN the way a file server serves files. With a regular file server, all the database data must be downloaded over the LAN to your PC so that the PC can pick out the information your application wants. With a database server, the server itself does the selecting, sending only the data needed to your PC.

Data Link layer   The second layer of the Open Systems Interconnection data communications model of the International Standards Organization. The Data Link layer is the level that puts messages together and coordinates their flow. Also refers to a connection between two computers over a phone line. See also *OSI model.*

datagram   A transmission method in which sections of a message are transmitted in scattered order and the correct order is reestablished by the receiving workstation.

DC600   A type of magnetic tape often used in backing up LAN file servers. Developed by 3M, DC600 tape is 1/4-inch wide and is enclosed in a cartridge the size of a paperback book.

DECnet   Digital Equipment Corporation's proprietary Ethernet LAN.

diskless PC   A PC without a disk drive. Used on a LAN, a diskless PC runs by booting DOS from a file server. The PC does this via a read-only memory chip on its network adapter card, called a *remote boot ROM.* Diskless PCs are cheaper than PCs with disks; they also are more compact and offer better security.

distributed data processing   The processing of information in separate locations equipped with independent computers. The computers are connected by a network. Often, this is a more efficient use of computer processing power because each CPU can be devoted to a certain task. A LAN is a perfect example of distributed processing.

electronic mail   A messaging system operating over some sort of communications medium, such as a LAN. Most E-mail systems enable users to write long notes and send them to other users on the system. Some E-mail systems are dial-up services, such as MCI Mail and CompuServe; others are applications running under a network operating system on a LAN.

Ethernet   A CSMA/CD, 10-megabit-per-second network using coaxial cable. Developed by Xerox Corporation, Ethernet is one of the most popular LANs in use.

fault tolerance   A method of making a computer or network system resistant to software errors and hardware problems. A fault-tolerant LAN system, as marketed by Novell under the System Fault Tolerant (SFT) name, tries to ensure that even in the event of a power failure, a disk crash, or a major user error, data isn't lost and the system can keep running. Cabling systems also can be fault-tolerant, using redundant wiring so that even if a cable is cut, the system can keep running. True fault tolerance is very difficult to achieve.

FDDI   Short for *fiber distributed data interface.* An emerging ANSI standard for a 100-megabits-per-second fiber optic LAN. FDDI is compatible with the standards for the Physical layer of the OSI model.

fiber optics   A data transmission medium consisting of glass fibers. Light-emitting diodes send light through the fiber to a detector, which then converts the light back into electrical signals. Fiber optics will be the predominant medium for LANs in the future. Fiber optic LANs offer immense bandwidth, as well as protection from eavesdropping, electro-magnetic interference, and radioactivity.

file locking   A method of ensuring data integrity. In a file-locking system, only one user can update a file at a time. Other users are locked out, unable to access the file. Contrast this system with *record locking.*

file server   A computer containing files shared by everyone connected to a LAN. In some LANs, the server is a dedicated personal computer. In other LANs, any PC can be a file server.

frame   A group of bits sent over a communications channel, usually containing its own control information, including address and error detection. The exact size and makeup of a frame depend on the protocol.

gateway   A computer system and its software that enable two networks using different protocols to communicate. Common gateways hook PC-based LANs into IBM mainframes (SNA gateways) or X.25 packet-switched public network systems (X.25 gateways).

hub   The center of a star topology network or cabling system. File servers often act as the hub of a LAN. They house the network software and direct communications within the network. They also may act as the gateway to another LAN.

hybrid network   A LAN with a mixture of topologies and access methods—for example, a network that includes both a token ring and a CSMA/CD bus.

IEEE   Abbreviation for the *Institute of Electrical and Electronic Engineers*, a publishing and standards-making body responsible for many standards used in LANs, including the 802 series.

IEEE 802.2   A Data Link layer standard used with the IEEE 802.3, 802.4, and 802.5 standards.

IEEE 802.3   A Physical layer standard specifying a LAN with a CSMA/CD access method on a bus topology. Ethernet follows the 802.3 standard.

IEEE 802.4   A Physical layer standard specifying a LAN with a token-passing access method on a bus topology. ARCnet works this way.

IEEE 802.5   A Physical layer standard specifying a LAN with a token-passing access method on a ring topology. Used by IBM's Token Ring hardware.

interrupt request line (IRQ)   The communications channel through which devices issue interrupts to the interrupt handler of a PC's microprocessor. The IRQ is the channel through which these devices get the microprocessor's attention. Different IRQs are assigned to different devices. This assignment pattern differs from PC to PC. Many LAN adapter cards use an IRQ to get to the microprocessor. You must be sure that your LAN adapter card is not trying to use the IRQ assigned to another peripheral, such as the hard disk controller or VGA card.

local area network (LAN)   A data communications network spanning a limited geographical area (a few miles at most). A LAN enables you to share disks, files, printers, communications, and other devices.

login   The process of identifying oneself to a computer system. Used to control access to computer systems or a network.

MAN   An acronym for *metropolitan area network*. A MAN is a wide area network that spans a city or large town.

NetBIOS   Short for *Network Basic Input Output System*, IBM's LAN communications protocol. NetBIOS has been adopted as an industry standard. It offers LAN applications a variety of ways to carry out interapplication communications and data transfer. To run an application that works with NetBIOS, a non-IBM network operating system or network adapter card must offer a NetBIOS emulator. More and more hardware and software vendors offer these emulators. These emulators aren't always perfectly compatible, however.

network adapter card   Electronic circuitry that connects a workstation to a network—usually a card that fits into one of the expansion slots inside a personal computer. A network adapter card works with the network software and computer operating system to send and receive messages on the network.

network layer   The third layer of the OSI model of data communications. It involves routing data messages through the network using alternative routes. See also *OSI standards*.

network operating system (NOS)   The software side of a LAN, a NOS is the program that controls the operation of a network. A NOS enables users to communicate and to share files and peripherals. It provides the user interface to the LAN, and it communicates with the LAN hardware or network adapter card. Notice that a network operating system is different from a network adapter card; IBM's Token Ring, for example, is an adapter card, not a NOS.

nodes   Points in a network at which service is provided, service is used, or communications channels are interconnected. *Node* sometimes is used interchangeably with *workstation*.

noise   Random electrical signals, generated by circuit components or by natural disturbances, that distort transmitted data and introduce errors. Noise can come from lightning, crossed cables, and electrical motors.

OSI model   Abbreviation for *Open Systems Interconnection*, a logical structure for network operations standardized within the ISO. See also *OSI standards*.

OSI standards   The International Standards Organization (ISO) has established the Open System Interconnection (OSI). OSI provides a network design framework, enabling equipment from different vendors to communicate. The OSI model is a design in which groups of protocols, or rules for communicating, are arranged as layers. Each layer performs a specific data communications function. Each of these steps, or OSI layers, builds on the one below it. Although each step must be performed in order, each layer provides several options. The OSI model contains seven layers. The first three layers are Physical, Data Link, and Network, all of which are concerned with data transmission and routing. The fourth layer, Transmission, provides an interface between the first three layers and last three layers. The last three layers are Session, Presentation, and Application. These layers focus on user applications.

packet   A group of bits, including address, data, and control elements, that are switched and transmitted together. Think of a packet as one sentence or one group of numbers being sent at the same time.

plenum   A type of cable jacket commonly used in forced air plenums, or ducts. Plenum cable is made so that if it catches fire, it does not circulate toxic smoke throughout the ventilation system.

Presentation layer   The sixth layer of the OSI model of data communications. This layer controls the formats of screens and files. Control codes, special graphics, and character sets work in this layer. See also *OSI standards*.

printer server   A computer or program providing LAN workstations with access to a centralized shared printer. Print requests from each workstation go to the printer server, which segregates the requests into individual print jobs. Print jobs usually are handled in the order in which they are received.

protocol   A set of rules for communicating among computers. These rules govern format, timing, sequencing, and error control.

protocol analyzer   A specialized computer or program that connects to a LAN and analyzes its traffic. Good protocol analyzers can record and display data on all levels of traffic on a LAN cable, from the lowest media access control packets to NetBIOS commands and application data.

Protocol analyzers are excellent for diagnosing network problems, but they require some expertise because their data output is rather obscure.

record locking   The most common and most sophisticated means for multiuser LAN applications to maintain data integrity. In a record-locking system, users are prevented from working on the same data record at the same time. That way, users don't overwrite other users' changes, and data integrity is maintained. Although record locking doesn't enable users to work with the same record at the same time, it does enable multiple users to work on the same file simultaneously; each workstation locks a particular *record* (a small part of the file) for only a brief time. Compare record locking with *file locking*, which enables a single user to work on one file at a time.

repeater   A device that amplifies signals from one piece of cable and passes them on to another piece of cable without changing the signals' contents. Repeaters increase the maximum length of LAN connections.

ring   A LAN topology (organization) in which each workstation is connected to two other workstations, forming a loop (or ring). Data is sent from workstation to workstation around the loop in the same direction. Each PC acts as a repeater by resending messages to other PCs. Rings have a predictable response time that is determined by the number of PCs.

router   A router is like a bridge but more protocol-dependent. A router usually can link only LANs with the identical protocol (such as two LANtastic LANs or two NetWare LANs). Like bridges, routers restrict a LAN's local traffic to itself, passing data on the bridged (routed) LAN only when that data is specifically intended for it. Compare a router with a *repeater*, which indiscriminately passes along all data, regardless of its destination. See also *bridge*.

RPC   An acronym for *remote procedure call*. Programmers take advantage of RPC technology to make different parts of one application run on different kinds of computers.

security   A way of ensuring that data on a LAN is protected from unauthorized use. Network security measures can be software-based, with passwords restricting users' access to certain data files or directories. This kind of security usually is implemented by the network operating system. Audit trails are another software-based security measure, maintaining an ongoing journal of which users did what with which files.

server A computer that provides a service to LAN users, such as shared access to disks, files, a printer, or an electronic mail system. Usually, a server is a combination of hardware and software. See also *file server* and *printer server*.

session A logical network connection between two workstations (typically, a user station and a server) for the exchange of data. Also a data conversation between two devices—for example, a dumb terminal and a mainframe. It is possible to have more than one session going between two devices simultaneously.

Session layer The fifth layer of the OSI model of data communications. The Session layer performs the log-keeping, security, and administrative tasks.

shielding The process of protecting a cable (consisting of one or more plastic-coated conductors) with a grounded metal sheath so that electrical signals outside the cable cannot interfere with transmission inside the cable.

star A LAN topology in which all workstations are wired to a central workstation that establishes, maintains, and breaks connections between the workstations. The center of a star is called the *hub*. The advantage of a star is that it makes isolating a problem node easy. If, however, the central node fails, the entire network fails.

TCP/IP Short for *Transmission Control Protocol/Internet Protocol*. TCP/IP is an important, established internetworking protocol that works at the third and fourth layers of the OSI model. Developed by the Department of Defense, TCP/IP is designed to be rugged and robust, and to guarantee delivery of data in the most demanding circumstances. TCP/IP is becoming more popular with networking and computer vendors who want to connect their equipment to a variety of other systems and protocols.

Thin Ethernet An Ethernet technology that uses a smaller-diameter coaxial cable than standard Ethernet. Also called *CheaperNet* because of the smaller cabling cost. Thin Ethernet systems tend to have transceivers located on the network adapter card rather than in external boxes. PCs connect to the Thin Ethernet bus via a T connector.

token A unique combination of bits. When a LAN workstation receives a token, it is given permission to transmit. See also *token passing*.

token bus   A LAN with a bus topology that uses token passing as its access method.

token passing   An access method in which a token is passed from workstation to workstation, giving permission to send a message. When you have the token, you can send. You attach your message to the token, which "carries" it around the LAN. Every station between you and the recipient "sees" the message, but only the receiving workstation accepts it. When the receiving station gets the message, the station generates another token.

token ring   A LAN with a ring topology that uses token passing as its access method.

topology   The description of the physical connections of a network, or the description of the possible logical connections between nodes, indicating which pairs of nodes are able to communicate. Examples of topology are bus, ring, star, and tree.

Transport layer   The fourth layer of the OSI model of data communications. High-level quality control (error checking) and some alternative routing are performed at this level.

tree   A LAN topology in which only one route exists between any two nodes on the network. The pattern of connections resembles a tree, in which all branches spring from one root.

twisted pair   Two insulated wires twisted around each other. The pair of wires may be surrounded by a shield, a jacket, additional insulation, or similar pairs of wires. Most twisted pair wire is not shielded, which makes it susceptible to electromagnetic interference. Twisted pair wiring is easier to install and change than coaxial cable, although its bandwidth (information-carrying capacity) usually is much smaller.

wide area network   A data communications network designed to serve an area of hundreds or thousands of miles. Public and private packet-switching networks and the nationwide telephone network are good examples of wide area networks, also called WANs.

workstation   A personal computer attached to a LAN.

Glossary

Index

Symbols